# Regulating Peer-to-Peer Lending in Vietnam

Yen Hai Nguyen

# Regulating Peer-to-Peer Lending in Vietnam

## A Comparative and Economics Perspective

Springer

Yen Hai Nguyen
Hanoi Law University
Hanoi, Vietnam

ISBN 978-981-96-9504-1 ISBN 978-981-96-9505-8 (eBook)
https://doi.org/10.1007/978-981-96-9505-8



This Springer imprint is published by the registered company Springer Nature Singapore Pte Ltd.
The registered company address is: 152 Beach Road, #21-01/04 Gateway East, Singapore 189721, Singapore

# Acknowledgments

The completion of this book has been made possible thanks to the support, guidance, and encouragement of many individuals and institutions, to whom I owe my deepest gratitude.

First and foremost, I would like to express my sincere appreciation to Professor Shinto Teramoto of Kyushu University, Japan, whose insightful guidance introduced me to legal research through a comparative and economic lens. During my Ph. D. journey, I learned invaluable lessons from him—how to approach research with rigor, how to question conventional thinking, and how to cultivate a habit of critical inquiry.

I am also especially grateful to Professor Steven Van Uytsel, also of Kyushu University, for his thoughtful academic advice, steady encouragement, and generous kindness. His mentorship has been instrumental in shaping the ideas and structure of this book.

My sincere thanks also go to Professor Toshiyuki Kono, Professor Han Sang Hee, Professor Ryu Kojima, and Professor Mark Fenwick for their support and constructive feedback at various stages of my research.

Among my mentors, a special note of heartfelt thanks goes to Dr. Nguyen Thanh Tran at the University of Economics Ho Chi Minh City (UEH), Vietnam. His intellectual generosity, insightful discussions, and unwavering support during the most challenging years of my Ph.D. have left a profound impact on both my academic and personal growth.

On a professional note, I would like to acknowledge my colleagues at Hanoi Law University and Vietthink Law Firm for the opportunities to collaborate on important legal issues and for encouraging me to pursue further studies in Japan. I am truly grateful for the many thought-provoking conversations and continued encouragement from these professional communities.

I also gratefully acknowledge the support of the Japanese Grant Aid for Human Resource Development Scholarship (JDS) for funding my research in Fukuoka. Without this generous scholarship from the Government of Japan, neither my academic journey in Japan nor this book would have been possible.

Finally, I wish to thank my family, friends, and loved ones for their unwavering love, patience, and support. Their quiet strength and encouragement have sustained me throughout this endeavor. Though I cannot name everyone individually, I am sincerely thankful to all those around me who have inspired and motivated me along the way.

Please note that the views expressed in this book are solely my own and do not necessarily reflect those of the individuals or institutions mentioned above.

**Competing Interests** The author has no competing interests to declare that are relevant to the content of this manuscript.

# Contents

# About the Author

**Yen Hai Nguyen** is a lecturer at the Department of Financial and Banking Law, Faculty of Economic Law, Hanoi Law University, Vietnam. She holds an LLD and an LLM from the Graduate School of Law in Kyushu University, Japan, as well as an LLM and an LLB from Hanoi Law University. Her previous experience includes working as a legal consultant for law firms. Her research has focused on financial law, banking law, securities law, with a particular emphasis on fintech law. Her current publications include Fintech in Vietnam and Its Regulatory Approach, Fenwick, Uytsel, and Ying (eds); Regulating Fintech in Asia: Global Context, Local Perspectives (Springer, 2020); Addressing AML Challenges in Vietnam's Fintech and DeFi Ecosystem: Bridging Regulatory Gaps for Financial Stability. International Journal of Law 11(3) 2025, pp. 1–6.

# List of Abbreviations

| | |
|---|---|
| 504 Loan Program | Real Estate and Equipment Loan Program of the US |
| 7(a) Loan Program | General Small Business Loan Program of the US |
| Agribank | Vietnam Bank for Agriculture and Rural Development |
| ASCAs | Accumulating Savings and Credit Associations |
| AUP | Acceptable Use Policy |
| BIDV | Bank for Investment and Development of Vietnam |
| CDCs | Certified Development Companies of the US |
| CFPB | Consumer Financial Protection Bureau of the US |
| CFR | Code of Federal Regulations of the US |
| CGCs | Credit Guarantee Corporations in Japan |
| CGFs | Credit guarantee funds of Vietnam |
| CIC | Credit Information Center |
| Construction Bank | Construction Commercial One Member Limited Liability Bank of Vietnam |
| CPTPP | Comprehensive and Progressive Agreement for Trans-Pacific Partnership |
| CRD | Japanese Credit Risk Database |
| CRIN | Credit Reporting Information Network of Japan |
| DATC | Vietnam Debt and Asset Trading Corporation |
| e-KYC | Electronic Know Your Customer |
| FILP | Japan's Fiscal Investment and Loan Program |
| Fintech | Financial Technology |
| FTC | US Federal Trade Commission |
| JFC | Japan Finance Corporation |
| JGAAP | Japanese Generally Accepted Accounting Principles |
| JICC | Japan Credit Information Reference Center Corp. |
| KYC | Know Your Customer |
| LSTA | Loan Syndication Trading Association of the US |
| M7 – MFI | M7 Microfinance Institution of Vietnam |
| MFIs | Microfinance Institutions |

| | |
|---|---|
| NAIC | US National Association of Insurance Commissioners |
| NGOs | Non-Governmental Organizations |
| NRSROs | Nationally Recognized Statistical Rating Organizations of the US |
| OTC | Over-the-Counter |
| OXFAM | Oxford Committee for Famine Relief |
| P2P Lending | Online Peer-to-Peer Lending |
| PSS | Japan's Postal Savings System |
| Rabobank | Coöperatieve Rabobank U.A. |
| ROSCAs | Rotating Savings and Credit Associations |
| SBA | Small Business Administration |
| SEC | US Securities and Exchange Commission |
| SMEs | Micro, Small, or Medium Enterprises |
| SOEs | State-Owned Enterprises |
| UCC | Uniform Commercial Code of the US |
| UNFPA | United Nations Population Fund |
| UNICEF | United Nations International Children's Emergency Fund |
| US | United States of America |
| USD | United States Dollar |
| USPAP | US Uniform Standards of Professional Appraisal Practice |
| VAMC | Vietnam Asset Management Company |
| VBSP | Vietnam Bank for Social Policies |
| VDB | Vietnam Development Bank |
| Vietinbank | Vietnam Joint Stock Commercial Bank for Industry and Trade |
| VND | Vietnamese Dong |
| WTO | World Trade Organization |
| Yen | Japanese Yen |

# List of Figures

# List of Tables

# Chapter 1
# Introduction

## 1.1 Background and Problem Statement

It is highly probable that there are always households and businesses in every country that require small amounts of funding. It can be easily presumed that households demand small funds to meet their various needs and small businesses demand small funds to enhance their flexibility in operations and investment decisions. It can also be presumed that the clear demand for small funds by households and small businesses has prompted them to seek ways to raise such funds. As has been noted, taking loans from loanable funds suppliers could be one way to help them meet their demand for small funds.[1]

On the supply side of the loanable funds market, there are several sources that can provide small funds for households and small firms. For example, financial intermediaries, such as commercial banks and other financial institutions, can provide lending services for households and small firms to access small funds.[2] Assessing borrowers' creditworthiness can pose a significant challenge for financial intermediaries when borrowers "lack collateral, steady employment, and verifiable credit history."[3] Also, bearing high transaction costs associated with making many small loans is likely to be a notable challenge that they often face.[4] They may, therefore, not find providing small funds as an economically viable option.

Another example of funding sources for individuals seeking to raise small funds includes those that are in close proximity to them, such as family members, relatives, neighbors, friends, pawnbrokers, and local moneylenders.[5] It has been noted that

[1] See Arun et al. (2009, p. 9) and Sundaresan (2008, p. 2).

[2] See Mankiw (2018, p. 544) and Allen et al. (2020), p. 39).

[3] See Ledgerwood (1999, p. 2), Raaij (2016, p. 59), and Westover (2008, p. 3).

[4] See Abor (2017, p. 114).

[5] See Sundaresan (2008, p. 3) and Nelson (2013, p. 150).

 
Y. H. Nguyen, *Regulating Peer-to-Peer Lending in Vietnam*,
https://doi.org/10.1007/978-981-96-9505-8_1

these sources have "existed long before the rise of lending institutions."[6] Among these sources, family members, relatives, neighbors, and friends are likely to be able to offer loans with flexible terms. Because of having personal relationships with borrowers, these lenders are likely to know borrowers' financial situation and repayment ability. They might be willing to adjust loan terms according to borrowers' specific needs and circumstances.[7] However, because the lenders' capital is likely to be very limited, the loans offered tend to be very small.[8]

Pawnbrokers can also provide individuals with small funds. They can provide loans through a pawn agreement, which involves a loan being provided on the condition that the borrower pledges an item of value as collateral. However, it is important to note that people who are struggling financially may have limited valuable assets to offer as collateral, which could negatively impact their ability to borrow from a pawnbroker.[9]

Local moneylenders including those who have some idle money and provide loans with the expectation of making some profits can be a source of small funds for individuals.[10] They are likely to offer small loans to those who urgently need capital through implicit agreements, which involve collecting borrowers' repayments in regular (daily, weekly, or monthly) installments and very high interest rates.[11] Because their capital is likely to be very limited, they might want to charge high interest rates to make more profits.[12] As has been noted, they tend not to lower their interest rates because they know that the borrowers linked with them are unlikely to have other options for raising small funds.[13] They are also likely to consider high interest rates to be necessary due to the high transaction costs associated with making many small loans and collecting regular installments.[14] Furthermore, the risk of borrower default, which is widely perceived as a probable outcome, may induce them to charge high interest rates to cover their losses.[15]

In addition to the abovementioned funding sources, institutions that offer microfinance[16] (hereinafter referred to as "microfinance institutions" or "MFIs") can provide low-income people with small funds. For example, Grameen Bank, which was established in 1983 "with the aim of alleviating poverty and empowering

---

[6]See Sundaresan (2008, p. 4) and Wang et al. (2009, p. 183).

[7]See Ledgerwood (1999, p. 13).

[8]See Robinson (2001, p. 150).

[9]See Arun et al. (2009), p. 8).

[10]See Robinson (2001, p. 173) and Sundaresan (2008, p. 23).

[11]See Rutherford (2011, p. 521).

[12]See Schmidt (2013, p. 51).

[13]See Robinson (2001, p. 183) and Robinson (2009, p. 45).

[14]See Schmidt (2013) and Robinson (2001, p. 184).

[15]See Rutherford (2011) and Robinson (2009, p. 50).

[16]Microfinance is widely referred to as small-scale financial services—primarily credit and savings—provided for low-income people. See Robinson (2001, p. 9) and Karlan and Goldberg (2011, p. 20).

the marginalized poor in Bangladesh through micro-credit",[17] has been considered the first MFI.[18] The Bank claimed that it provided microloans to millions of borrowers, primarily women, to help them improve their lives.[19] Another example is FINCA International, which was founded in 1984 as a nonprofit microfinance organization to help low-income individuals raise their standard of living and create jobs. The institution claimed to provide microloans to millions of people in poverty in several countries, such as Uganda, Zambia, and Tajikistan.[20] The provision of microfinance has been considered a significant tool for providing micro and/or small funds to low-income people and a means for poverty alleviation.[21]

It has been noted that there are two basic models of lending employed by MFIs, including group lending and individual lending.[22] The first model involves lending to groups of people, in which "each group member guarantees the other members' repayment. If any of the group members fail to repay their loans, the other group members must repay for them or face losing access to future credit."[23] For example, Grameen Bank organized groups of five members including those who could support each other's loans and provided loans to members of these groups.[24] In this lending model, the threat of losing access to future credit and peer pressure within lending groups can serve as a substitute for physical collateral.[25] The second lending model involves lending to individuals instead of groups. MFIs could offer individual loans to their established clients and first-time clients.[26] They may require borrowers to have collateral or collateral substitutes, such as compulsory savings, personal guarantees, or assets with low market value but high personal value to borrowers.[27] For example, M7 Microfinance Institution (hereinafter referred to as "M7 MFI"), which was established in 2012, has provided loans to low-income individuals in Vietnam. M7 MFI requires either compulsory savings or personal guarantees to secure individual loans.[28] As has been noted, in both group lending and individual lending models, MFIs offer loans at market interest rates that allow them to recover their costs but not so high that the poor cannot afford them.[29]

---

[17] Grameen Bank (2023).

[18] See Manos et al. (2013, p. 3), Armendáriz and Labie (2011, p. 5), and Sundaresan (2008, p. 4).

[19] See Grameen Bank (2023).

[20] See FINCA International (2023).

[21] See Armendáriz and Labie (2011, p. 1) and Sundaresan (2008).

[22] See Karlan and Goldberg (2011, p. 23).

[23] See Karlan and Goldberg (2011, p. 23).

[24] See Hassan (2002, p. 205).

[25] See Ghatak and Guinnane (1999, p. 200, p. 4).

[26] See Karlan and Goldberg (2011, p. 21).

[27] See Ledgerwood (1999, p. 138).

[28] See M7-MFI (2023).

[29] See Karlan and Goldberg (2011, p. 22).

It has also been noted that besides MFIs, other microfinance schemes, such as savings and credit cooperatives,[30] credit unions,[31] self-help groups,[32] and microfinance projects or programs,[33] have also been developed to meet the demand for micro and/or small funds by low-income people.[34] However, not all schemes labeled as microfinance can meet all the demand for small funds, as the matching of demand and supply of microfinance depends on several factors, such as the lending model, target group, and services offered.[35]

Furthermore, with the rise of innovative technologies over the past decades, online peer-to-peer lending (hereinafter referred to as "P2P lending") has emerged as a new source of micro and/or small funding. P2P lending platforms, such as Zopa[36] in the United Kingdom (founded in 2005) and Prosper[37] and LendingClub[38] (founded in 2006) in the United States, have provided lending services by directly or indirectly (usually via a bank) matching borrowers' demand with lenders' supply of small funds.[39] It has been noted that P2P lending schemes have targeted not only the poor but also individuals facing liquidity difficulties and self-employed borrowers running micro, small, and medium enterprises.[40] It is said that the lending schemes have enabled the raising of small funds among family members, relatives, friends, pawnshops, and local moneylenders or through MFIs, within the community

[30] A savings and credit cooperative is referred to as a financial organization, which is owned and controlled by its members who can borrow at low interest rates from an amount of money they have saved as a group. See Cambridge Dictionary Online (2025a, b).

[31] A credit union is referred to as a financial organization, which is owned and controlled by its members who can borrow at low interest rates from an amount of money they have saved as a group. Credit unions are cooperative financial organizations that are similar to credit cooperatives but are called by a different name in several countries like the United States, Canada, and Australia. See Cambridge Dictionary Online (2025a, b) and Ledgerwood (1999, p. 101).

[32] A self-help group is referred to as a group of people who come together voluntarily to pool their savings to help each other. Two basic types of self-help groups include rotating savings and credit associations (hereinafter referred to as "ROSCAs") and accumulating savings and credit associations (hereinafter referred to as "ASCAs"). Participating in ROSCAs, all the group members take turn to borrow a loan from the general pool. At each meeting (or round), the money is collected, and the total is given to one member on a rotating basis. When the last member has received the lump sum, the group can choose to start a new cycle or disband. Meanwhile, participating in ASCAs, group members save regularly, but the combined contributions are not distributed at each meeting. The group members borrow only when needed, in amounts that they and the rest of the members are confident will be repaid. See Arun et al. (2009, p. 10) and Ledgerwood (1999, p. 70).

[33] Microfinance projects or programs can be funded by governments, nongovernmental organizations (NGOs), and donors to provide loans to the poor for the purpose of poverty reduction. See Robinson (2009, p. 55).

[34] See Ledgerwood (1999, p. 13).

[35] See Karlan and Goldberg (2011, p. 20) and See Bateman (2010).

[36] See Zopa (2025).

[37] See Prosper (2025).

[38] See LendingClub (2025a).

[39] See Patwardhan (2017, p. 391) and Bachmann and Funk (2011, p. 6).

[40] See Patwardhan (2017, p. 395).

domain, on a larger scale by eliminating geographical limits.[41] Therefore, it is presumed that P2P lending can fill the credit gap for which conventional banks are often reluctant to provide finance.[42]

In the course of operation, P2P lending platforms have several advantages in comparison with conventional commercial banks. For example, P2P lending platforms are likely to have much lower transaction costs. This is because they are unlikely to require face-to-face meetings to identify borrowers like conventional banks.[43] They are also unlikely to need brick-and-mortar branches and human resources to run such branches, as they are very likely to match borrowers' demand with lenders' supply of small funds via online automated systems.[44] As a result, P2P lending platforms could enable potential lenders to make rapid decisions to provide loans at competitive interest rates, even without collateral. Therefore, they are likely to mitigate the barriers for potential borrowers to access credit and attract them. Moreover, it is reasonable to presume that P2P lending platforms could enable potential lenders to diversify their loan portfolios by investing in different loans with varying levels of risk and attract them. Also, they are likely to help potential lenders reduce the transaction costs of providing loans, which is likely to result in higher net returns for them.[45]

A typical P2P lending platform service provider (hereinafter referred to as "platform service provider" or, simply, "lending platform") rates the credibility of potential borrowers. The provider then provides these credit scores to potential lenders, who use them to make investment decisions. For example, LendingClub checks the creditworthiness of potential borrowers and splits their loans into multiple Notes with risk grades from A to C, which are then sold on its investment platform to potential investors (see Fig. 1.1).

It can be seen that P2P lending could pose several problems for those who invest in loans on P2P lending platforms (hereinafter referred to as "P2P lenders"). For example, P2P lenders might be put at risk of losing their money if those who borrow their money through P2P lending platforms (hereinafter referred to as "P2P borrowers") do not repay their loans. In this case, platform service providers do not usually bear the risk of default, as they typically do not invest their own capital in loans on their platforms. For example, if loans provided via LendingClub become default, the platform provider will not bear the risk of default. Instead, it may make efforts to collect outstanding payments and take other appropriate actions to prevent further deterioration of the loans' status. On the website of LendingClub, the platform announced:

> When members fall behind on their payments, LendingClub makes significant efforts to contact them, collect outstanding payments, and bring the loans back to "current" status. In

[41] See Wang et al. (2009) and Johnson et al. (2010, p. 27).

[42] See Patwardhan (2017, p. 395).

[43] See Davis and Murphy (2016, p. 38) and Calebe et al. (2016, p. 17).

[44] See Cummins et al. (2019, p. 18).

[45] See Davis and Murphy (2016), Yum et al. (2012, p. 470), and Wang et al. (2009).

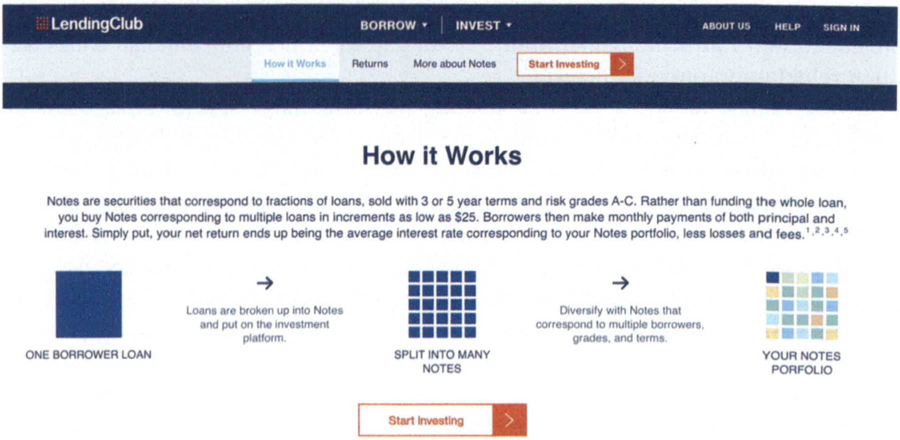


**Fig. 1.1** How LendingClub works (See LendingClub (2025b))

> addition to servicing and collections efforts, LendingClub reports delinquent borrowers to credit bureaus every month. This information may adversely impact a member's credit score and their ability to access credit in the future, which can incentivize borrowers to bring their loans back to "current" status.[46]

LendingClub may update lenders with any servicing and collection activity related to their Notes. However, lenders are not allowed to contact borrowers directly or be paid by the platform's money under any circumstances. LendingClub stated:

> We'll update you with any collection activity related to your Notes through the Loan Performance page in your Member Center. Under My Notes, click the status link of any Note to view its loan performance. Collections activities are strictly regulated according to federal, state, and municipal laws. Under no circumstance will an investor be permitted to contact borrowers directly.[47]

Moreover, P2P lenders might face the risk of making wrong lending decisions due to inaccuracies in borrowers' credibility assessments provided by platform service providers. It is easily presumed that platform service providers have a financial incentive to maximize loan origination to increase transaction fees, which are gained by platform service providers in proportion to the loan volume originated through their platforms. They, therefore, may provide P2P lenders with inaccurate information regarding borrowers' credibility to encourage P2P lenders' lending decisions and make more profits unless such behaviors are discouraged by appropriate regulations.

In Vietnam, P2P lending has emerged as a new source of micro and/or small funding since 2015, when Finsom Joint Stock Company started its P2P lending

---

[46] LendingClub (2025c).

[47] LendingClub (2025d).

platform "Loanvi."[48] There are several big names in the lending business, such as Tima,[49] Vaymuon,[50] Lendbiz,[51] Fiin Credit,[52] and LinkBank.[53] Individual loans provided through these platforms tend to be small and unsecured.[54]

At present, P2P lending platforms in Vietnam can perform the most basic function of a P2P lending model, which is connecting P2P borrowers and P2P lenders via their platforms. P2P lending is currently not included in the list of prohibited or conditional business lines under the Law on Investment 2020. Transactions between a platform service provider, a borrower, and a lender can be considered civil transactions under Article 116 of the Civil Code 2015.[55] Therefore, a P2P lender may lawfully lend to a P2P borrower as long as the transaction between them falls within the scope of a civil lending transaction. Accordingly, a P2P lender and a P2P borrower may establish a loan contract under Article 463 of the Civil Code 2015.[56] The interest rate agreed upon by both parties may not exceed 20% per year, as stipulated in Article 468, clause 1, of the Civil Code 2015.[57] However, if P2P lending platforms perform functions such as taking deposits, making loans, and providing intermediary payment services, they must satisfy stringent qualifications to be licensed by the State Bank of Vietnam.[58]

---

[48] See Fintechnews Vietnam (2018).

[49] Tima (2025).

[50] Vaymuon (2020).

[51] Lendbiz (2025a, b).

[52] Fiin Credit (2025a).

[53] LinkBank (2025a, b).

[54] For example, lending amounts range from VND 100 thousand to VND seven million on the LinkBank platform and from VND one million to VND 50 million on the Fiin Credit platform. All these P2P lending platforms do not require collateral. See LinkBank (2025b); Fiin Credit (2025b).

[55] A civil transaction is a contract or a unilateral legal act that gives rise to, changes, or terminates civil rights and/or obligations. See the Civil Code 2015 of Vietnam, Article 116.

[56] Vietnam's Civil Code 2015, Article 463 provides that "Contract for the loan of property means an agreement between parties whereby a lender delivers property to a borrower. When the loan falls due, the borrower must repay the lender property of the same type in accordance with the correct quantity and quality and must pay interest if so agreed or so provided by law."

[57] Vietnam's Civil Code 2015, Article 468, clause 1 provides that "The rate of interest for a loan shall be as agreed by the parties. The rate of interest for a loan agreed by the parties may not exceed 20% per year, unless otherwise prescribed by law. According to actual conditions and at the proposal of the Government, the Standing Committee of National Assembly shall adjust the above interest and send report to the National Assembly at the latest session. If the agreed interest exceeds the maximum interest prescribed in this Clause, the agreed interest shall become invalid."

[58] Vietnam's Law on Credit Institutions 2010 (as amended in 2017), Article 20, clause 1 provides that:

> [a] credit institution may obtain a license when fully meeting the following conditions:
>
> a/ Its charter or allocated capital is at least equal to the legal capital;
>
> b/ Its owner is a one-member limited liability company, its founding shareholders or members are legal entities which are lawfully operating and financially capable of capital contribution. Its founding shareholders or members are individuals with full civil act capacity and financially capable of capital contribution. The State Bank shall provide the

The online lending process begins when a potential borrower (hereinafter, sometimes referred to as "borrower" for the purpose of convenience) applies or registers for a specific amount of loan within a particular time frame via a P2P lending platform. The borrower is typically required to provide personal information, such as phone number, email address, age, gender, national identification number, job, and income. If the borrower is a company, it is required to provide company information, such as phone number, headquarters address, business lines, personal information of company representatives, bank account, and financial statements. The borrower then is required to upload photos of necessary documents, such as a national identification card or passport, salary slips, driver's license, or business registration certificate, to the lending platform via its website or application on a mobile device.

To verify the information provided by potential borrowers, a P2P lending platform may collect potential borrowers' personal information as well as their credit histories and debt-income ratios from various information sources.[59] These sources may include the websites of government authorities like the website of the General Department of Taxation[60] and the national business registration portal of the Ministry of Planning and Investment,[61] data on social network services (like Facebook, Instagram, and Zalo), credit history data systems built up by platform service providers, and data bought from phone carriers and e-commerce companies.[62]

After verifying potential borrowers' information, a P2P lending platform may use proprietary algorithms to rate their creditworthiness.[63] The lending platform then posts their scores on its lending platform for potential lenders' reference. Potential lenders can choose to fund loans available on the platform[64] or customize their preferences for risk, loan amount, and loan maturity and wait for a match made by the lending platform.[65] One borrower can receive a loan from a single or multiple lenders, whether private or institutional.[66] This means that the relationship between a

conditions for owners of credit institutions being one-member limited liability companies and founding shareholders and members;

c/ Its managers, executives and Control Board members fully meet the criteria and conditions under Article 50 of this Law;

d/ Its charter complies with this Law and other relevant laws; and

e/ It has an establishment plan and a feasible business plan which neither affects the safety and stability of the credit institution system nor creates monopoly or restrict competition or create unfair competition within the credit institution system.

[59] See Akkizidis and Stagars (2016, p. 49).

[60] The General Department of Taxation website: http://www.gdt.gov.vn/wps/portal/english.

[61] The National Business Registration portal: https://dangkykinhdoanh.gov.vn/en/Pages/default.aspx.

[62] Thắng (2019).

[63] Akkizidis and Stagars (2016).

[64] Such as via Tima and Vaymuon.

[65] Like via Lendbiz and Vnvon.

[66] See Statista (2025).

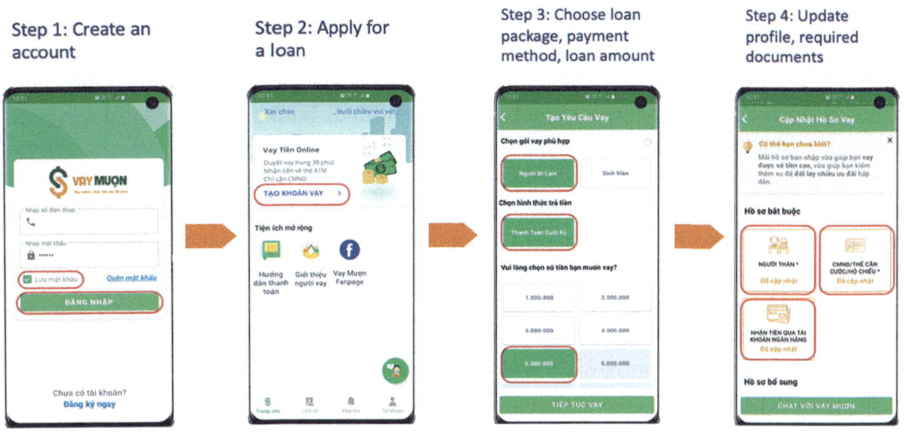


**Fig. 1.2** Loan application process via Vaymuon application

lender and a borrower could be one to one, one contributor to multiple borrowers, or multiple contributors to one borrower.

Vaymuon, a major P2P lending platforms in Vietnam, can be taken as an example. The lending platform does not require those who wish to apply for loans via its platform (or potential borrowers) to attend one-to-one meetings with it to verify their information. Instead, it requires them to download and install the Vaymuon Vaytien application on their mobile devices, create an account, and upload photos of necessary documents such as a national identification card or passport (see Fig. 1.2).

Vaymuon then automates the process of evaluating potential borrowers' credit-worthiness and posts their scores on its platform for potential lenders' reference. It requires those who wish to become an investor on its platform (or potential lenders) to install the Vaymuon Nha Dau Tu application, create an account, and link their accounts with the e-wallet Vimo. The platform also requires them to authorize it to transfer money from their e-wallets to the e-wallets or bank accounts of borrowers who have been approved for loans by them.[67]

After that, potential lenders can invest in loans available on the Vaymuon platform in a manual and/or automatic way based on the amount of money they have in their Vimo e-wallets. If they have less than VND 50 million, they should manually select loans themselves. If they have VND 50 million or more, they can provide loans both manually and automatically. In an automatic way, they are matched automatically with one or more individual borrowers by the Vaymuon

[67] The author directly contacted the platform via the Chatbox tool on the website http://vaymuon.vn on December 28, 2019.

platform. The platform then sends them a list of borrowers who have been matched with them based on their investment criteria.[68]

While the P2P lending scheme can become a source of micro and/or small funds, which may fill the credit gap for which conventional banks are often reluctant to provide finance as mentioned above, it also has several material issues. Some lending platforms function as information intermediaries between potential lenders and borrowers by providing information only, while others function as information and financial intermediaries by providing money or other financial resources in addition to information.[69] The latter may not meet the demand of potential borrowers in P2P lending, while the former may cause conflicts or discrepancies of interest between the platform service provider and P2P lenders. Some P2P lending platforms may simply match P2P borrowers with P2P lenders by assisting potential borrowers in providing potential lenders with their loan demands and creditworthiness. This allows P2P borrowers to obtain loan approvals from P2P lenders. Other P2P lending platforms may provide services that include both information and money through their platforms. In the latter case, P2P lending platforms function as financial intermediaries and are therefore subject to strict regulations as financial institutions. As a result, such P2P lending platforms are obliged to offer loans with stringent due diligence, high transaction costs, and collateral requirements. However, such loans may not be attractive to potential borrowers of P2P lending. If P2P lending platforms function as information intermediaries and provide only information, P2P lenders are likely to be exposed to credit risk caused by defaulted borrowers, while the platform providers themselves are not exposed to the same risk since they do not lend their own money to P2P borrowers via their lending platforms.

The second problem that inherently accompanies the P2P lending scheme is that P2P lending platforms cannot easily diversify the risk borne by lenders, as conventional banks can, if they only act as information intermediaries between P2P lenders and P2P borrowers by providing or helping to exchange information between them, without committing to the exchange or flow of money between them. On the one hand, in the traditional lending context, conventional commercial banks accept deposits from large-scale depositors at lower interest rates and allocate the pooled funds to make loans to large-scale borrowers at higher interest rates.[70] Some borrowers may have higher credibility, while others may have lower credibility. Additionally, some borrowers may borrow large amounts of money, while others may borrow small or very small amounts of money. Maturities can range from very short term (several days) to long term (several years). By combining such diversified funds provided by depositors and allocating them to make loans with varying amounts and maturities, ranging from short term (usually less than 1 year), medium

[68] The author directly contacted the platform via the Chatbox tool on the website http://vaymuon.vn on December 28, 2019.

[69] See Davis and Murphy (2016).

[70] See Freixas and Rochet (2008, p. 2), Greenbaum et al. (2019, p. 61), and Hughes and Mester (2020, p. 230).

term (usually from 1 year to 3 or 5 years), to long-term (usually more than 3 or 5 years), the risks for commercial banks and their depositors can be effectively mitigated.[71] On the other hand, in the context of P2P lending, it is difficult for P2P lending platforms to achieve diversification of various sums of money and borrowing periods, because they merely connect individual lenders and borrowers. Furthermore, it is commonly known that in traditional lending, lenders typically safeguard themselves by conducting due diligence, obtaining collateral, or diversifying their loans across various borrowers and situations. However, in P2P lending, loans are provided through P2P lending platforms, and it is the responsibility of the platform providers to identify potential borrowers and assess their credit scores. It is readily apparent that individual lenders are less capable of evaluating the risks associated with lending to individual borrowers. If borrowers are unbanked or non-banked and apply for loans via a P2P lending platform for the first time, the platform provider or lender(s) may find it impossible to obtain their track records. As a result, lending through P2P lending platforms can be risky.

The Vietnamese government recently announced its intention to develop a pilot program for P2P lending.[72] However, it can be seen that the major problems related to the P2P lending scheme, outlined above, make it difficult for the government to issue specific regulations governing the lending business. To establish a legal framework that encourages potential lenders to participate in lending via P2P lending platforms and facilitates P2P lending to become a source of small funds that can fill the credit gap in society, it is crucial for the government to consider legal solutions to the above major problems. In other words, it is important for the government to find legal solutions to the mitigation or diversification of risk borne by lenders in P2P lending in order to facilitate the sound development of the lending business. The next section will discuss approaches to the diversification of risk borne by lenders in the P2P lending scheme in Vietnam.

## 1.2 Diversifying Lenders' Risk in P2P Lending: Vietnamese Government's and Academic Debates

It is commonly understood that mitigating lenders' risk is essential for encouraging potential lenders to provide loans through P2P lending platforms.[73] According to the widely accepted understanding in the practice of finance, the risk associated with a financial investment is managed or mitigated through diversification, which can involve creating a portfolio of loans with various levels of risk, utilizing guarantees, insurance, and other methods. Therefore, diversification of risk borne by lenders is essential for facilitating lenders' provision of loans via P2P lending platforms.

[71] See Choudhry (2012, p. 393).

[72] See Viet Nam News (2019).

[73] See Lenz (2016, p. 688) and Cummins et al. (2019, p. 15).

The diversification of risk borne by lenders in P2P lending schemes has been examined by legal scholars across various jurisdictions.[74] In Vietnam, government officials, attorneys, and legal scholars have been exploring potential measures to diversify or mitigate the risk faced by P2P lenders. Some prevalent approaches are outlined below.

The first approach is to enhance the effectiveness of *due diligence* investigations conducted by P2P lending platforms, which can be achieved through the following methods: (i) integrating citizens' information into the national information system to enhance the accuracy of P2P lending platforms' evaluation of customer authentication; (ii) allowing P2P lending platforms' access to credit information held by the Credit Information Center of the State Bank of Vietnam; (iii) requiring P2P lending platforms to establish a transparent credit scoring system and due diligence process; and (iv) encouraging the development of credit rating companies to improve the quality of information disclosure.[75]

In practice, it can be challenging and costly for platform service providers to obtain enough data to establish reliable information systems for customer authentication. Moreover, platform service providers may encounter difficulties in obtaining the track records of potential borrowers who are unbanked or non-banked and are applying for loans via online lending platforms for the first time. In addition, the proprietary algorithms employed by platform service providers to evaluate borrowers' creditworthiness are still considered a "black box" underwriting method. The "black box" label comes from the lack of transparency regarding the data used, the factors that influence credit scores, and the weightings applied to determine borrowers' creditworthiness.[76] It is also difficult to determine the extent to which platform service providers should disclose potential borrowers' information in order to facilitate investment decisions made by potential lenders. Providing too much information on potential borrowers could lead to that information being shared, sold, or used for criminal purposes, which could be a concern for platform service providers.[77]

The second approach is to require P2P lending platforms to ensure the repayment of both the principal amount provided by P2P lenders and the accompanying interest through an agreement, in which platform service providers commit to guaranteeing the repayment of overdue debts in the case of borrower default. Specifically, platform service providers commit to directly acquiring or supporting P2P lenders in acquiring overdue debts from P2P borrowers in the case of default.[78]

---

[74] See Ahern (2018, p. 193), Wei (2016, p. 539), Lo (2016, p. 87), Davis and Murphy (2016), Samitsu (2017), Milne and Parboteeah (2016), and Kartika (2023, pp. 93–112).

[75] See Cuong (2022, p. 10), Dân (2019, p. 42), Hà and Thực (2019, p. 40), Ngoc (2020, p. 36), and Vũ (2019).

[76] See Eschholz and Djabbarpour (2018, p. 64) and Akkizidis and Stagars (2016).

[77] See Nhi (2019).

[78] See Allens Law Firm (2019, p. 2).

Theoretically, P2P lending platforms may help P2P lenders diversify credit risk associated with P2P lending by directly acquiring or supporting P2P lenders in acquiring loans provided by them (hereinafter referred to as "P2P loans") from P2P borrowers. It is possible for P2P lending platforms to directly acquire P2P loans from P2P borrowers because P2P lenders can assign their loan claims to platform service providers in accordance with Article 365 of the Civil Code 2015.[79] However, this approach is rarely employed in practice due to several reasons. Firstly, platform service providers are unlikely to have much incentive to collect outstanding debts from defaulted borrowers, as they are not exposed to the borrowers' default risk. Secondly, due to the relatively small value of P2P loans, it is economically inefficient for platform service providers to track down each delinquent borrower. As a result, the repayment of P2P loans primarily depends on the ability and cooperation of P2P borrowers.

To acquire P2P loans from P2P borrowers, platform service providers may demand that P2P borrowers have a guarantor to *guarantee* the repayment of P2P loans. This is possible under the current laws in Vietnam. Article 335 of the Civil Code 2015 provides that.

> [g]uarantee means an undertaking made by a third person (hereinafter referred to as the guarantor) to an obligee (hereinafter referred to as the creditor) to perform an obligation on behalf of an obligor (hereinafter referred to as the principal debtor) if the obligation falls due and the principal debtor fails to perform or performs incorrectly the obligation.[80]

If a guarantee is provided, "[t]he guarantor shall be entitled to receive remuneration if so agreed by the guarantor with the principal debtor."[81] In addition, Article 7 of the Law on Enterprises 2020 allows Vietnamese enterprises to provide commercial guarantees as one of their business rights.[82] Nevertheless, it has been noted that commercial guarantees are often used by holding companies to guarantee their subsidiaries' loans.[83]

---

[79] Vietnam's Civil Code 2015, Article 365 provides that: "Transfer of the right to claim:

1. The party having the right to claim the performance of an obligation may transfer that right to a subrogee as agreed upon, except for the following cases:

a/ The right to claim support money and to claim compensation for damage caused by infringement upon his/her/its life, health, honor, dignity or reputation;

b/ The obligee and obligor have agreed on the non-transfer or the transfer is not permitted by law.

2. When the party having the right to claim transfers that right, the subrogee shall become the party having the right to claim. The transfer of the right to claim is not subject to consent of the obligor. The transferor of the right to claim shall notify in writing the obligor of the transfer, unless otherwise agreed upon. In case the transferor of the right to claim fails to notify such transfer, thus making the obligor incur expenses, the transferor shall pay these expenses."

[80] Vietnam's Civil Code 2015, Article 335.

[81] Vietnam's Civil Code 2015, Article 337.

[82] Vietnam's Law on Enterprises 2020, Article 7 provides that "Rights of enterprises: Engage in business lines that are not prohibited by law; Decide on the method of raising and using capital...."

[83] See Pham Law Firm (2023).

Because P2P borrowers are unlikely to have holding companies that can provide commercial guarantees, they may be required to seek commercial guarantees from credit institutions[84] for borrowing P2P loans. Article 4, clause 2, of the Law on Credit Institutions 2024 stipulates that

> [b]ank guarantee means a form of credit extension under which a credit institution commits to the guarantee to fulfill financial obligations of its client in case the client fails to fulfill or fully fulfill its obligations as committed; the client shall acknowledge and repay the debt to the credit institution as agreed upon.[85]

However, credit institutions are unlikely to have much incentive to provide commercial guarantees for P2P borrowers because their borrowings will be small loans. It is easily predicted that the transaction costs associated with providing small-sized guarantees will become comparatively high against the available service charges and discourage credit institutions from providing them. Also, it should be noted that in Vietnam, credit institutions such as DongA Bank[86] and Bank for Investment and Development of Vietnam (BIDV)[87] typically require guaranteed debtors to provide collateral to secure their rights to have the guaranteed amount reimbursed.

Although P2P borrowers are unlikely to benefit from commercial guarantees provided by holding companies or credit institutions, if they are micro, small, or medium enterprises as defined below (hereinafter referred to as "SMEs"), they can potentially benefit from credit guarantee funds established by provincial authorities of Vietnam. According to Article 4 of the Law on Support for SMEs 2017:

> Small- and medium-sized enterprises include micro, small- and medium-sized enterprises, each having an average number of employees covered by social insurance not exceeding 200 a year and satisfying either of the following criteria: a) The total capital amount does not exceed VND 100 billion; or b) The total revenue of the preceding year does not exceed VND 300 billion.[88]

Provincial credit guarantee funds for SMEs have been established in accordance with Decree No. 34/2018/ND-CP of the government dated March 8, 2018, on the establishment, organization, and operation of credit guarantee funds for SMEs. Article 15, clause 1, of Decree No. 34/2018/ND-CP provides that SMEs to which provincial credit guarantee funds are available are those that have development potential but do not meet the requirements for accessing bank credit in the prioritized sectors.[89] However, it should be noted that SMEs can only benefit from provincial

[84] Vietnam's Law on Credit Institutions (2024), Article 4, clause 38 provides that "credit institutions include banks, non-bank credit institutions, microfinance institutions, and people's credit funds."

[85] Vietnam's Law on Credit Institutions (2024), Article 4, clause 2.

[86] See DongA Bank (2023).

[87] See BIDV (2025).

[88] The Law on Support for SMEs 2017 of Vietnam, Article 4.

[89] SMEs borrowing for investment and business production in the following sectors will be given priority for credit guarantee issuance: (a) sectors prioritized for credit issuance according to the State Bank' guidance in each period and (b) sectors prioritized for economic and social development in

credit guarantee funds when they borrow loans from credit institutions or state financial funds in accordance with Article 17, clause 2,[90] and Article 3, clause 5,[91] of Decree No. 34/2018/ND-CP. Because P2P loans are not provided by credit institutions or state financial funds, credit guarantee funds established by provincial authorities are not available to P2P borrowers.

It can be seen that P2P lending platform service providers might guarantee the repayment of P2P loans, or they could require P2P borrowers to arrange a guarantor to guarantee the repayment of P2P loans. These arrangements could potentially attract potential lenders to participate in lending via P2P lending platforms. However, as discussed above, it is highly unlikely that platform service providers guarantee the repayment of P2P loans. In addition, it is also highly unlikely that P2P borrowers can easily find guarantors to guarantee their repayment of P2P loans.

The third approach is to limit the investment of individual P2P lenders to a certain amount, or based on their total income and assets, in each transaction. It is expected that this approach can distribute the risk caused by one borrower among multiple P2P lenders when the amount of a P2P loan provided to one borrower exceeds such a limit.[92] A lending platform may limit the amount of each transaction between one borrower and one lender via its lending platform so that it will not be greater than a certain amount (e.g., USD 25), and one borrower is approved to borrow a total amount not exceeding a specific amount (e.g., USD 500) from 20 lenders. If a borrower fails to repay the principal of a loan in the amount of USD 500, each individual among the 20 lenders will only be exposed to a loss of no more than USD 25. In other words, the 20 lenders provide a syndicated loan to one borrower and collectively share the default risk of up to USD 500 caused by that borrower (see Fig. 1.3).

Indeed, the diversification of P2P lenders' loan portfolios, aimed at sharing default risk caused by defaulted borrowers among syndicated lenders, could be used. However, this approach is likely to be extremely costly and impractical. In order to make such a scheme viable, individual P2P lenders may be obliged to assess the creditworthiness of all prospective borrowers. However, this is not likely to be feasible. To avoid the time and cost involved in evaluating each borrower individually, P2P lenders can establish lending criteria based on risk level, loan maturity, interest rate, borrowers' professions or occupations, and the location of borrowers'

---

provinces in each period. The English translation of Decree No. 34/2018/ND-CP of Vietnam, Article 15, clause 2.

[90] Decree No. 34/2018/ND-CP, Article 17, clause 2 provides that "[t]he guarantees of the credit guarantee fund include: a) Guarantee for the principal of a loan taken out by the obligor from a lender; b) Guarantee for the interest of a loan taken out by the obligor from a lender; c) Guarantee for the principal and interest of a loan taken out by the obligor from a lender, specified in the credit guarantee contract."

[91] Decree No. 34/2018/ND-CP, Article 3, clause 5 provides that "lender refers to credit institutions and state financial funds having lending functions as per the law."

[92] See Trang et al. (2019, p. 217), Hiệu (2018, p. 16), Hà and Thực (2019), Ngoc (2020), and Dân (2019).

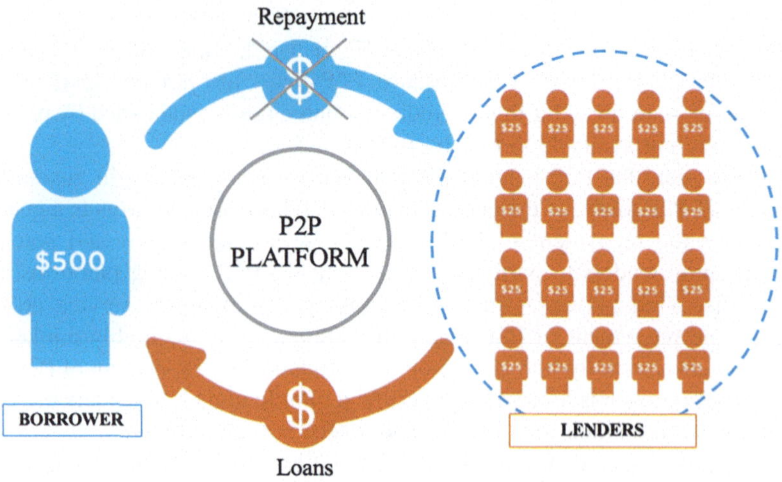


**Fig. 1.3** Model of sharing default risk caused by one borrower among lenders

businesses or residences. Then they can rely on the automatic matching provided by P2P lending platforms. Alternatively, P2P lending platforms can pool all P2P loans together and offer each potential lender the opportunity to spread their funds across the entire loan book. For example, SBI Social Lending in Japan, founded in 2008,[93] offered both manual and automated investment options for potential investors. However, it should be noted that this company provided relatively large-scale funding to somewhat organized fund seekers. Additionally, it is worth noting that this company already assigned its business to Bankers Co., Ltd., another Japanese company, in 2022.[94] Investors could either manually select loans available on the SBI Social Lending platform or wait for automatic matching by SBI Social Lending based on their investment amount and lending criteria.[95] If potential lenders set lending criteria and waited for automatic matching by SBI Social Lending, the cost of assessing borrowers' credibility might have been reduced. However, relying solely on automatic matching by P2P lending platforms may reduce P2P lenders' incentive to assess P2P borrowers' creditworthiness, which may potentially lead to risky and irredeemable investments for P2P lenders.

The fourth approach is to limit the risk borne by individual lenders by limiting the total amount of loans each lender can make through a single P2P lending platform.[96] Specifically, for example, a platform service provider may impose a cap on the total loan amount of individual lenders in all transactions via its platform. The maximum limit could be, for example, USD 500, and one lender may lend up to USD 500 to

[93] See SBI Social Lending (2023a).

[94] See SBI Social Lending (2023a).

[95] See SBI Social Lending (2023b).

[96] See Trang et al. (2019), Hiệu (2018), Hà and Thực (2019), Ngoc (2020), and Dân (2019).

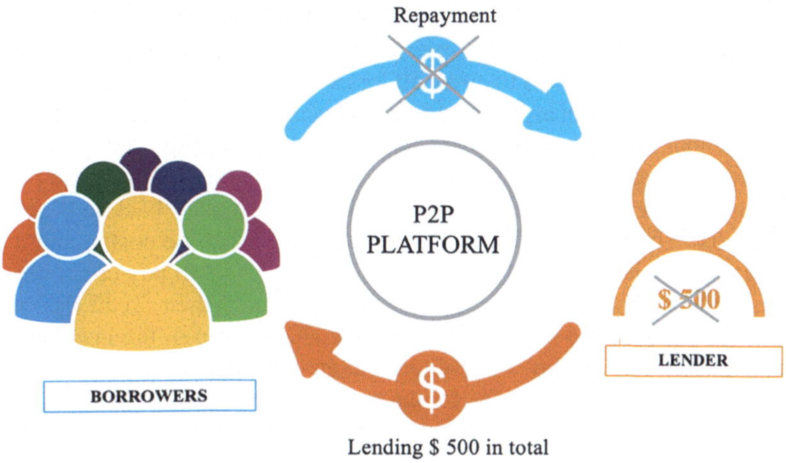


**Fig. 1.4** Model of the limitation of default risk caused by borrowers for one lender

one or more borrowers. In the event that any of these borrowers fail to repay such loan(s), the lender will be exposed to a maximum loss of up to USD 500 (see Fig. 1.4).

In this approach, platform service providers may set up a lending limit for each borrower or for all borrowers who apply for loans via their lending platforms to help P2P lenders limit their credit risk. If they set up a different lending limit for each borrower based on their assessment of the creditworthiness thereof, it would be costly for them. Moreover, if they set up a small lending limit for all potential borrowers, they are very likely to lose profitable opportunities to obtain charges from providing larger loans to potential borrowers.

The fifth approach is to encourage or request P2P lending platforms to establish and maintain provisional funds, which the platforms would use to offset bad debts and repay lenders in the case of credit default.[97] To help P2P lenders diversify credit risk caused by defaulted borrowers, P2P lending platforms may establish provisional funds to absorb the expected loss and reimburse lenders partly or completely for the principal and interest of disbursed loans. The provisional funds may be funded by either the contribution of platform service providers or the fees collected from P2P lenders and/or P2P borrowers. It is clear that platform service providers are unlikely to have much incentive to establish such provisional funds by their own contribution, as it simply increases the cost of operating their platforms. Moreover, the coverage for expected losses by means of reimbursing lenders could be limited by the ability of these funds. If total claims by P2P lenders to reimburse their loans exceed the size of the provisional funds, the funds will fail to cover all losses that lenders are exposed to, and the lenders will likely bear the uncovered losses. Suppose that the provisional funds are established by collecting fees from P2P lenders determined

[97] See Hiệu (2018), Hà and Thực (2019), Ngoc (2020), Dân (2019), and Lực (2018).

based on the size of the loans provided by themselves and/or fees from P2P borrowers determined based on the size of their borrowings. Suppose also that the provisional funds are designed to cover all losses of P2P lenders caused by defaults of P2P borrowers. Such charges are likely to become expensive, which may discourage potential lenders and borrowers from using the lending platforms.

The sixth approach is to encourage or request P2P lending platforms to purchase credit insurance to ensure that P2P lenders will get their money back in the event of credit defaults.[98] In practice, purchasing credit insurance can be costly, and it is not surprising that P2P lending platforms require P2P borrowers to pay credit insurance premiums.[99] This approach can help P2P lenders diversify their credit risk because losses caused by defaulted borrowers can be socialized through the insurance.

However, credit insurance is likely to motivate both P2P lending platforms and P2P lenders to provide riskier loans for the purpose of increasing their profits while discouraging them from conducting due diligence on potential borrowers. This could be deemed a kind of moral hazard, and, on the other hand, it is likely to discourage insurance companies from providing credit insurance to cover the potential losses of P2P loans. If insurance companies are discouraged from providing credit insurance, P2P lenders may not be able to rely on this approach to diversify their credit risk.

The seventh approach is for P2P lending platforms to set up a secondary market where primary lenders can assign their loan receivables to potential investors or other lenders before loan maturity.[100] Usually, P2P lending platforms do not provide P2P lenders with measures to collect and withdraw loans until their due dates.[101] However, if investors could purchase their loan receivables, P2P lenders would recover their funds. If P2P lending platforms facilitate a secondary loan market, they can help P2P lenders connect with potential investors who are ready to purchase loan receivables. However, a secondary market that enables P2P lenders to liquidate loans with a high probability of default before loan maturity may discourage them from carefully selecting lending occasions with a lower probability of default. This result could deteriorate the quality of the loan receivables traded on the secondary market and, accordingly, discourage potential investors from investing there. Furthermore, it is easily predicted that the receivables of defaulted loans will be difficult to sell on the secondary loan market unless at a nominal price, and, accordingly, P2P lenders are likely to be obliged to bear the losses caused by such defaults.

Based on the above discussion, it is easy to see the risks that P2P lenders are exposed to, though this is not necessarily an exhaustive itemization of possible approaches to mitigating such risks. Some of these approaches have been discussed by Vietnamese government officials, attorneys, and legal scholars to date. However,

[98] See Hiệu (2018), Hà and Thực (2019), Ngoc (2020), and Dân (2019).

[99] For example, some Vietnamese P2P lending platforms require borrowers to pay credit insurance premiums such as Lendbiz and Vnvon.

[100] See Allens Law Firm (2019).

[101] For example, Lendbiz and Fiin Credit do not allow lenders to withdraw their money before loan maturities. See Lendbiz (2025b) and Fiin Credit (2025a).

the approaches mentioned above have scarcely been implemented in actual P2P lending, and P2P lenders still face substantial risks. To the best of the author's knowledge, government officials, attorneys, and legal scholars in Vietnam rarely consider the practice of the P2P lending business and the social and economic conditions surrounding it.[102] However, it is obvious that these are essential factors when considering measures to mitigate the risks borne by P2P lenders. In light of these considerations, the author has attempted to examine the attitudes and behaviors of stakeholders in the P2P lending business with the aim of finding measures to diversify the risks borne by P2P lenders.

It is widely known that developed countries, such as the United States and Japan, have extensive experience in developing legal measures to diversify the risks borne by lenders and other investors. Therefore, the book has examined the legislations in the United States and Japan that are designed to mitigate problems related to micro- and/or small-sized finance and has considered whether the measures implemented therein are applicable to diversifying risks borne by P2P lenders in Vietnam.

## 1.3 Research Objectives, Methodology, and Book Structure

This book does not aim to suggest policy recommendations for diversifying the risks borne by lenders in the P2P lending scheme in Vietnam. Instead of seeking direct answers to the question "How to protect lenders in the P2P lending scheme in Vietnam?", the book aims to find answers to the following research questions:

(1) What are the specific risks to which lenders in the P2P lending scheme are exposed?
(2) How do the concepts of mutual funding, personal relationships, and professional management contribute to the diversification of risks borne by P2P lenders?
(3) What conditions are likely to enable P2P lenders to diversify their risks?

This book begins with a description of the current status of P2P lending and the risks associated with the P2P lending scheme in Vietnam. For this purpose, the book utilizes various sources, including government reports, statistics, academic articles, and comments by attorneys and industry experts. From a historical and comparative perspective, this books then examines the legislations in the United States and Japan,

[102] For example, Ha and Thuc briefly described the current situation of P2P lending business in Vietnam (just mentioning the number of P2P lending platforms operating in Vietnam, the information risk faced by the lenders, and the current governing regulations) in their article "Kinh Nghiệm Cho Vay Ngang Hàng Ở Một Số Quốc Gia Trên Thế Giới Và Bài Học Cho Việt Nam" [Experience on Peer-to-Peer Lending in Some Countries and Lessons for Vietnam]. Another example is that attorneys at Allens Law Firm discussed the model of P2P lending business and the P2P lending market in Vietnam, but they did not consider the social and economic conditions surrounding the lending business in their paper "Peer-to-Peer Lending in Vietnam." See Hà and Thực (2019) and Allens Law Firm (2019).

which are designed to mitigate problems related to micro- and/or small-sized finance. This book also examines the specific risks borne by lenders (and possible lenders) in the P2P lending scheme by means of comparison with conventional financing schemes. In addition, targeted in-depth interviews with Vietnamese middle-class people were conducted to gather firsthand insights into their attitudes toward a mutual funding scheme.

In light of the abovementioned background and considerations, this book is structured with six chapters besides the Introduction (Chap. 1) and the Conclusion (Chap. 9).

Chapter 2 begins with an observation and description of the historical background of micro- and/or small-sized finance in Vietnam. The author believes this is helpful for understanding why P2P lending, a new form of micro- and/or small-sized finance, has been developing rapidly despite existing risks and the absence of a regulatory framework. In the first section of this chapter, the background of micro- and/or small-sized finance in Vietnam is described, the reasons for its further development are examined, the legislative history of Vietnamese laws on micro- and/or small-sized finance is discussed, and the current laws on micro- and/or small-sized finance in Vietnam are outlined. In the second section, the growth of P2P lending in Vietnam is described, the current regulations governing the P2P lending business are outlined, and the regulatory approach to the P2P lending business in the country is presented.

Chapter 3 discusses the risks associated with micro- and/or small-sized finance and explores how P2P lending challenges existing risk mitigating frameworks for micro- and/or small-sized finance. The first section of this chapter focuses on the specific risks arising from micro- and/or small-sized finance via P2P lending platforms in Vietnam, which generally include risks related to micro- and/or small-sized finance, risks inherent to online platforms, and risks emerging from the combination of micro- and/or small-sized finance and online platforms. The second section of this chapter examines the exposure of individual participants in the P2P lending scheme—namely, P2P lenders, borrowers, and platform service providers—to the risks when engaging in micro- and/or small-sized finance through online lending platforms in Vietnam. It begins with a comparative analysis of the risks faced by P2P lenders and those faced by lenders in conventional financing schemes, followed by a comparison of the risks faced by P2P borrowers and borrowers in conventional financing schemes. The section finally examines the risks faced by platform service providers. In the third section of this chapter, the concern about the risks borne by P2P lenders is justified by using basic tools of economics (i.e., demand and supply curves).

Chapter 4 discusses approaches to risk diversification in micro- and/or small-sized financing schemes in Vietnam and demonstrates why these approaches are insufficient for managing the risks associated with P2P lending. This chapter firstly traces and summarizes the various micro- and/or small-sized financing schemes in Vietnam, along with their historical background. Then it outlines the approaches employed to diversify the risks involved in these micro- and/or small-sized financing schemes. Specifically, it examines various approaches to the diversification of risks, including collateral, due diligence, sharing risk among syndicated lenders, limiting risk by setting up a lending limit for a single borrower, provisional funds, credit insurance, and secondary markets. Additionally, it provides an overview of the laws governing these approaches in the country and analyzes their limitations in addressing the risks posed by P2P lending in Vietnam.

Chapter 5 provides a comparative and historical analysis of the approaches employed by the United States, Japan, and Vietnam to diversify the risks involved in various micro- and/or small-sized financing schemes. The chapter begins by tracing the historical development of various micro- and/or small-sized financing schemes in the United States and Japan and summarizing their key characteristics. It then examines various risk diversification strategies in the two countries, including the use of collateral, due diligence, risk sharing among syndicated lenders, lending limits for individual borrowers, provisional funds, credit insurance, and secondary markets. The chapter ends with a comparative summary of the approaches used by the United States, Japan, and Vietnam to diversify risks in various micro- and/or small-sized financing schemes.

Chapter 6 examines the role of mutual help and mutual funding in mitigating risks. The first section of this chapter explores the concept of mutual help, while the second section focuses on to an understanding of mutual funding. The third section discusses the role of personal relationships between members of a mutual funding scheme in mitigating the risks borne by P2P lenders. It also elaborates on the role of professional management of loans and borrowers in a mutual funding scheme in the current urbanized society in Vietnam, where the Internet is widely used. In light of this understanding, Chap. 6 proposes to employ the measures used in a mutual funding scheme to diversify risks borne by P2P lenders.

Chapter 7 describes an empirical study on P2P lending in Vietnam that aims to find evidence supporting the proposal made in Chap. 6. The empirical study focuses on attitudes toward a mutual funding scheme among middle-class citizens in Vietnam, as well as the role of personal relationships and professional management of loans and borrowers in the P2P lending business in the country. This chapter also explains the methodology used for the study and presents its results.

Chapter 8 discusses possible measures to diversify and mitigate risks borne by P2P lenders, P2P borrowers, and platform service providers in the course of mutual funding in Vietnam. The first section of this chapter clarifies the risks borne by P2P lenders, which can be mitigated by implementing some of the characteristics of a mutual funding scheme. This section also considers possible measures employed by US and Japanese laws to propose possible solutions to mitigate the risks borne by P2P lenders. The second and third sections of this chapter discuss the employ of possible solutions to mitigate the risks borne by P2P lenders to mitigate the risks borne by the other stakeholders of P2P lending, such as P2P borrowers and platform service providers. These sections further explain how mitigating the risk borne by P2P lenders can benefit the other stakeholders of P2P lending in Vietnam. Finally, this chapter employs a mutual funding scheme and adopts the measures employed by US and Japanese laws to propose possible solutions to mitigate the risks borne by P2P lenders, ensuring the sound development of the lending business in Vietnam.

## References

Abor JY (2017) Entrepreneurial finance for MSMES: A managerial approach for developing markets. Springer, Switzerland

Ahern D (2018) Regulatory arbitrage in a fintech world: devising an optimal EU regulatory response to crowdlending. J Bus Law 3:193–214

Akkizidis I, Stagars M (2016) Marketplace lending, financial analysis, and the future of credit: Integration, profitability and risk management. Wiley, New York

Allen F, Carletti E, Gu X (2020) The Roles of Banks in Financial Systems. In: Berger NA, Molyneux P, Wilson OSJ (eds) The Oxford handbook of banking, 3rd edn. Oxford University Press, Oxford

Allens Law Firm (2019) Peer-to-peer lending in Vietnam. https://www.allens.com.au/globalassets/pdfs/insights/asia/peer-to-peer-lending-in-vietnam.pdf. Accessed 20 Mar 2025

Armendáriz B, Labie M (2011) Introduction and Overview: An Inquiry into the Mismatch in Microfinance. In: Armendáriz B, Labie M (eds) The handbook of microfinance. World Scientific, Singapore

Arun T, Hulme D, Matin I, Rutherford S (2009) Finance for the Poor: The way forward? In: Hulme D, Arun T (eds) Microfinance: A reader. Routledge, London

Bachmann A, Funk B (2011) Online peer-to-peer lending—a literature review. J of Inter Bank and Comm 16:2

Bateman M (2010) Why doesn't microfinance work? the destructive rise of local neoliberalism. Zed Books, New York

BIDV (2025) Guarantee. https://bidv.com.vn/!ut/p/z0/04_Sj9CPykssy0xPLMnMz0vMAfIjo8ziDRw9jQw9DQz9_X0cjQzMDI0tzFw8TCxNDA31C7IdFQHJGMJY/. Accessed 2 Mar 2025

Calebe R, Loriana P, Paolo T (2016) How does p2p lending fit into the consumer credit market? https://papers.ssrn.com/sol3/papers.cfm?abstract_id=2848043. Accessed 20 Mar 2025

Cambridge Dictionary Online (2025a). https://dictionary.cambridge.org/dictionary/english/savings-and-credit-co-operative. Accessed 20 Mar 2025

Cambridge Dictionary Online (2025b). https://dictionary.cambridge.org/dictionary/english/credit-union. Accessed 20 Mar 2025

Choudhry M (2012) The principles of banking. Wiley, Singapore

Cummins M, Lynn T, Bhaird MC, Rosati P (2019) Addressing Information Asymmetries in Online Peer-to-Peer Lending. In: Lynn T, Mooney GJ, Rosati P, Cummins M (eds) Disrupting finance: fintech and strategy in the 21st century. Palgrave Pivot, Cham

Cuong NV (2022) Regulations on peer-to-peer lending in vietnam: status and recommendations. Legis. Stud. 22:10

Dân VĐ (2019) Peer-to-peer lending: new financial technology platform and suggestions for its operation in Vietnam. Finan and Mon Mar Rev 3:42

Davis TK, Murphy J (2016) Peer-to-peer lending: structure, risks and regulation. JASSA: The Finsia J of Appl Fin 3:37

DongA Bank (2023) Domestic Guarantee. https://www.dongabank.com.vn/en/service/897/domestic-guarantee. Accessed 2 May 2023

Eschholz S, Djabbarpour J (2018) Big data and scoring in the financial sector. In: Hoeren T, Barbara KR (eds) Big data in context: legal, social and technological insights. Springer, Cham

Fiin Credit (2025a) Đầu tư [Investment]. https://fiin.vn/dau-tu/. Accessed 20 Mar 2025

Fiin Credit (2025b) Vay tiền ngắn hạn [Borrowing short-term loans]. https://fiin.vn/vay-tien/vay-ngan-han/. Accessed 20 Mar 2025

FINCA International About FINCA. https://finca.org/about-finca. Accessed 20 Mar 2025

Fintechnews Vietnam (2018) P2P lending activity accelerates in Vietnam. https://fintechnews.sg/24833/vietnam/p2p-lending-activity-in-vietnam/. Accessed 20 Mar 2025

Freixas X, Rochet JC (2008). Microeconomics of banking, 2nd edn. The MIT Press, Massachusetts

Ghatak M, Guinnane WT (1999) The economics of lending with joint liability: theory and practice. J of Develop Eco 60:195
Grameen Bank (2023) About Grameen bank. https://grameenbank.org/about/introduction. Accessed 20 Apr 2023
Greenbaum IS, Thakor VA, Boot WAA (2019) Contemporary financial intermediation, 4th edn. Academic Press, London
Hà NTL, Thực VV (2019) Kinh nghiệm cho vay ngang hàng ở một số quốc gia trên thế giới và bài học cho Việt Nam [Experience on peer-to-peer lending in some countries and lessons for Vietnam]. Finan and Mon Mar Rev 19:40
Hassan MK (2002) The microfinance revolution and the grameen bank experience in Bangladesh. Financ Mark Institutions Instruments 11:205
Hiệu NV (2018) Cho vay ngang hàng - kinh nghiệm thế giới và hàm ý cho Việt Nam' [Peer-to-peer lending—experience in the world and implications for Vietnam]. Bank Rev 22:10
Hughes PJ, Mester JL (2020) The performance of financial institutions modeling, evidence, and some policy implications. In: Berger NA, Molyneux P, Wilson OSJ (eds) The Oxford Handbook of Banking, 3rd edn. Oxford University Press, Oxford
Johnson S, Arvind A, Assadi D (2010) Online or offline? the rise of peer-to-peer lending in microfinance. J of Elec Com in Org 8:26
Karlan D, Goldberg N (2011) Microfinance Evaluation Strategies: Notes on Methodology and Findings. In: Armendáriz B, Labie M (eds) The handbook of microfinance. World Scientific Publishing, Singapore
Kartika R (2023) Financial technology innovation—peer-to-peer (p2p) lending in the RCEP member states. In: Mahani H, Muhammad A, Norainie A (eds) Regional Comprehensive Economic Partnership. Bentham Books, Singapore
Ledgerwood J (1999) Sustainable banking with the poor, microfinance handbook: an institutional and financial perspective. World Bank Publications, Washington, D.C.
Lendbiz (2025a). https://lendbiz.vn/. Accessed 20 Mar 2025
Lendbiz (2025b) Câu hỏi thường gặp [Frequently asked questions]. https://lendbiz.vn/cau-hoi-thuong-gap/. Accessed 20 Mar 2025
LendingClub (2025a) About us. https://www.lendingclub.com/company/about-us. Accessed 20 Mar 2025
LendingClub (2025b) How it works. https://www.lendingclub.com/investing/peer-to-peer. Accessed 20 Mar 2025
LendingClub (2025c) What should an investor expect when a loan payment is late? https://help.lendingclub.com/hc/en-us/articles/216127917. Accessed 20 Mar 2025
LendingClub (2025d) Where can investors see ongoing collection activities on late notes? https://help.lendingclub.com/hc/en-us/articles/216127987-Where-Can-Investors-See-Ongoing-Collection-Activities-on-Late-Notes-. Accessed 20 Mar 2025
Lenz R (2016) Peer-to-peer lending: opportunities and risks. Eur J Risk Regul 7:688
LinkBank (2025a). https://linkbank.vn/. Accessed 20 Mar 2025
LinkBank (2025b) Vay tiền nhanh [Quick loans]. https://linkbank.vn/vay-tien-nhanh. Accessed 20 Mar 2025
Lo B (2016) It ain't broke: the case for continued SEC regulation of p2p lending. Harvard Bus Law Rev Online, 6: 87-110
Lực CV (2018) Quản lý cho vay ngang hàng: kinh nghiệm quốc tế và một số gợi ý cho Việt Nam [Peer-to-peer lending management: international experience and some suggestions for Vietnam]. https://cafef.vn/cac-nuoc-dang-quan-ly-cho-vay-ngang-hang-nhu-the-nao-20181017140302299.chn. Accessed 20 Mar 2025
M7-MFI (2025) About us. http://www.m7mfi.vn/en/about-us.html. Accessed 20 Mar 2025
Mankiw NG (2018) Principles of economics, 8th edn. Cengage Learning, Massachusetts
Manos R, Gueyie JP, Yaron J (2013) Dilemmas and directions in microfinance research. In: Gueyie JP, Manos R, Yaron J (eds) Microfinance in developing countries: issues, policies, and performance evaluation

Milne A, Parboteeah P (2016) The business models and economics of peer-to-peer lending. https://www.ceps.eu/download/publication/?id=9451&pdf=ECRI%20RR17%20P2P%20Lending.pdf. Accessed 20 Mar 2025

Nelson C (2013) Community-based providers. In: Joanna L, Alan G (eds) The new microfinance handbook: a financial market system perspective. World Bank Publications, Washington, DC.

Ngoc LH (2020) Peer-to-peer lending in china and recommendations for Vietnam. Indus and Trad Mag 2:36

Nhi LY (2019) Nhiều rủi ro với cho vay ngang hàng [Many risks in association with p2p lending]. https://tapchitaichinh.vn/nhieu-rui-ro-voi-cho-vay-ngang-hang.html. Accessed 20 Mar 2025

Patwardhan A (2017) Peer-to-peer lending. In: Chuen DKL, Deng R (eds) Handbook of Blockchain, digital finance, and inclusion, volume 1: cryptocurrency, fintech, insurtech, and regulation. Academic Press, London

Pham Law Firm (2023) Hoạt động cho vay và cấp bảo lãnh của doanh nghiệp [Lending business and guarantee provision services of enterprises]. https://phamlaw.com/hoat-dong-cho-vay-va-cap-bao-lanh-cua-doanh-nghiep.html. Accessed 20 Mar 2025

Prosper About us. https://www.prosper.com/about. Accessed 20 Mar 2025

Raaij FVW (2016) Understanding consumer financial behavior: money management in an age of Financial illiteracy. Palgrave Macmillan, London

Robinson SM (2001) The microfinance revolution. World Bank Publications, Washington, DC.

Robinson SM (2009) Supply and demand in microfinance: the case for a financial systems approach. In: David H, Thankom A (eds) Microfinance: a reader. Routledge, New York

Rutherford S (2011) Boosting the poor's capacity to save: a note on instalment plans and their variants. In: Beatriz A, Marc L (eds) The handbook of microfinance. World Scientific Publishing, Manchester

SBI Social Lending (2023a) Company information. https://sbsl.bankers.co.jp/pages/aboutus. Accessed 2 May 2023

SBI Social Lending (2023b) Transaction flow. https://sbsl.bankers.co.jp/pages/flow. Accessed 2 May 2023

Schmidt HR (2013) Core values of microfinance under scrutiny: back to basics? In: Köhn D (ed) Microfinance 3.0: reconciling sustainability with social outreach and responsible delivery. Springer, Heidelberg

Samitsu A (2017) Structure of p2p lending and investor protection: analyses based on an international comparison of legal arrangements. https://www.boj.or.jp/en/research/wps_rev/lab/lab17e06.htm. Accessed 20 Mar 2025

Statista (2025) Alternative lending transaction value by segment in Vietnam. https://www.statista.com/forecasts/1228504/alternative-lending-transaction-value-by-segment-vietnam. Accessed 20 Mar 2025

Sundaresan S (2008) The changing landscape of microfinance. In: Sundaresan S (ed) Microfinance: emerging trends and challenges. Edward Elgar Publishing, Cheltenham

Tima. https://tima.vn/. Accessed 20 Mar 2025

Thắng PH (2019) Đánh giá khách hàng vay tại các công ty p2p lending [Assessing borrowers' creditworthiness at p2p lending companies]. https://thoibaonganhang.vn/danh-gia-khach-hang-vay-tai-cac-cong-ty-p2p-lending-94334.html. Accessed 20 Mar 2025

The English translation of the Civil Code 2015 of Vietnam, Article 116 (trans: Luatvietnam.vn). https://english.luatvietnam.vn/law-no-91-2015-qh13-dated-november-24-2015-of-the-national-assembly-on-civil-code-101333-doc1.html. Accessed 20 Mar 2025

The English translation of Decree No. 34/2018/ND-CP of Vietnam, Article 15, clause 2 (trans: Thuvienphapluat). https://thuvienphapluat.vn/van-ban/Doanh-nghiep/Decree-34-2018-ND-CP-operation-of-credit-gurantee-funds-for-medium-and-small-enterprises-414270.aspx?v=d. Accessed 20 Mar 2025

The English translation of the Law on Support for SMEs 2017 of Vietnam, Article 4 (trans: the Supreme Court of Vietnam). https://www.toaan.gov.vn/webcenter/portal/spc/document-detail?Keyword=&dDocName=TOAAN011016. Accessed 20 Mar 2025

The General Department of Taxation website: https://www.gdt.gov.vn/wps/portal/english. Accessed 20 Mar 2025

The National Business Registration portal: https://dangkykinhdoanh.gov.vn/en/Pages/default.aspx. Accessed 20 Mar 2025

Trang NTT, Minh LX, Hà VTN (2019) Cho vay ngang hàng ở Việt Nam và bài học kinh nghiệm quản lý từ một số quốc gia [Peer-to-peer lending in vietnam and lessons on management from some countries]. Sci Tech Dev J – Eco Law Manag 3:211-217

Vaymuon (2020). https://vaymuon.vn/. Accessed 20 Mar 2020

Viet Nam News (2019) Government moves to legalise p2p lending. https://vietnamnews.vn/economy/506959/government-moves-to-legalise-p2p-lending.html. Accessed 20 Mar 2025

Vietnam's Law on Credit Institutions 2024 (trans: Thuvienphapluat). https://thuvienphapluat.vn/van-ban/Tien-te-Ngan-hang/Law-32-2024-QH15-Credit-institutions-606780.aspx?tab=1. Accessed 20 Mar 2025

Vietnam's Law on Enterprises 2020 (trans: Luatvietnam.vn). https://english.luatvietnam.vn/law-on-enterprises-no-59-2020-qh14-dated-june-17-2020-of-the-national-assembly-186272-doc1.html. Accessed 20 Mar 2025

Vũ L (2019) Loại hình cho vay ngang hàng: chuẩn hóa các quy định để giảm thiểu rủi ro [Types of peer-to-peer lending: standardize regulations to minimize risks]. https://thoibaotaichinhvietnam.vn/loai-hinh-cho-vay-ngang-hang-chuan-hoa-cac-quy-dinh-de-giam-thieu-rui-ro-27571.html. Accessed 20 Mar 2025

Wang H, Greiner M, Aronson J (2009) People-to-people lending: the emerging e-commerce transformation of a financial market. In: Matthew LN, Michael JS, Troy JS (eds) Value creation in e-business management. Springer, Heidelberg

Wei S (2016) Designing optimal regulation for financial innovation in capital raising—regulatory options for China's peer-to-peer lending sector. Bank Financ Law Rev 31:539–572

Westover J (2008) The record of microfinance: the effectiveness/ineffectiveness of microfinance programs as a means of alleviating poverty. Elec J of Socio

Yum H, Lee B, Chae M (2012) From the wisdom of crowds to my own judgment in microfinance through online peer-to-peer lending platforms. Elec Com Res and App 11:469

Zopa (2025) About us. https://www.zopa.com/. Accessed 20 Mar 2025

# Chapter 2
# Micro- and/or Small-Sized Finance and the Development of P2P Lending in Vietnam

## 2.1 Background of Micro- and/or Small-Sized Finance in Vietnam

### *2.1.1 Micro- and/or Small-Sized Finance in Vietnam*

Micro- and/or small-sized finance in Vietnam has been considered a significant tool for supporting poor and low-income individuals in accessing financial services.[1] It is said that, at the beginning of its development, micro- and/or small-sized finance in Vietnam primarily provided micro and/or small loans (or micro and/or small credit) to assist poor and low-income individuals in covering their daily expenses and engaging in small businesses.[2] However, it is important to note the impact of the country's socioeconomic changes throughout history on its financial offerings for poor and low-income individuals. Initially, these individuals were provided with micro and small loans, often referred to as micro and/or small finance. Over time, these services have expanded to include a broad array of financial options. These include savings, insurance, payment services, and money transfers. In addition to these, business advice has also been offered as part of the wider suite of financial services.[3]

It has been documented that prior to the invasion of French colonists in 1858, Vietnam did not have formal banking or credit institutions.[4] At that time, the economy was primarily self-sufficient, characterized by rudimentary and underdeveloped economic activities.[5] During the colonial period from 1858 to 1945, French

[1] See Duong and Nghiem (2022, p. 406).

[2] See Anh et al. (2014, p. 14).

[3] Anh et al. (2014, p. 18) and Nguyen (2020, p. 72).

[4] See Du et al. (2013, p. 2).

[5] Du et al. (2013).



Y. H. Nguyen, *Regulating Peer-to-Peer Lending in Vietnam*,
https://doi.org/10.1007/978-981-96-9505-8_2

colonists established a monetary and credit system to provide capital for their economic activities in Indochina.[6]

After the August Revolution in 1945, Vietnam gained independence and began to establish its own independent monetary and banking system.[7] The first credit institution in the country, the Production Credit Office, was formed in 1947 to provide funds for production and collective businesses.[8] In 1951, the Vietnam National Bank[9] was established to facilitate production and implement the state's credit policy. The Bank's main functions included issuing banknotes, mobilizing capital, and providing loans.[10]

After the Geneva Agreements in 1954, Vietnam was temporarily divided into the North and the South. Socialism was continued in the North, while capitalism was adopted in the South.[11] In the North, it is worth noting that credit and banking institutions were established to promote credit activities aimed at revitalizing the economy and developing the country. Rural credit cooperatives were established in 1956 to mobilize capital and provide loans to farmers.[12] In 1957, the Vietnam Construction Bank was formed (under the Ministry of Finance) to allocate loans for construction.[13] In 1959, socialist savings funds were established within state agencies and state-owned enterprises (hereinafter referred to as "SOEs"). These funds were designed to mobilize deposit savings, thereby providing banks with the necessary resources to extend loans to employees.[14] Furthermore, in 1962, the Vietnam Bank for Foreign Trade was established as a separate entity from the Foreign Exchange Bureau of the State Bank of Vietnam, with the specific aim of providing loans for foreign trade activities.[15]

In the South, it is noteworthy that a banking system, encompassing a central bank, commercial banks, and rural banks, was established. This system was designed to provide credit for economic activities, operating under the management of the South Vietnam government and the auspices of the United States.[16] The central bank was granted the authority to issue currency for circulation and to oversee banking

---

[6] See The State Bank of Vietnam (2025a) and Du et al. (2013).

[7] See The State Bank of Vietnam (2025a).

[8] Du et al. (2013).

[9] The Vietnam National Bank was renamed the State Bank of Vietnam in 1961. See The State Bank of Vietnam (2025b).

[10] The Vietnam Bank for Social Policies (2025b).

[11] The Vietnam Bank for Social Policies (2025b).

[12] Although the rural credit cooperative network expanded quickly and reached 5000 credit cooperatives by 1960, it collapsed and was reestablished in the late twentieth century. See Chính and Hoàng (2009, p. 82).

[13] See Du et al. (2013, p. 3), The Vietnam Bank for Social Policies (2025b), and BIDV (2022).

[14] See Chính and Hoàng (2009).

[15] See Du et al. (2013, p. 3) and The Vietnam Bank for Social Policies (2025b).

[16] Du et al. (2013, p. 3) and The Vietnam Bank for Social Policies (2025b).

activities in the region.[17] Before the country's reunification in 1975, the South was home to 40 commercial banks with 203 branches, primarily providing funds for commerce, imports, and consumer goods activities. Additionally, there were 87 rural banks, which primarily provided funds for the agricultural sector.[18] However, the banking system in the South was nationalized and merged into the banking system in the North after 1975 to unify the banking system throughout the country.[19]

It is pertinent to note that from 1976 to 1985, under the central planning regime, credit activities were developed to provide loans for the economy, especially for SOEs.[20] During this period, the banking system primarily served as a budgetary tool, and the government directly intervened in banking operations as well as determining credit supply.[21] In general, it has been found that the micro- and/or small-sized financial market "played a minimal role"[22] in providing loans for individuals and private businesses.

The development of the micro- and/or small-sized financial market in Vietnam "is historically marked by the 'Reform' in 1986,"[23] known as "Đổi Mới." Since the Đổi Mới, Vietnam has developed a socialist-oriented market economy and established a new credit and banking system. This system includes various providers designed to provide micro- and/or small-sized finance for the economy.[24] In the late 1980s, credit institutions were established to facilitate the implementation of the government's social protection measures aimed at supporting the poor and the agricultural sector.[25] For example, the Vietnam Agricultural Development Bank[26] was established in 1988 to meet the demand for credit by people working in the agricultural sector in rural areas.[27] It should be noted that, at that time, more than 90% of the country's poor population lived in rural areas,[28] where approximately 70% of the country's labor force worked in the agricultural sector.[29] In 1995, the establishment of the Vietnam Bank for the Poor[30] was announced. This institution

[17] See Hà (2017, p. 73).

[18] Hà (2017).

[19] See The Vietnam Bank for Social Policies (2025b).

[20] The Vietnam Bank for Social Policies (2025b).

[21] See Chính and Hoàng (2009, p. 77) and Du et al. (2013, p. 4).

[22] See Vuong (2019, p. 202) and Phan and Gan (2017, p. 24).

[23] Phan and Gan (2017).

[24] See The Vietnam Bank for Social Policies (2025b) and Du et al. (2013, p. 3).

[25] See Hansen and Diaz (2008, p. 21).

[26] Which was renamed the Vietnam Bank for Agriculture and Rural Development in 1996 in accordance with Decision No. 280/QD-NH5 dated October 15, 1996, of the State Bank of Vietnam.

[27] See Agribank (2025a, b).

[28] See World Bank (2023).

[29] See Mccaig and Pavcnik (2017, p. 82).

[30] Which was reorganized into the Vietnam Bank for Social Policies in 2002 by integrating all the operations of the Vietnam Bank for the Poor and other policy lending programs extended by the government, including loans to students, employment generation programs, and lending programs for small entrepreneurs. The bank operated for nonprofit purposes and poverty reduction. See The Vietnam Bank for Social Policies (2025a, b).

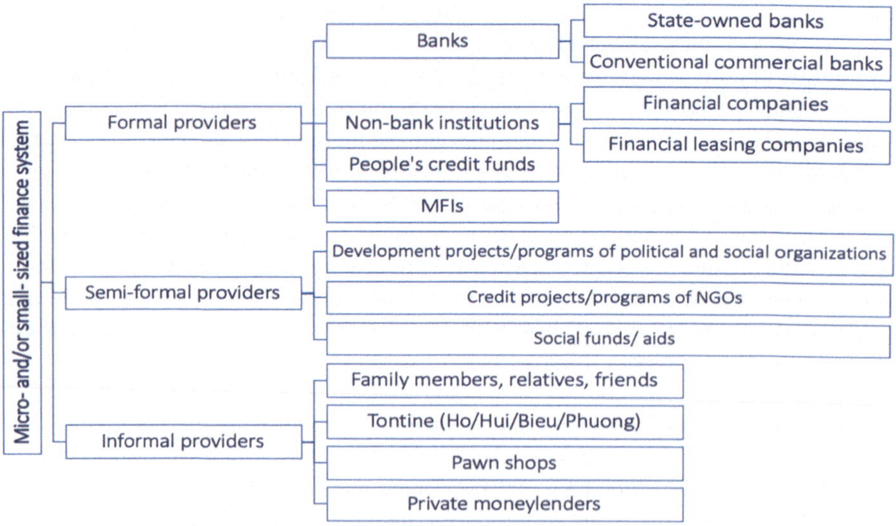


**Fig. 2.1** Micro- and/or small-sized finance system in Vietnam

aimed to serve low-income households across the country.[31] In addition to the aforementioned banks, people's credit funds were formed in 1993 to address the high demand for productive credit in rural areas.[32] In the early 1990s, nongovernmental organizations (NGOs) and international organizations, in cooperation with the Vietnamese government, developed various credit and savings programs and projects. These initiatives aimed to reduce poverty and income inequality in the country.[33]

The current credit and banking system in Vietnam includes formal, semiformal, and informal micro- and/or small-sized finance providers (as shown in Fig. 2.1). Among micro- and/or small-sized finance providers, those that are registered and subject to banking regulations and regular supervision by the State Bank have been considered formal providers.[34] A wide range of formal providers offering micro- and/or small-sized finance includes 4 state-owned commercial banks,[35] 2 policy

[31] See Duong and Nghiem (2022, p. 407).

[32] See Nghiem et al. (2007, p. 74).

[33] See Phan and Gan (2017, p. 24) and Anh et al. (2014).

[34] See Churchill and Frankiewicz (2006, p. 38), and Pham and Lensink (2007, p. 182).

[35] Including the Vietnam Bank for Agriculture and Rural Development (Agribank), the Construction Commercial One Member Limited Liability Bank (Construction Bank), the Global Petro Sole Member Limited Liability Commercial Bank, and the Ocean Commercial One Member Limited Liability Bank.

banks,[36] 9 wholly foreign-owned banks, 31 joint-stock commercial banks, Co-operative Bank of Vietnam, 26 nonbank credit institutions (including 16 finance companies and 10 leasing companies), 50 foreign bank branches, 67 representative offices of foreign credit institutions, 1182 people's credit funds, and 4 licensed MFIs[37] as of September 3, 2024.[38]

Semiformal service providers represent the second type of micro- and small-sized finance providers. While these entities are registered and subject to all relevant general laws, they are considered informal because they do not fall under banking regulations and supervision by the State Bank.[39] More than 450 semiformal micro- and/or small-sized finance development projects and programs, established by political organizations, sociopolitical organizations, and NGOs, were operating in 2019 to provide credit for poor and low-income individuals.[40] It has also been discovered that many of these development projects and programs are managed by sociopolitical organizations, such as the Vietnam Women's Union, the Vietnam General Confederation of Labor, and the Vietnam Farmers' Union.[41] In addition to development projects and programs, the SME Development Fund, which was established by the Prime Minister in 2013,[42] can be considered a semiformal micro- and/or small-sized finance provider. The Fund is an extra-budgetary state and not-for-profit financial institution and provides loans to innovative startup SMEs and SMEs involved in industrial linkage clusters and value chains.[43]

It is widely known that informal micro- and/or small-sized finance providers represent another category of micro- and/or small-sized finance providers. They can be entities, whether unregistered or registered with business registration authorities as financial institutions, that are not subject to banking regulations and supervision by the State Bank.[44] For example, unregistered entities, such as family members, relatives, friends, neighbors, and private moneylenders, provide individuals in local communities with microcredit in cash or kind with short maturities.[45] Registered

---

[36] Including the Vietnam Bank for Social Policies and the Vietnam Development Bank.

[37] Including the M7 Microfinance Institution, the Tinh Thuong One-member Limited Liability Microfinance Institution, the Thanh Hoa Microfinance Institution, and the Capital Aid for Employment of the Poor Microfinance Institution Limited.

[38] See The State Bank of Vietnam (2025c).

[39] See Churchill and Frankiewicz (2006, p. 38), and Pham and Lensink (2007, p. 182).

[40] See Mai et al. (2019, p. 23).

[41] Mai et al. (2019).

[42] The English translation of Decision No. 601/QD-TTg of Vietnam on the establishment of the SME Development Fund.

[43] Vietnam's Law on Support for SMEs 2017, Article 20.

[44] See Churchill and Frankiewicz (2006, p. 38), Pham and Lensink (2007, p. 182), and Schreiner (2001, p. 637).

[45] See Phan and Gan (2017, p. 25) and Bui (2017, p. 91).

entities such as pawnshops and tontines (Ho/Hui/Bieu/Phuong)[46] are also micro- and/or small-sized credit sources for individuals to cover their daily expenses and engage in small businesses.[47] In 2019, informal micro- and/or small-sized credit was estimated to account for approximately 20% of the total credit in the economy.[48]

It is worth noting that over the past 35 years, micro- and/or small-sized finance in Vietnam has made significant contributions to poverty reduction.[49] As has been explained, this is because the micro- and/or small-sized finance sector in Vietnam has a strength, compared with other sectors, in providing financial services to poor and low-income individuals living in rural and remote areas, thanks to the participation of various micro- and/or small-sized finance providers.[50] It has been noted that many of the providers have access points that are convenient for individuals in rural and remote areas and can offer financial products and services that are suitable for the needs of poor and low-income customers, with simple procedures and without physical collateral.[51]

Conventional micro- and/or small-sized finance framework in Vietnam has been regarded as a framework that is characterized by government control and subsidies.[52] One possible reason is that the framework consists of state-owned or state-directed institutions and development programs and projects managed by political organizations and sociopolitical organizations, as mentioned above. These institutions and development programs and projects have provided credit to the poor, low-income individuals, and SMEs under the direction of the state or in accordance with the state's policies.[53] In addition, it has been discovered that the provision of micro and/or small loans by state-owned institutions and development programs and projects managed by political organizations and sociopolitical organizations heavily relies on government subsidies.[54] During the period from 2008 to 2011, such subsidies have been estimated to cost the government approximately USD 200 million annually.[55] However, it should be noted that large-scale subsidized credit programs may result in significant challenges for the development of the micro- and/or

[46] Ho/Hui/Bieu/Phuong are local rotating savings and credit associations, which are known in Vietnam as Ho in the North, Bieu/Phuong in the Middle, or Hui in the South. They are a method of group financing, in which individuals who know and trust each other form a self-selected group and agree to contribute a regular fixed amount every period (usually a week or month). Members then take turns receiving the full amount collected in the period until all members have had a turn to receive funds. See, Pham and Lensink (2007, p. 186), and Phan and Gan (2017, p. 25).

[47] See Bui et al. (2018, p. 22).

[48] See Sơn (2019).

[49] See Anh et al. (2014, p. 16). As a result, Vietnam's poverty rate decreased from 58% in 1993 to less than 4% in 2019. See Trinh (2019, p. 74) and Anh (2019).

[50] See Mai et al. (2019, p. 23).

[51] Mai et al. (2019).

[52] See Bui et al. (2018, p. 27).

[53] See Asia-Pacific Economic Cooperation (2011, p. 1).

[54] Asia-Pacific Economic Cooperation (2011, p. 2).

[55] Asia-Pacific Economic Cooperation (2011).

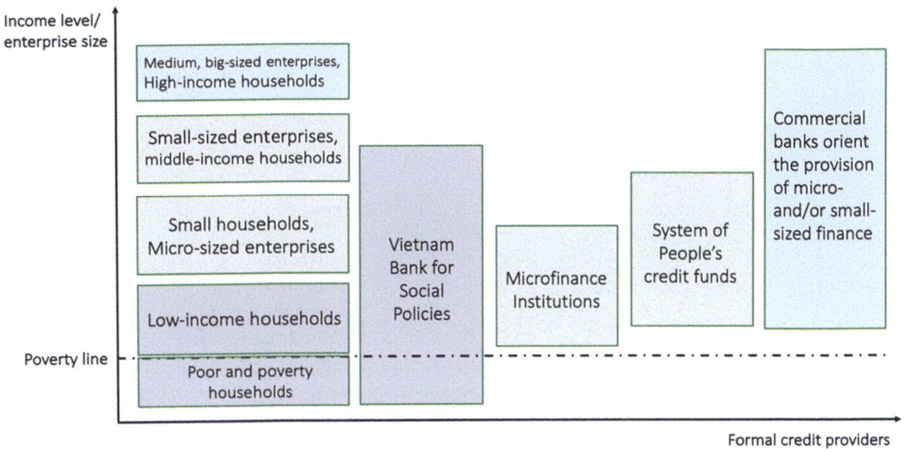


**Fig. 2.2** Formal micro- and/or small-sized finance segmentation in Vietnam

small-sized finance framework, such as a low repayment rate, corruption, and preferential loans being provided to better-off farmers or villagers rather than the poor.

### 2.1.2 *The Need for Further Enhancement of Micro- and/or Small-Sized Finance in Vietnam*

Several authors have noted that despite having a well-established system for providing micro- and small-sized finance services to households and small firms, Vietnam still faces a significant credit gap between the supply and demand sides of the market.[56]

On the supply side, it has been noted that the micro- and/or small-sized finance market is highly fragmented and exhibits overlapping characteristics in certain areas[57] (e.g., see Figs. 2.2 and 2.3).

In the formal micro- and/or small-sized finance sector, as shown in Fig. 2.2, conventional commercial banks tend to focus on providing services to medium- and large-sized enterprises, as well as high-income households. One reason for this tendency is that conventional commercial banks are unlikely to see the economic benefits of providing numerous micro and/or small loans to poor and low-income

[56] See Bui et al. (2018, p. 22), Nguyen and Le (2013, p. 63), and Hansen and Diaz (2008, p. 30).

[57] See Bui (2017), Nguyen and Le (2013, p. 64), Hansen and Diaz (2008, p. 11), and McCarty (2001, p. 3).

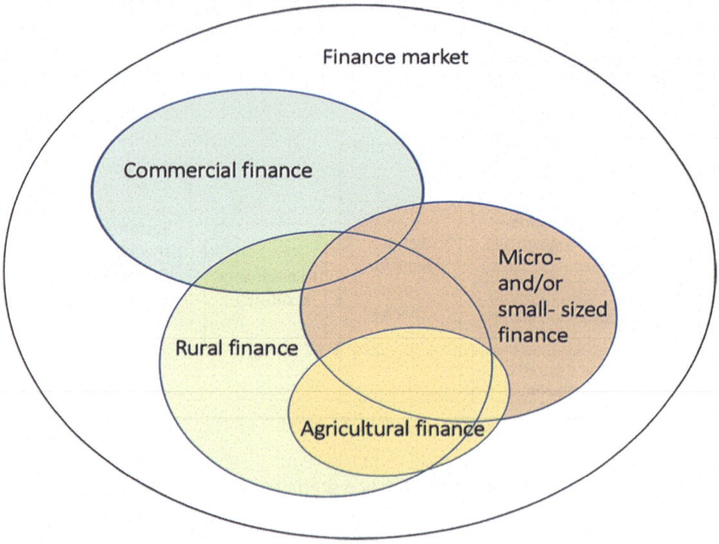


**Fig. 2.3** The overlapping of micro- and/or small-sized finance in Vietnam

households, which can involve high transaction costs. Another reason could be the absence of collateral among poor and low-income individuals to secure loans provided by conventional commercial banks. Consequently, this tendency is likely to leave a credit gap in the micro and/or small-sized finance market.

State-owned banks subsidized by the government have focused on providing micro- and/or small-sized finance in specific market segments to implement credit and banking policies of the government. For example, the Vietnam Bank for Agriculture and Rural Development (hereinafter referred to as "Agribank") and the Construction Commercial One Member Limited Liability Bank (hereinafter referred to as "Construction Bank") have received government subsidies to provide concessional loans for individuals and households in agriculture and rural areas[58] and the construction and housing industry,[59] respectively. The Vietnam Bank for Social Policies (hereinafter referred to as "VBSP") has focused on serving the poor, low-income, and other last-mile populations,[60] while the Vietnam Development Bank (hereinafter referred to as "VDB") has provided concessional loans with subsidized interest rates to government projects, SOEs, and, to a small extent, private SMEs (with the support of international donors) in the infrastructure and export sectors.[61] However, the provision of government subsidies to state-owned banks has been criticized by the NGO community for disregarding financial sustainability and

[58] See Agribank (2025a, b).

[59] See Construction Bank (2025).

[60] See The Vietnam Bank for Social Policies (2025a, b) and Nguyen and Le (2013, p. 72).

[61] See The Vietnam Development Bank (2025) and Hansen and Diaz (2008, p. 10).

distorting the credit market through concessional loans, which have low interest rates and minimal collateral requirements.[62] In particular, several experts from the Vietnam Microfinance Working Group, an NGO founded in Vietnam in 2004,[63] have denounced such government subsidies for impeding the potential development of other microfinance providers.[64]

Moreover, it is worth noting that the lending process of state-owned banks may involve biases in evaluating borrowers' creditworthiness and granting concessional loans.[65] For example, Agribank has been criticized for preferring providing large amounts of credit to SOEs to providing micro- and/or small-sized loans to rural individuals and households.[66] The reasons that have been noted for its preference include the perception that SOEs are regarded as clients with minimal risk due to the expectation of government bailouts in the event of default.[67] Another noteworthy reason is that extending substantial credit to SOEs involves lower transaction costs compared to providing numerous small loans to a significant number of rural individuals and households.[68] As a result, such problems are likely to impede the provision of micro- and/or small-sized loans by state-owned banks to poor and low-income individuals.

People's credit funds have been noted for their focus on serving small households in rural areas.[69] They are voluntarily established by legal entities, individuals, and households as cooperatives for mutual assistance among their members in production, business development, and life.[70] It is worth noting that the operation of people's credit funds mainly involves mobilizing capital from their members and providing them with micro- and/or small-sized loans.[71]

It is not surprising that people's credit funds do not specifically target low-income individuals and micro-sized enterprises. One possible reason could be the limited financial sources of people's credit funds. It has been noted that they may find it difficult to mobilize capital from other individuals and organizations because the interest rates on micro-savings offered by them are very likely to be lower compared to those offered by commercial banks.[72] Another reason that has been noted is that

---

[62] See Nghiem et al. (2007).

[63] The Vietnam Microfinance Working Group officially became a center under the Vietnam Association of Small and Medium Enterprises in September 2011. See Vietnam Microfinance Working Group (2020).

[64] See Nguyen and Le (2013, p. 170).

[65] See Phan and Gan (2017, p. 27).

[66] Phan and Gan (2017, p. 27).

[67] Phan and Gan (2017, p. 27).

[68] Phan and Gan (2017, p. 27).

[69] See Chi and Dung (2022).

[70] See Vietnam's Law on Credit Institutions 2010, Article 6, clause 4.

[71] See Hồng (2020).

[72] It can be seen that people's credit funds are likely to accept deposits and provide loans at lower interest rates in comparison with those offered by commercial banks for the purpose of assisting their members. See Bui et al. (2018, p. 26).

financial products and services offered by people's credit funds are relatively simple, primarily comprising microcredit, micro-savings, and micro-insurance.[73] They are not permitted to open payment accounts and provide via-account payment services.[74] The simplicity of their offerings is likely to make it difficult for them to meet the needs of low-income individuals and micro-sized enterprises. Furthermore, they provide loans to legal entities and individuals who are not their members, with the requirement that the borrowers maintain deposits with them and use their deposit books as collateral.[75] Such requirements may impede low-income individuals and micro-sized enterprises from accessing loans offered by them.

Among formal micro- and/or small-sized finance providers, MFIs are institutions specifically established to provide micro- and/or small-sized finance to low-income individuals and households and micro-sized enterprises.[76] It can be seen that MFIs have difficulties in serving low-income individuals and micro-sized enterprises, primarily due to their limited capital sources and the narrow scope of services they can provide. It has been noted that the restriction on the number of MFI members to five[77] is likely to limit the capital they can obtain from member contributions.[78] Also, MFIs may find it difficult to attract voluntary savings from their customers because the interest rates offered by them are very likely to be lower than those offered by commercial banks.[79] They, therefore, are likely to rely on compulsory savings, which is a requirement for joining microfinance operations through teams or group savings.[80] In addition, it has been found that financial products and services offered by MFIs are relatively simple, primarily comprising microcredit, micro-savings, and micro-insurance.[81] They are not permitted to open payment accounts and provide via-account payment services.[82] Furthermore, it has been noted that MFIs may find it difficult to compete with government-subsidized banks to provide loans for low-income individuals and micro-sized enterprises because they do not receive government subsidies.

[73] See Mai et al. (2019, p. 24) and Phan (2019, p. 28).

[74] See Hồng (2020).

[75] The English translation of Circular No. 13/VBHN-NHNN of Vietnam on people's credit funds, Article 37, clause 3, provides that "[p]eople's credit funds provide loans to legal entities and individuals who are not their members but have deposits with them, based on the security provided by deposit books issued by themselves."

[76] Vietnam's Law on Credit Institutions 2024, Article 6, clause 4, provides that "[m]icrofinance institution means a type of credit institution which mainly conducts some banking operations to meet the needs of low-income individuals and households and super small-sized enterprises."

[77] Vietnam's Law on Credit Institutions 2024, Article 70, clause 1.

[78] See Trinh (2019, p. 75).

[79] See Bui et al. (2018, p. 26).

[80] Bui et al. (2018 p. 26).

[81] See Mai et al. (2019, p. 24) and Phan (2019).

[82] Vietnam's Law on Credit Institutions 2024, Article 121.

In the semiformal micro- and/or small-sized finance sector, it has been observed that development programs and projects managed by sociopolitical organizations and NGOs and funded by bilateral or multilateral donors and social funds have attempted to reach poor and low-income populations.[83] It has been found that development projects and programs managed by sociopolitical organizations have made use of their existing networks to provide loans to poor and low-income individuals, thereby contributing to the implementation of the government's poverty alleviation objectives.[84] In addition, development projects and programs funded by NGOs and donors have primarily focused on delivering small and short-term loans with regular installment repayments to poor households in remote areas.[85]

However, it is easily predicted that ensuring the long-term financial sustainability of semiformal micro- and/or small-sized finance providers will be a significant challenge. This is due to several reasons as follows. Micro- and/or small-sized finance development projects and programs can mobilize compulsory and voluntary savings from their members. However, this capital source is likely to be very limited. It has been noted that these development projects and programs may find it difficult to borrow from conventional commercial banks because they are unlikely to have collateral to secure commercial loans.[86] Moreover, it has been explained that they have heavily relied on subsidies from sociopolitical organizations, NGOs, and donors, which are scarce and uncertain in the future.[87] For example, several significant credit programs, such as those of the Oxford Committee for Famine Relief (OXFAM), the United Nations International Children's Emergency Fund (UNICEF), the United Nations Population Fund (UNFPA), and the Coöperatieve Rabobank U.A. (Rabobank), ceased operating or phrased out of Vietnam since 2015.[88]

In the informal micro- and/or small-sized finance sector, it has been discovered that loans from family members, relatives, friends, neighbors, tontines, pawnshops, and private moneylenders are primarily provided for consumption purposes in daily life.[89] It has been noted that while loans from family members, relatives, friends, neighbors, and tontines are almost interest-free, loans from pawnshops and private moneylenders often come with higher interest rates compared to those offered by commercial banks. In case individuals have difficulties in accessing loans from formal and semiformal credit providers, as well as loans from family members, relatives, friends, neighbors, tontines, and pawnshops, they may rely on loans with extremely high interest rates (higher than the cap of interest rate allowed by the Civil

[83] See Phan and Gan (2017, p. 125) and Anh et al. (2014, p. 25).

[84] See Bui et al. (2018, p. 26).

[85] Bui et al. (2018, p. 26).

[86] See Nghiem et al. (2007, p. 71).

[87] Nghiem et al. (2007, p. 71).

[88] See Anh et al. (2014, p. 27).

[89] Nghiem et al. (2007, p. 74).

Code 2015) from private moneylenders, which are the so-called black credit.[90] It is important to note that black credit is not regulated by the government or any organizations. Instead, it operates on an implicit agreement between individuals who urgently need capital and private moneylenders.[91] It is likely to involve the use of strong-arm tactics for loan recovery.[92] The scale of black credit was estimated[93] to be about 30–35% of the total credit extended in the informal micro- and/or small-sized finance sector and equivalent to 6–8% of the total outstanding loans of the economy in 2018.[94]

On the demand side of the micro- and/or small-sized finance market, it is not surprising that low- and middle-income households have experienced a significant credit gap. Low- and middle-income households may find it difficult to obtain loans from both the formal and semiformal finance sectors, as mentioned above. It has been well documented that the growing demand for credit by poor and low-income households remains unmet.[95] In rural areas, over 63 million people (approximately 66% of the population in 2019) have faced difficulties in accessing financial services due to the limited coverage of conventional banks' networks of branches, transaction offices, and ATMs.[96]

It is worth noting that SMEs have limited access to the credit market.[97] Despite accounting for approximately 97% of all enterprises in the country[98] and about 37% of the workforce,[99] SMEs had less than 32% of the total business capital by the end of 2020.[100] In contrast, SOEs accounted for only 0.3% of all enterprises[101] and about 6.8% of the labor force[102] but around 21.4% of the total business capital.[103] It has been noted that the preferential treatment for SOEs by state-owned banks may have negatively influenced the capital allocation for private SMEs.[104] In addition, it has been reported that approximately 70% of SMEs have found it difficult to access loans provided by conventional commercial banks.[105] Several reasons for this

[90] See Mai (2022).

[91] See Mai (2022).

[92] See Ho Chi Minh City Police Department (2023).

[93] By Cấn Văn Lực, a member of the National Financial and Monetary Policy Advisory Council of Vietnam.

[94] See Sơn (2019).

[95] See Mai et al. (2019, p. 10) and Bui et al. (2018, p. 28).

[96] Central Population and Housing Census Steering Committee (2019, p. 14).

[97] Christine and Miao (2017, p. 13) and Viet Nam News (2017).

[98] Vietnam's Ministry of Planning and Investment (2022, p. 41).

[99] Vietnam's Ministry of Planning and Investment (2022, p. 37).

[100] Vietnam's Ministry of Planning and Investment (2022, p. 42).

[101] Vietnam's Ministry of Planning and Investment (2022, p. 41).

[102] Vietnam's Ministry of Planning and Investment (2022, p. 36).

[103] Vietnam's Ministry of Planning and Investment (2022, p. 41).

[104] See Rand and Tarp (2020, p. 1) and Đông (2019).

[105] See Nga (2023).

difficulty have also been reported, including the lack of collateral, unaudited financial statements, and inaccurate financial data.[106]

### 2.1.3 The Legislative History of Vietnamese Laws on Micro- and/or Small-Sized Finance

As mentioned in Sect. 2.1.1, the history of Vietnamese laws on micro- and/or small-sized finance started after Vietnam gained its independence in 1945. The regulations regarding micro- and/or small-sized finance have been developed since the Đổi Mới. In general, Vietnamese lawmakers have made significant efforts to establish a legal framework for the micro- and/or small-sized finance sector. Many legal documents were issued to regulate the provision of micro- and/or small-sized finance (see Table 2.1).

After the proclamation of independence in 1945, Vietnam gradually established its own independent monetary and banking system. In 1947, the Production Credit Office was formed under President's Decision No. 14/SL to provide funds for production and collective businesses. Later on, the Vietnam National Bank was established in 1951 under Decision No. 15/SL of the President to implement credit policies and facilitate production.

Rural credit cooperatives were established under Decision No. 739/TTg dated April 17, 1956, to mobilize capital and provide loans for farmers. In 1957, to promote construction in the North, the Vietnam Construction Bank was established to allocate loans for construction projects. To promote credit for SOEs, the Vietnam National Bank issued Decree No. 448-VP/NgD dated August 23, 1957, to regulate the provision of short-term loans for state-owned industrial enterprises.

In 1958, the Vietnam National Bank issued Decree No. 67-VNVNT to promulgate regulations on providing short-term loans for state-owned agricultural enterprises, national forest enterprises, and agricultural cooperatives. The Bank also issued Decree No. 81-NgD/NH on the provision of its long-term loans in the same year. Furthermore, it collaborated with the Ministry of Justice to issue Inter-Ministerial Circular No. 01-VHH-DS on policies and measures for debt collection, aiming to improve the effectiveness of debt collection.

In 1959, socialist savings funds were established under Decree No. 47/TTg of the Prime Minister to mobilize savings deposits and provide loans for workers and other employees. Three years later, Decree No. 115-CP of the Prime Minister was issued to establish the Vietnam Bank for Foreign Trade to provide loans for foreign trade activities. In 1972, the government issued Decision No. 197-CP to establish a socialist savings fund system to provide loans for public servants, officials, and workers, as well as cooperative members.

[106] See Lan (2023).

**Table 2.1** Key legal documents on the provision of micro- and/or small-sized finance

| Year | Legal document | Main content |
|---|---|---|
| 1947 | Decision No. 14/SL of the President | To establish the Production Credit Office to provide funds for production and collective business |
| 1951 | Decision No. 15/SL of the President | To establish the Vietnam National Bank and replace the Production Credit Office |
| 1956 | Rule No. 739-TTg of the Prime Minister | To establish a rural credit cooperative system |
| 1957 | Decree No. 177/TTg of the Prime Minister | To establish the Vietnam Construction Bank |
| 1957 | Decree No. 448-VP/NgD of the Vietnam National Bank | To issue rules concerning short-term loans provided by the Vietnam National Bank for state-owned industrial enterprises |
| 1958 | Decree No. 67-VNVNT of the Vietnam National Bank | To issue rules concerning short-term loans provided by the Vietnam National Bank for state-owned agricultural enterprises, national forest enterprises, and agricultural cooperatives |
| 1958 | Decree No. 81-NgD/NH of the Vietnam National Bank | To issue rules for long-term loans provided by the Vietnam National Bank |
| 1958 | Inter-Ministerial Circular of Ministry of Justice and the Vietnam National Bank | To issue policies and measures for debt collection of the National Bank |
| 1959 | Decree No. 312-TTg of the Prime Minister | To establish socialist savings funds |
| 1959 | Decree No. 47/TTg of the Prime Minister | To regulate the interest rates of individuals' deposits and savings and the Vietnam National Bank's short-term loans |
| 1962 | Decree No. 115-CP of the Prime Minister | To establish the Vietnam Bank for Foreign Trade |
| 1972 | Decision No. 197-CP of the government | To establish the socialist savings fund system and allow socialist savings funds to provide loans to public servants, officials, and workers |
| 1979 | Decision No. 114-CP of the government | To direct the nationalization of the banking system in the South of Vietnam |
| 1983 | Decision No. 24/NH-QD of the State Bank of Vietnam | To issue rules concerning socialist savings funds' loans provided for public servants and credit cooperatives' loans provided for members |
| 1983 | Decision No. 52/NH-QD of the State Bank of Vietnam | To promulgate regulations on the organization and operation of rural credit cooperatives |
| 1986 | Decision No. 67/NH-QD of the State Bank of Vietnam | To issue regulations on credit for individuals |
| 1988 | Decree No. 53/HDBT of the government | To establish specialized banks including the Vietnam Bank for Agricultural Development, the Vietnam Foreign Trade Bank, the Industrial and Commercial Bank of Vietnam, and the Bank for Investment and Construction of Vietnam to provide banking services in specific sectors according to the State's plans |

(continued)

**Table 2.1** (continued)

| Year | Legal document | Main content |
|---|---|---|
| 1990 | Ordinance No. 38-LCT/HNDN8 of the National Assembly | To regulate the establishment, organization, and operation of credit institutions including commercial banks, credit cooperatives, and finance companies to provide financial services to the people |
| 1993 | Decision No. 390/QD-TTg of the Prime Minister | To re-establish the system of people's credit funds to mobilize savings from and provide credit to rural households |
| 1995 | Decision No. 525/QD-TTg of the Prime Minister | To establish the Vietnam Bank for the Poor to provide preferential credit for poor households |
| 1995 | Circular No. 02/TT/LB of the Ministry of Trade and the State Bank of Vietnam | To direct the operation of pawn shops |
| 1997 | Law on Credit Institutions of the National Assembly | To uniformly manage all banking activities; To develop policy banks to serve the poor and other policy beneficiaries; To develop banks to serve agricultural and rural development |
| 2002 | Decision No. 131/2002/QD-TTg of the Prime Minister | To establish VBSP to provide preferential credit to the poor, low-income households, and SMEs in remote areas, aiming to contribute to poverty reduction and promote social welfare |
| 2004 | Amendment of Law on Credit Institutions 1997 of the National Assembly | To direct the establishment of leasing companies and recognize people's credit funds as one type of credit institutions |
| 2005 | Civil Code of the National Assembly | To set forth the cap on interest rates at 150% of the State Bank's announced rate in lending activities |
| 2005 | Decree No. 28/2005/ND-CP of the government | To direct the organization and operation of MFIs |
| 2006 | Decision No. 108/2006/QD-TTg of the Prime Minister | To establish VDB to implement policies on development investment credit and export credit |
| 2006 | Decree 144/2006/ND-CP of the government | To regulate tontine forms and the rights, obligations, and responsibilities of tontine participants |
| 2009 | Decree No. 56/2009/ND-CP of the government | To regulate the establishment of the SME Development Fund |
| 2010 | Law on Credit Institutions of the National Assembly | To incorporate MFIs into the credit institutions system |
| 2013 | Decision No. 601/QD-TTg of the Prime Minister | To establish the SME Development Fund |
| 2015 | Civil Code of the National Assembly | To set forth the cap on interest rates at 20% per year in lending activities, except credit institutions' lending activities |
| 2015 | Criminal Code of the National Assembly | To regulate crime relating to interest rates in lending transactions |
| 2015 | Circular No. 04/2015/TT-NHNN of the State Bank | To direct the establishment, organization, and operation of people's credit funds |

(continued)

**Table 2.1** (continued)

| Year | Legal document | Main content |
|---|---|---|
| 2015 | Circular 32/2015/TT-NHNN of the State Bank | To regulate limitations and prudential ratios for the operation of people's credit funds |
| 2015 | Circular 33/2015/TT-NHNN of the State Bank | To regulate prudential ratios for the operation of MFIs |
| 2016 | Decree No. 96/2016/ND-CP of the government | To provide conditions for the operation of pawn shops |
| 2016 | Decree No. 16/2016/ND-CP of the government | To promulgate regulations on the management and use of official development assistance and concessional loans granted by foreign sponsors |
| 2016 | Circular No. 39/2016/TT-NHNN of the State Bank | To direct lending activities and interest rates of credit institutions |
| 2017 | Decision No. 20/2017/QD-TTg of the Prime Minister | To direct the operation of microfinance programs and projects of political organizations, socio-political organizations, and NGOs |
| 2017 | Law on Support for SMEs | To regulate the establishment of the SME Development Fund |
| 2017 | Amendment of Criminal Code 2015 of the National Assembly | To amend some regulations on crime relating to interest rates in lending transactions |
| 2017 | Amendment of Law on Credit Institutions 2010 of the National Assembly | To amend and supplement some regulations on credit institutions' obligations to ensure the safety and stability of their operation |
| 2018 | Circular No. 03/2018/TT-NHNN of the State Bank of Vietnam | To direct the establishment, organization, and operation of MFIs |
| 2019 | Decree No. 19/2019/ND-CP of the government | To set forth detailed rules on interest rates in tontines |
| 2019 | Decree No. 39/2019/ND-CP of the government | To provide detailed instructions on the organization and operation of the SME Development Fund |
| 2019 | Circular No. 37/2019/TT-BTC of the Ministry of Finance | To give guidelines on the financial regime for microfinance programs and projects of political organizations, socio-political organizations, and NGOs |
| 2021 | Decree No. 80/2021/ND-CP of the government | To provide detailed instructions on the Law on Support for SMEs |
| 2024 | Law on Credit Institutions of the National Assembly | To establish a special control mechanism to proactively prevent and address risks in the banking sector |
| 2024 | Circular No. 12/2024/TT-NHNN of the State Bank | To direct lending transactions of credit institutions with customers |
| 2024 | Circular No. 13/2024/TT-NHNN of the State Bank | To regulate prudential ratios of people's credit funds |
| 2024 | Circular No. 24/2024/TT-NHNN of the State Bank | To regulate prudential ratios of MFIs |
| 2024 | Circular No. 29/2024/TT-NHNN of the State Bank | To direct the establishment, organization, and operation of people's credit funds |
| 2024 | Circular No. 33/2024/TT-NHNN of the State Bank of Vietnam | To direct the establishment, organization, and operations of MFIs |

To encourage the provision of loans to individuals and improve the quality of people's lives, the State Bank of Vietnam issued Decision No. 24/NH-QD in 1983. The Decision regulated the provision of loans from socialist savings funds to public servants, officials, and workers, as well as loans from cooperatives to their members. In the same year, the Bank also issued Decision No. 52/NH-QD on the organization and operation of rural credit cooperatives to improve the effectiveness of rural credit cooperatives' operation. The Bank then issued Decision No. 67/NH-QD on providing credit to individuals in 1986.

After the Đổi Mới, the Vietnamese banking system was reformed. In 1988, specialized banks, including the Vietnam Bank for Agricultural Development, Vietnam Foreign Trade Bank, Industrial and Commercial Bank of Vietnam, and Bank for Investment and Construction of Vietnam, were established under Decree No. 53/HDBT of the government. These banks provided banking services to specific sectors according to the government's plans, especially to poor and low-income individuals in the agricultural sector and rural areas. In 1990, to encourage the provision of financial services for individuals and businesses, the National Assembly promulgated Ordinance No. 38-LCT/HNDN8 on the establishment, organization, and operation of commercial banks, credit cooperatives, and finance companies. The system of people's credit funds was then reestablished in 1993 to mobilize savings from and provide credit to rural households under Decision No. 390/QD-TTg of the Prime Minister. Furthermore, the Vietnam Bank for the Poor was established in 1995 to provide preferential credit for poor households throughout the country.

In 1997, the National Assembly promulgated the Law on Credit Institutions to uniformly regulate banking activities and regulate the operations of policy banks. Accordingly, in 2002, the Prime Minister issued Decision No. 131/2002/QD-TTg to establish VBSP by integrating all the operations of the Vietnam Bank for the Poor and policy-based lending programs of the government (including loans to students, employment generation programs, and lending programs for small entrepreneurs) to contribute to poverty reduction and social welfare improvement. The Law on Credit Institutions 1997 was then amended and supplemented in 2004 to regulate the establishment of leasing companies. It also acknowledged people's credit funds as a type of credit institution. One year later, MFIs were officially regulated by Decree No. 28/2005/ND-CP, which was generally deemed a crucial milestone in the legal framework for the formalization of MFIs in Vietnam.

In 2010, the Law on Credit Institutions was passed by the National Assembly. The Law recognized MFIs as credit institutions, providing the legal foundation for MFIs to grow alongside other credit institutions and contribute to poverty alleviation and social welfare improvement in the country. Following the Law on Credit Institutions 2010, the State Bank issued Circular No. 04/2015/TT-NHNN on the establishment, organization, and operation of people's credit funds to facilitate credit access for low- and middle-income individuals. The Bank also issued Circular No. 32/2015/TT-NHNN and Circular No. 33/2015/TT-NHNN on prudential ratios for people's credit funds and MFIs to ensure their safety and stability. In 2017, the Law on Credit Institutions 2010 was amended, incorporating regulations on the responsibilities of credit institutions to ensure their safety and stability. In line with the amendment, the State Bank issued Circular No. 03/2018/TT-NHNN to guide the establishment, organization, and operation of MFIs in 2018.

A new Law on Credit Institutions was promulgated by the National Assembly in 2024, establishing a special control mechanism to proactively prevent and address risks in the banking sector. Following this law, the State Bank issued Circular No. 29/2024/TT-NHNN and Circular No. 33/2024/TT-NHNN to regulate the establishment, organization, and operation of people's credit funds and MFIs. Additionally, the State Bank issued Circular No. 13/2024/TT-NHNN and Circular No. 24/2024/TT-NHNN, setting prudential ratios for people's credit funds and MFIs to ensure their safety and stability. Furthermore, Circular No. 12/2024/TT-NHNN was introduced to regulate lending transactions between credit institutions and customers.

In the semiformal micro- and/or small-sized finance sector, the government issued Decree No. 56/2009/ND-CP in 2009 to regulate the establishment of the SME Development Fund. The Fund was officially established in 2013, under Decision No. 601/QD-TTg of the Prime Minister. In 2017, the Prime Minister promulgated Decision No. 20/2017/QD-TTg to provide guidance on the operations of microfinance programs and projects managed by political institutions, sociopolitical organizations, and NGOs. In addition, Decree No. 56/2009/ND-CP was abolished, and the Law on Support for SMEs 2017 and Decree No. 80/2021/ND-CP were promulgated to regulate the establishment of the SME Development Fund.

In the informal micro- and/or small-sized finance sector, the Ministry of Trade and the State Bank of Vietnam jointly issued Circular No. 02/TT/LB in 1995 to direct the operations of pawnshops. In 2006, the government issued Decree No. 144/2006/ND-CP to regulate tontine forms and the rights, obligations, and responsibilities of tontine participants. The Decree aimed to prevent tontines from being used for illegal lending activities, thus protecting the legitimate interests of tontine participants. Pawnshop services are considered conditional business lines, and the operations of pawnshops are currently governed by Decree No. 96/2016/ND-CP. In 2019, Decree No. 19/2019/ND-CP was promulgated to replace Decree No. 144/2006/ND-CP and set interest rates and other rules for tontines. According to Decree No. 19/2019/ND-CP, lending interest rates applied by pawnshops and tontines must not exceed 20% per year, as stipulated in the Civil Code 2015.

### *2.1.4 Current Vietnamese Laws on Micro- and/or Small-Sized Finance*

Up to now, Vietnam has issued numerous legal documents to regulate the provision of micro- and/or small-sized finance in the formal, semiformal, and informal sectors. In the formal sector, it can be seen that conventional commercial banks have been heavily regulated by the Law on Credit Institutions 2024 and related legal documents. In order to conduct banking activities, including deposit taking, credit extension, and via-account payment services provision,[107] commercial banks must meet requirements for capital, reserve, and liquidity.[108] They also have to perform due diligence,[109] establish provisional funds,[110] purchase deposit insurance,[111] as well as fulfill other obligations to protect the legitimate rights of their customers and ensure the safety and stability of their operations.[112] Commercial banks can apply lending interest rates agreed upon by the parties in accordance with the demand and supply on the capital market, as well as the loan demand and creditworthiness of borrowers, unless the State Bank has regulations on maximum interest rates in some cases.[113] For example, the State Bank has set a maximum interest rate for short-term VND loans at 4% per year in several specific cases, such as development credit for agriculture and rural areas, as well as credit for SMEs' development.[114]

Nonbank credit institutions can provide banking services under the Law on Credit Institutions 2024 and related legal documents. Nonbank credit institutions, such as finance companies and leasing companies, may conduct one or several banking operations, except taking deposits from individuals and providing via-account payment services.[115] Like conventional commercial banks, nonbank credit institutions must meet requirements for capital, reserve, and liquidity,[116] as well as fulfill legal obligations, such as performing due diligence,[117] establishing provisional funds,[118] and purchasing deposit insurance,[119] to protect the legitimate rights of their customers and ensure their safety and stability. They can also apply lending interest rates agreed upon by the parties in accordance with the demand and supply

---

[107] See Vietnam's Law on Credit Institutions 2024, Article 4, clause 17.

[108] See Vietnam's Law on Credit Institutions 2024, Article 28 and Article 138.

[109] See Vietnam's Law on Credit Institutions 2024, Article 102.

[110] See Vietnam's Law on Credit Institutions 2024, Article 147.

[111] See Vietnam's Law on Credit Institutions 2024, Article 10, clause 1.

[112] See Vietnam's Law on Credit Institutions 2024, Article 10, Article 134 to Article 137, Article 139 to Article 140.

[113] See Vietnam's Law on Credit Institutions 2024, Article 100, and The English translation of Circular No. 39/2016/TT-NHNN of Vietnam, Article 13.

[114] See The English translation of Decision No. 1125/QD-NHNN on the maximum interest rate for short-term loans in VND in some specific cases according to Circular No. 39/2016/TT-NHNN, Article 1.

[115] Vietnam's Law on Credit Institutions 2024, Article 4, clause 41, provides that "[n]on-bank credit institution means a type of credit institution which may conduct one or some banking operations under this Law, except taking deposits from individuals and providing services of payment via client accounts. Non-bank credit institutions include general and specialized finance companies."

[116] See Vietnam's Law on Credit Institutions 2024, Article 28 and Article 138.

[117] See Vietnam's Law on Credit Institutions 2024, Article 102.

[118] See Vietnam's Law on Credit Institutions 2024, Article 131.

[119] See Vietnam's Law on Credit Institutions 2024, Article 10, clause 1.

on the capital market, as well as the loan demand and creditworthiness of borrowers, unless the State Bank has regulations on maximum interest rates in some cases.[120]

Policy banks, including VBSP and VDB, operate for nonprofit purposes to implement the state's socioeconomic policies.[121] They receive capital from the government and can mobilize capital from domestic and foreign individuals and organizations.[122] They are exempt from taxes and state budget contributions and are not required to hold reserve ratios. They do not have to purchase deposit insurance, and their payment capacity is guaranteed by the government.[123] In the course of its operation, VBSP provides loans for the poor and other policy beneficiaries,[124] while VDB focuses on providing loans for SMEs operating in the development investment and export sectors.[125]

People's credit funds are voluntarily established by legal entities, individuals, and households as cooperatives for mutual assistance among their members in production, business development, and life in accordance with the Law on Credit Institutions 2024 and Circular No. 04/2015/TT-NHNN (2015, as amended) issued by the State Bank. They can conduct several banking activities, such as taking deposits, providing loans, and offering collection and payment services, as well as remittances for their members.[126] People's credit funds must meet capital, reserve, and liquidity requirements,[127] perform due diligence,[128] establish provisional funds,[129] and purchase deposit insurance[130] when providing lending services. They can apply lending interest rates agreed upon by the parties in accordance with the demand and supply on the capital market, as well as the loan demand and creditworthiness of borrowers, unless the State Bank has regulations on maximum interest rates in some cases.[131] For example, the State Bank has set a maximum interest rate for short-term loans in VND at 5% per year in several specific cases, such as development credit for agriculture and rural areas, as well as credit for SMEs' development.[132]

[120] See Vietnam's Law on Credit Institutions 2024, Article 100 and Circular No. 39/2016/TT-NHNN, Article 13.

[121] See Vietnam's Law on Credit Institutions 2024, Article 16, clause 1.

[122] See The English translation of Decision No. 131/2002/QD-TTg of Vietnam, Article 2, and The English translation of Decision No. 108/2006/QD-TTg of Vietnam, Article 3.

[123] See Vietnam's Decision No. 131/2002/QD-TTg, Article 3, and Vietnam's Decision No. 108/2006/QD-TTg, Article 2.

[124] See Vietnam's Decision No. 131/2002/QD-TTg, Article 2.

[125] See Vietnam's Decision No. 108/2006/QD-TTg, Article 4.

[126] See Vietnam's Law on Credit Institutions 2024, Article 126.

[127] See The English translation of Circular No. 32/2015/TT-NHNN, Article 5 to Article 8, and the English translation of Circular No. 13/2024/TT-NHNN, Article 1, clauses 7 and 9.

[128] See The English translation of Circular No. 29/2024/TT-NHNN, Article 26.

[129] See The English translation of Decree No. 86/2024/ND-CP on establishing risk provisions, Chap. 2.

[130] See Vietnam's Law on Credit Institutions 2024, Article 10, clause 1.

[131] See Circular No. 39/2016/TT-NHNN, Article 13.

[132] See Decision No. 1125/QD-NHNN dated June 16, 2023, Article 1.

MFIs can conduct several banking activities to serve the needs of individuals, low-income households, and micro-sized enterprises in accordance with the Law on Credit Institutions 2024 and Circular No. 03/2018/TT-NHNN (2018, as amended) issued by the State Bank. They can take deposits, provide loans, and offer collection and payment services, as well as remittances.[133] Like people's credit funds, when providing lending services, MFIs must also meet capital, reserve, and liquidity requirements,[134] perform due diligence, establish provisional funds,[135] and purchase deposit insurance.[136] They must be established as limited liability companies,[137] with the total number of members not exceeding 5.[138] According to Circular No. 33/2024/TT-NHNN of the State Bank, MFIs impose loan limits based on borrower categories, providing up to 100 million VND for microenterprises and poor/near-poor households, while limiting loans to low-income individuals and households to 50 million VND. They ensure that loans to poor and near-poor households comply with residency requirements and official poverty classification standards.[139] Like people's credit funds, they can apply lending interest rates agreed upon by the parties in accordance with the demand and supply on the capital market, as well as the loan demand and creditworthiness of borrowers, unless the State Bank has regulations on maximum interest rates in some cases.[140]

In the semiformal micro- and/or small-sized finance sector, microfinance programs and projects managed by political institutions, sociopolitical organizations, and NGOs are regulated by Decision No. 20/2017/QD-TTg dated June 12, 2017. Accordingly, these projects and programs serve various customer groups, including low-income individuals, poor households, near-poverty households, households just escaping the poverty line, middle-income households, and micro-sized enterprises.[141] They may provide lending services and accept voluntary and compulsory savings.[142] "The total amount of voluntary saving deposits must not exceed 30% of the total capital granted to a microfinance program or project,"[143] and "[t]he maximum amount of loans granted to a microfinance customer must not exceed VND

[133] See Vietnam's Law on Credit Institutions 2024, Article 4, clause 37, Article 127, and Article 130, clause 1, paragraph c.

[134] See The English translation of Circular No. 33/2015/TT-NHNN, Article 4 to Article 8, and the English translation of Circular No. 24/2024/TT-NHNN, Article 1.

[135] See The English translation of Decree No. 86/2024/ND-CP on establishing risk provisions, Chap. 2.

[136] See Vietnam's Law on Credit Institutions 2024, Article 10, clause 1.

[137] See Vietnam's Law on Credit Institutions 2024, Article 6, clause 6.

[138] See Vietnam's Law on Credit Institutions 2024, Article 77, clause 1.

[139] Circular No. 33/2024/TT-NHNN, Article 24, clauses 4 and 5.

[140] See Circular No. 39/2016/TT-NHNN, Article 13.

[141] See The English translation of Decision No. 20/2017/QD-TTg of Vietnam, Article 2, clause 3.

[142] See Vietnam's Decision No. 20/2017/QD-TTg, Article 3, clause 1.

[143] Vietnam's Decision No. 20/2017/QD-TTg, Article 13, clause 1(b).

50 million."[144] Lending interest rates applied by microfinance projects and programs "must comply with the law, specific conditions of each microfinance program or project and microfinance plan, fully cover operational and growth expenses, and serve not-for-profit purposes."[145]

In addition, the SME Development Fund is managed according to Decree No. 39/2019/ND-CP dated May 10, 2019. The Fund is established as a single-member limited liability company, and its chartered capital is wholly owned by the state.[146] It grants loans directly or indirectly (through entrusting its capital to commercial banks) to SMEs. SMEs eligible to receive loans from the Fund must have feasible production and business projects and plans belonging to the priority and encouragement domains of the state.[147] The lending interest rate for a loan provided by the Fund shall be equal to 80% of the lowest commercial interest rate among the

---

[144] Vietnam's Decision No. 20/2017/QD-TTg, Article 13, clause 2(c).

[145] Vietnam's Decision No. 20/2017/QD-TTg, Article 13, clause 2(a).

[146] See The English translation of Decree No. 39/2019/ND-CP of Vietnam, Article 2, clause 2.

[147] Vietnam's Decree No. 39/2019/ND-CP, Article 16 governs direct lending requirements as below:

> 1. Small and medium enterprises running innovative startups shall be entitled to loans granted by the Fund provided that they meet the following requirements:
>
> a) Meet regulations set forth in Article 4 in the Law on Support for Small and Medium Enterprises;
>
> b) Have feasible production and business projects and plans, exploit intellectual property assets prescribed in the Intellectual Property Law or new technologies prescribed in the Law on Technology Transfer or new business models according to regulations of law;
>
> c) Ensure the equity participation in a production and business project or plan makes up at least 20% of the total investment capital to implement that production and business project or plan, and ensure sufficient capital for implementation of a production and business project or plan; and
>
> d) Meet regulations on loan guarantee laid down herein.
>
> 2. Small and medium enterprises participating in inter-sectoral complexes shall be entitled to loans extended by the Fund when meeting the following requirements:
>
> a) Comply with regulations set forth in points a, c and d of clause 1 of this Article; and
>
> b) Have feasible production and business projects or plans, locate their offices within geographical areas of inter-sectoral complexes and have cooperation or business contracts with other enterprises in these inter-sectoral complexes or jointly build and use regional brands. Identification of inter-sectoral complexes shall be subject to provisions enshrined in the Law on Support for Small and Medium Enterprises and other documents giving instructions on implementation thereof.
>
> 3. Small and medium enterprises participating in value chains shall be entitled to loans extended by the Fund when meeting the following requirements:
>
> a) Comply with regulations set forth in points a, c and d of clause 1 of this Article; and
>
> b) Have production and business projects or plans that are feasible and are put to use to directly create the additional value of products in these value chains or have cooperation and business contracts with enterprises directly creating the additional value of products in these value chains. Identification of value chains shall be subject to regulations laid down in the Law on Support for Small and Medium Enterprises and other relevant documents providing instructions on implementation thereof.

Article 23 provides that indirect lending requirements include:

commercial interest rates of four state-owned commercial banks at the time of determining the Fund's lending interest rate.[148] Loans provided to each production and business plan or project must not be greater than 80% of the total investment of each plan or project, and loan terms must not be longer than 7 years. Each SME cannot be granted more than 15% of the actual chartered capital of the Fund.[149]

In the informal micro- and/or small-sized finance sector, the provision of pawnshop services is governed by Decision No. 96/2016/ND-CP dated July 1, 2016. Pawnshop service providers may provide loans to borrowers who pledge their legitimate property as collateral at pawnshops.[150] Pawnshop service is a conditional business line,[151] and pawnshop service providers must meet security and social order conditions, including establishing property pledge agreements and accepting only pledged property with legitimate ownership.[152] Pawnshops may apply an interest rate agreed upon by the parties, which must not exceed 20% per year, in accordance with the Civil Code 2015. If a pawnshop sets an interest rate that is five times or more higher than the interest rate cap provided by the Civil Code 2015, earns an illegal profit of VND 30 million or more, or recommits this offense despite being previously imposed with administrative sanctions or having a criminal record that has not been cleared by the court, the pawnshop will be subject to punishments under the Criminal Code (2015, amended in 2017).[153]

Tontines can be organized into tontine groups solely for the purpose of mutual assistance among participants under Decree No. 19/2019/ND-CP of the

---

1. Small and medium enterprises running innovative startups may be entitled to loans derived from the Fund's available capital when meeting the following requirements:

a) Comply with provisions laid down in point a, point b and point c of clause 1 of Article 16 herein; and

b) Meet regulations on loan guarantee under relevant laws.

2. Small and medium enterprises participating in inter-sectoral complexes may have access to loans derived from the Fund's available capital when meeting the following requirements:

a) Comply with provisions laid down in point a and point c of clause 1 and point b of clause 2 of Article 16 herein; and

b) Meet regulations laid down in point b of clause 1 of this Article.

3. Small and medium enterprises participating in inter-sectoral complexes may have access to loans derived from the Fund's available capital when meeting the following requirements:

a) Comply with provisions laid down in point a and point c of clause 1 and point b of clause 3 of Article 16 herein; and

b) Meet regulations laid down in point b of clause 1 of this Article.

[148] See Vietnam's Decree No. 39/2019/ND-CP, Article 17, clause 1.

[149] See Vietnam's Decree No. 39/2019/ND-CP, Article 18.

[150] See The English translation of Decision No. 96/2016/ND-CP, Article 3, clause 4.

[151] See The English translation of Vietnam's Law on Investment 2020, Article 7 and Appendix IV (List of Conditional Business Lines).

[152] See Vietnam's Decision No. 96/2016/ND-CP, Article 29.

[153] See The English translation of Vietnam's Criminal Code 2015, Article 201, and The English translation of Vietnam's Criminal Code amended in 2017, Article 2, clause 2.

government.[154] A tontine group is "formed according to specific agreements between tontine participants in terms of time, annuity share, annuity-contributing and -receiving procedures, and rights and obligations of tontine holder (if any) and tontine members."[155] Participants must be at least 15 years old and possess legal capacity. If those between the ages of 15 and 18 own real estate or movable property and wish to participate in tontine groups by using such property as collateral, they must obtain the consent of their legal representatives.[156] A tontine holder must be at least 18 years old, possess legal capacity, and inform the local people's committee if they organize a tontine group where a member would receive VND 100 million or more at each tontine opening time or if they organize two or more tontine groups.[157] Similar to pawnshops, tontine groups may set lending interest rates that are agreed upon by the participants, but these rates must not exceed 20% per year, in accordance with the Civil Code 2015.

## 2.2 The Development of P2P Lending in Vietnam

### *2.2.1 The Development of P2P Lending in Vietnam*

As mentioned in Sect. 1.1, with the recent development of technological innovation, P2P lending has become a new source of small funding. This is expected to fill the credit gap that conventional banks have been hesitant to serve. It is evident that Vietnam's P2P lending market has grown significantly since 2015.[158] The number of P2P lending platforms registered with business registration authorities increased dramatically, from 1 in 2015 to around 100 by the end of 2022 (see Chart 2.1 and Appendix A).

Most of the P2P lending platforms are likely operating nationwide through the Internet, while several platforms are primarily serving households and SMEs in major cities. For example, Huydong has provided lending services to SMEs in Ho Chi Minh and Hanoi,[159] and Lendbiz has mainly served individuals and SMEs in Hanoi and Da Nang.[160] P2P lending platforms operating in Vietnam, both domestic and foreign owned, reportedly provided P2P lending services for more than 3.3 million local citizens by May 2019.[161] It is worth noting that the total transaction value in the P2P lending sector increased from USD 2.5 billion in 2015 to USD 7.8

[154] See The English translation of Decree No. 19/2019/ND-CP, Article 3, clause 2.

[155] Vietnam's Decree No. 19/2019/ND-CP, Article 4, clause 1.

[156] See Vietnam's Decree No. 19/2019/ND-CP, Article 5.

[157] See Vietnam's Decree No. 19/2019/ND-CP, Article 6 and Article 14, clause 1.

[158] See Uyen and Ha (2017, p. 84).

[159] See Huydong (2020a, b).

[160] See Lendbiz (2025).

[161] See The State Bank of Vietnam (2019).

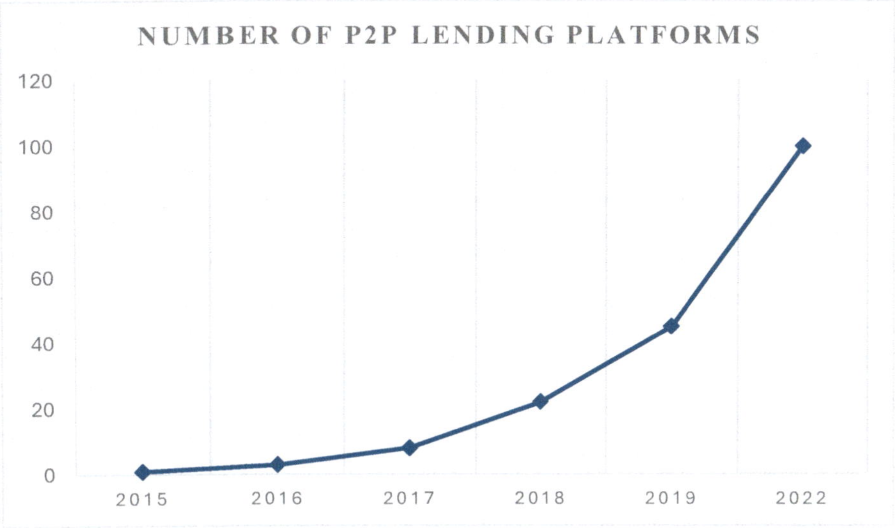


**Chart 2.1** The number of P2P lending platforms in Vietnam (Author's own synthesis from 2015 to 2019 as Appendix A. See Hằng et al. (2022))

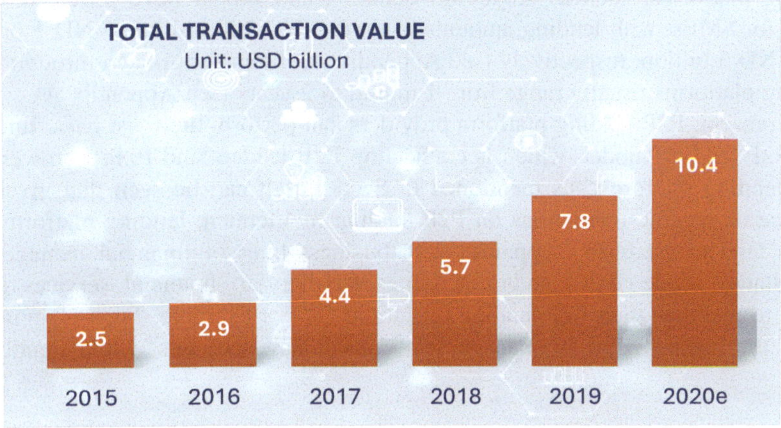


**Chart 2.2** Total transaction value via P2P lending platforms in Vietnam (See Hartung (2019))

billion in 2019 and was expected to reach USD 10.4 billion in 2020[162] (see Chart 2.2).

Among the registered P2P lending companies, several platforms are prominent due to their reach and transaction size. For example, Vaymuon stated that, by July

[162] See Hartung (2019), and Cao (2019).

2019, it had connected over two million borrowers to more than 400,000 lenders.[163] Another example is Tima, which claimed to be the largest P2P lending platform in Vietnam in terms of transaction size, with a total disbursement of more than VND 94,000 billion by the end of November 2022.[164] The platform also stated that it served more than 64,000 lenders and up to eight million borrowers.[165]

It can be seen that P2P lending platforms have enabled individuals and SMEs to obtain loans from single or multiple private or institutional lenders. P2P lending platforms like Huydong, Lendbiz, Eloan, and Growth Wealth have focused on serving SMEs, while others such as Tima, Vaymuon, Mofin, Fiin Credit, and Vnvon have primarily provided loans to individual borrowers.[166] Particularly, Interloan has offered P2P loans to employees in enterprises or entities, and Trust Circle has organized rotating savings and credit groups.[167] It is worth noting that P2P loans can be provided for several purposes, such as consumer loans without collateral for students, freelancers, workers, and households to cover their living costs; mortgage loans for taxi drivers and small traders to enable them to engage in small businesses; or business capital for SMEs to conduct their operations.

It has been noted that loans provided via P2P lending platforms in Vietnam tend to be small in amount and short term in duration.[168] Some P2P lending platforms, such as Vaymuon, Mofin, Eloan, and Cash Money, have mainly provided very small and small loans, with amounts of less than VND 20 million.[169] Some other P2P lending platforms, such as Huydong, Lendbiz, and Eloan, have provided larger funds for SMEs, with lending amounts of up to VND 100 million, VND 1 billion, and VND 5 billion, respectively (see Appendix A). Loans originated through these lending platforms usually range from 1 month to 2 years (see Appendix A).

At present, P2P lending platform providers can perform the most basic function of a P2P lending model, which is connecting P2P lenders and P2P borrowers via their lending platforms, as mentioned in Sect. 1.1. It can be seen that given the absence of specific regulations on P2P lending in Vietnam, lending platform providers tend to establish companies with business lines of financial management consultancy (code 7020) and/or activities auxiliary to financial services (code 6619) to facilitate their P2P lending operations.[170] For example, Tima is registered under the business line of management consultancy activities, while Lendbiz is

[163] See Fintechnews Vietnam (2019).

[164] See Tima (2025) and Phong (2022).

[165] See Phong (2022).

[166] See Tima (2025), Mofin (2020), and Vnvon (2023).

[167] See Huydong (2020a, b), Lendbiz (2025), Eloan (2020), Growth Wealth (2020), Interloan (2023), and Trust Circle (2020).

[168] See Home Office of the UK's government (2018, p. 10).

[169] See Mofin (2020), Eloan (2020), and Cash Money (2020).

[170] In accordance with Decision No. 27/2018/QD-TTg of Vietnam on Vietnam's standard industrial classification.

registered for both management consultancy and activities auxiliary to financial services.

In practice, P2P lending platforms may employ various tactics to verify borrowers' information and evaluate their creditworthiness. For example, some P2P lending platforms, such as Huydong, Vaymuon, Mofin, and Vdong, have reported using AI and big data to verify information provided by P2P borrowers and collect information on their credit history within a few hours or a couple of days.[171] Some other lending platforms, such as Avay, VayVND, and Oncredit, request potential borrowers to allow them to use cookies to collect all information from their devices.[172] Notably, Lendbiz may require face-to-face meetings with potential borrowers to perform due diligence (see Appendix A).

It can be presumed that several P2P lending platforms have announced their cooperation with commercial banks and/or insurance companies in order to attract potential lenders to use P2P lending services. The cooperation with commercial banks is expected to provide bank accounts for customers, while the collaboration with insurance companies is believed to offer credit insurance for loans originated through P2P lending platforms. For example, Tima has signed partnership agreements with Nam A Bank, Bao Minh Insurance, and Vietinbank Insurance.[173] Another example is Lendbiz, which has collaborated with Vietnam International Bank, Petrolimex Group Bank, and Bao Viet Insurance.[174]

It is easily predicted that P2P lending has developed rapidly in Vietnam in recent years due to the high demand for small funds by individuals and SMEs. It is worth noting that many Vietnamese people are currently unbanked (without bank accounts) or underbanked (struggling to access formal financial services). By the middle of 2019, approximately 43% of the population (around 41 million people) had payment accounts, 27% of the population owned debit cards, and only 4% of the population had credit cards.[175] In addition, although SMEs have played a key role in stimulating economic growth since the Đổi Mới,[176] with the number of operating enterprises exceeding 857,000 as of 2021,[177] only about 30% of them can access bank loans.[178] Approximately 25% of SMEs indicated that "insufficient capital due to the difficulty in accessing finance is still the most critical constraint to their business growth."[179] Among the SMEs that have access to bank loans, approximately 20% can borrow only 25% of their capital needs.[180] From the above analysis,

[171] See Huydong (2020a, b), Mofin (2020), and Vdong (2023).

[172] See Avay (2023), VayVND (2023) and Oncredit (2023).

[173] See Tima (2025), ICTnews (2019).

[174] See Investing.vn (2019).

[175] See Vietnam Microfinance Working Group (2019, p. 3) and Nguyen (2019).

[176] See Rand and Tarp (2020) and Dang and Chuc (2019, p. 1).

[177] See Vietnam's Ministry of Planning and Investment (2022, p. 20).

[178] See Thương (2023).

[179] Dang and Chuc (2019, p. 1).

[180] See Dang and Chuc (2019, p. 5).

it can be seen that a significant credit gap between supply and demand for small funding is very likely to exist in Vietnamese society, and P2P lending companies have an opportunity to fill this gap.

In the long run, the P2P lending sector in Vietnam probably has a high potential for development. It can be seen that P2P lending companies have the ability to easily serve unbanked and underbanked customers, especially those living in rural and remote areas. This is because the lending process of P2P lending companies can be conducted entirely online, which is likely to make it faster and more convenient than that of conventional commercial banks, people's credit funds, or MFIs. In addition, it is readily apparent that the demand for small funding by low- and middle-income households and SMEs remains very high. As mentioned in Sect. 2.1.2, low- and middle-income households are very likely experiencing a significant credit gap, while it has been reported that approximately 70% of SMEs find it difficult to access loans provided by conventional commercial banks. Meanwhile, it can be predicted that there is an upward trend in the number of Vietnamese people who have some idle money and are attracted to supplying credit via P2P lending platforms. It has been observed that the number of middle-class people[181] in Vietnam has increased rapidly in recent years.[182] This number accounted for 13.3% of the population in 2016 and reached 18.2% in 2018.[183] It is projected to account for 26% by 2026.[184] It has been noted that these people are very likely to be attracted to investing in loans via P2P lending platforms for potential returns.[185] Furthermore, it is worth noting that the high rates of Internet penetration and smartphone usage in Vietnam are expected to make significant contributions to the development of the P2P lending sector.[186] As of 2022, both rates were reported to account for more than 73% of the population.[187]

## 2.2.2 *Current Regulations Governing P2P Lending in Vietnam*

In Vietnam, companies that are legally established can provide P2P lending services according to current laws. Article 33 of the Constitution 2013 recognizes the right of every individual to freely conduct business in sectors and business lines not

[181] Middle class is referred to as the social class whose members are neither very rich nor very poor and that includes professional and business people. See Oxford Learner's Dictionaries (2025).

[182] See An (2021).

[183] The middle class is considered households with per-capita spending from USD 15 a day. See The World Bank (2018, p. 2) and Quân and Lý (2022).

[184] See Dương (2022).

[185] See Lien (2017) and Nga (2018).

[186] See MB Securities Joint Stock Company (2018, p. 9).

[187] See The Ministry of Information and Communication of Vietnam (2022) and Vũ (2022).

prohibited by laws.[188] Under the Law on Investment 2020, P2P lending is not listed as a banned or conditional business activity. P2P lending platform service providers, therefore, can establish a company and exercise the right to conduct P2P lending business in accordance with the Law on Enterprises 2020. Specifically, P2P lending companies have the autonomy to conduct their business, determine their organizational structure, business lines, and business location, and make decisions regarding business scale and methods of raising and utilizing capital.[189]

P2P lending companies that are not licensed as credit institutions are prohibited from providing banking operations regularly. Article 8 of the Law on Credit Institutions 2024 provides that "organizations that fully meet the conditions under this Law and other relevant laws and are licensed by the State Bank may conduct one or some banking operations according to regulations of this Law."[190] In addition, since banking operations are listed as a conditional business line according to the Law on Investment 2020,[191] companies that conduct banking operations must satisfy business conditions stipulated by laws.[192] They must also fulfill these requirements throughout their operations.[193] If P2P lending companies wish to conduct any banking operations, such as taking deposits, making loans, or providing intermediary payment services, they must satisfy stringent qualifications to be licensed by the State Bank.[194]

---

[188] Vietnam's Constitution 2013, Article 33 provides that "[e]veryone has the right to freedom of enterprise in the sectors and trades that are not prohibited by law."

[189] Vietnam's Law on Enterprises 2020, Article 7 provides that "[r]ights of enterprises:

1. To enjoy freedom of enterprise in the sectors and trades that are not banned by law;
2. To enjoy business autonomy and select forms of business organization; to take the initiative in selecting sectors and trades, locations and forms of business; to take the initiative in adjusting the scale of business and business lines;
3. To select forms and methods of capital raising, distribution and use;
4. To freely seek markets and customers and enter into contracts;
5. To conduct export and import business;
6. To recruit, hire and employ employees in accordance with the labor law;
7. To take the initiative in applying science and technology to raise business effectiveness and competitiveness; to have intellectual property rights protected in accordance with the law on intellectual property;
8. To possess, use and dispose of their assets;
9. To reject unlawful requests of agencies, organizations or individuals for supply of resources;
10. To lodge complaints and participate in legal proceedings in accordance with law; and
11. Other rights as prescribed by law."

[190] Vietnam's Law on Credit Institutions 2024, Article 8. It should be noted that Vietnam's Law on Credit Institutions 2024, Article 4, clause 17, provides that "[b]anking operations means the trading in and regular provision of one or some of the following services: a) Deposit taking; b) Credit extension; and c) Via-account payment."

[191] See Vietnam's Law on Investment 2020, Article 7 and Appendix IV (List of Conditional Business Lines).

[192] See Vietnam's Law on Enterprises 2020, Article 8, clause 1.

[193] Vietnam's Law on Enterprises 2020, Article 8, clause 1.

[194] Vietnam's Law on Credit Institutions 2024, Article 29, clause 1, provides that:

At present, P2P lending platform providers can perform the most basic function of a P2P lending model, which is connecting P2P lenders and P2P borrowers via their lending platforms. Transactions between a P2P lending company, a P2P borrower, and a P2P lender can be considered civil transactions according to Article 116 of the Civil Code 2015, as mentioned in Sect. 1.1. To engage in P2P lending business, a P2P lending platform service provider may establish a company and register business lines that are not listed as banned business lines under Article 6 of the Law on Investment 2020. These business lines may include financial management consultancy activities (code 7020) and activities auxiliary to financial services (code 6619).[195] These business lines are also open for foreign investment in Vietnam under Vietnam's WTO Commitments on Services and the Comprehensive and Progressive Agreement for Trans-Pacific Partnership (CPTPP).

It can be seen that a P2P lender may lawfully lend to a P2P borrower if the transaction between them falls within a civil lending transaction. In this case, the lender is not required to obtain a banking license, and the loan granted to the borrower could be conducted via a loan contract in accordance with the Civil Code 2015. Article 463 of the Civil Code 2015 states:

> [a] loan contract means an agreement between parties whereby a lender delivers property[196] to a borrower. When the loan falls due, the borrower must repay the lender the same type of property in terms of quantity and quality and repay the lender an interest agreed upon by both parties or provided by laws.[197]

However, it is apparent that a transaction between a P2P lender and a P2P borrower is not classified as a civil lending transaction if it is the primary business activity of the lender, conducted regularly for profit-making purposes, and generates the majority of the lender's income. If P2P lenders frequently lend and earn most of their income via P2P lending platforms, their lending transactions may no longer be

---

> [a] credit institution may obtain a license when fully meeting the following conditions:
> a/ Its charter or allocated capital is at least equal to the legal capital;
> b/ Its owner is a one-member limited liability company, its founding shareholders or members are legal entities which are lawfully operating and financially capable of capital contribution. Its founding shareholders or members are individuals with full civil act capacity and financially capable of capital contribution;
> c/ Its managers, executives and Control Board members fully meet the criteria and conditions under Article 41 of this Law;
> d/ Its charter complies with this Law and other relevant laws; and
> e/ It has an establishment plan and a feasible business plan which neither affects the safety and stability of the credit institution system nor creates monopoly or restrict competition or create unfair competition within the credit institution system.

[195] In accordance with the Prime Minister's Decision No. 27/2018/QD-TTg on promulgating the Vietnam's Standard Industrial Classification.

[196] Vietnam's Civil Code 2015, Article 105, provides that "[p]roperty comprises objects, money, valuable papers and property rights."

[197] Vietnam's Civil Code 2015, Article 463.

classified as civil transactions. Also, they are very likely to be accused of conducting banking activities illegally without a banking license.

Lending interest rates of P2P loans must be in compliance with current laws. Article 468 of the Civil Code 2015 provides that:

> [t]he interest rate of a loan agreed upon by the parties may not exceed 20% per year, unless otherwise prescribed by laws. Based on the actual conditions and government proposal, the Standing Committee of the National Assembly shall make a decision on adjusting the above cap of interest rates and submit a report to the National Assembly at the nearest meeting session. If the interest rate agreed upon by the parties exceeds the cap of interest rates provided by this Article, such interest rate shall become invalid.[198]

Accordingly, the lending interest rates of P2P loans must not be higher than 20% per year. A lender who violates this rule and sets an interest rate that is five times or more higher than the interest rate cap provided by the Civil Code, earns an illegal profit of between VND 30 million and VND 100 million, or recommits this offense despite being previously imposed with administrative sanctions or having a criminal record that has not been cleared by the court will be fined from VND 50 million to VND 200 million or be imposed with a noncustodial sentence of up to 3 years. A lender who earns an illegal profit of VND 100 million or more will be fined from VND 200 million to VND 1 billion or be imposed with a custodial sentence ranging from 6 months to 3 years.[199]

### 2.2.3 Regulatory Approach to P2P Lending in Vietnam in the Future

The Vietnamese government has taken an incremental approach toward the P2P lending business so far. In March 2019, the government announced that it would issue a pilot P2P lending program to establish a transparent legal framework for the P2P lending business in Vietnam.[200] The pilot program is expected to cover the following key points[201]:

(1) P2P lending companies will be restricted to connecting lenders and borrowers.
(2) P2P lending companies will be prohibited from directly taking deposits, making loans, or providing intermediary payment services.
(3) Financial institutions will not be allowed to take part in P2P lending.

---

[198] Vietnam's Civil Code 2015, Article 468.

[199] See Vietnam's Criminal Code 2015, Article 201, and Vietnam's Criminal Code amended in 2017, Article 2, clause 2.

[200] See Viet Nam News (2019).

[201] Viet Nam News (2019).

Considering the potential risks associated with the cooperation between credit institutions and P2P lending companies, the State Bank issued Official Dispatch No. 5228/NHNN-CSTT on July 8, 2019. In the document, the State Bank recommended that credit institutions carefully assess the risks related to the P2P lending model. The authority also requested credit institutions to report information regarding their cooperation with P2P lending companies in a fully transparent and honest manner.

On June 1, 2020, the government released the first draft of the Decree on the controlled testing mechanism for financial technology activities (fintech) in the banking sector. P2P lending would be included in this testing mechanism. The mechanism has several objectives, including (i) modernizing banking activities and promoting innovation and financial inclusion; (ii) establishing a testing environment to develop and enhance fintech solutions in line with market demand and the legal framework; (iii) preventing risks and safeguarding customers who use non-licensed services; and (iv) establishing and improving the appropriate legal framework for fintech services (including P2P lending) based on the results of the testing mechanism. The testing period is expected to last for 1–2 years.

According to the first draft of the Decree, after the testing period, the State Bank will evaluate and approve P2P lending solutions based on the following criteria: (i) the absence of a comprehensive or partial legal framework governing such solutions at present; (ii) solutions that are developed and applied in Vietnam for the first time or that demonstrate creativity and benefits for users, contributing to improving financial inclusion; (iii) solutions that do not pose risks to the stability of the financial and banking market, as well as the overall economy; and (iv) solutions that exhibit sound risk management and are less likely to have an adverse impact on financial institutions.[202]

On April 1, 2022, the second draft of the Decree on the controlled testing mechanism for financial technology activities (fintech) in the banking sector was released by the government.[203] The second draft added several main points to the first draft as follows. Firstly, in the process of participating in the pilot mechanism, P2P lending companies would not be allowed to perform the following acts:

> providing loan security; providing the service of information brokerage for borrowing loans for stock investment and other high-risk activities; and using funds mobilized from customers in an unauthorized manner. Acts of abusing Fintech solutions to alter information, commit swindling or fraud or appropriate property would be prohibited.[204]

Secondly, "managerial staffs of P2P lending companies must neither be owners, managers or administrators of financial or credit service companies, pawnshops and multi-level marketing firms nor perform jobs related to banking, payment intermediary or e-wallet services."[205]

---

[202] See Vietnamese Government (2020).

[203] See Vietnamese Government (2022).

[204] Vietnam Law and Legal Forum (2022).

[205] Vietnam Law and Legal Forum (2022).

Thirdly, P2P lending companies would be required to protect the legitimate rights of their customers by (i) providing customers with guidelines on preventing risks when participating in using P2P lending services; (ii) ensuring accurate and complete information on lending services, service fees, as well as the rights and responsibilities of customers participating in P2P lending; (iii) ensuring the safety and confidentiality of customers' information during and after the process of participating in the pilot mechanism; and (iv) establishing a customer care and complaint management department.[206]

On March 4, 2024, a newly draft of the Decree on the controlled testing mechanism for financial technology activities (fintech) in the banking sector was released by the government. This newly draft provides several main points as follows:

First, fintech companies registering for P2P lending will be considered for a **participation certificate** if they meet specific criteria and conditions. According to Article 9 of the new draft of the Decree, the proposed P2P lending **solution** must (i) address technical and business aspects that are not yet clearly regulated under existing laws; (ii) be innovative and beneficial, particularly in promoting financial inclusion; (iii) include a risk management framework that mitigates potential negative impacts on the banking system and foreign exchange activities; (iv) undergo evaluation by participating entities in terms of operation, functionality, and utility; (v) be feasible for market deployment after completing the **Regulatory Sandbox**; (vi) implement measures to identify and manage the maximum outstanding loan balance for an individual borrower within a P2P lending solution, as well as the total outstanding loan balance for a borrower across all P2P lending solutions participating in the Regulatory Sandbox; and (vii) carry out the disbursement, repayment of principal and interest, and payment of fees for transactions conducted by borrowers through a P2P lending solution via payment accounts at credit institutions, branches of foreign banks, or e-wallets provided by licensed payment intermediary service providers.

Second, according to Article 10, clause 3, of the newly drafted Decree, a company must meet several strict requirements to register as a P2P lending provider. Firstly, it must be a legally established and operational entity in Vietnam, without foreign investment, and must not have undergone division, merger, consolidation, conversion, dissolution, or bankruptcy. Additionally, it cannot be engaged in the pawnshop business. Secondly, the legal representative and general director (director) must meet stringent eligibility criteria, including having no criminal record or past sanctions for financial, banking, or cybersecurity violations. They cannot concurrently be an owner or manager of a financial service business, credit institution, pawnshop, multilevel marketing company, or tontine group. Furthermore, they must not hold key positions, such as board member or supervisory board member, in credit institutions, foreign bank branches, or payment intermediary service providers.

[206] See Vietnamese Government (2022).

Thirdly, the legal representative and general director (director) must hold at least a bachelor's degree in economics, business administration, law, or information technology, have a minimum of 2 years of experience as a manager or executive in the financial or banking sector, and must not be subject to any legal prohibitions. Finally, companies must meet technical and infrastructure standards for their P2P lending platforms. These include maintaining IT and data storage systems within Vietnam to ensure safe and uninterrupted operation, particularly in the event of technical issues; securely storing and sharing customer and related data in compliance with transparency and confidentiality laws; conducting technology testing and evaluation before deployment; and employing a technical team proportional to the system's scale to ensure stable and continuous operation.

Third, according to Article 7, clause 3, of the newly drafted Decree, a P2P lending company is strictly limited to providing a platform that connects borrowers and lenders and must not engage in prohibited activities. These include offering its own guarantees for customer loans, operating beyond the scope of its regulatory sandbox approval, or acting as a borrower or lender itself. Additionally, the company cannot issue debt securities, introduce borrowers or lenders, engage in false advertising, or charge fees for handling complaints. It is also prohibited from collecting and consolidating lenders' funds, splitting loan terms, independently selling financial products to raise capital, exaggerating profits, or providing brokerage services for high-risk loan activities. Furthermore, the company must not use lenders' funds or borrowers' repayments for investment or business purposes, disclose borrower and lender information to unauthorized parties, or offer P2P lending services to pawnshops. Other restrictions include requesting or encouraging borrowers and lenders to grant access to their personal data, such as contacts, photos, friend lists, or social media accounts. Lastly, the company must refrain from any other activities explicitly prohibited by law.

Fourth, according to Article 3, clause 10, of the newly drafted Decree, participation in the P2P lending is strictly limited to domestic entities, excluding foreign-invested enterprises. This regulation is designed to protect Vietnamese investors and borrowers from potential risks and fraud associated with overseas entities.

## 2.3 Interim Conclusion

This chapter provides a historical overview of micro- and/or small-sized finance in Vietnam. It explains why, since the Đổi Mới, micro- and/or small-sized finance has been regarded as a critical tool in assisting poor and low-income individuals to access financial services. This chapter concludes that the micro- and/or small-sized finance sector in Vietnam excels at providing financial services to individuals residing in rural or remote areas. However, it is noteworthy that the sector is characterized by substantial government control and subsidies. In addition, this chapter scrutinizes the significant credit gap in the micro- and/or small-sized finance market in Vietnam from both supply and demand perspectives. It further underscores the necessity for the continued development of this sector. From the supply perspective, the micro- and/or small-sized finance market exhibits significant fragmentation, with overlapping services in some areas. Meanwhile, from the demand perspective, the substantial credit gap predominantly affects low- and middle-income households as well as private SMEs. Furthermore, this chapter outlines the legislative history of micro- and/or small-sized finance in Vietnam and the current Vietnamese laws on micro- and/or small-sized finance.

Subsequently, this chapter details the rapid growth of P2P lending in Vietnam, which is highlighted by the increasing number of P2P lending platforms emerging in the market.

It explains why P2P lending may fill the credit gap for which conventional banks are often reluctant to provide finance. This can be attributed to two main reasons: (i) the high demand for small funds by individuals and SMEs and (ii) the high potential for the P2P lending sector to develop. This chapter continues by outlining the regulations that govern P2P lending in Vietnam. Until now, Vietnam has not enacted specific regulations pertaining to the operations of P2P lending platforms. P2P lending companies have the option to register their business under management consultancy activities or activities auxiliary to financial services, in accordance with the Law on Enterprises 2020. Additionally, P2P lenders may lawfully lend to P2P borrowers if the transactions between them via online lending platforms fall within a civil lending transaction under the Civil Code 2015. The regulatory approach to P2P lending in Vietnam is also outlined in this chapter. Since the Vietnamese government has taken a very cautious approach to the P2P lending business so far, the government has just announced the development of a pilot program for the P2P lending scheme.

## References

An P (2021) Vietnam among world's fastest middle class growth nations. https://e.vnexpress.net/news/business/data-speaks/vietnam-among-world-s-fastest-middle-class-growth-nations-4351459.html. Accessed 20 Mar 2025

Agribank (2025a) About Agribank. https://www.agribank.com.vn/en/ve-agribank/gioi-thieu-agribank. Accessed 20 Mar 2025

Agribank (2025b) History. https://www.agribank.com.vn/en/ve-agribank/lich-su-dinh-huong. Accessed 20 Mar 2025

Anh NK, Tam LT, Cuong NM, Thuyet NV, Mai NTT (2014) Microfinance in Vietnam: the real situation and policy recommendations. https://microfinance.vn/study-report-on-microfinance-in-vietnam-the-real-situation-and-policy-recommendations-2/?lang=en. Accessed 10 Apr 2020

Anh X (2019) Tỷ lệ hộ nghèo bình quân cả nước còn dưới 4% [The national average rate of poor households is below 4%]. https://www.nhandan.org.vn/xahoi/item/42750402-ty-le-ho-ngheo-binh-quan-ca-nuoc-con-duoi-4.html. Accessed 5 May 2023

Asia-Pacific Economic Cooperation (2011) Promoting sustainable, market-based microfinance: Viet Nam case study and lessons learned for APEC economies. https://www.apec.org/Publications/2011/01/Promoting-Sustainable-Marketbased-Microfinance-Viet-Nam-Case-Study-and-Lessons-Learned-for-APEC-Econ. Accessed 20 Mar 2025

Avay (2023). https://avay.vn/. Accessed 5 May 2023

BIDV (2022) Early Days of Bank for Construction - Hanoi Branch. https://www.bidv.com.vn/bidv_en/tin-tuc/bidvstories/mot-vai-ky-niem-ve-thua-ban-dau-cua-chi-hang-kien-thiet-ha-noi. Accessed 20 Mar 2025

Bui TL, Lucía M, Bernadette AOC (2018) Microfinance notes in the context of Vietnam. Adv Nat Appl Sci 12:22

Bui TT (2017) Factors affecting microfinance development in Vietnam. https://www.theses.fr/2017USPCD065.pdf. Accessed 20 Mar 2025

Cao H (2019) P2P loans finding favor. https://vietnamnet.vn/en/p2p-loans-finding-favor-582700.html. Accessed 20 Mar 2025

Cash Money (2020). https://cashmoney.vn/. Accessed 10 Apr 2020

Central Population and Housing Census Steering Committee (2019) The result of Vietnam population and housing census of 00:00 hours on 1 April 2019. Statistical Publishing House, Hanoi

Chi LHD, Dung TTT (2022) Recommendations for the sustainable development of the people's credit fund system. https://tapchinganhang.gov.vn/nhung-khuyen-nghi-nham-phat-trien-ben-vung-he-thong-quy-tin-dung-nhan-dan-viet-nam.htm. Accessed 20 Mar 2025

Chính PM, Hoàng VQ (2009) Kinh tế Việt Nam: thăng trầm và đột phá [Vietnam's economy: vicissitudes and breakings]. National Political Publishing House, Hanoi

Christine NN, Miao C (2017) Differentials in market constraints and value addition among micro, small, and medium enterprises in Viet Nam. https://www.wider.unu.edu/publication/differentials-market-constraints-and-value-addition-among-micro-small-and-medium. Accessed 20 Mar 2025

Churchill C, Frankiewicz C (2006) Making microfinance work: managing for improved performance. International Labour Organization, Geneva

Construction Bank (2025) About. https://www.cbbank.vn/Pages/About.aspx. Accessed 20 Mar 2025

Dang LN, Chuc AT (2019) Challenges in implementing the credit guarantee scheme for small and medium-sized enterprises: the case of Viet Nam. https://www.adb.org/publications/challenges-implementing-credit-guarantee-scheme-sme-vietnam. Accessed 20 Mar 2025

Đông PT (2019) Rào cản nào trong tiếp cận vốn tín dụng của doanh nghiệp nhỏ và vừa ở Việt Nam? [What are the barriers to the access credit of small and medium enterprises in Vietnam?]. https://tapchitaichinh.vn/rao-can-nao-trong-tiep-can-von-tin-dung-cua-doanh-nghiep-nho-va-vua-o-viet-nam.html. Accessed 20 Mar 2025

Du HT, Kiều NM, Tuấn DTA (2013) Hệ thống tài chính Việt Nam [Vietnam's financial system]. https://fsppm.fulbright.edu.vn/attachment.aspx?Language=2&ID=54229. Accessed 5 May 2023

Duong HA, Nghiem HS (2022) The impact of microfinance on poverty reduction in Vietnam: a dynamic panel-data analysis, Poverty & Public Policy 14:406

Dương N (2022) Việt Nam s⊠ có 26% dân số thuộc tầng lớp trung lưu vào năm 2026 [Vietnam is projected to have a middle-class population of 26% by 2026]. https://vneconomy.vn/viet-nam-se-co-26-dan-so-thuoc-tang-lop-trung-luu-vao-nam-2026.htm. Accessed 20 Mar 2025

Eloan (2020). https://eloan.vn/. Accessed 10 Apr 2020

Fintechnews Vietnam (2019) Vietnamese p2p lender vaymuon.vn eyes US$ 10 million series A for global ambitions. https://fintechnews.sg/32611/vietnam/vietnames-p2p-lender-vaymoun-eyes-us-10-million-series-for-global-ambitions/. Accessed 20 Mar 2025

ICTnews (2019) Tima hợp tác Bảo Minh cung cấp bảo hiểm cho người đầu tư và người vay [Tima cooperates with Bao Minh to provide insurance for investors and borrowers]. https://vietnamnet.vn/tima-hop-tac-bao-minh-cung-cap-bao-hiem-cho-nguoi-dau-tu-va-nguoi-vay-i38549.html. Accessed 20 Mar 2025

Interloan (2023). https://interloan.vn/. Accessed 5 May 2023

Investing.vn (2019) Đánh giá công ty cho vay ngang hàng Lendbiz [Reviewing Lendbiz p2p lending company]. https://investing.vn/danh-gia-cong-ty-cho-vay-ngang-hang-lendbiz.html. Accessed 5 May 2023

Growth Wealth (2020). https://www.growth-wealth.com/. Accessed 10 Apr 2020

Hà PTH (2017) Hệ thống ngân hàng ở miền nam Việt Nam (1954-1975) [The banking system in the south of Vietnam (1954-1975)]. https://repository.vnu.edu.vn/flowpaper/simple_document.php?subfolder=11/98/31/&doc=119831481745877218502314088918456557 85&bitsid=ebf6e92e-be46-45bc-9fc9-5aff98f6656d&uid=. Accessed 20 Mar 2025

Hằng BT, Dũng PX, Anh PTH (2022) Peer-to-peer lending in Vietnam. https://tapchinganhang.gov.vn/hoat-dong-cho-vay-ngang-hang-tai-viet-nam.htm. Accessed 20 Mar 2025

Hansen L, Diaz L (2008) Microfinance industry report: Vietnam. https://www.findevgateway.org/paper/2008/01/microfinance-industry-report-vietnam. Accessed 20 Mar 2025

Hartung R (2019) Vietnam's retail loan market to reach $145 billion by 2020. https://tabinsights.com/article/vietnams-retail-loan-market-to-reach-145-billion-by-2020. Accessed 20 Mar 2025

Home Office of the UK's government (2018) Country policy and information note: fear of illegal moneylenders in Vietnam.https://assets.publishing.service.gov.uk/government/uploads/system/uploads/attachment_data/file/766760/Vietnam_-_Moneylenders_-_CPIN_-_v1.0__December_2018__ex__002_.pdf. Accessed 20 Mar 2025

Huydong (2020a). http://huydong.com/. Accessed 14 Jul 2020

Huydong (2020b) Apply SME loans. https://www.huydong.com/apply-sme-loans. Accessed 10 Apri 2020

Ho Chi Minh City Police Department (2023) Đấu tranh ngăn ngừa các hoạt động tín dụng đen & tội phạm cho vay nặng lãi [Fight against black credit activities & loan crimes]. https://phunu.hochiminhcity.gov.vn/tai-lieu-tuyen-truyen-dau-tranh-ngan-ngua-cac-hoat-dong-tin-dung-den-toi-pham-cho-vay-nang-lai-post1262.html. Accessed 20 Mar 2025

Hồng A (2020) Quỹ tín dụng nhân dân không thể dần dần biến thành ngân hàng [People's credit funds cannot gradually turn into banks]. https://tuoitre.vn/quy-tin-dung-nhan-dan-khong-the-dan-dan-bien-thanh-ngan-hang-20200110180422928.htm. Accessed 20 Mar 2025

Lan H (2023) Vì sao doanh nghiệp nhỏ và vừa khó tiếp cận vốn ngân hàng? [Why do SMEs find it difficult to access bank loans?]. https://vneconomy.vn/vi-sao-doanh-nghiep-nho-va-vua-kho-tiep-can-von-ngan-hang-832937.htm. Accessed 20 Mar 2025

Lendbiz (2025) Gọi vốn cùng Lendbiz [Raising capital with Lendbiz]. https://lendbiz.vn/goi-von-cung-lendbiz/. Accessed 20 Mar 2025

Lien T (2017) Thriving online lending carries potential risks. https://vir.com.vn/thriving-online-lending-carries-potential-risks-51014.html. Accessed 20 Mar 2025

Mai NN (2022) Tín dụng đen là gì? người hoạt động tín dụng đen bị xử lý thế nào? [What is black credit? How is it treated?]. https://thuvienphapluat.vn/chinh-sach-phap-luat-moi/vn/thoi-su-phap-luat/tu-van-phap-luat/41284/tin-dung-den-la-gi-nguoi-hoat-dong-tin-dung-den-bi-xu-ly-the-nao. Accessed 20 Mar 2025

Mai NTT, Ejigu SN, Huyen TT, Lan DTN, Linh LM, Linh NTV (2019) Report on microfinance products and services: the influences of mfis' organizational current state and development solution characteristics and performances on financial inclusion in Vietnam. https://microfinance.vn/research-report-on-microfinance-products-and-services-current-state-and-development-solution/?lang=en. Accessed 10 Apr 2020

MB Securities Joint Stock Company (2018) Vietnam fintech report. https://mbs.com.vn/media/g5edvk1i/1_-vietnam-fintech-report_22102018.pdf. Accessed 20 Mar 2025

Mccaig B, Pavcnik N (2017) Moving out of agriculture: structural change in Vietnam. In: Margaret SM, Rodrik D, Sepúlveda C (eds) Structural change, fundamentals, and growth: a framework and case studies. International Food Policy Research Institute, Washington, D.C.

McCarty A (2001) Microfinance in Vietnam: a survey of schemes and issues. https://ideas.repec.org/p/wpa/wuwpfi/0110001.html. Accessed 20 Mar 2025

Mofin (2020). https://mofin.vn/. Accessed 10 Apr 2020

Nga H (2018) Tiềm năng kinh doanh từ tầng lớp trung lưu Việt Nam [Business potential arising from Vietnam's middle class]. https://tapchitaichinh.vn/tiem-nang-kinh-doanh-tu-tang-lop-trung-luu-viet-nam.html. Accessed 20 Mar 2025

Nga N (2023) 70% doanh nghiệp vừa và nhỏ khó tiếp cận vay vốn [70% of SMEs find it difficult to access loans]. https://thanhnien.vn/70-doanh-nghiep-vua-va-nho-kho-tiep-can-vay-von-185230316161658602.htm. Accessed 20 Mar 2025

Nghiem HS, Tim C, Prasada R (2007) The efficiency of microfinance in Vietnam: evidence from NGO schemes in the north and the central regions. Int J Environ Cult Econ Soc Sustain 2:74

Nguyen D (2019) Businesses have long wait to cash in on cashless Vietnam. https://e.vnexpress.net/news/business/data-speaks/businesses-have-long-wait-to-cash-in-on-cashless-vietnam-3868565.html. Accessed 20 Mar 2025

Nguyen KA, Le TT (2013) The sustainability of microfinance institutions in Vietnam: circumstances and implications. Transport Publishing House, Hanoi

Nguyen QMA (2020) Financial services for the poor in Vietnam: a comprehensive analysis on the performance and sustainability of microfinance sector. https://microfinance.vn/study-report-on-microfinance-in-vietnam-the-real-situation-and-policy-recommendations-2/?lang=en. Accessed 20 Mar 2025

Oncredit (2023). https://oncredit.vn/. Accessed 5 May 2023

Oxford Learner's Dictionaries (2025). https://www.oxfordlearnersdictionaries.com/definition/english/middle-class_1?q=middle+class. Accessed 20 Mar 2025

Pham TTT, Lensink R (2007) Lending policies of informal, formal and semiformal lenders. Econ Transit Institutional Chang 15:182

Phan DK and Gan C (2017) Rural credit market and microfinance in Vietnam. In: Gan C, Gilbert VN (eds) Microfinance in ASIA. World Scientific Publishing, Singapore

Phan THT (2019) Activities of official micro finance institutions in Vietnam. Finan and Mone Mar Rev 6:28

Phong L (2022) P2P lending đua lãi suất, gồng thanh khoản [P2P lending companies in a race for interest rate and liquidity]. https://www.tinnhanhchungkhoan.vn/p2p-lending-dua-lai-suat-gong-thanh-khoan-post311255.html. Accessed 20 Mar 2025

Quân DV, Lý DTM (2022) Phát triển tầng lớp trung lưu Việt Nam [Developing the middle class in Vietnam]. http://lyluanchinhtri.vn/home/index.php/dien-dan/item/4686-quan-tri-dia-phuong-ung-pho-voi-bien-doi-khi-hau-o-khu-vuc-dong-bang-song-cuu-long.html. Accessed 20 Mar 2025

Rand J, Tarp F (2020) Introduction. In: Rand J, Tarp F (eds) Micro, small, and medium enterprises in Vietnam. Oxford University Press, New York

Schreiner M (2001) Informal finance and the design of microfinance. Develop in Prac 11:637

Sơn H (2019) Ứng xử phù hợp tín dụng phi chính thức [Behaving properly in the informal credit sector]. https://tapchitaichinh.vn/ung-xu-phu-hop-tin-dung-phi-chinh-thuc.html. Accessed 20 Mar 2025

The English translation of Circular No. 24/2024/TT-NHNN of Vietnam (trans: Thuvienphapluat). https://thuvienphapluat.vn/van-ban/Tien-te-Ngan-hang/Circular-24-2024-TT-NHNN-amending-certain-articles-of-Circular-33-2015-TT-NHNN-645140.aspx?tab=1. Accessed 20 Mar 2025

The English translation of Circular No. 33/2015/TT-NHNN of Vietnam (trans: Thuvienphapluat). https://thuvienphapluat.vn/van-ban/EN/Tien-te-Ngan-hang/Circular-33-2015-TT-NHNN-prudential-ratios-of-microfinance-institutions/433097/tieng-anh.aspx. Accessed 20 Mar 2025

The English translation of Circular No. 39/2016/TT-NHNN of Vietnam (trans: Luatvietnam.vn). https://english.luatvietnam.vn/circular-no-39-2016-tt-nhnn-dated-december-30-2016-of-the-state-bank-of-vietnam-prescribing-lending-transactions-of-credit-institutions-and-or-forei-112177-doc1.html. Accessed 20 Mar 2025

The English translation of Decision No. 20/2017/QD-TTg of Vietnam (trans: Luatvietnam.vn). https://english.luatvietnam.vn/decision-no-20-2017-qd-ttg-dated-june-12-2017-of-the-prime-minister-on-regulating-operations-of-microfinance-programs-and-projects-of-political-orga-114982-doc1.html. Accessed 20 Mar 2025

The English translation of Decision No. 96/2016/ND-CP of Vietnam (trans: Luatvietnam.vn). https://english.luatvietnam.vn/decree-no-96-2016-nd-cp-dated-july-01-2016-of-the-government-on-security-and-order-conditions-for-a-number-of-conditional-business-lines-107490-doc1.html. Accessed 20 Mar 2025

The English translation of Decision No. 108/2006/QD-TTg of Vietnam (trans: Luatvietnam.vn), https://english.luatvietnam.vn/decision-no-108-2006-qd-ttg-dated-may-19-2006-of-the-prime-minister-establishing-the-vietnam-development-bank-18691-doc1.html. Accessed 20 Mar 2025

The English translation of Decision No. 131/2002/QD-TTg of Vietnam (trans: Luatvietnam.vn). https://english.luatvietnam.vn/decision-no-131-2002-qd-ttg-dated-october-4-2002-of-the-prime-minister-on-the-establishment-of-the-social-policy-bank-14162-doc1.html. Accessed 20 Mar 2025

The English translation of Decision No. 601/QD-TTg of Vietnam on the establishment of the SME Development Fund (trans: Thuvienphapluat). https://thuvienphapluat.vn/van-ban/Doanh-nghiep/Decision-No-601-QD-TTg-to-establish-the-medium-and-small-enterprise-development-183331.aspx?tab=1. Accessed 20 Mar 2025

The English translation of Decision No. 1125/QD-NHNN of Vietnam on the maximum interest rate for short-term loans in VND in some specific cases according to Circular No. 39/2016/TT-NHNN (trans: Thuvienphapluat). https://thuvienphapluat.vn/van-ban/Tien-te-Ngan-hang/Decision-1125-QD-NHNN-2023-maximum-interest-rates-in-Vietnamese-Dong-according-Circular-39-2016-TT-NHNN-570224.aspx?tab=1. Accessed 20 Mar 2025

The English translation of Decree No. 19/2019/ND-CP of Vietnam (trans: Luatvietnam.vn), https://english.luatvietnam.vn/decree-no-19-2019-nd-cp-dated-february-19-2019-of-the-government-on-tontine-170756-doc1.html. Accessed 20 Mar 2025

The English translation of Decree No. 39/2019/ND-CP of Vietnam (trans: Luatvietnam.vn), https://english.luatvietnam.vn/decree-no-39-2019-nd-cp-dated-may-10-2019-of-the-government-on-organization-and-operation-of-small-and-medium-enterprise-development-fund-172694-doc1.html. Accessed 20 Mar 2025

The English translation of the Criminal Code 2015 of Vietnam (trans: Luatvietnam.vn). https://english.luatvietnam.vn/code-no-100-2015-qh13-dated-november-27-2015-of-the-national-assembly-on-criminal-101324-doc1.html. Accessed 20 Mar 2025

The English translation of the Criminal Code amended in 2017 of Vietnam (trans: Luatvietnam.vn). https://english.luatvietnam.vn/law-no-12-2017-qh14-dated-june-20-2017-of-the-national-assembly-on-amending-the-criminal-code-no-100-2015-qh13-115503-doc1.html. Accessed 20 Mar 2025

The English translation of the Law on Credit Institutions 2024 of Vietnam (trans: Thuvienphapluat). https://thuvienphapluat.vn/van-ban/Tien-te-Ngan-hang/Law-32-2024-QH15-Credit-institutions-606780.aspx?tab=1. Accessed 20 Mar 2025

The Ministry of Information and Communication of Vietnam (2022) Viet Nam has over 72 million internet users. https://english.mic.gov.vn/Pages/TinTuc/156626/Viet-Nam-has-over-72-million-Internet-users.html. Accessed 20 Mar 2025

The English translation of the Law on Investment 2020 of Vietnam (trans: Luatvietnam.vn). https://english.luatvietnam.vn/law-on-investment-no-61-2020-qh14-dated-june-17-2020-of-the-national-assembly-186270-doc1.html#_ftn1. Accessed 20 Mar 2025

The State Bank of Vietnam (2019) Vietnam's fintech trend and ongoing policies. https://www.fintechweek.or.kr/download.php?downloadfilename=Vietnams%20Fintech%20Trend%20and%20ongoing%20Policies%20-%20State%20Bank%20of%20Vietnam20190515.pdf. Accessed 28 Dec 2019

The State Bank of Vietnam (2025a) History of the State Bank of Vietnam, https://www.sbv.gov.vn/webcenter/portal/en/home/sbv/aboutsbv/history?_afrLoop=23151389246858224#%40%3F_afrLoop%3D23151389246858224%26centerWidth%3D80%2525%26leftWidth%3D20%2525%26rightWidth%3D0%2525%26showFooter%3Dfalse%26showHeader%3Dfalse%26_adf.ctrl-state%3Dxnhc3z5ed_4. Accessed 20 Mar 2025

The State Bank of Vietnam (2025b) History and Development of the Central Bank, https://www.sbv.gov.vn/webcenter/portal/en/home/rm/museum/hadotcb?centerWidth=80%25&

leftWidth=20%25&rightWidth=0%25&showFooter=false&showHeader=false&_adf.ctrl-state=3hltvxt7u_9&_afrLoop=20472523887458466. Accessed 20 Mar 2025
The State Bank of Vietnam (2025c) System of Credit Institutions. https://www.sbv.gov.vn/webcenter/portal/m_en/home/fm/socins?_afrLoop=19267569961733023#%40%3F_afrLoop%3D19267569961733023%26centerWidth%3D100%2525%26leftWidth%3D0%2525%26rightWidth%3D0%2525%26showFooter%3Dfalse%26showHeader%3Dfalse%26_adf.ctrl-state%3D16zezr5myc_78. Accessed 20 Mar 2025
The Vietnam Bank for Social Policies (2025a) History. https://eng.vbsp.org.vn/history.html. Accessed 20 Mar 2025
The Vietnam Bank for Social Policies (2025b) Vision. https://eng.vbsp.org.vn/vision.html. Accessed 20 Mar 2025
The Vietnam Development Bank (2025) About Vietnam Development Bank. https://en.vdb.gov.vn/VDB/about-vdb. Accessed 20 Mar 2025
The World Bank (2018) Bước tiến mới giảm nghèo và thịnh vượng chung ở Việt Nam [A new step towards poverty reduction and overall prosperity in Vietnam]. https://documents1.worldbank.org/curated/en/826021522843528151/pdf/124916-WP-PUBLIC-VITENAMESE-P161323-VietnamPovertyUpdateReportVIE.pdf. Accessed 20 Mar 2025
Thương N (2023) Tăng khả năng tiếp cận vốn tín dụng cho doanh nghiệp nhỏ và vừa [Increasing access to credit for SMEs]. https://congthuong.vn/tang-kha-nang-tiep-can-von-tin-dung-cho-doanh-nghiep-nho-va-vua-246440.html. Accessed 20 Mar 2025
Tima (2025) About Tima. https://tima.vn/Home/About/. Accessed 20 Mar 2025
Trinh TT (2019) Issues about development of microfinance models in Vietnam. Rev of Finan 714:74
Trust Circle (2020). http://www.trustcircle.com. Accessed 10 Apr 2020
Uyen TD, Ha H (2017) The sharing economy and collaborative finance: the case of p2p lending in Vietnam. J Eko Bis. 22:84
VayVND (2023). https://vayvnd.vn/. Accessed 5 May 2023
Vdong (2023). https://vdong.vn/pc/index. Accessed 5 May 2023
Viet Nam News (2017) SMEs hard to access bank loans. https://vietnamnews.vn/economy/379890/smes-hard-to-access-bank-loans.html. Accessed 20 Mar 2025
Vietnam Law & Legal Forum (2022) Regulatory Fintech Sandbox for Banking Activities Proposed. https://vietnamlawmagazine.vn/regulatory-fintech-sandbox-for-banking-activities-proposed-48532.html?utm_source=link.gov.vn#source=link.gov.vn. Accessed 20 Mar 2025
Vietnam Microfinance Working Group (2019) Financial inclusion note 2. https://microfinance.vn/wp-content/uploads/2019/06/FINANCIAL-INCLUSION-NOTE.pdf. Accessed 10 Apr 2020
Vietnam Microfinance Working Group (2020) Introduction. https://microfinance.vn/introduction/?lang=en. Accessed 10 Apr 2020
Vietnam's Constitution 2013 (trans: Luatvietnam.vn). https://english.luatvietnam.vn/constitution-of-the-socialist-republic-of-vietnam-2013-83320-doc1.html. Accessed 20 Mar 2025
Vietnam's Ministry of Planning and Investment (2022) 2022 Vietnamese Enterprises White Book. Statistical Publishing House, Hanoi
Vietnamese Government (2020) Dự thảo bộ hồ sơ lập đề nghị xây dựng Nghị định về cơ chế thử nghiệm fintech trong hoạt động ngân hàng để trình Thủ tướng chính phủ [Draft proposal dossier for establishing a Decree on the controlled testing mechanism for financial technology activities (fintech) in the banking sector]. http://chinhphu.vn/portal/page/portal/chinhphu/congdan/DuThaoVanBan?_piref135_27935_135_27927_27927.mode=detail&_piref135_27935_135_27927_27927.id=3619. Accessed 1 Jun 2020
Vietnamese Government (2022) Dự thảo nghị định quy định về cơ chế thử nghiệm có kiểm soát hoạt động công nghệ tài chính trong lĩnh vực ngân hàng [Draft Decree on the controlled testing mechanism for financial technology activities (Fintech) in the banking sector]. https://chinhphu.vn/?pageid=30187&vbid=4880&title=du-thao-nghi-dinh-quy-dinh-ve-co-che-thu-nghiem-co-kiem-soat-hoat-dong-cong-nghe-tai-chinh-trong. Accessed 20 Mar 2025
Vnvon (2023). https://vnvon.com/. Accessed 20 May 2023

Vũ D (2022) Việt Nam Hiện Có 93,5 Triệu Thuê Bao Sử Dụng Smartphone [Vietnam currently has 93.5 million smartphone subscribers]. https://vietnamnet.vn/viet-nam-hien-co-935-trieu-thue-bao-su-dung-smartphone-i407583.html. Accessed 20 Mar 2025

Vuong QH (2019) The financial economy of Viet Nam in an age of reform, 1986-2016. In: Volz U, Peter JM, Yoshino N (eds) Routledge handbook of banking and finance in ASIA. Routledge, New York

World Bank (2023) Rural Population (% of Total Population)—Vietnam, https://data.worldbank.org/indicator/SP.RUR.TOTL.ZS?locations=VN. Accessed 20 Mar 2025

# Chapter 3
# Risks Related to Micro- and/or Small-Sized Finance Via P2P Lending Platforms

## 3.1 General Risks Related to Micro- and/or Small-Sized Finance

Although the P2P lending scheme is expected to bridge the credit gap in society and improve financial inclusion in the country, it also contains potential risks. It can be seen that risks related to micro- and/or small-sized finance via P2P lending platforms might come from micro- and/or small-sized finance, using online lending platforms, and the combination of micro- and/or small-sized finance and online lending platforms. The following subsections will clarify the specific risks related to micro- and/or small-sized finance via P2P lending platforms in Vietnam.

### *3.1.1 Risks Related to Micro- and/or Small-Sized Finance*

It can be seen that P2P lenders are exposed to several potential risks due to the nature of micro- and/or small-sized finance. For example, it is widely perceived that default risk is an inherent problem that accompanies micro- and/or small-sized finance in general and micro- and/or small-sized finance via P2P lending platforms in particular. If a P2P borrower comes into default, the corresponding P2P lenders are very likely to lose their money, either partly or entirely. This is because P2P loans tend to be unsecured, and P2P lenders usually have no collateral to recoup the loans, as mentioned in Sect. 1.1. Another example of a possible risk related to micro- and/or small-sized finance is that P2P borrowers may delay their repayments to P2P lenders. The delays caused by P2P borrowers may happen frequently, and the duration of the delays can be lengthy. It is foreseeable that it might take P2P lenders a significant amount of time and effort to recoup the delayed loans. In both examples, it is reasonable to presume that pursuing a legal process could be time-consuming if P2P lenders bring their cases to court. Also, the amount of money they could claim is



Y. H. Nguyen, *Regulating Peer-to-Peer Lending in Vietnam*,
https://doi.org/10.1007/978-981-96-9505-8_3

likely to be minimal, because P2P loans are typically of a very small and/or small size.

Meanwhile, it can be reasonably predicted that P2P lenders may find it challenging to rely on platform service providers for loan recovery. This is likely because loan contracts are often established solely between P2P lenders and P2P borrowers. Platform service providers may merely act on behalf of both parties to transfer money based on their orders or authorities, facilitating loan disbursement and payments. Platform service providers, therefore, might not have direct recourse to borrowers in the event of a default. Suppose lenders authorize their right of recourse to platform service providers. In this case, they may directly have claims against defaulted borrowers to assist P2P lenders in recouping defaulted loans. However, as mentioned in Sect. 1.1, platform service providers are unlikely to have much incentive to pursue the repayment from each borrower in default.

It is readily apparent that platform service providers do not have the same obligations to safeguard lenders' funds as conventional commercial banks. Unlike commercial banks, platform service providers are not subject to the same level of supervision by the State Bank. The operations of P2P lending platforms are also not governed by banking regulations. This means that platform service providers are not obligated to protect lenders' money in the same way that commercial banks are obligated to protect depositors' money. Since transactions between platform service providers and P2P lenders are considered civil transactions, platform service providers are not required to protect lenders' money in accordance with the Civil Code.

In addition, it is obvious that platform service providers do not have the same obligations to employ all possible measures to ensure the safety of lenders' money as conventional commercial banks. Specifically, platform service providers are not obligated to exercise strict due diligence before loan origination, establish provisional funds, buy credit insurance, or establish a secondary market to protect lenders' money. In practice, some platform service providers report employing various measures, such as due diligence, provisional funds, credit insurance, and a secondary loan market, to attract potential lenders. However, as examined in Sect. 1.2, P2P lenders may not be able to rely on platform service providers' tactics to ensure the safety of their money.

### *3.1.2 Risks Associated with Using Online Platforms*

When potential lenders and borrowers register on online lending platforms, they are likely to enter into contracts containing ambiguous and unfair terms with platform service providers. This is due to the likelihood that potential lenders and borrowers must accept the terms of use presented by platform service providers as a nonnegotiable condition for creating an account on these lending platforms. It is highly probable that to successfully register, potential lenders have to create an account through P2P lending websites or investor-focused applications by providing platform service providers with the necessary information. Likewise, potential

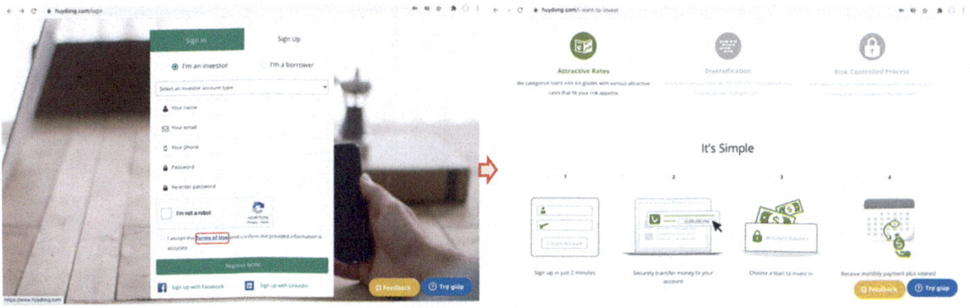


**Fig. 3.1** Investor registration process via Huydong

borrowers have to register via P2P lending websites or borrower-focused applications by providing platform service providers with the required information. Also, both potential lenders and borrowers are very likely to be required to accept the terms of use presented by platform service providers by checking the designated checkbox. For example, an individual lender can create an account on the Huydong platform's website by providing the required information (including name, email address, phone number, and password), checking the "I'm not a robot" checkbox, and accepting the "Terms of Use" offered by Huydong (see Fig. 3.1).

It seems likely that potential lenders and borrowers may find it convenient to complete the registration process, even without downloading and reading the terms of use. In some cases, they may even be unable to find the terms of use before completing the registration process. For example, when clicking on the "Terms of Use" on Huydong's website, potential lenders are presented with an interface introducing the investment process through the lending platform, rather than the actual contents of the terms (see Fig. 3.1).

It is evident that when P2P lenders and borrowers create an account on online lending platforms, they are likely to enter into an adhesion contract with platform service providers. In such transactions, platform service providers may easily prefix all the conditions and terms arbitrarily, as P2P lenders and borrowers can only accept or reject the offered terms. Without any possibility of negotiation and manifesting knowing and voluntary consent to all the terms of the contract, P2P lenders and borrowers are likely to be subject to contracts containing ambiguous and unfair terms prefixed by platform service providers.

Besides the risk of entering into contracts containing ambiguous and unfair terms with platform service providers, P2P lenders and borrowers are also likely to face the risk of high intermediary fees imposed by platform service providers. This is because platform service providers can establish and freely adjust transaction fees, which may cause financial harm to P2P lenders and borrowers. In practice, some P2P lending platforms[1] do not provide disclosure regarding the lending interest rates they impose on P2P borrowers. However, the repayment amounts clearly indicate that the

[1] Such as Money Bank, Cash Money, and Avay. See Money Bank, Cash Money, and Avay.

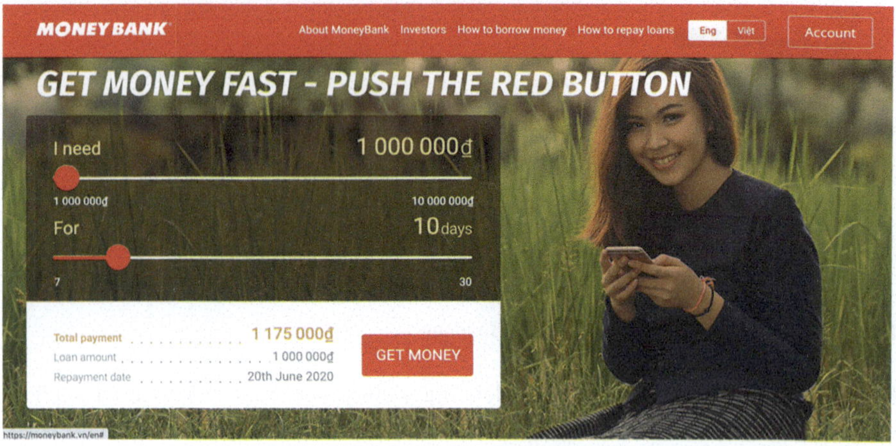


**Fig. 3.2** A loan via Money Bank

interest rates can exceed 600% per year, significantly surpassing the legally permitted interest rate cap of 20% per year in the country. The case of Money Bank can be taken as an example. If a P2P borrower borrows VND one million for 10 days via the Money Bank platform, they would be required to repay VND 1.175 million (see Fig. 3.2). In this scenario, the interest rate amounts to 1.75% per day or 630% per year.

It can be observed that some other P2P lending platforms declare imposing lending interest rates of no more than 20% per year on borrowers, but they also impose consulting and/or transaction fees. This makes the total cost that P2P borrowers eventually have to pay substantially higher than the legally regulated interest rate cap. For example, Vaydi announces an interest rate of 18% per year and charges 5% per transaction[2]; Tamo promotes an interest rate of 20% per year, but the total cost that P2P borrowers ultimately have to bear can exceed 500% per year.[3] In some cases, platform service providers deduct lending interest and transaction fees before transferring the loans to P2P borrowers, resulting in reduced disbursement of the P2P loans. As an example, a borrower registered for a loan of VND three million via the Cashwagon platform but only received VND 1.9 million.[4]

It is reasonable to assume that P2P lenders and borrowers face the risk of having their personal information misappropriated by platform service providers, potentially leading to identity theft and data breaches by unauthorized individuals. Misappropriation by platform service providers is possible because they could collect and store information from P2P lenders and borrowers to facilitate loans originated through their platforms. In practice, platform service providers usually require P2P

[2] See Vaydi (2020).

[3] See Tamo (2023).

[4] See Lê (2020).

lenders and borrowers to provide personal data, for example, national identification numbers, occupation, phone numbers, email addresses, age, and gender, for their verification process.[5] Some P2P lending platforms, such as Avay, VayVND, and Oncredit,[6] also request permission from P2P borrowers to use cookies for collecting information from their devices (see Appendix A). It is foreseeable that platform service providers may use the personal information of P2P lenders and borrowers to make unauthorized transactions without their awareness and consent. Furthermore, in the absence of standardized information security requirements in the P2P lending business, P2P lenders and borrowers are likely to be exposed to additional risks of identity theft and data breaches, unless platform service providers implement well-established security measures to protect their platforms.[7]

In addition to the risks mentioned above, P2P lenders are also exposed to the risk of adverse selection due to information asymmetry between them and P2P borrowers. It can be seen that this is possible because P2P borrowers may provide P2P lenders with limited information, or even false or inaccurate information, regarding their creditworthiness for the purpose of increasing their chances of obtaining loans. Platform service providers may further contribute to this information asymmetry by providing P2P lenders with false or inaccurate information regarding P2P borrowers' creditworthiness. This provision of false or inaccurate information can occur in cases where platform service providers fail to conduct proper due diligence on P2P borrowers and/or intentionally provide misleading information to maximize loan origination and revenue, which is often tied to the volume of loans originated. It is reasonable to presume that platform service providers face financial incentives to maximize loan origination, even at the expense of credit standards, while they are unlikely to be exposed to the direct financial consequences of borrower defaults. In such cases, P2P lenders are highly likely to be at risk of making wrong lending decisions.

It is not surprising that P2P lenders are likely to bear the risk of losing their money if P2P lending platforms cease their operations, whether temporarily or permanently. It can be predicted that the cessation of P2P lending platforms can happen due to various reasons, such as software failures within P2P lending platforms, the

[5] For example, Tima, Vnvon, and Eloan.

[6] See Avay, VayVND, and Oncredit.

[7] See The State Bank of Vietnam (2020, p. 2).

platforms' unprofitable operations, or the operators of the platforms being arrested for police investigation.[8] For example, Cashwagon,[9] a P2P lending platform in Vietnam, abruptly shut down its website on June 3, 2020.[10] As has been reported, the platform was ceased after its operators were arrested.[11] In the event of a P2P lending platform's cessation, it remains unclear how the management of borrowers' ongoing repayments and their transmission to respective lenders could be handled. Although the transfer and assignment of the loan books and lenders' accounts to another P2P lending platform could be one possible solution under the direction of an administrator or liquidator, this measure seems likely to result in significant losses for P2P lenders.

It is easily predicted that in the absence of a legal framework for the operations of P2P lending platforms in Vietnam, these platforms could be fertile ground for illegal lending activities. Some P2P lending platforms have been reported to provide loans at exorbitant interest rates via the Internet.[12] It has also been reported that after China tightened the management of P2P lending, some Chinese P2P lending platforms moved to Vietnam and illegally operated P2P lending businesses.[13] In April 2020, the Criminal Police Department of Ho Chi Minh Public Security arrested a group of individuals from China who were involved in the illegal provision of loans with interest rates of more than 1000% per year via three lending platforms, including Vaytocdo, Moreloan, and VD Online.[14] These lending platforms had provided more than VND 100 billion to approximately 60,000 borrowers since April 2019.[15] In case of borrower default, these lending platforms used strong-arm methods, such as kidnapping or threatening defaulted borrowers' family members and defaming

---

[8] To the best of the author's knowledge, official statistical data on the default rate for P2P lending in Vietnam has not yet been made available. This lack of official statistical data could be attributed to several factors, including:

(i) The P2P lending industry in Vietnam is relatively new and still developing. Collecting accurate and comprehensive data on default rates may pose challenges, especially when P2P lending companies operate with varying levels of transparency.

(ii) Regulatory oversight of the P2P lending sector in Vietnam is still evolving. As the government continues to develop a pilot program for P2P lending as mentioned in Sect. 2.2.3, it has not yet implemented reporting requirements specifically focused on default rates.

(iii) There is a lack of research and analysis conducted by independent parties or government agencies specifically focused on default rates in the P2P lending sector. The author has tried to search for such statistical data but has failed to find it.

[9] The Cashwagon platform was established by Cashwagon Limited Company in Vietnam in 2017. The company registered its operation under the business line of management consultancy activities (code 7020).

[10] See Thuận (2020).

[11] It should be noted that the Cashwagon platform was accused of providing loans with exorbitant interest rates and using strong-arm methods for debt collection. See Duong Gia Law Firm (2023).

[12] See Tùng (2020, p. 24).

[13] See Vietnam Net (2020) and Thiện (2020).

[14] See Hồng and Thiện (2020).

[15] See Online Newspaper of the Government (2020).

defaulted borrowers on the Internet or at their living places.[16] It has been noted that some P2P lending platforms illegally conducted banking operations such as mobilizing capital and providing loans via their platforms.[17] For example, some P2P lending platforms, such as Finizi, Oneclickmoney, Doctor Dong, and Viet Than Tai, used their own capital to illegally provide P2P loans without accepting investments or funding from potential lenders via their lending platforms.[18] They claimed that they simply attract potential borrowers and refer them to pawnshops or finance companies for loan provision.[19] However, it can be easily seen that it seems likely risky for pawnshops or finance companies to provide small loans to many P2P borrowers without collateral or due diligence performance. If they require collateral or strictly perform due diligence, they may find it difficult to take advantages, such as a quick lending process, low transaction costs, and the potential to reach individuals in rural and remote areas, of the P2P lending model.

Furthermore, it is worth noting that P2P lending platforms can be exploited for money laundering and terrorist financing.[20] It is possible to presume that P2P lending platforms may transfer money to P2P borrowers for the purpose of conducting such illegal activities, especially when P2P loans are provided without involving investments or funding from potential lenders. Another possibility is that P2P lenders and borrowers themselves engage in such illegal activities by transferring money to each other via P2P lending platforms. This is possible because P2P lending platforms simply act as intermediaries to facilitate transactions between P2P lenders and P2P borrowers, acting on behalf of both parties to move money and process loan payments. Even though P2P loans are transferred via online lending platforms, platform service providers are currently not required to comply with the Law on Anti-Money Laundering 2022. This means that they are not obligated to monitor and/or prevent money laundering and terrorist financing activities. If regulations were introduced requiring that all loan disbursements, repayments, and fee payments on P2P lending platforms be processed through payment accounts at credit institutions, foreign bank branches, or licensed e-wallet service providers, this could improve oversight and reduce financial crime risks. However, such requirements could also limit access to P2P loans for individuals in remote and underbanked areas.

[16] See Tùng (2020).

[17] See Duong Gia Law Firm (2023).

[18] See Finizi (2023), Oneclickmoney (2020), Doctor Dong (2020), and Viet Than Tai (2020).

[19] For example, Finizi P2P lending application operated by Finizi Technology Solutions Limited Company with the registered business line of activities auxiliary to financial service activities (code 6619) claimed that it cooperated with EasyCredit, a finance company, to provide loans to borrowers.

[20] See The State Bank of Vietnam (2020).

### 3.1.3 Risks Associated with Micro- and/or Small-Sized Finance on Online Platforms

It is reasonable to presume that P2P lenders face the risk of losing the opportunity to make continuous investments. During a severe economic recession or a pandemic disease (like COVID-19), for example, P2P borrowers may give up their chance of doing business and want to request early loan repayment before the loans mature. In this case, P2P lenders are not subject to any loss of disbursed loans, but they are likely to lose the opportunity to make continuous investments with their money.

Besides the risk of losing the opportunity to make continuous investments, P2P lenders are likely to be exposed to liquidity risk. In P2P lending, it is highly unlikely that P2P lenders can withdraw their money before loan maturities. Although platform service providers may provide a secondary loan market where P2P lenders can sell their loan claims, they can liquidate their loans only when potential investors are willing to take over the loans. It is apparent that P2P lenders might not always find a potential investor to immediately buy their loan claims via the secondary loan market when they urgently need to liquidate the loans.

It can be seen that P2P lenders are also likely to be exposed to interest rate risk. This is because there is no secondary market with continuous pricing for P2P loans, as is available for securities. Any change in market interest rates or the borrower's credit risk assessment is unlikely to visibly affect the current interest rates of P2P loans. If market interest rates increase during loan terms, P2P lenders are likely to miss the opportunity to earn a higher income.

In addition to the aforementioned risks, the risks associated with the combination of micro- and/or small-sized finance and online lending platforms also include the risk of losing potential lenders' investments, which are likely to be faced by platform service providers. It can be presumed that potential lenders no longer want to provide loans to potential borrowers via online lending platforms. In this case, platform service providers might have to restrict the amount of new loans via their lending platforms or even stop the operation of their lending platforms. It can be seen that there are several reasons why P2P lenders may no longer want to provide P2P loans. The first reason is that a loss in P2P lenders' trust could occur if they have experienced high rates of P2P borrowers' default. If so, they may no longer trust the credit ratings provided by platform service providers and, therefore, are likely to stop investing in loans available on lending platforms. Another reason is that lenders' confidence in P2P lending could be destroyed if any operational risk like false identification, privacy infringements, cyberattacks, or operational disruption of lending platforms were to happen. The third reason could be the rise in consulting fees or transaction fees that platform service providers charge P2P lenders, which makes the return associated with P2P loans less attractive to them.

Moreover, both platform service providers and P2P lenders are likely to be put at legal risk in the absence of a legal framework for the P2P lending business. It has been noted that this is because platform service providers transfer P2P lenders' money to P2P borrowers without a payment intermediary license granted by the

State Bank.[21] They are, therefore, likely to be subject to administrative fines and confiscation of proceeds.[22] In addition, if P2P lenders frequently lend to P2P borrowers and get most of their income from providing P2P loans, their lending transactions may no longer fall under civil transactions. As mentioned in Sect. 2.2, P2P lenders are likely to be accused of illegally conducting banking activities without a banking license.

## 3.2 Risks Faced by Stakeholders in P2P Lending Schemes

As mentioned above, stakeholders in P2P lending schemes face potential risks when engaging in micro- and/or small-sized finance via P2P lending platforms in Vietnam. It is evident that these potential risks could impede the growth of the P2P lending business in the country. The reason likely lies in the fact that these risks could make stakeholders hesitate to participate in the lending schemes. It is, therefore, important to examine the risks that individual participants might face in order to consider how we can mitigate these risks and facilitate the development of the P2P lending business.

### *3.2.1 Risks Faced by P2P Lenders*

It can be seen that P2P lenders face substantial risks when providing small loans through P2P lending platforms. These risks are outlined below.

It is evident that potential lenders may be easily solicited by platform service providers to enter into a service contract, the enforceability of which can be challenged later due to its inequitable and substantially disadvantageous terms and conditions to P2P lenders (hereinafter, for the purpose of convenience, referred to as an "unfair service contract"). Such solicitation to an unfair service contract can happen under various conditions. For example, the providers may arbitrarily prefix all the terms and conditions of the service contracts between them and P2P lenders, and what potential lenders can do is either accept the given terms and conditions by checking the designated checkbox or give up using online lending platforms. Moreover, it is highly likely that potential lenders can enter into service contracts with platform service providers even without downloading and reading the said terms and conditions. Also, the providers may arbitrarily change and amend the said terms and conditions, including, without limitation to, the transaction fees charged to P2P lenders using their lending platforms, without obtaining individual lenders' consent. Such arbitrary changes to the terms and conditions might cause financial

[21] See Hai (2023).

[22] Hai (2023).

damages to P2P lenders. If P2P lenders want to claim compensation for financial damages arising from their use of lending platforms, they might struggle to find the exact terms and conditions at the time they entered into the service contracts with platform service providers, as these terms may have been repeatedly changed thereafter. Even if P2P lenders could restore the exact terms and conditions at the time of entering into the service contracts, the terms may authorize the providers to amend them from time to time.[23]

Like any lender in conventional financing schemes, those who provide loans via online lending platforms are exposed to the risk of losing lent money partly or fully due to borrowers' defaults. If a borrower defaults on a loan provided through an online lending platform, the corresponding lender is likely to have difficulties in recouping the principal amount and accompanying interest due to several reasons. For example, because the principal amount and accompanying interest of individual P2P loans are likely to be considerably small, the cost necessary to recoup the loan is unlikely to pay off. Additionally, usually, the loans provided through P2P lending platforms are unsecured,[24] and, accordingly, P2P lenders can hardly expect the recouping of principal amounts and accompanying interest of P2P loans unless the borrowers autonomously make repayments. In practice, some P2P borrowers have even attempted to avoid paying their debts by various means, such as stopping using their SIM cards, running away, or faking their deaths.[25]

It is evident that the temporary or permanent cessation of platform service providers' operations can result in P2P lenders losing part or all of their lent money, even when P2P borrowers are not in default. For example, if a platform experiences a temporary cessation due to Internet connection issues, software failures, or server system failures,[26] transactions through the platform might not be recorded promptly and accurately. As a result, lending data might be altered or lost, which can lead to inaccuracies or suspension of loan repayments to P2P lenders. In this scenario, P2P lenders may find it challenging to hold platform service providers liable for compensation for their damages or losses. This is because the providers often include terms in their service contracts with P2P lenders that disclaim liability. These terms typically state that the providers will not be held liable for any damages or losses arising from errors, delays in connection, transmission, and data storage within their online lending systems, or any illegal actions by third parties.[27]

Another example is the permanent cessation of platform service providers' operations due to unprofitable businesses, software failures, or server system

[23] For example, Lendbiz may, at its sole discretion, modify and supplement or replace any part of its terms of use. Another example is Vdong, which reserves the right to change its terms and conditions at any time without prior notice. See Lendbiz (2025b) and Vdong (2023).

[24] Many P2P lending platforms, such as Lendbiz, Fiin, SHA, and Vnvon, provide unsecured loans. See Lendbiz (2025a), Fiin Credit (2023c), SHA (2023), and Vnvon (2025a).

[25] See Trường and Linh (2021) and Anh (2021).

[26] Internet connection failures may include a disrupted Internet connection or limited transmission capacity, while software or server system failures could result from cyberattacks or power outages.

[27] See Lendbiz (2025b), Fiin Credit (2023b), and Tima (2018).

failures.[28] In such cases, the providers might not collect loan repayments from P2P borrowers and allocate them to the corresponding lenders.[29] As mentioned above, the terms and conditions of service contracts between the providers and P2P lenders are usually prefixed by the providers themselves. The terms governing the providers' responsibilities for collecting and allocating loan repayments in the case of permanent cessation of their operations are, therefore, likely to exempt themselves from these responsibilities or not define these responsibilities clearly. The terms that facilitate P2P lenders in collecting repayments directly from P2P borrowers in the event of permanent cessation of the providers' operations are also unlikely to exist. P2P lending differs from lending that does not involve a P2P platform in that lenders often find it difficult to directly interact with borrowers and ascertain the location of recourse assets. It should be paid close attention to that, in most cases, P2P lenders must transfer their funds to the bank accounts or e-wallets of platform service providers and authorize these providers to allocate their funds to selected P2P borrowers. P2P lenders are also required to delegate their rights to enforce loan collection to the providers. Likewise, P2P borrowers are required to make repayments to the platform service providers' bank accounts or e-wallets and authorize them to transfer such repayments to the corresponding lenders.[30] While platform service providers act as intermediaries between P2P lenders and borrowers, facilitating the collection and transfer of loan repayments, this arrangement often makes it challenging for P2P lenders to collect repayments directly from the corresponding borrowers.

From the analysis above, it is clear that P2P lenders face the risk of partial or total loss of lent money, regardless of whether they engage in conventional micro- and/or small-sized financing schemes or online P2P lending schemes. However, in the case of P2P lending, lenders especially face difficulties in obtaining the necessary or useful information to enforce their rights against borrowers. To address these difficulties, platform service providers may employ several tactics that are commonly used by conventional lenders. These tactics include limiting the amount lent to a single P2P borrower and promoting syndicated lending to distribute the risk among multiple P2P lenders. While these tactics can limit and reduce P2P lenders' losses, they may still face losses on money lent to borrowers who default. Besides tactics for limiting and sharing risk, platform service providers may also utilize provisional funds and/or credit insurance to secure P2P loan repayments. However, the amounts that P2P lenders can recoup hinge on the size of the provisional funds

[28] For example, many lending platforms, such as Moreloan, Vaytocdo, VD online, Trust Circle, Mofin, Eloan, Cashwagon, Doctor App, Vdong, Openvay, Tiennhanh, Vietdong, Movay, and Vaymoney, have recently ceased operations and disappeared. See Cao (2020).

[29] See Liên (2020).

[30] For example, Vaymuon requires investors to authorize it to allocate their money to selected borrowers and to transfer the rights to enforce loan collection to the platform. Likewise, Lendbiz and Fiin Credit ask investors to authorize them to allocate their money to borrowers and to transfer the rights to enforce loan collection to the platforms. See Vaymuon (2021a), Lendbiz (2020), and Fiin Credit (2023a).

and/or the extent of credit insurance coverage. If the total amount of defaulted loans surpasses the size of the provisional funds, or if each defaulted loan exceeds the credit insurance coverage limit, P2P lenders are likely to shoulder the remaining loss.

In addition to the aforementioned financial risks, P2P lenders also face the risk of their personal information being misappropriated by platform service providers or stolen by hackers. Unlike conventional financing schemes where lenders are typically financial institutions or loans are made directly between a lender and a borrower, in online P2P lending, lenders can be ordinary citizens with their personal information registered on Internet-connected platforms. In the course of their operations, platform service providers collect, use, and save P2P lenders' personal information for various purposes. These may include, but are not limited to, verification of identity, detection of money laundering and terrorist financing, and prevention of fraud and other financial crimes. During the registration process on online lending platforms, potential lenders are typically required to provide certain personal information. This may include, but is not limited to, name, email address, phone number, government-issued ID, date of birth, and other relevant details.[31] It is evident that platform service providers can misappropriate such information to commit fraud, such as making unauthorized transactions or purchases, without the awareness or consent of individual P2P lenders. Additionally, without the implementation of well-established security systems by platform service providers, online lending platforms are unsurprisingly vulnerable to information theft, which can potentially expose P2P lenders to identity theft by hackers.[32] Meanwhile, in conventional financing schemes where transactions between financial institutions and their customers are not always conducted online, customers still face the risk of personal information leakage by institutional staff and/or identity theft by hackers. For example, when commercial banks accept money from depositors, who hold a position similar to P2P lenders, they collect and store the depositors' personal information. In practice, depositors' personal information can be leaked due to the misconduct or negligence of commercial bank staff. This is similar to the case in May 2021 when a staff of Military Bank disclosed the personal information and account statement of a popular artist.[33] Additionally, depositors' personal information can be compromised by unauthorized intruders, as evidenced by the October

[31] For example, Fiin Credit asks potential lenders to provide their personal information, including but not limited to name, gender, email address, age, phone number, residential address, and government-issued ID. Likewise, Vaymuon requires users of its platform to provide information such as name, gender, email address, contact information, phone number, government-issued ID, date of birth, Facebook account, bank account, credit card number, information about computer, phone, network device, IP address, location information, camera, microphone, call logs, video, and photo library. See Fiin Credit (2023a) and Vaymuon (2021b).

[32] For example, in May 2021, 17 GB of data containing photos of identity cards or citizen identification cards, along with photos and videos of around 10,000 Vietnamese people, was traded on a forum. According to the preliminary opinion of the investigation agency under the Ministry of Public Security, the data might have been hacked from online platforms, such as online lending platforms and virtual currency exchanges. See Xuân (2021) and Phạm (2021).

[33] See Tuấn (2021).

2019 incident with Maritime Bank, where details of two million bank accounts were posted on a forum dedicated to trading stolen data.[34] In such instances, financial institutions are held accountable for damages incurred by their customers in accordance with prevailing regulations.

It is important to note that for those investing in P2P loans or lending through P2P platforms, there is a risk of making wrong lending decisions due to the challenge of distinguishing between reliable borrowers and riskier ones. This difficulty stems from the information asymmetry between P2P lenders and borrowers, a phenomenon also observed in the relationship between lenders and borrowers in conventional lending schemes. To help P2P lenders mitigate the risk of making incorrect lending decisions, platform service providers can exercise due diligence in evaluating the creditworthiness of P2P borrowers.[35] However, when potential borrowers are unbanked or non-banked and apply for loans on a P2P lending platform for the first time, both the platform service provider and P2P lenders might not be able to access their track record. Additionally, P2P lenders face the risk of making wrong lending decisions in two scenarios. First, if platform service providers carelessly assess borrowers' creditworthiness.[36] Second, if these providers, exploiting P2P lenders' lack of sophistication, intentionally provide misleading information about the creditworthiness of P2P borrowers. The latter might be done to encourage lending, thereby increasing profit through origination fees. After all, P2P lenders run the risk of making wrong investment decisions, which might result in losses from their investments.

Furthermore, like lenders in conventional financing schemes, P2P lenders also face liquidity risk since they are typically not entitled to withdraw the lent money before the loan's maturity date.[37] In both conventional financing schemes and P2P lending schemes, lenders can liquidate their loans before the due date, provided there are investors willing to take over the outstanding balances. This practice is practically feasible under Vietnamese laws because lenders can assign their loan claims to other lenders or investors,[38] or sell the rights to collect debts to debt collection

[34] See Lam (2019).

[35] For example, Tima's terms of use state that the platform requires its users to provide personal information, which will be used to verify users' identity. Another example is SHA, which verifies the identity of potential borrowers who apply for loans via its platform. Similarly, Lendbiz automatically examines the identity of borrowers via its platform to evaluate their creditworthiness. See Tima (2018), SHA (2021), and Lendbiz (2025b).

[36] In practice, some online lending platforms, such as Avay and MoneyCat, advertise the provision of unsecured loans without conducting appraisals by contacting borrowers' family members, relatives, or friends. See Avay (2023) and MoneyCat.

[37] For example, Tima and Fiin Credit prefix the length of loan periods that lenders/investors can choose to invest in, such as 1 month, 3 months, 9 months, and 12 months, while Vnvon prefixes the terms that lenders/investors are not allowed to withdraw their investment before loan maturity. See Tima (2025), Fiin Credit (2023a), Vnvon (2025b), and Chương (2021).

[38] Vietnam's Civil Code 2015, Article 365 provides that:

service providers,[39] without needing the consent of the respective borrowers. However, when P2P lenders assign their loan claims to other lenders or investors, they must provide a written notice to inform the respective borrowers of the assignment. If they fail to do so, resulting in expenses for the borrowers, they are obligated to cover those expenses. To mitigate liquidity risk, a platform service provider might establish a secondary market, akin to the secondary loan market used by financial institutions, to connect P2P lenders with potential investors. However, while defaulted loans from financial institutions can still be traded on the secondary loan market to recover principal and interest, defaulted loans from P2P lending platforms are seldom sold on this market. Consequently, P2P lenders are more likely to bear the loss if the corresponding borrowers default.

### 3.2.2 *Risks Faced by P2P Borrowers*

From the perspective of P2P borrowers, several risks arise when participating in online P2P lending schemes. Unlike borrowers in conventional lending schemes, where lenders are often financial institutions with standardized contracts, P2P borrowers face the risk of being solicited by platform service providers to enter into a service contract. The enforceability of such a contract can be challenged later if its terms and conditions are inequitable and substantially disadvantageous to P2P borrowers. This kind of solicitation can occur under various circumstances. For example, platform service providers might unilaterally set the terms and conditions of the service contracts with P2P borrowers. Potential borrowers then either accept these terms by checking the designated checkbox or opt out of using the platforms.

---

1) A party having the right to demand the performance of an obligation may transfer such right to demand to a subrogatee [of the obligee] as agreed, except in the following cases: (a) The right is the right to demand support or the right to demand compensation for any loss and damage resulting from harm to life, health, honour, dignity or reputation; (b) The obligee and the obligor agree or the law provides that the right to demand may not be transferred.

2) Where a person having a right to demand transfers such right to a subrogatee, the subrogatee [of the obligee] shall become the person having the right to demand. The transfer of the right does not require the consent of the obligor. A person transferring a right to demand must provide a written notice to the obligor of such transfer, unless otherwise agreed. Where the party transferring the right to demand fails to provide a notice of the transfer, giving rise to expenses to the obligor, then the party transferring the right to demand must pay such expenses.

[39] Vietnam's Civil Code of 2015, Article 450 provides that:

1) Where property rights are sold and purchased, a seller must deliver the relevant documents and complete the procedures for transferring the ownership right to the purchaser and the purchaser must pay the seller.

2) Where property rights are the right to demand payment of a debt and the seller has guaranteed the ability to pay of the debtor, the seller must be jointly liable for payment if the debt falls due and the debtor fails to pay.

Potential borrowers might enter into a service contract with a platform service provider without downloading or reading its terms and conditions. Additionally, platform service providers may unilaterally modify the terms and conditions, including but not limited to transaction fees charged to P2P borrowers, without seeking individual borrowers' consent. These arbitrary changes might result in financial damages for P2P borrowers.

Based on the experience of conventional lending, it is evident that P2P borrowers are likely to be exposed to high interest rates and exorbitant intermediary fees. This is because the transaction costs for making many small loans are essentially costly, and P2P borrowers have low bargaining power and few other loan raising options, similar to the case of lending provided by local moneylenders.[40] Additionally, if platform service providers offer vague or overly complicated explanations of the interest rates and transaction fees of P2P loans, the risks may increase. In practice, there are those who were enticed to take P2P loans with the promise of a rapid loan approval process and attractive interest rates, but without receiving a detailed explanation of transaction fees, from platform service providers.[41] In such situations, P2P borrowers are likely to end up paying really high transaction fees, which may include, but are not limited to, service charges,[42] loan insurance, late fees,[43] late payment interest, overdue interest, and early repayment charges.[44] For example, a borrower applied for a loan of VND four million for 10 days via Vdong but, in fact, only received VND 2.9 million. The Vdong platform explained that it had already collected the interest and service charges, with a total amount of VND 1.1 million, before loan disbursement.[45] Similarly, another borrower applied for a loan of VND 1.5 million for 7 days via Moreloan, and an amount of VND 600,000 was deducted before loan disbursement for the interest and service fees. Additionally, a late payment interest rate of 5% per day was imposed on the overdue loan.[46] It is evident that P2P borrowers face significantly high interest rates, service charges, and late payment interest.

In addition to the aforementioned financial risks, P2P borrowers are at risk of facing strong-arm methods employed by platform service providers, P2P lenders, assignees of P2P loan receivables, or debt collection service providers. These strong-arm methods involve the use of force and threats to compel P2P borrowers to repay their overdue debts, and they can also be employed in black credit practices. In online P2P lending, service contracts between P2P borrowers and platform service providers are often unilaterally set by the providers. As mentioned, this can mean that P2P borrowers are compelled to grant platform service providers access to the

[40] See Robinson (2001, p. 150).

[41] See Phòng (2021) and ANTV (2021).

[42] Imposed if potential borrowers' loan applications are approved.

[43] Imposed on borrowers who fail to make loan repayments by the due date.

[44] See Cao and Tuấn (2020) and Phòng (2021).

[45] See Cao and Tuấn (2020).

[46] See Anh (2020).

contact information of their family members, relatives, and other associated individuals. Additionally, they may allow platform service providers to use cookies to collect information from their devices for loan recovery purposes.[47] If a borrower fails to repay a P2P loan on time, the provider may resort to aggressive methods. These can include threats, physical violence, asset seizure (such as houses, land, or vehicles), defamation, or even kidnapping the borrower's family members to recover the loan.[48] The case of a lecturer from Kien Giang province, Vietnam, who committed suicide in May 2020 due to the aggressive tactics of a platform service provider, serves as a poignant example. The lecturer borrowed a loan of VND five million for 7 days via an online lending platform but could not repay it on time. The platform service provider constantly threatened him with phone calls and made him extremely anxious. The provider also threatened his colleagues and students to smear and discredit him.[49] If P2P borrowers fall victim to platform service providers, P2P lenders, assignees of P2P loan receivables, or debt collectors using strong-arm methods, they can lodge complaints or file denunciations with competent authorities, seeking action in line with current laws.

It is reasonable to presume that P2P borrowers face the risk of having their personal information misappropriated by platform service providers and P2P lenders and/or hacked by hackers. Unlike borrowers in conventional financing schemes, where lending transactions are not necessarily conducted online, P2P borrowers are very likely to register their personal information on Internet-connected lending platforms. When applying for P2P loans, P2P borrowers are often required to provide personal information, which may include, but is not limited to, name, email address, phone number, residence, government-issued ID, date of birth, job, family details, financial situation, devices used for loan applications, and other relevant details.[50] This data can be collected and saved by platform service providers for various purposes, which may include, but are not limited to, identity verification, creditworthiness assessment, debt collection, detection of money laundering and terrorist financing, and prevention of fraud and other financial crimes. However, the data can also be misappropriated by platform service providers for fraudulent purposes, such as making unauthorized transactions, without the awareness and

[47] For example, in the terms and conditions of use applied for borrowers, Vaymuon requires P2P borrowers using its platform to allow it to collect their personal information and the information of their family members and relatives, as well as to accept all kinds of penalties and measures imposed by the platform, to collect overdue loans. Likewise, Tienoi requires borrowers using its platform to accept the terms and conditions of use that give the platform the right to collect their personal information and the information of their related persons, as well as other information collected from their devices using cookies, to recover loans. See Vaymuon (2021c) and Tienoi (2021).

[48] See Thư (2021) and Thanh (2021).

[49] See Thủy (2020).

[50] For example, Tienoi requires borrowers using its platform to provide their personal information, including name, email address, phone number, residence, government-issued ID, date of birth, job, family information, financial situation, information about their employers and colleagues, GPS information, social media profiles, and devices used for loan applications. See Tienoi (2021).

consent of individual borrowers. Additionally, platform service providers may share the collected data about P2P borrowers with P2P lenders to facilitate their lending decisions[51] or debt collection.[52] Such data about P2P borrowers may also be misappropriated by P2P lenders for the purpose of committing fraud or privacy infringement. Furthermore, P2P borrowers' personal information, which is collected and stored by platform service providers, can be exposed to the risk of identity theft by hackers, unless the providers protect their platforms by implementing well-established security systems.

### *3.2.3 Risks Faced by Platform Service Providers*

From the perspective of platform service providers, they face the risk of losing their business profit and/or their own money due to P2P borrowers' default. This could happen for several reasons as outlined below. For example, suppose that the terms and conditions of the service contract between a P2P borrower and a platform service provider allow the borrower to pay the service fee in installments, such as weekly or monthly, or in full on the due date of the loan. If the borrower defaults on the service fee, the provider is likely to have difficulties in recouping that money. This is because the service fee is considerably small and, accordingly, the cost necessary to enforce the provider's rights to recoup the fee is not likely to pay off. Additionally, because the loans provided via online lending platforms are usually unsecured, platform service providers can hardly expect to recoup the service fees unless P2P borrowers make repayments voluntarily. Moreover, if the providers establish provisional funds to secure repayments of P2P loans using their own funds, any losses arising from borrowers' defaults will be absorbed by the providers' provisional funds.

It should also be noted that platform service providers are at risk of identity fraud committed by both P2P lenders and borrowers using P2P lending platforms for illegal purposes, such as stealing money, money laundering, terrorist financing, or other illicit activities. Some borrowers may provide fake identity information during loan applications via online lending platforms. If the providers fail to detect such identity fraud, these borrowers might be approved to receive loans via the platforms. In case these borrowers disappear after obtaining the loans, it becomes difficult for the providers to track and collect the disbursed loans. In practice, several borrowers have used fake identity information, junk SIM cards, and cloned accounts on social

[51] For example, Tima can share potential borrowers' personal information, including name, phone number, residence, government-issued ID, date of birth, job, workplace, and income, with potential lenders to facilitate lending transactions, provided that the platform obtains the consent of potential borrowers. See Tima (2017).

[52] For example, Vaymuon shares P2P borrowers' personal information with the corresponding P2P lenders to facilitate their loan recovery if P2P borrowers fail to make repayments on time. See Vaymuon (2021c).

networks like Facebook, Instagram, or Zalo to apply for loans via some lending platforms, such as ATM Online and Senmo, and then disappeared after obtaining the loans.[53] Notably, in some P2P lending schemes, P2P lenders and borrowers can contact and transfer money directly,[54] and they may establish accounts on lending platforms with fake identity information for the purpose of money laundering and terrorist financing. They even scale up lending transactions for such purposes by using a number of different accounts and lending platforms. If the providers cannot detect the identity fraud committed by P2P lenders and borrowers using their platforms, they can hardly prevent such crimes.

Platform service providers are also exposed to the risk of their platforms being attacked by spies and hackers. These attacks may aim to steal personally identifiable information of P2P lenders and borrowers, interrupt the platforms' operations, or even destroy the entire lending system. Potential malicious actors and hackers may attempt to access the personal information of P2P lenders and borrowers, irrespective of whether the data is stored on computer servers or in online storage. They might use various methods, including, but not limited to, spoofing, phishing, and exploiting unintentional disclosures by platform employees.[55] For example, in a spoofing attack, attackers may send emails with a forged sender address, pretending to be from a lending platform. They ask recipients to provide sensitive information, such as accounts on the real lending platform, passwords, and other details. Alternatively, spoofed emails may include a link that, if clicked, installs malware on the recipients' devices to steal their personal information.[56] Another example is phishing, wherein fraudsters establish a counterfeit lending platform to lure gullible individuals into sharing their sensitive information with the fake lending platform, such as accounts on a real lending platform, passwords, and other details. The information thus obtained by fraudsters might be used to access the real lending platform and transfer funds.[57] Additionally, unauthorized actors and hackers might penetrate the operating system of P2P lending platforms, causing significant disruptions in their operations, along with potential business losses and reputational damage. The purposes of such attacks may include, but are not limited to, drawing attention to a cause through relatively minor disruption, manipulating the operation of lending platforms, demanding a ransom in exchange for ending the attacks, and even attempting to destroy online lending systems.[58]

[53] See Trường and Linh (2021).

[54] For example, Tima allows direct communication between potential lenders and potential borrowers to facilitate lending transactions, and the platform can provide potential lenders with potential borrowers' contact information if it obtains the consent of potential borrowers. See Tima (2017).

[55] See Lagazio (2016, p. 39).

[56] See Eastwood (2022) and Crowdstrike (2021).

[57] See Alkhalil et al. (2021) and Groot (2022).

[58] See Lagazio (2016, p. 29).

It is important to note that platform service providers face the risk of losing potential investors or lenders who are willing to invest in or provide loans through their lending platforms. From the viewpoint of investors or lenders on P2P lending platforms, they may be hesitant to lend more money if they have previously incurred financial losses, big or small, due to P2P borrower defaults. Likewise, they are likely to be reluctant to invest in loans posted on P2P lending platforms if they have suffered identity theft by hackers through lending platforms or have experienced lending platforms' operational disruptions due to hacker attacks. Therefore, it can be easily presumed that platform service providers might lose potential investors or lenders due to their fear of financial loss, identity theft, or lending platforms' operational disruptions. Consequently, the loss of potential investors or lenders who could have been willing to invest in or provide loans via lending platforms can cause a loss of business profit and potential dissolution of lending platforms.

## 3.3 Interim Conclusion

Considering the operations of Vietnam's P2P lending companies, this chapter clarifies general risks related to micro- and/or small-sized finance via P2P lending platforms. These risks might arise from micro- and/or small-sized finance, online platforms, and the combination of micro- and/or small-sized finance and online platforms. First, risks related to micro- and/or small-sized finance include default risk and the risk of late payments. Second, risks associated with online platforms include the risk of entering into an unfair contract with platform service providers; the risk of adverse selection due to information asymmetry between P2P lenders and P2P borrowers; the risk of losing P2P lenders' money due to P2P lending platforms' cessation or temporary closure and/or the failure of their software; the risk of identity theft and data breaches; and the risk of terrorist financing and money laundering. Third, risks associated with the combination of micro- and/or small-sized finance and online platforms include the risk of losing the opportunity to make continuous investments, liquidity risk, interest rate risk, the risk of losing potential lenders, and legal risk.

In the second section of this chapter, the risks associated with P2P lending are defined as potential risks that encompass all participants of P2P lending schemes, including P2P lenders, P2P borrowers, and platform service providers. These risks arise when they partake in micro- and/or small-sized finance through P2P lending platforms.

From the standpoint of P2P lenders, they encounter several risks. These risks include the risk of entering into an unfair contract with platform service providers, the risk of losing lent money partly or fully due to borrower default and/or the temporary or permanent cessation of P2P lending platforms' operations, the risk of having personal information misappropriated by platform service providers and/or stolen by hackers, the risk of making wrong lending decisions due to information asymmetry between P2P lenders and P2P borrowers, and liquidity risk. In comparison with lenders in conventional finance schemes, P2P lenders are facing similar risks. On the one hand, using the Internet may enable P2P lenders to avoid or mitigate such risks. On the other hand, the use of the Internet may also accelerate or increase such risks. Therefore, fundamentally and historically, the risks faced by P2P lenders are not different from those encountered by lenders in conventional financing schemes. For example, in a P2P lending scheme, because the platform service provider can easily match individual borrowers and individual lenders via its lending platform, possibly, more and more individual lenders or investors are easily subject to the above risks. However, because more ordinary citizens are making investments or loans via P2P lending platforms, or platform service providers can offer investment opportunities or lending opportunities to more and more people, the number of P2P lenders may increase, allowing more lenders to share the risks to which they are exposed.

From the perspective of P2P borrowers, they are exposed to several risks. These risks include the potential for entering into an inequitable contract with platform service providers, facing high interest rates and exorbitant intermediary fees set by these providers, dealing with aggressive collection tactics employed by platform service providers or P2P lenders, and the threat of their personal information being misappropriated by both platform providers and P2P lenders or stolen by hackers.

From the perspective of platform service providers, they face several risks. These risks include the risk of losing business profit and/or their own money due to borrower default, the risk of identity fraud committed by P2P lenders and borrowers for the purpose of stealing money, money laundering, terrorist financing, or other illicit activities, the risk of having their platforms attacked by spies and hackers, and the risk of losing potential lenders who are willing to invest in their platforms.

## References

Alkhalil Z, Hewage C, Nawaf L and Khan I (2021) Phishing Attacks: a recent comprehensive study and a new anatomy. https://www.frontiersin.org/articles/10.3389/fcomp.2021.563060/full. Accessed 20 Mar 2025

Anh T (2020) Triệt phá đường dây cho vay qua mạng lãi 1.000%/năm [Dismantle online lending that imposed an interest rate of 1,000% per year]. https://thuongtruong.com.vn/news/triet-pha-duong-day-cho-vay-qua-mang-lai-1-000-nam-do-nguoi-trung-quoc-cam-dau-27635.html. Accessed 20 Mar 2025

Anh T (2021) Không trả được nợ, nhiều người rủ nhau… bùng công ty tài chính, app vay tiền: luật sư nói gì? [Unable to repay debts, many debtors call each other to avoid paying debts through finance companies and lending platforms: what lawyers say?]. https://cafef.vn/khong-tra-duoc-no-nhieu-nguoi-ru-nhaubung-cong-ty-tai-chinh-app-vay-tien-luat-su-noi-gi-20210903140713619.chn. Accessed 20 Mar 2025

ANTV (2021) Cẩn trọng khi vay tiền qua các ứng dụng trực tuyến [Being careful of loans via online lending platforms]. https://www.antv.gov.vn/tin-tuc/kinh-te/can-trong-khi-vay-tien-qua-cac-ung-dung-truc-tuyen-358290.html. Accessed 20 Mar 2025

Avay (2023) Duyệt vay siêu tốc [Fast loans appraisal]. https://avay.vn/?flow=v2910. Accessed 28 Jul 2023

Cao H (2020) Vay tiền qua app: nhiều app đột ngột ngưng hoạt động và ngưng giải ngân [Borrowing money via online lending platforms: Many lending platforms suddenly stopped working and stopped disbursing]. https://laodong.vn/kinh-te/vay-tien-qua-app-nhieu-app-dot-ngot-ngung-hoat-dong-va-ngung-giai-ngan-809096.ldo. Accessed 20 Mar 2025

Cao H and Tuấn T (2020) Vay tiền qua app: tiết lộ những khoản thu cắt cổ gọi là phí dịch vụ [Borrowing money via online platforms: Reveal exorbitant charges called service fees]. https://laodong.vn/xa-hoi/vay-tien-qua-app-tiet-lo-nhung-khoan-thu-cat-co-goi-la-phi-dich-vu-814564.ldo. Accessed 20 Mar 2025

Chương B (2021) Đầu tư vốn vào các công ty cho vay ngang hàng: coi chừng mất cả chì lẫn chài [Investing via P2P lending platforms: Beware of losing hook, line and sinker]. https://laodong.vn/kinh-te/dau-tu-von-vao-cac-cong-ty-cho-vay-ngang-hang-coi-chung-mat-ca-chi-lan-chai-962947.ldo. Accessed 20 Mar 2025

Crowdstrike (2021) Spoofing attacks. https://www.crowdstrike.com/cybersecurity-101/spoofing-attacks/. Accessed 20 Mar 2025

Doctor Dong (2020). https://doctordong.vn/. Accessed 10 Jun 2020

Duong Gia Law Firm (2023) Đánh giá thực tiễn hoạt động cho vay ngang hàng ở Việt Nam [Evaluating the practice of P2P lending in Vietnam]. https://luatduonggia.vn/danh-gia-thuc-tien-hoat-dong-cho-vay-ngang-hang-o-viet-nam/. Accessed 20 Mar 2025

Eastwood B (2022) Spoofing: what it is and how to prevent it. https://www.mimecast.com/blog/spoofing-what-it-is-and-how-to-prevent-it/. Accessed 28 Jul 2023

Fiin Credit (2023a) Đầu tư [Investment]. https://fiin.vn/dau-tu/. Accessed 28 Jul 2023

Fiin Credit (2023b) Terms of use, part XII (3). https://fiin.vn/dieu-khoan/. Accessed 28 Jul 2023

Fiin Credit (2023c) Vay tiền ngắn hạn [Borrowing short-term loans]. https://fiin.vn/vay-tien/vay-ngan-han/. Accessed 28 Jul 2023

Finizi (2023). https://finizi.vn/. Accessed 5 May 2023

Groot JD (2022) Phishing attack prevention: how to identify & avoid phishing scams in 2022. https://digitalguardian.com/blog/phishing-attack-prevention-how-identify-avoid-phishing-scams. Accessed 20 Mar 2025

Hai HT (2023) Legal issues on peer-to-peer lending business in Vietnam. http://www.bizconsult.vn/legal-issues-peer-peer-lending-business-vietnam/. Accessed 20 Mar 2025

Hồng A, Thiện Đ (2020) Cho vay nặng lãi Trung Quốc tràn vào Việt Nam, lãi suất hơn 1.000%/năm [Usury loans from China flooded into Vietnam, the interest rates were over 1,000% per year]. https://tuoitre.vn/cho-vay-nang-lai-trung-quoc-tran-vao-viet-nam-lai-suat-hon-1-000-nam-20200508082046595.htm. Accessed 20 Mar 2025

Lagazio M (2016) A taxonomy of cyber crime in the financial sector: a comprehensive approach to countermeasures. In: Taplin R (ed) Managing cyber risk in the financial sector: lessons from Asia, Europe and the USA. Routledge, New York

Lam B (2019) Two million account details from major Vietnamese bank leaked online. https://e.vnexpress.net/news/news/two-million-account-details-from-major-vietnamese-bank-leaked-online-4016176.html. Accessed 20 Mar 2025

Lendbiz (2020) Transfer agreement. https://lendbiz.vn/wp-content/uploads/2020/07/thoa-thuan-chuyen-quyen-nha-dau-tu-ban-docx.pdf. Accessed 20 Mar 2025

Lendbiz (2025a) Capital call with Lendbiz. https://lendbiz.vn/en/capital-call-with-lendbiz/. Accessed 20 Mar 2025

Lendbiz (2025b) Terms of use, section I. https://lendbiz.vn/en/transaction-terms/. Accessed 20 Mar 2025

Lê Đ (2020) Vay qua app: quá kinh hoàng! [Loans through lending app: Too horrible!]. https://plo.vn/vay-qua-app-qua-kinh-hoang-post578476.html. Accessed 20 Mar 2025

Liên L (2020) Vay tiền qua app: app mất hút, người vay bỗng dưng hết nợ [Borrowing money via online lending platforms: Lending platforms disappeared, borrowers suddenly got debt cancellation]. https://dantri.com.vn/kinh-doanh/vay-tien-qua-app-app-mat-hut-nguoi-vay-bong-dung-het-no-20200706060856527.htm. Accessed 20 Mar 2025

Oneclickmoney (2020). https://oneclickmoney.vn/. Accessed 10 Jun 2020

Online Newspaper of the Government (2020) Đánh sập đường dây cho vay qua mạng lãi 1.000%/ năm [Shutting down an online loan line with the interest rate of 1,000% per year]. https://baochinhphu.vn/triet-pha-duong-day-cho-vay-qua-mang-lai-1000-nam-102271519.htm. Accessed 20 Mar 2025

Phạm H (2021) Lộ thông tin cá nhân—vấn đề nhức nhối khi các app vay, tiền ảo ngày càng phát triển và biến tướng [Personal information leak—a serious problem when lending platforms and virtual currency exchange grow and deform]. https://vnfinance.vn/lo-thong-tin-ca-nhan%2D%2Dvan-de-nhuc-nhoi-khi-cac-app-vay-tien-ao-ngay-cang-phat-trien-va-bien-tuong-26604.html. Accessed 20 Mar 2025

Phòng B (2021) Sai lầm khi vay tiền online nhiều người mắc phải hiện nay [Mistakes that many people make when they apply for loans via online lending platforms]. https://www.bienphong.com.vn/sai-lam-khi-vay-tien-online-nhieu-nguoi-mac-phai-hien-nay-post444778.html. Accessed 20 Mar 2025

Robinson MS (2001) The microfinance revolution. World Bank Publications, Washington. DC.

SHA (2021) Quy trình xử lý khoản vay [Loan processing]. https://tietkiemonline.vn/quy-trinh-xu-ly-khoan-vay/. Accessed 20 Oct 2021

SHA (2023) Câu hỏi thường gặp [Frequently asked questions]. https://tietkiemonline.vn/cau-hoi-thuong-gap/. Accessed 28 Jul 2023

Tamo (2023). https://www.tamo.vn/. Accessed 5 May 2023

Thanh PV (2021) Rủi ro pháp lý và hệ lụy từ các app vay tiền online [Legal risks and consequences from online lending platforms]. https://lsvn.vn/rui-ro-phap-ly-va-he-luy-tu-cac-app-vay-tien-online1624607482.html. Accessed 20 Mar 2025

The State Bank of Vietnam (2020) Dự thảo cáo đánh giá tác động chính sách về việc xây dựng nghị đinh về cơ chế thử nghiệm có kiểm soát hoạt động công nghệ tài chính trong lĩnh vực ngân hàng [Draft report on the impact evaluation of the establishment of the Decree on the controlled testing mechanism for financial technology activities in the banking sector]. https://sbv.gov.vn/webcenter/portal/vi/menu/fm/ddnhnn/lykdtvbqppl/ctlykdtvbqppl?centerWidth=80%25&dDocName=SBV411672&dID=413921&expired=false&leftWidth=20%25&rightWidth=0%25&showFooter=false&showHeader=false&_adf.ctrl-state=10ki8qlzp8_95&_afrLoop=8195045440752412#%40%3F_afrLoop%3D8195045440752412%26centerWidth%3D80%2525%26dDocName%3DSBV411672%26dID%3D413921%26expired%3Dfalse%26leftWidth%3D20%2525%26rightWidth%3D0%2525%26showFooter%3Dfalse%26showHeader%3Dfalse%26_adf.ctrl-state%3D197e9enmaz_4. Accessed 10 Jun 2020

Thiện Đ (2020) App Trung Quốc 'truy sát', vay 2 triệu phải trả 54 triệu, chậm trả bị ghép ảnh sex tung lên mạng [Chinese app chased borrowers. Borrowed VND 2 million, the borrowers were required to repay VND 54 million. Due to delayed repayments, the borrowers' sex collage pictures were uploaded on the Internet]. https://tuoitre.vn/app-trung-quoc-truy-sat-vay-2-trieu-phai-tra-54-trieu-cham-tra-bi-ghep-anh-sex-tung-len-mang-20200531083045949.htm. Accessed 20 Mar 2025

Thuận H (2020) Công an khám xét công ty cashwagon chuyên cho vay tiền qua app [The public security authority searched Cashwagon, a company specializing in lending money through apps]. https://dantri.com.vn/phap-luat/cong-an-kham-xet-cong-ty-cashwagon-chuyen-cho-vay-tien-qua-app-20200603203021675.htm. Accessed 20 Mar 2025

Thủy T (2020) Vay 5 triệu đồng trả 200 triệu chưa hết, thầy giáo cùng đường tìm cái chết [Borrowed VND 5 million, a lecturer who could not pay VND 200 million committed suicide]. https://dantri.com.vn/kinh-doanh/vay-5-trieu-dong-tra-200-trieu-chua-het-thay-giao-cung-duong-tim-cai-chet-20201107063104480.htm. Accessed 20 Mar 2025

Thư A (2021) Đủ chiêu trò thu hồi nợ của các app vay tiền: nỗi thống khổ của nạn nhân [All kinds of online lending platforms' tactics for loan recovery: Victims' suffering]. https://laodong.vn/phap-luat/du-chieu-tro-thu-hoi-no-cua-cac-app-vay-tien-noi-thong-kho-cua-nan-nhan-970368.ldo. Accessed 20 Mar 2025

Tima (2017) For investors. https://tima.vn/Home/Support/. Accessed 20 Mar 2025

Tima (2018) Terms of use, Article 5. https://tima.vn/dieu-khoan.html. Accessed 20 Mar 2025

Tima (2025) Nhà đầu tư [Investors]. https://tima.vn/nha-dau-tu. Accessed 20 Mar 2025
Tienoi (2021) Privacy policy, section 3 and section 4. https://tienoi.com.vn/chinh-sach-bao-mat/. Accessed 20 Mar 2025
Tuấn A (2021) Hoai Linh's account information leaked: mb handled employees with serious violations. https://en.spress.net/hoai-linh-account-information-leaked-mb-handled-employees-with-serious-violations/. Accessed 20 Mar 2025
Trường Đ, Linh C (2021) Nghề bùng nợ các ứng dụng cho vay tiền [The flare-up of avoiding debts through lending platforms]. https://laodong.vn/kinh-te/nghe-bung-no-cac-ung-dung-cho-vay-tien-905840.ldo. Accessed 20 Mar 2025
Tùng NQ (2020) Hoạt động cho vay ngang hàng tại Việt Nam và một số vấn đề đặt ra [P2P lending in Vietnam and some emerging issues]. Democracy and Law 5:20-24
Vaydi (2020). https://www.vaydi.vn/. Accessed 6 Jun 2020
Vaymuon (2021a) Investor agreements, Article 3. https://vaymuon.vn/thoa_thuan_nha_dau_tu. Accessed 20 Oct 2021
Vaymuon (2021b) Privacy policy, section 1. https://vaymuon.vn/chinh_sach_quyen_rieng_tu. Accessed 20 Oct 2021
Vaymuon (2021c) Terms of use for borrowers, section 4.2. https://vaymuon.vn/thoa_thuan_nguoi_vay. Accessed 5 Nov 2021
Vdong (2023) Terms of service of Vdong.Vn website, Section IIIf. 1.1.1. https://app-api.vdong.vn/Wap/Agreement?name=web&system=Vdong. Accessed 28 Jul 2023
Viet Than Tai (2020). https://vietthantai.xyz/. Accessed 10 Jun 2020
Vietnam Net (2020) Ứng dụng cho vay nặng lãi online của Trung Quốc đang tràn vào Việt Nam [China's online usury lending apps are flooding into Vietnam]. https://vietnamnet.vn/ung-dung-cho-vay-nang-lai-online-cua-trung-quoc-dang-tran-vao-viet-nam-638991.html. Accessed 20 Mar 2025
Vnvon (2025a) Câu hỏi thường gặp [Frequently asked questions]. https://vnvon.com/cau-hoi-thuong-gap/. Accessed 20 Mar 2025
Vnvon (2025b) Huy động vốn [Capital mobilization]. https://vnvon.com/huy-dong-von/. Accessed 20 Mar 2025
Xuân T (2021) Lộ thông tin từ sàn vàng, app vay, tiền ảo [Information leak from online platforms like gold trading platforms, lending platforms, and virtual currency exchange]. https://vietstock.vn/2021/05/lo-thong-tin-tu-san-vang-app-vay-tien-ao-4260-858517.htm. Accessed 20 Mar 2025

# Chapter 4
# Risk Diversification as the Traditional Tool for Reducing Risk in Vietnam's Micro- and/or Small-Sized Finance

## 4.1 Micro- and/or Small-Sized Financing Schemes in Vietnam

As mentioned in Sect. 2.1.1, Vietnam began establishing its independent banking system in 1945. Under the central planning regime before the Đổi Mới in 1986, the Vietnamese banking system encompassed a state bank, state-owned banks, rural credit cooperatives, and socialist savings funds.[1] These financial institutions offered micro- and/or small-sized loans through several financing schemes as follows.

Firstly, the state bank and state-owned banks provided loans to cooperative businesses, state-owned enterprises (SOEs), and individuals under the direction of the government.[2] These banks received capital from the state budget and mobilized idle capital from cooperatives, socialist savings funds, and individuals alike.[3] To make loan decisions for cooperative businesses and SOEs, the banks specifically considered borrowers' business plans and evaluated their basic materials and

[1] See The State Bank of Vietnam (2025) and Chính and Hoàng (2009).

[2] Decree No. 81-NgD/NH, Section IV, provides borrowers who can borrow long-term loans from the State Bank:

1. Cooperatives, progressive groups, and labor exchange groups regularly engage in agricultural and fishery production, as well as land reclamation organizations;
2. Cooperatives and progressive groups engage in crafts;
3. Cooperatives and progressive groups engage in transportation;
4. Trading cooperatives; and
5. People in mountainous areas…

Decree No. 177-TTg, Article 2, regulates the tasks of the Vietnam Construction Bank: "…To provide short-term loans to state-owned enterprises in accordance with the loan plan approved by the government… ."

[3] See Decree No. 81-NgD/NH, Section IV, Decree No. 312-Ttg, Article 4, Decree No. 177-TTg, Article 2, Decree No. 47-TTg.

 
Y. H. Nguyen, *Regulating Peer-to-Peer Lending in Vietnam*,
https://doi.org/10.1007/978-981-96-9505-8_4

equipment.[4] After loan disbursement, the banks closely monitored the condition of borrowers' assets and equipment in order to make adjustments to loan amounts.[5] This monitoring involved reviewing borrowers' reports, invoices, receipts, and balance sheets, as well as conducting inspections at borrowers' production sites.[6] The banks also monitored how the disbursed loans were utilized to ensure that they were being used for the intended purposes.[7] If borrowers were unable to fulfill their payment obligations, the banks deducted debts directly from their payment accounts. If the outstanding funds in their payment accounts were insufficient to repay the debts, the banks would impose overdue debt penalties and suspend further loan disbursements.[8]

Secondly, rural credit cooperatives provided loans to their members. Rural credit cooperatives were established under Rule No. 739-TTg in 1956. They received mandatory shares from their members[9] and accepted deposits from both members and nonmembers.[10] Credit cooperatives could also borrow from the State Bank when facing financial difficulties.[11] They provided loans to their members in accordance with the government's policies.[12] Right before the Đổi Mới, the State Bank issued Decision No. 67-NH/QD, which stipulated the lending activities of rural credit cooperatives. Pursuant to this Decision, borrowers obtaining loans from credit cooperatives were required to provide collateral to secure their loans for business purposes but not for personal needs.[13] After loan disbursement, credit cooperatives closely monitored the use of disbursed loans.[14] If borrowers could not fulfill their payment obligations, credit cooperatives would impose overdue debt penalties and suspend further loan disbursements.[15]

Thirdly, socialist savings funds provided loans to individuals. The funds were established by the State Bank under Decree No. 312-TTg in 1959. They mobilized savings deposits and idle money from urban and rural inhabitants[16] and provided loans to public servants, officials, and workers to support their production and livelihood.[17] To be eligible for borrowing loans from socialist savings funds,

---

[4] See Decree No. 448-VP/NgD, Article 15, Circular No. 06-TC/NHKT dated April 10, 1973, Section V, on lending activities of the Vietnam Construction Bank.

[5] See Decree No. 448-VP/NgD, Article 40, Circular No. 376-TC/NHKT/TT, Article 32.

[6] See Decree No. 448-VP/NgD, Article 41, Circular No. 376-TC/NHKT/TT, Article 33.

[7] Decree No. 448-VP/NgD, Article 41, Circular No. 376-TC/NHKT/TT, Article 33.

[8] See Decree No. 448-VP/NgD, Article 43, Circular No. 376-TC/NHKT/TT, Article 36.

[9] See Rule No. 739-TTg, Article 18.

[10] Rule No. 739-TTg, Article 18.

[11] See Decision No. 52-NH/QD, Article 5, clause 1.

[12] See Rule No. 739-TTg, Article 2.

[13] See Decision No. 67-NH/QD, Article 5.

[14] See Decision No. 67-NH/QD, Article 11.

[15] Decision No. 67-NH/QD, Article 11.

[16] See Decree No. 312-TTg, Article 1.

[17] See Decision No. 24-NH/QD, Article 2.

borrowers must have a minimum amount of capital and make monthly deposits with the savings funds.[18] After loan disbursement, the savings funds closely monitored the use of disbursed loans. If loans were found to be misused, the borrowers must immediately repay the loans.[19] In case, borrowers failed to repay their loans, they would face social pressure from their teams or groups, receive criticism and warnings from local people's committees, or even be subject to legal action.[20]

As mentioned in Sect. 2.1.1, before the Đổi Mới, the efficiency of micro- and/or small-sized financing schemes was considered to be limited. The reasons that have been noted are that loans were primarily provided based on the state's policies and plans, and the government determined credit supply and directly intervened in banking operations.[21] In the event that micro- and/or small-sized finance providers faced financial difficulties, the state would provide them with financial support.[22]

As mentioned above, since the Đổi Mới in 1986, Vietnam has developed its market for micro- and/or small-sized finance with a variety of providers. In the formal micro- and/or small-sized finance sector, conventional banks, general finance companies, and specialized finance companies (including factoring finance companies, consumer credit finance companies, and financial leasing companies) can mobilize capital from individuals and organizations[23] to offer loans through a range of micro- and/or small-sized financing schemes. These include lending via loan agreements, bank guarantees, discounting valuable papers, finance leasing, and issuing lines of credit, credit cards, or debit cards.[24]

In the financing scheme of lending via loan agreements, conventional banks or finance companies provide loans through loan agreements. These agreements contain terms and conditions under which conventional banks or finance companies give or commit to giving borrowers specific sums of money for specific purposes and defined periods.[25] Loans provided by conventional banks or finance companies can be either secured or unsecured. Additionally, the loans can have varying durations,

---

[18] See Rules on Lending public servants, officials, workers, and cooperative members for doing business and solving difficulties in life attached Decision No. 24-NH/QD, Article 6.

[19] See Rules on Lending public servants, officials, workers, and cooperative members for doing business and solving difficulties in life attached Decision No. 24-NH/QD, Article 14.

[20] See Inter-Ministerial Circular No. 01-VHH-DS, Section III (A) (1).

[21] See Chính and Hoàng (2009).

[22] Chính and Hoàng (2009).

[23] It should be noted that conventional banks and nonbank credit institutions (including general finance companies, factoring finance companies, consumer credit finance companies, and financial leasing companies) can mobilize capital by accepting deposits, issuing deposit certificates, promissory notes, treasury bills, and bonds, as well as borrowing from other financial institutions and the State Bank. While conventional banks can mobilize capital from both individuals and organizations, nonbank credit institutions can mobilize capital from only organizations. See Vietnam's Law on Credit Institutions 2024, Article 107, Article 108, Article 115, Article 116, Article 120, and Article 121.

[24] See Vietnam's Law on Credit Institutions 2024, Article 4, clause 4.

[25] See Vietnam's Law on Credit Institutions 2024, Article 4, clause 7, provides that "[l]ending means a form of credit extension whereby the lender gives or commits to give the borrower a sum of

categorized as short term, medium term, or long term, based on the agreed-upon repayment periods. The principle of payment for these loans includes the repayment of both the principal amounts and accompanying interest.[26]

In a bank guarantee scheme, a conventional bank or finance company extends credit through a guarantee agreement. In this agreement, they commit to guarantee the fulfillment of financial obligations on behalf of their customer in the event that the customer fails to fulfill their obligations, either partly or entirely, as committed.[27] The customer is required to acknowledge and repay the debt to the bank or finance company as agreed upon.[28] In practice, conventional banks and finance companies may require collateral or the guarantee of another party to secure guaranteed obligations. For example, Sacombank requires customers to have collateral for guaranteed obligations,[29] while PVcombank can provide bank guarantee services either with or without collateral for guaranteed obligations.[30]

In a scheme involving the discounting of valuable papers, conventional banks and finance companies provide loans through contracts of discount.[31] Under these contracts, banks and finance companies purchase valuable papers from the beneficiaries and acquire ownership of these valuable papers for a specific term.[32] Alternatively, they can purchase outstanding valuable papers for the remaining duration

---

money for use for a specific purpose in a certain period on the principle of payment of both principal and interest as agreed."

[26] Vietnam's Law on Credit Institutions 2024, Article 4, clause 7.

[27] Vietnam's Law on Credit Institutions 2024, Article 4, clause 2, provides that "[b]ank guarantee means a form of credit extension to a client whereby a credit institution or foreign bank's branch undertakes to act on behalf of the obligor to fulfill their financial obligations to the obligee in the event the obligor fails to fulfill or insufficiently fulfills their obligations as agreed; the client shall have the obligation to repay the debt to the credit institution or the foreign bank's branch as agreed."

[28] Vietnam's Law on Credit Institutions 2024, Article 4, clause 2.

[29] See Sacombank (2025).

[30] See Pvcombank (2019).

[31] Vietnam's Law on Credit Institutions 2024, Article 4, clause 6, provides that "[d]iscount means a form of credit extension by purchase of on a definite term or purchase of the right to collect negotiable instruments and other valuable papers of beneficiaries prior to their due date."

[32] The English translation of Circular No. 04/2013/TT-NHNN (2013, as amended) of Vietnam, Article 10, regulates the following methods of discounting:

> Credit institutions, foreign banks' branches and customers shall agree on, select one of the following discount methods:
>
> 1. Purchase of negotiable instruments, other valuable papers for terms means that credit institutions or foreign banks' branches shall purchase and receive transfer of ownership of negotiable instruments, other valuable papers which are not yet matured from customers, together with customers' commitment on their repurchase of those negotiable instruments, other valuable papers after a duration defined in the contract of discount.
>
> 2. Purchase with reservation for the recourse of negotiable instruments, other valuable papers means that credit institutions, foreign banks' branches shall purchase and receive ownership of negotiable instruments, other valuable papers which are not yet matured from customers; customers shall return discount amount, discount interest and other lawful costs relating to discount activities in case credit institutions, foreign banks' branches do not

until their due dates and acquire ownership of these papers while having recourse to these papers in case they are not paid in full when due.[33] The contracts also include terms and conditions regarding discount prices, terms, interest rates, and relevant costs.[34] The borrowers commit to repurchasing the discounted valuable papers after a specific term in accordance with the discount contracts or return discount amounts, discount interests, and other lawful costs relating to discount activities in case the discounted valuable papers are not paid in full when due.[35]

In a financial leasing scheme, the fund seeker, known as the lessee, enters into a lease contract with a leasing company, referred to as the lessor. Under a lease contract, the lessor provides the lessee with the use of specific machines, equipment, or assets based on the lessee's requirements.[36] The lessee leases these machines, equipment, or assets from the lessor, and the leasing charges may cover the cost of acquiring the machines, equipment, or assets, as well as other affiliated disbursements of the lessor. The lease term for an asset is at least 60% of the time required for its depreciation for tax purpose,[37] and the total leasing charges specified in the lease contract are equal to or greater than the value of the asset at the time of signing the lease contract. At the end of the lease term, ownership of the asset is transferred to the lessee, or the lessee is entitled to the option to continue the lease, as agreed upon by the lessor and the lessee. Alternatively, the lessee is prioritized to purchase the leased asset at a nominal price that is lower than its actual value at the time of purchase.[38] The lessor has the ownership of the leased asset and the right to examine the use and management of the leased asset by the lessee during the lease term.[39] If the lessee fails to pay the leasing charges, the lessor can seize the machines, equipment, or assets in accordance with the lease contract.[40]

In addition to the aforementioned financing schemes, conventional banks and finance companies also offer loans to individuals and enterprises through agreements related to card issuance and usage. Under these agreements, banks and finance companies provide cardholders with lines of credit, credit cards, or debit cards,

receive the full amount allowed for payment from the persons who are responsible for payment of negotiable instruments, persons who issue other valuable papers.

[33] See Circular No. 04/2013/TT-NHNN (2013, as amended) of Vietnam, Article 10.

[34] See Circular No. 04/2013/TT-NHNN (2013, as amended), Article 11.

[35] See Circular No. 04/2013/TT-NHNN (2013, as amended), Article 15, clause 2.

[36] The English translation of Circular 26/2024/TT-NHNN of Vietnam, dated 28 June, 2024, Article 3, clause 1, provides that "finance leasing" means the extension of medium and long-term credit under a finance leasing contract between a finance lessor and a finance lessee. The finance lessor purchases finance leased assets at the request of the finance lessee and takes over ownership of the finance leased assets during the lease term. The finance lessee uses the finance leased assets and pays rentals therefor throughout the lease term under the finance leasing contract.

[37] See The English translation of Lease Accounting Standard No. 6 under Decision No.165/2002/QD-BTC of Vietnam.

[38] The English translation of Circular 26/2024/TT-NHNN of Vietnam, Article 18.

[39] See The English translation of Circular 26/2024/TT-NHNN of Vietnam, Article 16.

[40] See The English translation of Circular 26/2024/TT-NHNN of Vietnam, Article 16.

which can be used for purchasing goods and services, as well as withdrawing cash.[41] The agreements also include terms and conditions regarding the usage of the cards and repayment of debts, such as card limit, card term, payment limit, cash withdrawal limit, interest rate, interest calculation method, minimum repayment rate, debt repayment term, and overdue penalty fees.[42] Banks and finance companies can issue lines of credit, credit cards, or debit cards either with or without collateral, depending on borrowers' creditworthiness.[43]

It is worth noting that several commercial banks, such as the Joint Stock Commercial Bank for Investment and Development of Vietnam (BIDV) and the Vietnam Joint Stock Commercial Bank for Industry and Trade (Vietinbank), have been using the Internet to provide customers with banking services, such as remittances, account balances, and account statements, since 2004.[44] It has been noted that, up to now, all conventional banks and most finance companies in Vietnam have been using the Internet to serve their customers. Internet banking or digital banking services provided by banks and finance companies might include lending, bank guarantees, issuing lines of credit, and payment.[45]

As mentioned in Sect. 2.1.4, conventional banks, finance companies, and leasing companies are required to meet capital, reserve, and liquidity requirements when extending credit. They are also obligated to perform due diligence and fulfill other obligations to safeguard the legitimate rights of their customers and ensure the safety and stability of their operations.

Besides conventional banks and finance companies, people's credit funds also provide loans through loan agreements.[46] They can mobilize capital by means of receiving mandatory shares from their members, accepting savings and deposits from members and nonmembers, and borrowing loans from other financial institutions.[47] People's credit funds primarily provide loans to their members for mutual assistance among members in production, business development, and life.[48] People's credit funds can provide loans to nonmembers, but they require borrowers to have deposits with them as collateral.[49] Similar to conventional banks and finance companies, people's credit funds are required to meet capital, reserve, and liquidity requirements, as mentioned in Sect. 2.1.4. They also have to perform due diligence, establish provisional funds, and fulfill other obligations to ensure the safety of their operations. It has been noted that people's credit funds have not offered Internet

[41] See Vietnam's Law on Credit Institutions 2024, Article 107, clause 3 (d), Article 115, clause 6, and Article 120, clause 2 (a).

[42] See The English translation of Circular No. 15/VBHN-NHNN of Vietnam, Article 15, clause 1.

[43] See Circular No. 15/VBHN-NHNN of Vietnam, Article 15, clause 1.

[44] See Vương and Nguyễn (2016, p. 45).

[45] See Hang and Mai (2021) and the State Bank of Vietnam (2023).

[46] See Vietnam's Law on Credit Institutions 2024, Article 126, clause 2.

[47] Except for other people's credit funds. See Circular No. 04/2015/TT-NHNN, Article 36.

[48] See Vietnam's Law on Credit Institutions 2024, Article 118, clause 1.

[49] See Circular No. 29/2024/TT-NHNN, Article 26, clause 3.

banking services to their customers. This has been attributed to several factors, including their primary objective of mutual assistance among members, the simplicity of their services, the small scale of their operations, and their limited capital resources.[50]

Similar to people's credit funds, MFIs can offer loans only through loan agreements.[51] They accept both mandatory and voluntary savings and also borrow loans from individuals and organizations.[52] MFIs provide loans in two forms, group lending and personal loans, catering to the needs of individuals, low-income households, and micro-sized enterprises.[53] Loans provided by MFIs can be secured by collateral and mandatory savings and guaranteed by lending groups.[54] Like people's credit funds, MFIs are required to meet capital, reserve, and liquidity requirements and fulfill obligations to ensure the safety of their operations, as mentioned in Sect. 2.1.4. It has been noted that although MFIs have been making efforts to improve their information technology systems and the quality of their services, they have struggled to keep up with the growing demand for small funds from their customers.[55] Furthermore, their experience in using the Internet to provide loans to customers residing in rural and remote areas has been considered to be limited. This limitation has been attributed to the shortage of financial and human resources within MFIs.[56]

In the semi-formal micro- and/or small-sized finance sector, development projects and programs provide loans to poor and low-income individuals through loan agreements.[57] These projects and programs receive refundable or nonrefundable aid from the government and domestic and foreign organizations and individuals. They also mobilize capital from other sources, including mandatory or voluntary savings from borrowers and loans borrowed from financial institutions.[58] Similar to MFIs, these lending projects and programs can offer both group lending loans and personal loans, provided loans can be secured by mandatory savings of borrowers and/or guarantees by lending groups.[59] It has been noted that the provision of these loans through the Internet has been almost nonexistent, as development projects and

[50] See Hồng (2020).

[51] See Vietnam's Law on Credit Institutions 2024, Article 127, clause 2.

[52] Vietnam's Law on Credit Institutions 2024, Article 4, clause 37, provides that "Microfinance institution means a credit institution which mainly conducts one or some banking operations to meet the needs of low-income individuals and households, and super small-sized enterprises."

[53] See Vietnam's Law on Credit Institutions 2024, Article 127, clause 1.

[54] See Circular 33/2024/TT-NHNN, Article 24, clause 3, Vietnam Microfinance Working Group (2018, p. 150).

[55] See Vietnam Microfinance Working Group (2018, p. 88).

[56] Vietnam Microfinance Working Group (2018, p. 88).

[57] See Decision No. 20/2017/QD-TTg, Article 13, clause 2.

[58] See Decision No. 20/2017/QD-TTg, Article 13, clause 1.

[59] See Decision No. 20/2017/QD-TTg, Article 13, clause 2.

programs have primarily focused on providing loans to poor and low-income individuals in rural and remote areas.[60]

In addition, the SME Development Fund offers loans directly (via loan agreements) or indirectly (through indirect loan agreements with commercial banks) to SMEs. As mentioned in Sect. 2.1.4, SMEs eligible to receive loans from the Fund must have feasible production and business projects and plans belonging to the priority and encouragement domains of the state. In the direct lending scheme, the Fund offers loans to SMEs based on loan agreements.[61] These agreements contain terms and conditions regarding interest rates, lending terms, loan purposes, loan disbursement, loan repayment, and loan security measures.[62] Borrowers are required to provide collateral or obtain guarantees from a third party.[63] In the indirect lending scheme, the Fund selects commercial banks and enters into indirect lending agreements with them.[64] Under these agreements, designated banks borrow loans from the Fund to provide loans to eligible SMEs. The banks assume responsibility for any risks associated with their lending decisions for SMEs and are obligated to repay the principal amounts and accompanying interest to the Fund.[65]

In the informal micro- and/or small-sized finance sector, it is widely perceived that borrowers can obtain loans from family members, friends, neighbors, relatives, or moneylenders based on loan agreements with the lenders. Borrowers may write promissory notes and provide them to lenders as evidence of their debt repayment obligations. Loan terms can vary, and loans can be secured or unsecured. In practice, it seems likely common for lenders and borrowers to transfer money directly in cash or through bank accounts.

As mentioned in Sect. 1.1, pawnshops provide individuals with small loans through pawn agreements. Under these agreements, borrowers can obtain loans by pledging an item of value as collateral. If borrowers fail to repay their loans, pawnshops can sell the pledged property to recover the loan amounts, as agreed upon by the two parties. It has been noted that recently, an increasing number of pawnshops have been using the Internet to provide their services to customers.[66] For example, F88, a Vietnamese company established in 2016, has been using the Internet to provide pawnshop services. The company receives customer requests, appraises the value of pledged assets, and then offers loans corresponding to the appraised value through its website. Once customers accept loan offers, the company collects the pledged assets and disburses the loans accordingly.[67]

[60] See Nguyễn (2020a, b).

[61] See Decree 39/2019/ND-CP, Article 15, clause 1.

[62] See Decree 39/2019/ND-CP, Article 20.

[63] See Decree 39/2019/ND-CP, Article 21.

[64] See Decree 39/2019/ND-CP, Article 27.

[65] See Decree 39/2019/ND-CP, Article 22.

[66] See Nguyễn (2020a, b).

[67] See F88 (2025).

Individuals can also borrow small loans from tontine schemes, as mentioned in Sect. 2.1.1. In a tontine scheme, individuals who are in close proximity, know, and trust each other can establish a self-selected lending group for mutual assistance.[68] Participants contribute and lend to each other based on agreements regarding interest rates, lending terms, contribution and distribution procedures, participants' rights and obligations, and other terms, if applicable.[69] Under these agreements, they regularly contribute a fixed amount at specific intervals and take turns receiving the total amount collected in each interval. It can be seen that collateral is not necessarily required, as peer pressure within lending groups and the threat of social punishment can serve as security for the loans.

It can be observed that recently, department stores, shops, and online commercial websites like Pico,[70] FPT shop,[71] and Lazada[72] have been cooperating with commercial banks and finance companies to offer customers installment loans that are linked to purchase programs. Under these purchase programs, borrowers have the opportunity to acquire assets such as laptops, vehicles, or smartphones from department stores, shops, or commercial websites, with commercial banks and finance companies providing loans to cover the cost of the purchased items. The borrowers then repay the loans in installments over agreed-upon terms. To be eligible for these installment loans, borrowers are typically required to have credit cards issued by cooperating commercial banks or finance companies. Alternatively, they may be required to demonstrate stable income and provide necessary documents such as a national identification card, driver's license, and salary slips. Additional requirements from commercial banks and finance companies may apply, if applicable. Interest rates on these installment loans can vary, depending on the borrowers' creditworthiness.

Furthermore, online lending platforms have been providing P2P loans via their lending platforms since 2015, as mentioned in Sect. 1.2. In this lending scheme, borrowers apply for or register specific loan amounts within particular time frames and provide the required information. P2P lending platform service providers verify the information provided by borrowers and collect information on their credit history and debt-income ratios from various information sources to evaluate their creditworthiness. P2P lending platforms then post the information on borrowers' creditworthiness on their lending platforms for potential lenders' reference. Potential lenders can choose to fund loans available on P2P lending platforms or customize their preferences for risk, loan amount, and loan maturity and wait for a match made by P2P lending platforms. One borrower can receive a loan from single or multiple lenders, and P2P loans can be secured or unsecured.

[68] See Decree No. 19/2019/ND-CP, Article 3, clause 2.

[69] See Decree No. 19/2019/ND-CP, Article 8.

[70] See PiCo (2024).

[71] See FPT Shop (2025).

[72] See Lazada (2024).

## 4.2 Approaches to Risk Diversification in Micro- and/or Small-Sized Financing Schemes in Vietnam

### *4.2.1 Collateral*

Collateral is widely accepted as an effective method for diversifying credit risk.[73] Collateral typically involves borrowers pledging valuable assets, which can be easily converted into cash, as a guarantee for loan repayments to lenders. When a borrower defaults on a secured loan, the lender can sell the collateral and use the proceeds to recover the loan amount, thereby mitigating the risk associated with borrowers.[74] Additionally, it can be reasonably predicted that collateral may provide borrowers with an incentive to use loans effectively, potentially reducing the likelihood of borrower default.[75]

In Vietnam, collateral has long been utilized to diversify risk in micro- and/or small-sized financing schemes.[76] Since the development of Vietnam's current banking system, the use of collateral to secure loans has been officially regulated. For example, Decree No. 448-VP/NgD, dated August 23, 1957, stipulated that loans provided to SOEs for purchasing basic materials must be secured by those materials.[77] Another example is Decision No. 24/NH-QD, which was issued by the State Bank of Vietnam in 1983. The Decision stipulated that members of socialist savings funds or credit cooperatives must contribute monthly compulsory savings to secure their loans.[78]

Currently, collateral is governed by the Civil Code 2015 and related regulations. The subject of a security interest can include objects, money, valuable papers, and property rights.[79] A property can be accepted as collateral as long as it meets the following conditions: (i) being under legal ownership of the securing party, except in the case of retention of title or reservation of ownership rights; (ii) being identifiable; and (iii) not being subject to prohibited transactions.[80] Collateral can be movable or immovable, tangible or intangible, and existing or future formed.[81] The realization of collateral can occur under the following circumstances: (i) when an obligator fails to fulfill an agreed-upon obligation within a specified timeframe; (ii) when an obligator is required to fulfill the secured obligation ahead of the due date due to a violation of the agreed terms or as prescribed by law; and (iii) in other cases as

---

[73] See Horcher (2005, p. 112), Esch et al. (2005, p. 18), Mülbert (2015, p. 393), and Sena (2008).

[74] See Bessis (2015, p. 202), Brigo et al. (2013, p. 38), Fleisig et al. (2006, p. 3), and Ettinger and Golieb (1962, p. 47).

[75] See Sena (2008, p. 8).

[76] See Lea and Nguyen (2019, p. 104) and Dinh et al. (2011, p. 8).

[77] See Decree No. 448-VP/NgD, Article 2, clause 3.

[78] See Decision No. 24/NH-QD of Vietnam, Article 3, clause 4.

[79] See Vietnam's Civil Code 2015, Article 105.

[80] See Vietnam's Civil Code 2015, Article 295, clause 1, clause 2, and clause 4.

[81] See Vietnam's Civil Code 2015, Article 295, clause 3.

agreed upon by the parties or prescribed by law.[82] Furthermore, the forms of collateral available under the Code include mortgages, pledges, credit guarantees, and other forms as regulated by law.[83]

A mortgage is an agreement established between a mortgagor and a mortgagee. Under this agreement, the mortgagor uses a property they own as security for the performance of an obligation to the mortgagee. This does not involve the transfer of title to the property. The parties may agree to entrust the mortgaged property to a third party for retention.[84] The mortgagor is obligated to inform the mortgagee of any third-party rights associated with the mortgaged property. Failure to do so may grant the mortgagee the right to cancel the mortgage agreement and seek compensation for losses or uphold the agreement while acknowledging the rights of the third party concerning the mortgaged property.[85] The mortgagee can require the mortgagor to provide information regarding the mortgaged property's current status, and they also have the right to directly examine and inspect the property.[86] Additionally, the mortgagee may retain documents related to the mortgaged property as agreed upon by the parties, unless otherwise provided by law.[87] The mortgagor assumes the responsibility for maintaining and preserving the mortgaged property. If the property is at risk of depreciation due to its exploitation, the mortgagor must take appropriate remedial actions, which may include discontinuing the exploitation. Furthermore, in the event of any damage to the property, the mortgagor is obligated to promptly repair or replace the property with another of equal value within a reasonable timeframe.[88]

A pledge is a contractual agreement between a pledger and a pledgee. Under this agreement, the pledger delivers a property under their ownership as security for the performance of an obligation to the pledgee.[89] The pledger is obligated to inform the pledgee of any third-party rights related to the pledged property. Failure to do so may grant the pledgee the right to cancel the pledge agreement and seek compensation for losses or uphold the agreement while acknowledging the rights of the third party concerning the pledged property.[90] The pledgee assumes the responsibility for maintaining and preserving the property. They are not allowed to sell, exchange, or transfer it nor can they use it as security for the performance of another obligation.

---

[82] See Vietnam's Civil Code 2015, Article 299.

[83] Vietnam's Civil Code 2015, Article 292, provides that "[t]ypes of security for the performance of obligations comprise the following: 1. Pledge of property; 2. Mortgage of property; 3. Deposit; 4. Security collateral; 5. Escrow deposit; 6. Title retention; 7. Guarantee; 8. Fidelity guarantees; and 9. Lien on property."

[84] See Vietnam's Civil Code 2015, Article 317.

[85] See Vietnam's Civil Code 2015, Article 320, clause 7.

[86] See Vietnam's Civil Code 2015, Article 323, clause 1 and clause 2.

[87] See Vietnam's Civil Code 2015, Article 323, clause 6.

[88] See Vietnam's Civil Code 2015, Article 323, clause 2, clause 3, and clause 4.

[89] See Vietnam's Civil Code 2015, Article 309.

[90] See Vietnam's Civil Code 2015, Article 311, clause 2.

Unless otherwise agreed upon by the pledger and the pledgee, this prohibition includes the lease or exploitation of the benefits or income derived from the pledged property.[91] If the property is lost or damaged, the pledgee is obligated to provide compensation to the pledger.[92]

A guarantee refers to an undertaking that involves three parties: the guarantor, the obligor, and the obligee. In this arrangement, the guarantor commits to fulfilling an obligation on behalf of the obligor should the obligor fail to fulfill the guaranteed obligation.[93] The guarantee may cover the entire guaranteed obligation or a portion of it. In the case of a loan repayment obligation, the guarantee may cover the principal amount, the accompanying interest, fines, compensation for any loss or damage, and interest on late payments.[94] The parties involved may agree to establish a security interest on the guarantor's property to secure the guarantee obligation.[95] If the obligor fails to fulfill the secured obligation, the guarantor must do so instead. If the guarantor also fails to fulfill their obligation, the obligee has the right to claim the value of the secured obligation from the guarantor and seek compensation for any losses or damages incurred.

It is worth noting that notarization or authentication is prescribed as a condition of validity for certain types of security agreements.[96] These include security agreements with respect to real estate and residential housing. The effective date of a security agreement is indicated by notarization or authentication. In cases where notarization or authentication is not mandatory, a security agreement can become effective upon its signing or at another mutually agreed-upon time between the related parties.

Additionally, registration with the competent authority is a condition of enforceability for certain types of security interest.[97] A security interest shall be enforceable against a third party after the relevant security agreement has entered into force. The

---

[91] See Vietnam's Civil Code 2015, Article 313.

[92] See Vietnam's Civil Code 2015, Article 312, clause 3.

[93] See Vietnam's Civil Code 2015, Article 335.

[94] See Vietnam's Civil Code 2015, Article 336, clause 1 and clause 2.

[95] See Vietnam's Civil Code 2015, Article 336, clause 3.

[96] See The English translation of Decree No. 21/2021/ND-CP of Vietnam, Article 22.

[97] See Vietnam's Civil Code 2015, Article 298, clause 1.

The English translation of Decree No. 102/2017/ND-CP of Vietnam, Article 4, clause 1, provides that "[t]he following security interests are subject to registration: a) Mortgage of land use rights; b) Mortgage of property on land whose ownership has been stated in the certificate of rights to use land, ownership of house and property on land (hereinafter referred to as land use right certificate); c) Pledge or mortgage of aircrafts; d) Mortgage of seagoing ships."

Decree No. 99/2022/ND-CP, Article 4, clause 1, provides that:

> [t]he following security interests are subject to registration:
>
> a) Registration of mortgage of property, pledge of property, title retention as prescribed in the Civil Code, and relevant laws;
>
> b) Registration under the agreement between the grantor and the secured party or at the request of the secured party, except for property lien;

timing of enforceability against a third party depends on either the time the secured party holds the security property or the date of registration. While possessory security (e.g., in the form of a pledge) can be enforceable from the time the secured party takes possession of the security property, non-possessory security (e.g., in the form of a mortgage) can be enforced against a third party from the time of registration.[98]

In addition to the Civil Code 2015, a security transaction can also be subject to additional regulations specific to the type of security property and the parties to the transaction. For example, while security property is real estate, a security agreement over it can be subject to the Law on Land 2024 and the Law on Residential Housing 2023. If residential housing has been developed by a company in the form of an investment project, the parties may have to consider the Law on Enterprises 2020, the Law on Investment 2020, and the Law on Real Estate Business 2024.

It can be seen that mortgages, pledges, and guarantees can be employed to diversify credit risk in micro- and/or small-sized financing schemes. However, in a P2P lending scheme, P2P lenders can hardly employ mortgages and pledges to diversify credit risk. This is because of several reasons. For example, P2P lending platforms may find it challenging to require borrowers to provide collateral through the Internet to secure their loans, especially in cases where they reside in remote areas. Additionally, potential borrowers, such as poor and low-income individuals, are likely to lack substantial assets to use as collateral to secure their loans. In such cases, P2P lenders may accept a third party's credit guarantee to provide P2P loans to borrowers.

Individual borrowers and SMEs can receive credit guarantees from several sources. Individual borrowers can receive third-party guarantees and credit guarantees in the form of joint liability of lending groups. Meanwhile, SMEs can receive credit guarantees from a third party, such as parent companies, the Vietnam Development Bank's credit guarantee fund (hereinafter referred to as "VDB credit guarantee fund"), and local credit guarantee funds (hereinafter referred to as "CGFs").

As mentioned in Sect. 4.1, in group lending models, each member guarantees the repayment of the other members. If any member fails to repay their loan, the other members must repay instead or face losing access to future credit. However, in practice, joint liability among lending group members is often established among those who are in close proximity to each other. These individuals also know and trust each other, as well as have a shared need for establishing lending groups for mutual assistance. In cases where individuals and SMEs apply for loans provided via a P2P

---

c) Registration of notice of realization of collateral in case an asset is used to secure the performance of many obligations but many parties jointly receive the security or in cases where the grantor and the secured party have reached an agreement;

d) Registration of changes to registered information (hereinafter referred to as change registration); deregistration of registered information (hereinafter referred to as deregistration) for the case specified at Points a, b, and c of this Clause.

[98] See Vietnam's Civil Code 2015, Article 297, clause 1.

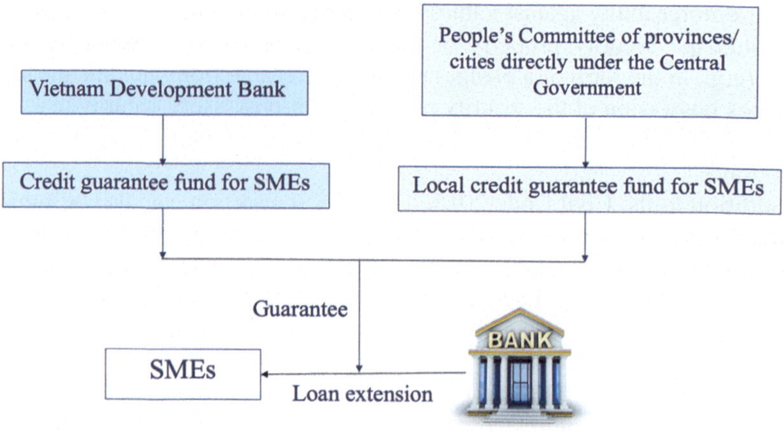


**Fig. 4.1** Public credit guarantee models in Vietnam

lending scheme, they may not know each other, and they therefore may find it difficult to establish such lending groups.

It can be seen that SMEs can receive credit guarantees from their parent companies. As has been noted in Sect. 1.2, credit guarantees are often utilized by holding companies to guarantee the loans of their subsidiaries. However, P2P borrowers are unlikely to have holding companies that can provide credit guarantees to obtain P2P loans.

In addition to credit guarantees from parent companies, SMEs can also receive credit guarantees from the VDB credit guarantee fund. In 2009, the VDB began offering credit guarantees[99] to support SMEs in accessing loans from commercial banks for their production and business development (see Fig. 4.1). To be eligible for credit guarantees from the VDB, the charter capital of SMEs should not exceed VND 100 billion, or they should employ between 10 and 300 employees.[100] SMEs must also meet the following conditions: (i) having a viable business project or plan appraised by the VDB; (ii) having no overdue debts; and (iii) maintaining equity capital of at least 15% of the project or plan's total investment, which must be entirely invested in fixed assets to be used as collateral at the VDB.[101]

Credit guarantees provided by the VDB can cover both the principal amount and companying interest of guaranteed loans. The maximum guarantee amount is 85% of a project or plan's total investment capital (excluding working capital).[102] In practice, the VDB provided credit guarantees to SMEs with government sponsorship during the financial crisis and economic recession from 2009 to 2011. However,

---

[99] See The English translation of Resolution No. 30/2008/NQ-CP of Vietnam and the English translation of Decision No. 03/2011/QD-TTg of Vietnam.

[100] See Decision No. 03/2011/QD-TTg, Article 3, clause 1.

[101] See Decision No. 03/2011/QD-TTg, Article 5.

[102] See Decision No. 03/2011/QD-TTg, Article 6.

since then, the bank has not provided guarantees for SMEs to borrow capital from commercial banks. It has been noted that this is due to the small size of the VDB credit guarantee fund and the bank's inclination to provide loans directly to SMEs in alignment with the government's policies.[103]

Local CGFs can also be a source of credit guarantees for SMEs (see Fig. 4.1). These CGFs were initially established in 2011 under Decision No. 193/2001/QD-TTg and are currently governed by Decree No. 34/2018/ND-CP. Provincial People's Committees establish CGFs in the form of a one-member limited company with a minimum charter capital of VND 100 billion. CGFs operate for nonprofit purposes and to ensure the safety of their initial capital.[104] In order to be eligible for credit guarantees from CGFs, SMEs should satisfy the following conditions: (i) having a viable investment project or production and business plan appraised by CGFs; (ii) maintaining equity capital of at least 20% of the project or plan's total investment; (iii) having no tax debt for 1 year or more, as well as no overdue debts at credit institutions; and (iv) having security measures for the guaranteed loans.[105]

CGFs consider and make decisions on providing credit guarantees to SMEs. These Funds may guarantee up to 100% of a project or plan's total investment capital (including working capital, medium- and long-term capital).[106] To make decisions on providing credit guarantees, the Funds may (i) require SMEs to use their existing property, property rights, and property to be formed in the future or a third party's existing property as collateral for the performance of their obligations; (ii) assess the viability of SMEs' investment projects and business plans; and (iii) assess SMEs' capability of debt repayment.[107]

In the course of their operation, CGFs are obligated to comply with the following limits: (i) the total amount of credit guarantees granted to an SME or an SME and its related entities must not exceed 15% or 20% of the actual charter capital of each CGF, respectively; (ii) the maximum credit guarantee for an SME's working capital must not exceed the amount of its equity as represented in its financial statement submitted to the tax authority the year before; and (iii) the total amount of credit guarantees extended to SMEs must not exceed three times the actual charter capital of each CGF.[108]

It has been observed that the operational effectiveness of CGFs is limited due to a variety of reasons.[109] Firstly, there is a lack of concrete cooperation and risk sharing between CGFs and lenders that provide loans to SMEs. CGFs assess the loan repayment capacity and creditworthiness of SMEs. They have the freedom to select SMEs for credit guarantees. It is important to note that lenders are not involved in the

---

[103] See VDB (2023).

[104] See Decree No. 34/2018/ND-CP of Vietnam, Article 4 and Article 5, clause 1.

[105] See Decree No. 34/2018/ND-CP, Article 16.

[106] See Decree No. 34/2018/ND-CP, Article 17, clause 1.

[107] See Decree No. 34/2018/ND-CP, Article 25.

[108] See Decree No. 34/2018/ND-CP, Article 19, clause 2, clause 3, and clause 4.

[109] See Dang and Chuc (2019, p. 16) and Dao (2017, p. 40).

selection of these guaranteed SMEs. If guaranteed SMEs default, the credit risk falls onto CGFs.[110] Secondly, ambiguous regulations regarding the guarantee coverage ratio may hinder SMEs' access to loans from credit institutions. Currently, CGFs can guarantee SMEs' loans partly or entirely. If the guarantee coverage ratio is less than 100% of the loan amount, lenders may refuse to provide loans to guaranteed SMEs.[111] Alternatively, if this ratio is set at 100% of the loan amount, lenders have little incentive to carefully assess and monitor loans granted to guaranteed SMEs. Consequently, the CGF must bear credit risk when a credit default occurs.[112]

It can be seen that, in a P2P lending scheme, P2P lenders may find it difficult to rely on the credit guarantee of CGFs to diversify their credit risk. This is because, under current laws, CGFs only provide credit guarantees for SMEs to borrow loans from credit institutions. If SMEs access loans provided via a P2P lending scheme, they are not eligible for CGFs' credit guarantees. Even if SMEs were guaranteed by CGFs to borrow loans via P2P platforms, P2P lenders are unlikely to effectively reduce their credit risk due to the abovementioned limitations of CGFs.

### *4.2.2 Due Diligence*

Due diligence has been widely recognized as a method to diversify risk in lending transactions.[113] It involves lenders systematically verifying and assessing borrowers' financial statements and other relevant information.[114] Prior to finalizing lending contracts, lenders may perform due diligence to evaluate loan applicants' ability to fulfill their repayment obligations. Based on this evaluation, lenders can select applicants who demonstrate the ability to fulfill repayment obligations to provide loans.[115] After loan disbursement, lenders may continue to perform due diligence to monitor borrowers' operations and make necessary adjustments to contractual arrangements.[116] The purpose of due diligence is to identify potential risks associated with lending transactions and implement risk prevention and mitigation measures.[117]

At the beginning of the due diligence process, lenders typically investigate and collect both financial and nonfinancial information on loan applicants. This stage may involve conducting procedures known as Know Your Customer (hereinafter

---

[110] See Dang and Chuc (2019, p. 20) and Dao (2017, p. 42).

[111] See Honohan (2010, p. 8) and Gozzi and Schmukler (2016, p. 6).

[112] See Dao (2017, p. 45), Dang and Chuc (2019, p. 21), and Yoshino and Hesary (2016, p. 3).

[113] See Lawson (2016, p. 9), Colquitt (2007, p. 53), Shain (2008), and OECD (2019, p. 14).

[114] Lawson (2016, p. 9), Colquitt (2007, p. 53), Shain (2008), and OECD (2019, p. 14).

[115] See Kelly (2006, p. 42), Andriole (2009, p. 1), and Bing (2008, p. 1).

[116] See Hassink (2010, p. 34), OECD (2019, p. 36), and Colquitt (2007, p. 128).

[117] See Abas (2010, p. 12), Lawson (2016, p. 27), Colquitt (2007, p. 8), OECD (2019, p. 17), and Bank for International Settlement (2001).

referred to as "KYC") or electronic Know Your Customer (hereinafter referred to as "e-KYC").[118] Under these procedures, lenders typically require individual applicants to provide their personal information such as name, phone number, age, gender, home address, job, and income. Additionally, individual applicants can be required to provide copies of identification documents, such as national identification cards, passports, or driver's licenses.[119] For SME applicants, lenders typically request specific information, including product portfolio details,[120] market information,[121] financial information,[122] personnel information,[123] execution information,[124] and legal information.[125]

During the due diligence process, lenders typically evaluate loan applicants' creditworthiness to determine loan eligibility, amounts, and conditions.[126] This evaluation may involve lenders using internal credit scoring systems and/or external resources, such as credit scores and credit ratings. Lenders may develop their own internal credit scoring systems using various scoring models[127] to assess loan applicants' credit scores.[128] Also, lenders may use credit scores and credit information provided by credit information companies or credit reporting companies to increase the effectiveness of due diligence performance. In addition to credit scores,

---

[118] See Lawson (2016, p. 27) and Colquitt (2007, p. 54). According to the Basel Committee on Banking Supervision, KYC programs should be formulated with four following key elements: (i) customer acceptance policy, (ii) customer identification, (iii) ongoing monitoring of high risk accounts, and (iv) risk management. See Bank for International Settlement (2025).

[119] Lawson (2016, p. 27), Colquitt (2007, p. 54), and Bank for International Settlement (2025).

[120] Which cover existing and former products, product quality, and product and service development plans.

[121] Such as the competitive landscape, competing strategies, customers, and competitors.

[122] Including capital structure, income statements, profit and loss statements, balance sheets, cash flow statements, account receivables, sales figures, financial projections, taxes, net losses, revenue recognition, related party transactions, proprietary technology, and facilities.

[123] Such as information about the entrepreneur, the executive team, the organization, the workforce, compensation, equity programs, incentive compensation, employee benefits, and retirement plans.

[124] Which covers sales, outbound marketing and corporate communication, revenue and customer information, general operational processes, manufacturing and supply chain systems, quality and compliance, services delivery and support, and customer journey.

[125] Including basic company documents, documents related to indebtedness, contracts and commitments, and litigation and claims. See Lawson (2016, p. 27).

[126] As mentioned above, lenders may also monitor borrowers' operations and make necessary adjustments to lending agreements. See Hassink (2010, p. 33) and OECD (2019, p. 37).

[127] It is worth noting several prevalent scoring models such as (i) the application scoring model which summarizes all available information of each applicant at the time of application into one overall score to facilitate lenders' decisions on granting new loans or not; (ii) the fraud scoring model which is used to detect fraudulent information provided by loan applicants; and (iii) the performance scoring model which evaluates the risk of existing borrowers during the loan term and helps make decisions on actions such as increasing credit limits, providing customer assistance, debt restructuring, requiring additional collateral, or reducing credit limits to mitigate credit risk. See Gestel and Baesens (2009, pp. 97–99).

[128] See Thomas et al. (2017, p. 1).

lenders may utilize credit ratings assigned by credit rating agencies to evaluate loan applicants' creditworthiness.[129] These agencies typically analyze a range of default risk factors[130] and employ their own methodologies[131] to assign specific credit ratings to individual loan applicants.[132] It has been noted that credit scores and ratings can make it easier for lenders to compare loan applicants' creditworthiness and assess their likelihood of default for effective fund allocation and risk management.[133] It should be noted that, during the due diligence process, lenders may also monitor borrowers' operations to mitigate risks associated with lending transactions.[134]

In Vietnam, due diligence has been regulated to mitigate risk in micro- and/or small-sized financing schemes. Currently, it is primarily governed by the Law on Anti-Money Laundering 2022 and the relevant regulations. The main aspects of due diligence that are regulated include KYC, credit scores, and credit ratings.

According to the Law on Anti-Money Laundering 2022, reporting entities including financial institutions[135] and relevant nonfinancial businesses and professions[136] are obligated to conduct KYC and maintain and update customer

---

[129] See Abrahams and Zhang (2009, p. 227), Galai et al. (2000, p. 259), Bessis (2015, p. 230), and Colquitt (2007, p. 288).

[130] Including financial ratios such as cash flow, debt-to-capital ratio, and debt coverage ratio.

[131] Such as accounting data and market information.

[132] It is worth noting that each rating agency usually has a specific rating scale or system of symbols for ranking the risk of default that goes from extremely safe (such as AAA, AA+, or AA, etc.) to highly risky (such as CCC, CC, or D, etc.). See Naciri (2015, p. 19) and Kruck (2011, p. 23).

[133] See Naciri (2015, p. 19) and Kruck (2011, p. 23).

[134] See OECD (2019, p. 17).

[135] Financial institutions are referred to organizations that are licensed to conduct one or more of the following activities or operations: (a) acceptance of deposits; (b) lending; (c) financial leasing; (d) payment services; (dd) payment intermediary services; (e) issuing negotiable instruments/ transferable securities, bank cards, and fund/money transfer/wire transfer orders; (g) bank guarantees and financial commitments; (h) providing foreign exchange services and money market instruments; (i) securities brokerage, advice to security investment, and provision of security for securities issues; (k) investment fund and portfolio management; (l) life insurance business; and (m) money and currency changing. See Vietnam's Law on Anti-Money Laundering 2022, Article 4, clause 1.

[136] Relevant nonfinancial businesses and professions are referred to entities that conduct one or more of the following activities or operations: (a) prize-awarding games, including electronic games, telecommunications network-based games, Internet-based games, casinos, lottery tickets, and betting; (b) real estate business, except leasing or subleasing of real property and real estate consulting; (c) dealing in precious metals and jewels; (d) supply of accounting services, provision of notarial services, and provision of legal services rendered by lawyers and legal professional organizations; and (dd) providing business formation, management, and administration services, services of acting as (or arranging for another person to act as) a director or secretary of a company to third parties, and legal arrangement services. See Vietnam's Law on Anti-Money Laundering 2022, Article 4, clause 1.

identification data.[137] Customer identification data collected includes the customer's identity, details about the beneficial owner, and information regarding business relationships with reporting entities.[138] These entities can verify customer identification data through the use of identification documents,[139] outsourcing to other entities,[140] or with third-party assistance.[141] Additionally, reporting entities are required to update customer identification data to ensure the consistency of their information systems regarding customer identification, customers' business activities, levels of money laundering risk, and the origin of their assets.[142]

In addition to KYC, credit scores provided by credit information companies can be used in the due diligence process. These companies can collect credit information from various sources to provide credit scores to participating organizations that have established agreements with them. Information sources may include participating organizations, other credit information companies, state authorities, and other lawful sources.[143] The collected data may include borrowers' identification information, credit extension history, debt repayment details, information on security for repayment obligations, and other relevant information.[144] Notably, credit information companies can only gather credit information of borrowers from participating organizations if the organizations have obtained written permission from the borrowers in accordance with the laws.[145]

Credit scores and reports provided by the Credit Information Center can also be used in due diligence. The Center was established under Decision No. 3289/QD-NHNN in 2008 by the State Bank. It collects credit information from credit institutions and provides credit scores and reports to credit institutions and other organizations in accordance with the law.[146] Additionally, the Center can rate and issue

---

[137] Financial institutions are required to conduct KYC when customers initially open accounts or establish business relations, as well as conduct occasional transactions that equal or exceed the designated threshold. Additionally, KYC is necessary when money laundering suspicions exist or when financial institutions have doubts about the accuracy of the obtained customer identification data. Relevant nonfinancial businesses and professions are required to conduct KYC when they get involved in certain activities or when transaction amounts of their customers equal or exceed designated thresholds. See Vietnam's Law on Anti-Money Laundering 2022, Article 9, clause 2 and clause 3.

[138] See Vietnam's Law on Anti-Money Laundering 2022, Article 10.

[139] For example, acceptable identification documents for individuals may include ID cards, passports, and other papers issued by a competent authority. Required documents for organizations may include establishment decisions, business registration certificates, decisions on reorganization or dissolution, appointment decisions for directors or general directors, and data on the founder or legal representative. See Vietnam's Law on Anti-Money Laundering 2022, Article 12, clause 1.

[140] See Vietnam's Law on Anti-Money Laundering 2022, Article 13.

[141] See Vietnam's Law on Anti-Money Laundering 2022, Article 14d.

[142] See Vietnam's Law on Anti-Money Laundering 2022, Article 11.

[143] See The English translation of Decree No. 58/2021/ND-CP of Vietnam, Article 18, clause 1.

[144] See Decree No. 58/2021/ND-CP, Article 18, clause 2.

[145] See Decree No. 58/2021/ND-CP, Article 4, clause 4.

[146] See Decision No. 3289/QD-NHNN, Article 2, clause 4.

credit scores for individuals and organizations that have borrowed from credit institutions.[147]

It is worth noting that credit rating companies can facilitate lenders' due diligence by issuing credit ratings. According to current laws, the credit rating process involves several essential steps, including (i) negotiating and signing a credit rating contract with a rated organization; (ii) selecting and assigning analysts; (iii) establishing a credit rating council; (iv) collecting and evaluating information to rate the rated organization's capacity to fulfill debt obligations; (v) approval of credit rating results; (vi) publishing a credit rating report; (vii) periodically evaluating the rating report until the rating contract expires; and (viii) concluding the rating contract.[148] Credit rating methodologies are designed to evaluate fundamental risks and their impact on the ability of rated organizations to fulfill debt obligations.[149] The evaluated risks must include macro risks, market and business environment risks, strategic risks, governance risks, personnel risks, financial risks, and other risks.[150] Furthermore, credit rating companies are obligated to apply their methodologies systematically and consistently to each debt obligation or business line. They must also periodically review these methodologies and make necessary adjustments.[151]

It is important to note that the due diligence process of credit institutions is also regulated by the Law on Credit Institutions 2024 and the related regulations. Credit institutions can conduct either KYC or e-KYC when their customers initially open accounts or establish business relations. When conducting e-KYC, credit institutions are required to meet the following requirements: (i) adopting appropriate solutions or technologies for collecting, checking, and verifying customers' identification information and biometric data; (ii) implementing technical methods to certify clients' consent to agreements with them; (iii) establishing risk management and control procedures to prevent identity impersonation and falsification; and (iv) adequately storing and managing clients' data.[152] The collected data must be securely stored, treated with confidentiality, and backed up to ensure its adequacy and integrity for purposes such as inspection, examination, trace requests, handling complaints and disputes, and addressing requests from competent authorities.[153]

Additionally, credit institutions[154] are required to establish their own internal credit rating systems to evaluate customers' creditworthiness before extending

[147] See Decision No. 3289/QD-NHNN, Article 2, clause 5.

[148] See The English translation of Decree No. 88/2014/ND-CP of Vietnam, Article 26, clause 1.

[149] See Decree No. 88/2014/ND-CP, Article 32, clause 1.

[150] See Decree No. 88/2014/ND-CP, Article 32, clause 2.

[151] See Decree No. 88/2014/ND-CP, Article 32, clause 3 and clause 4.

[152] See The English translation of Circular No. 17/2024/TT-NHNN of Vietnam, Article 16, clause 1.

[153] The protection of customers' identification information is also regulated by Decree No. 117/2018/ND-CP.

[154] Except nonbank credit institutions. See The English translation of Circular No. 31/2024/TT-NHNN of Vietnam, Article 5, clause 3.

loans.[155] Internal credit rating systems comprise sets of financial and nonfinancial indicators. These indicators are used in the evaluation of borrowers' payment ability through qualitative and quantitative analyses of their finance, business, governance, and reputation. The systems also include methods for assessing and rating specific groups of borrowers, including those with credit line constraints and their related persons.[156] The establishment of the systems must adhere to the following principles: (i) based on data and information collected from all customers within at least 1 year before the establishment of the system; (ii) the system should be updated annually; (iii) credit ratings corresponding to risk levels ranging from low to high should be established; and (iv) approval from the Board of Directors or Members' Council is required.[157]

It should be noted that credit institutions are required to conduct due diligence both before and after extending loans to borrowers. They are required to request customers to provide documents that demonstrate the feasibility of their capital use plans, financial capability, legality of capital use, and loan security measures. Additionally, credit institutions have the right and responsibility to inspect and monitor the utilization of loans and the repayment by borrowers. They may also request borrowers to provide reports on loan usage and evidence of appropriate utilization.[158]

It is evident that P2P lending platforms face challenges in enhancing the effectiveness of their due diligence. The reasons for this are as follows.

One notable reason is that P2P lending platforms are not granted access to the credit information held by the Credit Information Center. Currently, the Center exclusively provides credit information and ratings to credit institutions and also offers personal credit scoring services to individual borrowers. It does not extend its services to other lenders and lending platforms beyond credit institutions. Moreover, as of the end of 2022, the Center's database is still limited in scope and covers credit information for approximately 53 million borrowers, including corporate borrowers, individual borrowers, and credit card holders.[159]

Another reason is the lack of support from credit information companies in Vietnam. Currently, only the Vietnam Credit Information Joint Stock Company is authorized to provide credit information services in the market. While the company has signed agreements to share credit information with 26 out of 46 commercial banks, it has not extended this service to P2P lending platforms.[160]

Furthermore, P2P lending platforms can hardly rely on credit ratings issued by credit rating companies to evaluate potential borrowers' creditworthiness. Currently, only three credit rating companies have been established in Vietnam, including

[155] See Vietnam's Law on Credit Institutions 2024, Article 101, clause 2 (e).

[156] See Circular No. 31/2024/TT-NHNN, Article 5, clause 1.

[157] See Circular No. 31/2024/TT-NHNN, Article 5, clause 2.

[158] See Vietnam's Law on Credit Institutions 2024, Article 102.

[159] See Mạnh (2019, p. 14) and the State Bank of Vietnam (2022).

[160] See Vietnam Credit Information Joint Stock Company (2025) and Minh (2017).

SaigonRatings, FiinGroup, and VIS Rating. Among these companies, SaigonRatings and FiinGroup have issued credit ratings for a limited number of enterprises.[161] SaigonRatings, which was licensed in 2015, has provided around 125 solicited ratings and 50 unsolicited ratings for enterprises,[162] while FiinGroup, which was licensed in 2020, has issued credit ratings for just 90 enterprises.[163] VIS Rating was established in September 2023 and has provided credit ratings for nine enterprises.[164]

Finally, it is worth noting that the establishment of internal credit scoring systems for assessing potential borrowers' credit risk can be costly and ineffective. Apparently, obtaining sufficient data for establishing reliable information systems is a significant challenge for P2P lending platforms. As mentioned above, if potential borrowers are unbanked or nonbanked and applying for loans via P2P lending platforms for the first time, lending platforms can hardly obtain their track records. It becomes particularly ineffective to estimate credit scores for potential borrowers with limited data available in credit scoring systems. Developing internal credit scoring systems is also costly because it requires investment in information technology systems, personnel training, and support facilities.

### *4.2.3 Risk Limiting Measures*

In lending transactions, credit limits have been employed as a technique to limit credit risk borne by individual lenders.[165] It has been noted that these limits can be determined based on individual lenders' capital, borrowers' creditworthiness, collateral, loan type, loan maturity, or loan purpose. By establishing lending limits that one lender can lend to a single borrower or a group of borrowers, the credit risk faced by one lender can be limited.[166]

In Vietnam, the Law on Credit Institutions 2024 regulates credit limits applied to credit institutions. For example, finance companies and leasing companies must not extend a total amount exceeding 15% of their capital to a single borrower and 25% to a single borrower and affiliated persons.[167] Other credit institutions must not extend a total outstanding amount exceeding 14% of their own capital to a single borrower and 23% to a single borrower and affiliated persons until the end of 2025.[168]

[161] See Hiếu (2020).

[162] See SaigonRatings (2025) and SaigonRatings (2023).

[163] See FiinGroup (2025).

[164] See VIS Rating (2025).

[165] See Horcher (2005, p. 115) and Bessis (2015, p. 8).

[166] See Gregory (2012, p. 35), Bessis (2015, p. 9), and Colquitt (2007, p. 37).

[167] See Vietnam's Law on Credit Institutions 2024, Article 136, clause 2.

[168] See Vietnam's Law on Credit Institutions 24, Article 136, clause 1 (a).

Additionally, credit institutions are required to adhere to the following credit limits: (i) the total outstanding loans that credit institutions provide to the following must not exceed 5% of their own capital: audit institutions and auditors that are auditing them, inspectors that are inspecting them, their insiders (such as chief accountants, major shareholders, and founding shareholders), enterprises in which one of the abovementioned insiders of credit institutions owns more than 10% of charter capital, their staff who appraise and approve credit extensions, and their subsidiaries and affiliated companies over which they have control; (ii) the outstanding loans to a single subsidiary or affiliated company must not exceed 10% of each credit institution's capital; and (iii) the total outstanding loans to all subsidiaries and affiliated companies must not exceed 20% of each credit institution's capital.[169]

Notably, the total outstanding credit provided to borrowers for investment in corporate bonds or shares should not exceed 5% of the charter capital of credit institutions other than people's credit funds and MFIs.[170]

As mentioned in Sect. 1.2, P2P lending platforms can employ credit limits to limit the risk faced by individual P2P lenders. However, this approach could be costly if different lending limits were established for individual borrowers. Alternatively, setting up a single lending limit for all potential borrowers may cause P2P lending platforms to lose profitable opportunities by not providing larger loans to potential borrowers.

### 4.2.4 Risk Sharing

Loan syndication has been considered a traditional way to *share the credit risk* of making a very large loan to one borrower among syndicated lenders.[171] By providing a syndicated loan, syndicated lenders together share the credit risk caused by one borrower. It has been noted that syndicated loans can be either secured or unsecured, and they are usually governed by a common agreement or a single set of documentation. Providing syndicated loans can enable syndicated lenders to avoid costly duplication in monitoring the use of syndicated loans and the repayment of borrowers.[172]

In Vietnam, the provision of syndicated loans by credit institutions has been governed by Circular No. 42/2011/TT-NHNN. Syndicated loans are provided on the basis of voluntary participation, with the principle of co-appraisal, joint decision-making on credit extension, and shared responsibility for the outcome of the credit

[169] See Vietnam's Law on Credit Institutions 2024, Article 135.

[170] See The English translation of Circular No. 22/2019/TT-NHNN of Vietnam, Article 11 and Article 12, and the English translation of Circular No. 23/2020/TT-NHNN of Vietnam, Article 11 and Article 12.

[171] See Crouhy et al. (2014, p. 423), and Colquitt (2007, p. 8).

[172] Crouhy et al. (2014, p. 423) and Colquitt (2007, p. 8).

extension.[173] The credit outstanding of each credit institution participating in the provision of a syndicated loan to one borrower is the credit outstanding of each credit institution to the customer, which is determined at a certain time.[174]

As mentioned in Sect. 1.2, P2P lending platforms can limit the investment of individual P2P lenders to a certain amount in each transaction. When the amount of a P2P loan provided to one borrower exceeds this limit, multiple lenders can participate in a syndicated loan and collectively share the default risk caused by that borrower. However, this approach is likely to be extremely costly and impractical. If a credit limit is set up for each borrower, it could be expensive to evaluate the creditworthiness of all prospective borrowers. Alternatively, if a credit limit is set up for all borrowers, this may reduce P2P lenders' incentive to assess P2P borrowers' creditworthiness, potentially leading to risky and irredeemable investments.

### *4.2.5 Provisional Funds*

Setting up provisional funds has been considered a means to diversify the credit risk in lending transactions. Since the risk of losses on loans can hardly be estimated with certainty, lenders can establish provisional funds to offset future losses. These funds reflect expected future losses on loans in lenders' existing portfolios, thereby increasing lenders' risk tolerance and helping them stabilize and develop their business in the case of credit defaults.[175]

In Vietnam, the establishment and use of provisional funds for credit institutions were initially introduced under the Law on Credit Institutions 1997.[176] Currently, these funds are primarily regulated by the Law on Credit Institutions 2024. As part of their risk management, credit institutions are required to establish provisional funds.[177] These funds include specific provisions and general provisions, which are accounted for as operating costs.[178] Specific provisions refer to amounts of money that are set aside to provide against potential risks to each debt,[179] while general provision refers to amounts of money that are set aside to provide against potential risks that are not determined yet when a specific provision is established.[180]

---

[173] See The English translation of Circular No. 42/2011/TT-NHNN of Vietnam, Article 3, clause 1.

[174] Circular No. 42/2011/TT-NHNN, Article 2, clause 11.

[175] See Skoglund and Chen (2015, p. 326), Colquitt (2007, p. 333), Bessis (2015, p. 210), Quỳnh and Tuấn (2019, p. 112), and Nga (2010, p. 7).

[176] See Vietnam's Law on Credit Institutions 1997, Article 82.

[177] See Vietnam's Law on Credit Institutions 2024, Article 147.

[178] See Decree No. 86/2024/ND-CP of Vietnam, Article 3, clause 4.

[179] See Decree No. 86/2024/ND-CP of Vietnam, Article 3, clause 5.

[180] See Decree No. 86/2024/ND-CP of Vietnam, Article 3, clause 6.

To establish provisional funds, credit institutions are required to classify their debts and make adequate provisions corresponding to the levels of risks from debt classification. Debts are classified based on quantitative and qualitative methods. The qualitative method involves evaluating borrowers' creditworthiness based on nonfinancial indicators[181] and subjective criteria,[182] while the quantitative method relies on financial indicators[183] and objective data to assess borrowers' credit risk.[184] Debts are classified into five groups, including Group 1 (standard debts),[185] Group 2 (debts that need special attention),[186] Group 3 (substandard debts),[187] Group

[181] Such as borrower's reputation, business model, management capabilities, and governance structure.

[182] See Circular No. 11/2021/TT-NHNN, Article 10.

[183] Such as financial ratios, financial statements, and cash flow projections.

[184] See Circular No. 11/2021/TT-NHNN, Article 11.

[185] Includes (i) any unmatured debt with principal and interest which are rated likely to be fully recovered by due date; (ii) any debt which is less than 10 days past due and whose overdue principal and interest are rated likely to be fully recovered while its remaining principal and interest are rated likely to be fully recovered by due date; and (iii) any debt classified into Group 1 as prescribed in clause 2 of this Article. Circular No. 36/2024/TT-NHNN, Article 9, clause 1 (a).

[186] Includes (i) any debt which is up to 90 days past due, except the debts specified in point a(ii) of this clause and clause 3 of this Article; (ii) any debt with first-time adjusted repayment terms that is unmatured, except the debts specified in point b clause 2 and clause 3 of this Article; and (iii) any debt classified into Group 2 as prescribed in clauses 2 and 3 of this Article. Circular No. 36/2024/TT-NHNN, Article 9, clause 1(b).

[187] Includes (i) any debt which is from 91 to 180 days past due, except the debts specified in clause 3 of this Article; (ii) any debt with first-time extended repayment term that is unmatured, except the debts specified in point b clause 2 and clause 3 of this Article; (iii) any debt on which interest is exempted or reduced due to the customer's inability to pay the agreed-upon interest in full, except the debts specified in clause 3 of this Article; (iv) any debt which falls in one of the following cases and has not yet been recovered within a period of less than 30 days from the date on which the credit institution that is a cooperative signs the debt recovery document (hereinafter referred to as "debt recovery decision"):

- A debt violating provisions of clauses 1, 3, and 6, Article 134, of the Law on Credit Institutions
- A debt violating provisions of clauses 1, 2, 3, and 4, Article 135, of the Law on Credit Institutions
- A debt violating provisions of clauses 1, 5, and 9, Article 136, of the Law on Credit Institutions
- A debt violating SBV's regulations on lending operations of people's credit funds

(v) Any debt which is being recovered according to inspection conclusions; (vi) any debt which needs to be recovered under a premature debt recovery decision issued by a credit institution that is a cooperative due to the customer's breach of agreements made with that credit institution but is not yet recovered within a period of less than 30 days from the effective date of the debt recovery decision; (vii) any debt classified into Group 3 as prescribed in clauses 2 and 3 of this Article;and (viii) any debt which must be classified into Group 3 as prescribed in clause 2 Article 4 of this Circular. Circular No. 36/2024/TT-NHNN, Article 9, clause 1(c).

4 (doubtful debts),[188] and Group 5 (potentially irrecoverable debts).[189] Specific provisions for credit institutions (except for microfinance institutions) are made based on the ratios for each debt group, including 0%, 5%, 20%, 50%, and 100%, respectively. Specific provisions for MFIs are made based on the ratios for each debt group, including 0%, 2%, 25%, 50%, and 100%, respectively.[190] Additionally, general provisions account for 0.75% of the total outstanding amounts from Group 1 to Group 4.[191]

In certain cases, credit institutions can use provisional funds to offset bad debts, though they must adhere to regulated principles. Provisional funds can be used in cases where individual borrowers have died, gone missing, or have had permanent disability which causes loss of their earning capacity, organizational borrowers have been dissolved or declared bankrupt, or debts have been classified into Group 5.[192] Credit institutions are required to use specific provisions to offset bad debts in corresponding debt groups and handle collateral for debt recovery. In cases where

---

[188] Includes (i) any debt which is from 181 to 360 days past due, except the debts specified in clause 3 of this Article; (ii) any first-time rescheduled debt which is up to 90 days past due from the first-time rescheduled maturity date, except the debts specified in clause 3 of this Article; (iii) any second-time rescheduled debt which is unmatured, except the debts specified in point b clause 2 and clause 3 of this Article; (iv) the debt specified in point c(iv) clause 1 of this Article which is not yet recovered in a period of 30–60 days from the effective date of the recovery decision; (v) any debt which needs to be recovered under an inspection conclusion but is not yet recovered in a period of up to 60 days after the expiration of the prescribed recovery deadline; (vi) any debt which needs to be recovered under a premature debt recovery decision issued by a credit institution that is a cooperative due to the customer's breach of agreements made with that credit institution but is not yet recovered within a period of 30 to less than 60 days from the effective date of the debt recovery decision; (vii) any debt classified into Group 4 as prescribed in clauses 2 and 3 of this Article; and (viii) any debt which must be classified into Group 4 as prescribed in clause 2 Article 4 of this Circular. Circular No. 36/2024/TT-NHNN, Article 9, clause 1(d).

[189] Includes (i) any debt which is more than 360 days past due; (ii) any first-time rescheduled debt which is at least 91 days past due from the first-time rescheduled maturity date; (iii) any second-time rescheduled debt which is past due from the second-time rescheduled maturity date; (iv) any third- or more-time rescheduled debt, except the debts specified in point b clause 2 of this Article; (v) the debt specified in point c(iv) clause 1 of this Article which is not yet recovered in a period of more than 60 days from the effective date of the recovery decision; (vi) any debt which needs to be recovered under an inspection conclusion but is not yet recovered in a period of more than 60 days after the expiration of the prescribed recovery deadline; (vii) any debt which needs to be recovered under a premature debt recovery decision issued by a credit institution that is a cooperative due to the customer's breach of agreements made with that credit institution but is not yet recovered within a period of more than 60 days from the effective date of the debt recovery decision; (viii) any debt owned by a customer that is a credit institution placed under special control or FBB of which capital and assets are frozen; (ix) any debt classified into Group 5 as prescribed in clause 3 of this Article; and (x) any debt which must be classified into Group 5 as prescribed in clause 2 Article 4 of this Circular. Circular No. 36/2024/TT-NHNN of Vietnam, Article 9, clause 1 (dd).

[190] See Decree No. 86/2024/ND-CP, Article 4, clause 2 and clause 3.

[191] See Decree No. 86/2024/ND-CP, Article 7, clause 1.

[192] See Decree No. 86/2024/ND-CP, Article 11, clause 1 and clause 2.

specific provisions and proceeds from collateral handling are not sufficient, general provisions can be used to offset bad debts.[193]

In P2P lending, provisional funds may be funded by either the contribution of lending platforms or the fees collected from P2P lenders and/or P2P borrowers, as mentioned in Sect. 1.2. However, the establishment of provisional funds can be costly. While lending platforms are unlikely to have much incentive to establish provisional funds by their own contribution, the fees collected from P2P lenders and/or P2P borrowers to establish the funds may discourage them from using the lending platforms.

### 4.2.6 *Credit Insurance*

Credit insurance has been widely considered a measure to diversify credit risk borne by lenders in lending transactions.[194] Lenders may purchase credit insurance and/or require borrowers to pay credit insurance premiums to secure their loans. In case of credit defaults, insurance companies will reimburse partly or fully default loans to lenders according to the credit insurance contracts.[195] It is clear that credit insurance companies absorb partly or fully the losses borne by a small number of lenders and spread such losses over a large number of lenders or borrowers who pay for credit insurance premiums.[196]

Currently, credit insurance is not legally required in lending transactions in Vietnam. This enables lenders and borrowers to freely negotiate about purchasing credit insurance. Currently, nonlife insurance companies[197] can offer credit insurance as one of their business activities in accordance with the Law on Insurance Business 2022.[198] It has been noted that insurance premiums typically range from 5% to 6% of loan amounts, and insurance coverage can be up to 100%.[199] For example, Bao Minh Insurance has partnered with Easy Credit (EVN Finance Company) to provide credit insurance with up to 90% coverage for credit default and 100% coverage for cases where borrowers are missing, deceased, or seriously injured.[200] Another example is the case of Mirae Asset Finance Company collaborating with several insurance companies, such as PG Insurance, OPES Insurance,

---

[193] See Decree No. 86/2024/ND-CP, Article 11, clause 3.

[194] See Bodie et al. (2012, p. 314) and Hanna (1931, p. 521).

[195] Covering instances where individual borrowers are deceased or missing or organizational borrowers are dissolved or bankrupt. See Bình (2020).

[196] See Jus (2013, p. 9).

[197] Nonlife insurance refers to a type of insurance designed to offer protection against property and other losses or to provide third-party civil liability cover.

[198] See Vietnam's Law on Insurance Business 2022, Article 4, clause 14.

[199] See Bình (2020) and Nhã (2015).

[200] See Bao Minh Insurance (2025) and Banking Plus (2020).

and Vietnam National Aviation Insurance Corporation (VNI), to offer unsecured loans with a 5.5% premium and loan terms of up to 36 months.[201]

In P2P lending, as mentioned in Sect. 1.2, credit insurance may incentivize P2P lending platforms and lenders to offer riskier loans for higher profits, reducing the diligence in assessing potential borrowers' credit risk. This moral hazard might discourage insurance companies from covering potential P2P loan losses, which may hinder risk diversification for P2P lenders.

### *4.2.7 Secondary Market*

Secondary markets, where primary lenders sell off all or a portion of the loans they have originated, offer a way of diversifying the credit risk borne by primary lenders. By repackaging credit risk into new pools and classes of loans sold to a broad range of investors, the secondary market facilitates the distribution of credit risk from primary lenders to one or more lenders or investors who receive the assignment of loan claims. This allows primary lenders to recover part or all of their capital and reduce their credit risk.[202]

In Vietnam, the establishment of the secondary debt market began with the formation of the Vietnam Debt and Asset Trading Corporation (DATC) under Decision No. 109/2003/QD-TTg.[203] DATC assists in diversifying credit risk associated with debts of wholly SOEs to support them in restructuring their operations and transforming their legal form in accordance with the policies of the state. DATC operates under Decree No. 129/2020/ND-CP, which allows it to purchase debts from individual and organizational lenders, focusing on wholly SOEs' debts.[204] After acquiring debts on the secondary market, DATC may undertake the following measures to manage them: (i) directly collecting debts from debtors; (ii) managing, investing, exploiting, and disposing of collateral to recover debts; (iii) selling debts to individual and/or organizational investors; (iv) converting debts into equity in enterprises; (v) restructuring debts through adjustments in debt repayment terms, debt rescheduling, and debt interest rate adjustment; and (vi) other measures in accordance with laws and decisions made by competent authorities.[205] It is important to note that DATC can only purchase debts on the secondary market based on the designation of competent authorities or after its debt purchase plan receives approval from competent authorities.[206]

---

[201] See Mirae Asset Finance Company (2025)

[202] See Colquitt (2007, p. 10) and Crouhy et al. (2014, p. 431).

[203] See Anh (2019, p. 135) and Ngân (2019).

[204] See The English translation of Decree No. 129/2020/ND-CP of Vietnam, Article 13, clause 2.

[205] See Decree No. 129/2020/ND-CP, Article 16.

[206] See Decree No. 129/2020/ND-CP, Article 15.

Additionally, the Vietnam Asset Management Company (VAMC), established in 2013 under Decree No. 53/2013/ND-CP, helps credit institutions diversify the risk of bad debts. VAMC purchases bad debts from credit institutions based on specific conditions: (i) bad debts must be secured with collateral, (ii) all documentation related to bad debts and collateral must be legal and valid, (iii) individual debtors must be alive, and organizational debtors must still exist, and (iv) the balance or outstanding bad debts of debtors must meet the State Bank's regulated specific level.[207] VAMC can use its own capital or issue 0% interest rate special bonds[208] with a maximum 5-year duration to pay for bad debts acquired from credit institutions.[209] However, it can only use its own capital for such payment if it deems the capital recoverable and if the collateral securing the debts can be sold or if debtors show the potential to recover their payment ability.[210] VAMC handles bad debts through various measures, such as direct debt collection, managing collateral, selling debts to investors, debt-to-equity conversions, debt restructuring, and legal actions.[211] It has been noted that, while VAMC can use its limited government-granted capital to assist credit institutions in reducing credit risk from bad debts, issuing special bonds at 0% interest likely gives little incentive to handle the purchased bad debts. When these bonds mature, if VAMC fails to settle the debts, credit institutions remain responsible for repurchasing the bad debts and facing the risk of default.[212]

Before January 1, 2021, debt trading activities and related activities on the secondary loan market were governed by Decree No. 69/2016/ND-CP and Circular No. 53/2017/TT-BTC. These regulations required strict compliance for establishing a debt trading floor. However, with the Law on Investment 2020 taking effect on January 1, 2021, debt trading activities and the establishment of a debt trading floor are no longer considered conditional business lines. Despite this, there are no debt trading floors established in Vietnam yet. According to Decision No. 2024/QD-NHNN dated November 27, 2020, the State Bank has assigned VAMC to set up and operate the first debt trading floor in Vietnam by 2026.

As mentioned in Sect. 1.2, the existence of a secondary market allowing P2P lenders to sell loans with a high risk of default before their maturity may lead them to be less cautious about selecting loans with lower default probabilities. This behavior could negatively impact the quality of loan receivables traded on the secondary market, making potential investors less interested in investing there. Additionally, defaulted loan receivables are likely to be challenging to sell on the secondary

---

[207] See The English translation of Decree No. 53/2013/ND-CP of Vietnam, Article 8, clause 1.

[208] See Decree No. 53/2013/ND-CP, Article 7, clause 1 and clause 2.

[209] In the case of bad debts purchased from credit institutions that are implementing restructuring plans or facing financial difficulties, the maximum duration of special bonds is no longer than 10 years.

[210] See The English translation of Decree No. 34/2015/ND-CP of Vietnam, Article 1, clause 1.

[211] See Decree No. 53/2013/ND-CP, Article 12 and Article 16.

[212] See Thành and Yến (2018, p. 68).

market unless at a very low price, ultimately leaving P2P lenders responsible for the losses resulting from such defaults.

## 4.3 Interim Conclusion

As outlined above, since the establishment of Vietnam's independent banking system in 1945, and particularly after the Đổi Mới in 1986, various micro- and/or small-sized financing schemes have been developed to provide credit to households and small businesses. These initiatives, offered through both formal and informal sectors, have contributed significantly to improving financial access. However, despite these efforts, a substantial credit gap persists in society.

This chapter finds that conventional micro- and/or small-sized financing schemes in Vietnam employ several risk diversification methods, including the use of collateral, guarantees, credit insurance, provisional funds, and participation in secondary markets. While these approaches can achieve some success, they remain insufficient when applied to the specific risks faced by P2P lenders in Vietnam. These limitations highlight the urgent need for new, tailored regulatory approaches to address risks to which P2P lenders are exposed.

The chapter then presents the unique challenges faced by P2P lenders in applying the aforementioned risk diversification methods in Sect. 4.2. First, P2P lenders can hardly employ mortgages and pledges to diversify credit risk. Additionally, CGFs, which support SMEs borrowing from traditional credit institutions, do not extend their guarantees to loans obtained through P2P platforms under current regulations. Even if such guarantees were available, the limitations inherent in CGFs would prevent P2P lenders from effectively mitigating credit risk.

Furthermore, accessing reliable credit information remains a significant challenge for P2P lenders in conducting due diligence. Credit information companies can only collect borrower data with prior written consent, and many potential P2P borrowers—especially the unbanked—lack sufficient financial history to build reliable credit scores. The development of internal credit scoring systems by platform service providers is costly and complicated by a lack of data.

Other risk diversification approaches present additional limitations. The use of credit limits, while theoretically helpful, can be both costly and impractical to implement effectively. Syndicating loans among multiple P2P lenders may spread risk but would also raise operational expenses and lower efficiency. Similarly, the establishment of provisional funds or credit insurance mechanisms may inadvertently create moral hazard problems or disincentivize platform service providers use due to increased costs. Finally, although secondary markets could provide an exit for P2P lenders, they risk undermining overall loan quality by encouraging the transfer of high-risk loans.

# References


Abrahams C, Zhang M (2009) Credit risk assessment: the new lending system for borrowers, lenders, and investors. Wiley, New Jersey

Abas P (2010) Client life cycle management. In: Grinsven JHMV (ed) Risk management in financial institutions: formulating value propositions. IOS Press, Amsterdam

Andriole SJ (2009) Technology due diligence: best practices for chief information officers, venture capitalists, and technology vendors. Information Science Reference, New York

Anh TTV (2019) Xây dựng thị trường mua bán nợ: giải pháp xử lý nợ xấu [Establishment of the secondary loan market: Solutions for dealing with bad debts]. Bank Rev 2+3:135

Bank for International Settlement (2001) Customer due diligence for banks. https://www.bis.org/publ/bcbs85.pdf. Accessed 20 Mar 2025

Bank for International Settlement (2025) The Basel Committee—Overview. https://www.bis.org/bcbs/. Accessed 20 Mar 2025

Banking Plus (2020) Easy Credit hợp tác với bảo hiểm Bảo Minh [Easy Credit cooperates with Bao Minh insurance]. https://thoibaonganhang.vn/easy-credit-hop-tac-voi-bao-hiem-bao-minh-96953.html. Accessed 20 Mar 2025

Bao Minh Insurance (2025) Bảo hiểm tín dụng thương mại [Commercial credit insurance]. https://www.baominh.com.vn/bao-hiem-tin-dung-thuong-mai. Accessed 20 Mar 2025

Bessis J (2015) Risk management in banking, 4th edn. Wiley, West Sussex

Bing G (2008) Due diligence: planning, questions, issues. Praeger, Connecticus

Bình T (2020) Chia sẻ phí bảo hiểm khoản vay [Sharing credit insurance premium]. https://sbv.gov.vn/webcenter/portal/vi/menu/rm/apph/tbnh/tbnh_chitiet?leftWidth=20%25&showFooter=false&showHeader=false&dDocName=SBV414045&rightWidth=0%25&centerWidth=80%25&_afrLoop=18837441763619755#%40%3F_afrLoop%3D18837441763619755%26centerWidth%3D80%2525%26dDocName%3DSBV414045%26leftWidth%3D20%2525%26rightWidth%3D0%2525%26showFooter%3Dfalse%26showHeader%3Dfalse%26_adf.ctrl-state%3Dttf4dwm1o_9. Accessed 20 Mar 2025

Bodie Z, Merton RC, Cleeton DL (2012) Hedging, insuring, and diversifying. In: Bodie Z, Merton RC, Cleeton DL (eds) Financial economics, 2nd edn. Pearson, Boston

Brigo D, Morini M, Pallavicini A (2013) Counterparty credit risk, collateral and funding: with pricing cases for all asset classes. Wiley, Croydon

Chính PM, Hoàng VQ (2009) Kinh tế Việt Nam: thăng trầm và đột phá [Vietnam's economy: vicissitudes and breakings]. National Political Publishing House, Hanoi

Circular No. 06-TC/NHKT dated April 10, 1973 of Vietnam. https://thuvienphapluat.vn/van-ban/Tien-te-Ngan-hang/Thong-tu-06-TC-NHKT-huong-dan-cho-vay-cap-phat-von-dau-tu-xay-dung-co-ban-tinh-hinh-moi-23275.aspx. Accessed 20 Mar 2025

Circular No. 21/2019/TT-NHNN of Vietnam. https://thuvienphapluat.vn/van-ban/tien-te-ngan-hang/thong-tu-21-2019-tt-nhnn-sua-doi-thong-tu-ngan-hang-hop-tac-xa-quy-tin-dung-nhan-dan-428626.aspx. Accessed 20 Mar 2025

Circular No. 376-TC/NHKT/TT of Vietnam. https://thuvienphapluat.vn/van-ban/Tien-te-Ngan-hang/Thong-tu-376-TC-NHKT-TT-quyet-dinh-tien-hanh-cong-tac-cho-vay-ngan-han-kien-thiet-co-ban-22531.aspx. Accessed 20 Mar 2025

Colquitt J (2007) Credit risk management: how to avoid lending disasters and maximize earnings, 3rd edn. McGraw Hill, New York

Crouhy M, Galai D, Mark R (2014) The essentials of risk management, 2nd edn. McGraw Hill, New York

Dang LN, Chuc AT (2019) Challenges in implementing the credit guarantee scheme for small and medium-sized enterprises: the case of Viet Nam. https://www.adb.org/publications/challenges-implementing-credit-guarantee-scheme-sme-vietnam. Accessed 20 Mar 2025

Dao HHT (2017) Credit guarantee for small and medium enterprises the case of municipal credit guarantee funds in Vietnam. ASIAN J Poverty Stud 3: 40

Decision No. 24-NH/QD of Vietnam. https://thuvienphapluat.vn/van-ban/Tien-te-Ngan-hang/Quyet-dinh-24-NH-QD-the-le-cho-vay-voi-Can-bo-Cong-Nhan-Vien-Chuc-NN-xa-vien-thuoc-to-chuc-kinh-te-tap-the-lam-gia-dinh-giai-quyet-doi-song-kho-khan-44732.aspx?v=d. Accessed 20 Mar 2025

Decision No. 52-NH/QD of Vietnam. https://thuvienphapluat.vn/van-ban/Tien-te-Ngan-hang/Quyet-dinh-52-NH-QD-Dieu-le-to-chuc-hoat-dong-hop-tac-xa-tin-dung-nong-thon-44441.aspx. Accessed 20 Mar 2025

Decision No. 67-NH/QD of Vietnam. https://thuvienphapluat.vn/van-ban/Tien-te-Ngan-hang/Quyet-dinh-67-NH-QD-The-le-tin-dung-ca-the-tu-nhan-san-xuat-kinh-doanh-dich-vu-37103.aspx. Accessed 20 Mar 2025

Decree No. 47-TTg of Vietnam. https://thuvienphapluat.vn/van-ban/Tien-te-Ngan-hang/Nghi-dinh-047-TTg-an-dinh-muc-loi-suat-tien-gui-tu-nhan-tien-tiet-kiem-tinh-vao-so-du-tai-khoan-thanh-toan-cho-vay-ngan-han-cua-ngan-hang-quoc-gia-22782.aspx. Accessed 20 Mar 2025

Decree No. 81-NgD/NH of Vietnam. https://thuvienphapluat.vn/van-ban/Tien-te-Ngan-hang/Nghi-dinh-81-NgD-NH-ban-bien-phap-cho-vay-dai-han-20649.aspx. Accessed 20 Mar 2025

Decree No. 177-TTg of Vietnam. https://thuvienphapluat.vn/van-ban/Tai-chinh-nha-nuoc/Nghi-dinh-177-TTg-thanh-lap-Ngan-hang-kien-thiet-Viet-Nam-tai-Bo-Tai-chinh-21076.aspx?v=d. Accessed 20 Mar 2025

Decree No. 312-Ttg of Vietnam. https://thuvienphapluat.vn/van-ban/Tai-chinh-nha-nuoc/Nghi-dinh-312-TTg-thanh-lap-quy-tiet-kiem-xa-hoi-chu-nghia-21116.aspx. Accessed 20 Mar 2025

Decree No. 448-VP/NgD of Vietnam. https://thuvienphapluat.vn/van-ban/Doanh-nghiep/Nghi-dinh-448-VP-NgD-ban-the-le-va-bien-phap-cho-vay-ngan-han-doi-voi-cac-xi-nghiep-cong-nghiep-quoc-doanh-55646.aspx. Accessed 20 Mar 2025

Dinh T, Hainz C,Kleimeier S (2011) Collateral and its determinants: evidence from Vietnam. https://www.econstor.eu/bitstream/10419/48306/1/36_hainz.pdf. Accessed 20 Mar 2025

Esch L, Kieffer R, Lopez T (2005) Asset and risk management: risk oriented finance. Wiley, West Sussex

Ettinger RP, Golieb DE (1962) Credits and collections, 5th edn. Prentice Hall, New Jersey

F88 (2025) Về F88 [About F88]. https://f88.vn/ve-f88. Accessed 20 Mar 2025

FiinGroup (2025) Rating results. https://fiinratings.vn/RatingResult/en. Accessed 20 Mar 2025

Florack AJ, Dworkin CM, Jackson LV, Troconis A (2022) Banking & Finance 2022 USA: Law & Practice and USA: Trends and developments. https://www.davispolk.com/insights/articlesbooks/banking-finance-2022-usa. Accessed 20 Mar 2025

Fleisig H, Safavian M, Pena N (2006) Reforming collateral laws to expand access to finance. World Bank Publications, Washington, DC

FPT Shop (2025) Chính sách trả góp [Installment policy]. https://fptshop.com.vn/ho-tro/chinh-sach-tra-gop. Accessed 20 Mar 2025

Galai M, Dan C, Mark R (2000) Risk Management. McGraw Hill, New York

Gestel TV, Baesens B (2009) Credit risk management - basic concepts: financial risk components, rating analysis, models, economic and regulatory capital. Oxford University Press, New York

Gozzi JC, Schmukler S (2016) Public credit guarantees and access to finance. https://ideas.repec.org/p/ags/uwarer/269324.html. Accessed 20 Mar 2025

Gregory J (2012) Counterparty credit risk and credit value adjustment: a continuing challenge for global financial markets, 2nd edn. Wiley, New Jersey

Hanna J (1931) Credit insurance. Univ PA Law Rev 79:521

Hassink A (2010) The basics of credit risk management. In: Grinsven JHMV (ed) Risk management in financial institutions: formulating value propositions. IOS Press, Amsterdam

Hang LTT, Mai HQ (2021) Practical development of digital banking in Vietnam. Rev Financ 765:45

Hiếu NT (2020) Hoạt động của các tổ chức xếp hạng tín nhiệm doanh nghiệp tại Việt Nam và so sánh với các quốc gia châu Á [The performance of Vietnam's credit rating companies in comparison with that of other Asian countries]. https://tapchicongthuong.vn/bai-viet/hoat-dong-cua-cac-to-chuc-xep-hang-tin-nhiem-doanh-nghiep-tai-viet-nam-va-so-sanh-voi-cac-quoc-gia-chau-a-72860.htm. Accessed 20 Mar 2025

Honohan P (2010) Partial credit guarantees: principles and practice. J Financ Stab 6:8

Hồng A (2020) Quỹ tín dụng nhân dân không thể dần dần biến thành ngân hàng [People's credit funds cannot gradually turn into banks]. https://tuoitre.vn/quy-tin-dung-nhan-dan-khong-the-dan-dan-bien-thanh-ngan-hang-20200110180422928.htm. Accessed 20 Mar 2025

Horcher KA (2005) Essentials of financial risk management. Wiley, New Jersey

Inter-Ministerial Circular No. 01-VHH-DS of Vietnam. https://thuvienphapluat.vn/van-ban/Tien-te-Ngan-hang/Thong-tu-lien-bo-01-VHH-DS-chu-truong-duong-loi-giai-quyet-cong-tac-thu-no-Ngan-hang-Quoc-gia-21406.aspx. Accessed 20 Mar 2025

Jus M (2013) Credit Insurance. Elsevier, Massachusetts

Kelly M (2006) Risk management systems: the framework and practice in Asia. In: OECD (ed) Credit risk and credit access in Asia. OECD Publishing, Paris

Kruck A (2011) Private ratings, public regulations: credit rating agencies and global financial governance. Palgrave Macmillan, Hampshire

Lazada (2024) Làm thế nào để tham gia chương trình "trả góp 0% lãi suất của Lazada? [How to join the purchase program with installment interest rate of 0% of Lazada?]. https://www.lazada.vn/helpcenter/lam-the-nao-de-tham-gia-chuong-trinh-%E2%80%9Ctra-gop-0-lai-suat%E2%80%9D-cua-lazada-9052.html?spm=a2o4n.helpcenter-topic.articles-list.1.16ba5cb5D9PXpx. Accessed 20 Mar 2025

Lawson BC (2016) Due diligence for startups: a step-by-step guide. CreateSpace Independent Publishing, South Carolina

Lea CHA, Nguyen HL (2019) Collateral quality and loan default risk: the case of Vietnam. Comp Econ Stud 61:104

Mạnh H (2019) CIC - Những dấu ấn trên chặng đường 20 năm xây dựng và phát triển [CIC- the hallmarks of 20-year construction and development]. Bank Rev 19:14

Minh T (2017) Đề xuất thành lập thêm ít nhất 2 công ty thông tin tín dụng tại Việt Nam [Proposing to establish at least 2 more credit information companies in Vietnam]. https://vietnambiz.vn/de-xuat-thanh-lap-them-it-nhat-2-cong-ty-thong-tin-tin-dung-tai-viet-nam-28563.htm. Accessed 20 Mar 2025

Mirae Asset Finance Company (2025) Bảo hiểm khoản vay [Credit insurance]. https://mafc.com.vn/bao-hiem-khoan-vay/. Accessed 20 Mar 2025

Mülbert PO (2015) Managing risk in the financial system. In: Moloney N, Ferran E, Payne J (eds) The Oxford handbook of financial regulation. Oxford University Press, New York

Naciri A (2015) Credit rating governance: global credit gatekeepers. Routledge, Oxford

Nga ĐTT (2010) Pháp luật về các biện pháp hạn chế rủi ro trong hoạt động cho vay của các ngân hàng thương mại ở Việt Nam [Regulations on measures for risk reduction in lending activities of commercial banks in Vietnam]. https://repository.vnu.edu.vn/bitstream/VNU_123/6441/1/00050000474.pdf. Accessed 20 Mar 2025

Ngân B (2019) Phát triển thị trường mua bán nợ đúng nghĩa để "phá băng" nợ xấu [Development of secondary loan market to "break" bad debts]. https://nhandan.vn/phat-trien-thi-truong-mua-ban-no-dung-nghia-de-pha-bang-no-xau-post380740.html. Accessed 20 Mar 2025

Nhã U (2015) Bảo hiểm khoản vay—có bắt buộc mua khi vay tín chấp hay không? [Credit insurance—Is it compulsory to buy when borrowing unsecured loans?]. https://fecredit.com.vn/taichinh/bao-hiem-khoan-vay-co-bat-buoc-mua-khi-vay-tin-chap-hay-khong/. Accessed 20 Mar 2025

Nguyễn D (2020a) Cầm đồ từ truyền thống đến hiện đại: 'bóng tối' trở mình thành 'ngàn tỉ'? [From traditional to modern pawnshops: From the 'darkness' to the 'light'?]. https://thesaigontimes.vn/cam-do-tu-truyen-thong-den-hien-dai-bong-toi-tro-minh-thanh-ngan-ti/. Accessed 20 Mar 2025

Nguyễn K (2020b) Tổ chức tài chính vi mô: chuyển đổi để phát triển an toàn, bền vững [Microfinance institution: Transforming for safe and sustainable development]. https://thoibaonganhang.vn/to-chuc-tai-chinh-vi-mo-chuyen-doi-de-phat-trien-an-toan-ben-vung-98523.html. Accessed 20 Mar 2025

OECD (2019) Due diligence for responsible corporate lending and securities underwriting key considerations for banks implementing the OECD guidelines for multinational enterprises. http://mneguidelines.oecd.org/due-diligence-for-responsible-corporate-lending-and-securities-underwriting.pdf. Accessed 20 Mar 2025

PiCo (2024) Mua trả góp đơn giản, dễ dàng và tiết kiệm cùng Pico [Installment purchase is simple, easy and saving with pico]. https://pico.vn/mua-tra-gop-don-gian-de-dang-va-tiet-kiem-cung-pico-RRKP5027.b. Accessed 20 Mar 2025

Pvcombank (2019) Biểu phí dịch vụ tín dụng và bảo lãnh dành cho doanh nghiệp trong nước [Credit and guarantee service fee schedule for domestic enterprises]. https://www.pvcombank.com.vn/static/BieuPhi/2109Doanhnghiepbieuphi.pdf. Accessed 20 Mar 2025

Quỳnh PX, Tuấn Đ (2019) Nghiên cứu dự phòng rủi ro tín dụng tại các ngân hàng thương mại Việt Nam [Researching risk credit provision at commercial banks of Vietnam]. Rev Financ 700:112

Rule No. 739-TTg of Vietnam. https://thuvienphapluat.vn/van-ban/Doanh-nghiep/Quy-tac-739-TTg-to-chuc-hop-tac-xa-tin-dung-nong-thon-55492.aspx. Accessed 20 Mar 2025

Sacombank (2025) Guarantee. https://www.sacombank.com.vn/en/corporate/guarantee.html. Accessed 20 Mar 2025

SaigonRatings (2025) About Us. https://saigonratings.com/en/about/#:~:text=Saigon%20Ratings%20aims%20to%20promote,and%20individual%20investors%20in%20the. Accessed 20 Mar 2025

SaigonRatings (2023) Credit rating information. https://phatthinhrating.com/en/credit-rating/rating-list/. Accessed 10 Jul 2023

Sena V (2008) Credit and Collateral. Routledge, New York

Shain R (2008) Hedge fund due diligence: professional tools to investigate hedge fund managers. Wiley, New Jersey

Skoglund J, Chen W (2015) Financial risk management: applications in market, credit, asset and liability management and firmwide risk. Wiley, New Jersey

Thành HV, Yến NH (2018) Status quo of the law on dealing with bad debts of credit institutions in Vietnam at present and recommendations for improvement. Jurisprud J 7: 68

The English translation of Circular No. 03/2018/TT-NHNN of Vietnam (trans: Luatvietnam.vn). https://english.luatvietnam.vn/circular-no-03-2018-tt-nhnn-dated-february-23-2018-of-the-state-bank-of-vietnam-on-licensing-organization-and-operation-of-microfinance-institution-159765-doc1.html. Accessed 20 Mar 2025

The English translation of Circular No. 04/2013/TT-NHNN (2013, as amended) of Vietnam (trans: Thuvienphapluat). https://thuvienphapluat.vn/van-ban/Tien-te-Ngan-hang/Circular-No-04-2013-TT-NHNN-providing-on-discount-activities-of-negotiable-inst-174874.aspx?tab=1. Accessed 20 Mar 2025

The English translation of Circular No. 04/2015/TT-NHNN of Vietnam (trans: Thuvienphapluat). https://thuvienphapluat.vn/van-ban/Tien-te-Ngan-hang/Circular-No-04-2015-TT-NHNN-on-people-s-credit-funds-361625.aspx?tab=1. Accessed 20 Mar 2025

The English translation of Circular No. 11/2021/TT-NHNN of Vietnam (trans: Thuvienphapluat). https://thuvienphapluat.vn/van-ban/Tien-te-Ngan-hang/Circular-11-2021-TT-NHNN-management-of-risks-arising-from-operations-of-credit-institutions-486450.aspx?tab=1. Accessed 20 Mar 2025

The English translation of Circular No. 15/VBHN-NHNN of Vietnam (trans: Thuvienphapluat). https://thuvienphapluat.vn/van-ban/Tien-te-Ngan-hang/Integrated-document-15-VBHN-NHNN-2021-Circular-band-card-operations-500855.aspx?tab=1. Accessed 20 Mar 2025

The English translation of Circular No. 16/2020/TT-NHNN of Vietnam (trans: Thuvienphapluat). https://thuvienphapluat.vn/van-ban/EN/Tien-te-Ngan-hang/Circular-16-2020-TT-NHNN-amendments-Circular-23-2014-TT-NHNN-opening-checking-accounts/459239/tieng-anh.aspx. Accessed 20 Mar 2025

The English translation of Circular No. 17/2024/TT-NHNN of Vietnam (trans: Thuvienphapluat). https://thuvienphapluat.vn/van-ban/Tien-te-Ngan-hang/Circular-17-2024-TT-NHNN-on-opening-checking-accounts-at-payment-service-providers-616720.aspx?tab=1. Accessed 20 Mar 2025

The English translation of Circular No. 22/2019/TT-NHNN of Vietnam (trans: Thuvienphapluat). https://thuvienphapluat.vn/van-ban/Tien-te-Ngan-hang/Circular-22-2019-TT-NHNN-limits-and-prudential-ratios-of-banks-and-foreign-bank-branches-430840.aspx?tab=1. Accessed 20 Mar 2025

The English translation of Circular No. 23/2020/TT-NHNN of Vietnam (trans: Thuvienphapluat). https://thuvienphapluat.vn/van-ban/Tien-te-Ngan-hang/Circular-23-2020-TT-NHNN-regulating-prudential-limits-and-ratios-of-non-bank-credit-institutions-469659.aspx?tab=1. Accessed 20 Mar 2025

The English translation of Circular No. 26/2024/TT-NHNN of Vietnam (trans: Thuvienphapluat). https://thuvienphapluat.vn/van-ban/Tien-te-Ngan-hang/Circular-26-2024-TT-NHNN-providing-for-finance-leasing-activities-of-general-finance-companies-624324.aspx?tab=1. Accessed 20 Mar 2025

The English translation of Circular No. 29/2024/TT-NHNN of Vietnam (trans: Thuvienphapluat). https://thuvienphapluat.vn/van-ban/Tien-te-Ngan-hang/Circular-29-2024-TT-NHNN-people-s-credit-funds-618417.aspx?tab=1. Accessed 20 Mar 2025

The English translation of Circular No. 31/2024/TT-NHNN of Vietnam (trans: Thuvienphapluat). https://thuvienphapluat.vn/van-ban/Tien-te-Ngan-hang/Circular-31-2024-TT-NHNN-prescribing-classification-of-assets-in-operations-of-commercial-banks-622831.aspx?tab=1. Accessed 20 Mar 2025

The English translation of Circular No. 33/2024/TT-NHNN of Vietnam (trans: LuatVietnam). https://english.luatvietnam.vn/tai-chinh/circular-33-2024-tt-nhnn-c-359766-d1.html. Accessed 20 Mar 2025

The English translation of Circular No. 36/2024/TT-NHNN of Vietnam (trans: Thuvienphapluat). https://thuvienphapluat.vn/van-ban/Tien-te-Ngan-hang/Circular-36-2024-TT-NHNN-prescribing-classification-of-assets-of-credit-institutions-that-are-cooperatives-622894.aspx?tab=1. Accessed 20 Mar 2025

The English translation of Circular No. 42/2011/TT-NHNN of Vietnam (trans: Thuvienphapluat). https://thuvienphapluat.vn/van-ban/Tien-te-Ngan-hang/Circular-No-42-2011-TT-NHNN-providing-for-the-provision-of-syndicated-loans-by-135565.aspx?tab=1. Accessed 20 Mar 2025

The English translation of Decision No. 03/2011/QD-TTg of Vietnam (trans: Thuvienphapluat). https://thuvienphapluat.vn/van-ban/EN/Doanh-nghiep/Decision-No-03-2011-QD-TTg-promulgating-the-regulation-on-guaranteeing-loans/169119/tieng-anh.aspx. Accessed 20 Mar 2025

The English translation of Decision No. 20/2017/QD-TTg of Vietnam (trans: Luatvietnam.vn). https://english.luatvietnam.vn/decision-no-20-2017-qd-ttg-dated-june-12-2017-of-the-prime-minister-on-regulating-operations-of-microfinance-programs-and-projects-of-political-orga-114982-doc1.html. Accessed 20 Mar 2025

The English translation of Decree No. 21/2021/ND-CP of Vietnam (trans: Thuvienphapluat). https://thuvienphapluat.vn/van-ban/Quyen-dan-su/Decree-21-2021-ND-CP-elaborating-regarding-security-for-fulfillment-of-obligations-473188.aspx?tab=1. Accessed 20 Mar 2025

The English translation of Decree No. 34/2015/ND-CP of Vietnam (trans: Thuvienphapluat). https://thuvienphapluat.vn/van-ban/EN/Doanh-nghiep/Decree-No-34-2015-ND-CP-amendments-Decree-No-53-2013-ND-CP/272754/tieng-anh.aspx. Accessed 20 Mar 2025

The English translation of Decree No. 39/2014/ND-CP of Vietnam (trans: Thuvienphapluat). https://thuvienphapluat.vn/van-ban/Doanh-nghiep/Decree-No-39-2014-ND-CP-on-operation-of-financial-company-financial-leasing-company-229081.aspx?tab=1. Accessed 20 Mar 2025

The English translation of Decree 39/2019/ND-CP of Vietnam (trans: Thuvienphapluat). https://thuvienphapluat.vn/van-ban/Doanh-nghiep/Decree-39-2019-ND-CP-Organization-and-Operation-of-Small-and-Medium-Enterprise-Development-Fund-417435.aspx?tab=1. Accessed 20 Mar 2025

The English translation of Decree No. 53/2013/ND-CP of Vietnam (trans: Thuvienphapluat), https://thuvienphapluat.vn/van-ban/EN/Doanh-nghiep/Decree-No-53-2013-ND-CP-on-establishment-organization-and-operation-of-Vietnam/189128/tieng-anh.aspx. Accessed 20 Mar 2025
The English translation of Decree No. 58/2021/ND-CP of Vietnam (trans: Thuvienphapluat). https://thuvienphapluat.vn/van-ban/Doanh-nghiep/Decree-58-2021-ND-CP-provision-of-credit-information-service-479190.aspx?tab=1. Accessed 20 Mar 2025
The English translation of Decree No. 86/2024/ND-CP of Vietnam (trans: Thuvienphapluat). https://thuvienphapluat.vn/van-ban/Tien-te-Ngan-hang/Decree-86-2024-ND-CP-amounts-of-establishing-risk-provisions-from-operations-of-credit-institutions-618065.aspx?tab=1. Accessed 20 Mar 202s
The English translation of Decree No. 88/2014/ND-CP of Vietnam (trans: Thuvienphapluat). https://thuvienphapluat.vn/van-ban/EN/Doanh-nghiep/Decree-No-88-2014-ND-CP-on-credit-rating-services/271887/tieng-anh.aspx. Accessed 20 Mar 2025
The English translation of Decree No. 99/2022/ND-CP of Vietnam (trans: Thuvienphapluat). https://thuvienphapluat.vn/van-ban/Quyen-dan-su/Decree-99-2022-ND-CP-registration-of-security-interests-547660.aspx?tab=1. Accessed 20 Mar 2025
The English translation of Decree No. 102/2017/ND-CP of Vietnam (trans: Thuvienphapluat). https://thuvienphapluat.vn/van-ban/Quyen-dan-su/Decree-102-2017-ND-CP-on-registration-of-security-interests-362321.aspx?tab=1. Accessed 20 Mar 2025
The English translation of Decree No. 117/2018/ND-CP (trans: Thuvienphapluat). https://thuvienphapluat.vn/van-ban/Tien-te-Ngan-hang/Decree-117-2018-ND-CP-protection-confidentiality-provision-of-client-information-of-credit-institutions-396521.aspx?tab=1. Accessed 20 Mar 2025
The English translation of Decree No. 129/2020/ND-CP of Vietnam (trans: Thuvienphapluat). https://thuvienphapluat.vn/van-ban/EN/So-huu-tri-tue/Decree-129-2021-ND-CP-amendments-Decrees-penalties-for-violations-against-on-tourism/501618/tieng-anh.aspx. Accessed 20 Mar 2025
The English translation of Lease Accounting Standard No. 6 under Decision No.165/2002/QD-BTC of Vietnam (trans: Thuvienphapluat). https://thuvienphapluat.vn/van-ban/Ke-toan-Kiem-toan/Decision-No-165-2002-QD-BTC-of-December-31-2002-promulgating-and-publicizing-six-06-Vietnamese-accounting-standards-phase-2-74819.aspx?tab=1. Accessed 20 Mar 2025
The English translation of Resolution No. 30/2008/NQ-CP of Vietnam (trans: Thuvienphapluat). https://thuvienphapluat.vn/van-ban/EN/Bo-may-hanh-chinh/Resolution-No-30-2008-NQ-CP-of-December-11-2008-on-urgent-measures-to-curb-economic-decline-maintain-economic-growth-and-ensure-social-welfare/87044/tieng-anh.aspx. Accessed 20 Mar 2025
The English translation of Vietnam's Civil Code 2015 (translated by Thuvienphapluat). https://thuvienphapluat.vn/van-ban/Quyen-dan-su/Law-No-91-2015-QH13-The-Civil-Code-303230.aspx?tab=1. Accessed 20 Mar 2025
The English translation of Vietnam's Law on Anti-Money Laundering 2022 (trans: Thuvienphapluat). https://thuvienphapluat.vn/van-ban/EN/Tien-te-Ngan-hang/Law-14-2022-QH15-Anti-Money-Laundering/547270/tieng-anh.aspx. Accessed 20 Mar 2025
The English translation of Vietnam's Law on Credit Institutions 2024 (trans: Thuvienphap luat). https://thuvienphapluat.vn/van-ban/Tien-te-Ngan-hang/Law-32-2024-QH15-Credit-institutions-606780.aspx?tab=1. Accessed 20 Mar 2025
The English translation of Vietnam's Law on Insurance Business 2022 (trans: Thuvienphap luat). https://thuvienphapluat.vn/van-ban/EN/Doanh-nghiep/Law-08-2022-QH15-insurance-business/524310/tieng-anh.aspx. Accessed 20 Mar 2025
The State Bank of Vietnam (2022) CIC tổng kết hoạt động thông tin tín dụng năm 2022 [CIC provided a summary of its credit information activities in 2022]. https://sbv.gov.vn/webcenter/portal/vi/menu/trangchu/ttsk/ttsk_chitiet?leftWidth=20%25&showFooter=false&

showHeader=false&dDocName=SBV551639&rightWidth=0%25&centerWidth=80%25&_afrLoop=25668660884520023#%40%3F_afrLoop%3D25668660884520023%26centerWidth%3D80%2525%26dDocName%3DSBV551639%26leftWidth%3D20%2525%26rightWidth%3D0%2525%26showFooter%3Dfalse%26showHeader%3Dfalse%26_adf.ctrl-state%3D1b0twxkib_9. Accessed 20 Mar 2025

The State Bank of Vietnam (2025) History of the State Bank of Vietnam, https://www.sbv.gov.vn/webcenter/portal/en/home/sbv/aboutsbv/history?_afrLoop=2315138924685822 4#%40%3F_afrLoop%3D23151389246858224%26centerWidth%3D80%2525%26leftWidth%3D20%2525%26rightWidth%3D0%2525%26showFooter%3Dfalse%26showHeader%3Dfalse%26_adf.ctrl-state%3Dxnhc3z5ed_4. Accessed 20 Mar 2025

The State Bank of Vietnam (2023) Tăng cường tài chính số, thúc đẩy tài chính toàn diện cho các nhóm yếu thế tại Việt Nam [Fostering digital finance, promoting financial inclusion for disadvantaged groups in Vietnam]. https://www.sbv.gov.vn/webcenter/portal/vi/menu/trangchu/ttsk/ttsk_chitiet?leftWidth=20%25&showFooter=false&showHeader=false&dDocName=SBV569253&rightWidth=0%25&centerWidth=80%25&_afrLoop=22198629760615466#%40%3F_afrLoop%3D22198629760615466%26centerWidth%3D80%2525%26dDocName%3DSBV569253%26leftWidth%3D20%2525%26rightWidth%3D0%2525%26showFooter%3Dfalse%26showHeader%3Dfalse%26_adf.ctrl-state%3Da7ygnorl2_14. Accessed 20 Mar 2025

Thomas L, Crook J, Edelman D (2017) Credit scoring and its applications, 2nd edn. Society for Industrial and Applied Mathematics, Philadelphia

VDB (2023) Credit guarantee operation of VDB. https://wqw.vdb.gov.vn/ThongTinKH.aspx?ID=20. Accessed 10 Jul 2023

Vietnam Credit Information Joint Stock Company (2025) Quá trình phát triển [Development process]. https://www.pcb.vn/gioi-thieu/gioi-thieu-pcb/qua-trinh-phat-trien.html. Accessed 20 Mar 2025

Vietnam Microfinance Working Group (2018) Sản phẩm dịch vụ tài chính vi mô: thực trạng và giải pháp phát triển [Microfinance products and services: Current state and development solution]. http://vietedmfi.com.vn/wp-content/uploads/2018/03/VMFWG_Bao-cao-nghien-cuu-Phat-trien-san-pham-va-dich-vu-TCVM.pdf. Accessed 20 Mar 2025

VIS Rating (2025) Rating results. https://visrating.com/rating-results. Accessed 20 Mar 2025

Vương ĐHQ, Nguyễn TQ (2016) Vai trò internet banking và bài học kinh nghiệm cho ngân hàng thương mại Việt Nam [The role of Internet banking and lessons from experience for commercial banks in Vietnam]. Van Hien Univ J Sci 10: 42-45

Yoshino N, Hesary FT (2016) Optimal credit guarantee ratio for Asia. https://www.adb.org/publications/optimal-credit-guarantee-ratio-asia. Accessed 20 Mar 2025

# Chapter 5
# Vietnam's Traditional Risk Diversification Tools Compared to the Ones in the United States and Japan

## 5.1 Micro- and/or Small-Sized Financing Schemes in the United States and Japan

### *5.1.1 The United States*

It can be seen that, in comparison with the micro- and/or small-sized finance market in Vietnam, the US market has a very long history, with extensive and diverse financing schemes. It has been noted that lending within the circle of family and friends or person-to-person lending has existed for a long time,[1] while the modern system of micro- and/or small-sized financing schemes has its roots in the nineteenth century.[2] It is worth noting that, from the supply side, micro- and/or small-sized finance can be provided by financial institutions such as conventional banks, finance companies, leasing companies, and credit unions, supported by the federal and local governments, and funded by informal providers such as family and friends, pawn shops, and private lenders.[3]

It is widely known that one of the most common sources of small funds for households and small firms is commercial banks.[4] The United States has a dual banking system that consists of federally chartered and state-chartered commercial banks. "National banks are chartered and regulated under federal law and supervised by federal agencies,"[5] while "state banks are chartered and regulated under state laws and supervised by their respective states' banking departments."[6] Commercial banks

[1] See (2001, p. 27).

[2] See Calder (1999, p. 14) and Mason (2004, p. 2).

[3] See Kapoor et al. (2019, p. 175), Kiisel (2013), Vance (2005, p. 4) and Mylenbusch (1999, p. 1).

[4] See Sherman (2012, p. 135), Burk and Lehmann (2006, p. 72), Vinturella and Erickson (2013, p. 42) and Constand et al. (1991, p. 29).

[5] See Malloy and Lovett (2019, p. 11).

[6] See Malloy and Lovett (2019, p. 9).



Y. H. Nguyen, *Regulating Peer-to-Peer Lending in Vietnam*,
https://doi.org/10.1007/978-981-96-9505-8_5

accept deposits from depositors and use these funds to offer loans to individuals and businesses.[7] They provide loans through several financing schemes as follows.

Firstly, commercial banks provide loans to borrowers through lending agreements for consumer and business purposes. These loans have different durations, which are classified as short, intermediate, and long terms, and can be secured or unsecured. Various repayment methods can be applied for these loans, including installment, single payment, and discount. Installment loans, which have a fixed interest rate and a specific due date, require borrowers to make fixed monthly payments that include interest and a portion of the principal amount.[8] Single-payment loans allow borrowers to borrow a specific amount of money for a predetermined duration and repay the principal amount, along with the accompanying interest, in a single lump sum at the end of the loan term. The interest rates for these loans can be fixed or adjustable, the latter of which is typically tied to the prime rate of commercial banks.[9] With discount loans, borrowers receive an amount of money that has already been reduced by the interest charged by commercial banks. In other words, the total interest due over the loan term is deducted from the principal amount before the loan is disbursed to the borrower.[10]

In addition to providing loans through lending agreements, commercial banks also offer individuals and businesses lines of credit or credit cards. Lines of credit or credit cards have been considered flexible sources of credit that allow borrowers to access loans at their convenience, up to the maximum limit determined by commercial banks, without having to re-apply for loans each time.[11] Borrowers are required to repay the full amount of their loans by the due date to avoid paying any interest. If they fail to do so, they will be charged the predetermined interest rates on the remaining debt until the full amount is paid off.[12] To obtain a line of credit or credit card, borrowers should have an established credit history, stable income, and a residential address, or hold savings accounts with commercial banks.[13] Having a good track record of credit repayment, stable employment, sufficient income, and a high spending capacity may increase the likelihood of customers being eligible for luxury cards such as Gold, Titanium, and Black cards. Holders of these luxury cards can access a wide range of premium services.[14]

The provision of home equity loans by commercial banks is another financing scheme. This financing scheme allows homeowners to borrow against the accumulated equity in their homes, which is the market value of the home minus any outstanding debt against it. A home equity loan can be structured as a fixed-term

---

[7] See Vinturella and Erickson (2013, p. 51).

[8] See Mylenbusch (1999, p. 3) and Billingsley et al. (2013, p. 271).

[9] Mylenbusch (1999, p. 3) and Billingsley et al. (2013, p. 271).

[10] See Gallagher and Andrew (2007, p. 568).

[11] See Mylenbusch (1999, p. 34), Brigham and Houston (2015, p. 564).

[12] Mylenbusch (1999, p. 34), Brigham and Houston (2015, p. 564).

[13] See Mylenbusch (1999, p. 83).

[14] See Creditcards (2025) and DeMatteo (2021).

installment loan or a line of credit, and the interest on these loans is tax-deductible. Borrowers are required to secure the loan with their home as a second mortgage.[15]

It is worth noting that commercial banks are extensively regulated under federal and state laws. They fall under the supervision and regulation of their chartering authority, at either the federal or state level.[16] Commercial banks are required to comply with various requirements, such as minimum capital requirements, capital adequacy ratios, lending limits, and reserve requirements, under the National Bank Act of 1864 and the Dodd-Frank Act (2010, as amended). They are also required to perform due diligence and fulfill other obligations[17] under the PATRIOT Act of 2001 to ensure their safety and soundness and protect their consumers.[18] Notably, commercial banks are subject to usury laws, which are largely enforced at the state level. In specific, the interest rate charged by a national commercial bank[19] may not exceed

> the rate permitted by the state in which the bank is located or 1% above the discount rate on 90-day commercial paper in effect in the bank's Federal Reserve district. If the state where the bank is located does not prohibit usurious interest, the bank may not charge interest exceeding the greater of 7% or 1% above the discount rate on 90-day commercial paper in effect in the bank's Federal Reserve district.[20]

As for state-chartered banks, they are permitted to charge the same interest rate as national banks.[21]

It is well-documented that thrift institutions, including mutual savings banks, savings and loan associations, and credit unions, serve as another source of small loans for borrowers.[22] Mutual savings banks, which originated in 1816 with the aim of assisting the poor in saving for the future, have been considered the first thrift institutions to flourish.[23] Savings and loan associations were introduced in the United States in 1831 as a means to assist working-class individuals in meeting their consumer finance needs and achieving homeownership.[24] Credit unions were first established in 1909 to cater to the need for small funds of their members.[25] Thrift institutions offer small loans through several financing schemes as follows.

---

[15] See Gup (2011, p. 164) and Mylenbusch (1999, p. 57).

[16] See Malloy and Lovett (2019) and Baker McKenzie (2024, p. 6).

[17] Such as establishing a customer identification program and a risk-based system of internal control and complying with disclosure requirements and privacy safeguards for borrowers and depositors. See Malloy and Lovett (2019, p. 143) and Sahni and Byrne (2020, p. 290).

[18] See Office of the Comptroller of the Currency (2025a).

[19] It should be noted that the interest charged by commercial banks may also include overdrafts and late fees.

[20] See Onda (2013, p. 533) and Pistrang, Barker and Humphreys (2008, p. 110).

[21] Florack et al. (2022, p. 14).

[22] See Malloy and Lovett (2019, p. 287).

[23] Malloy and Lovett (2019, p. 299).

[24] Malloy and Lovett (2019, p. 301).

[25] Malloy and Lovett (2019, p. 335).

The first financing scheme involves mutual savings banks providing loans to their members through loan agreements. These banks accept regular savings from their members and offer short-term loans without requiring collateral, as well as long-term mortgage loans. In addition to providing loans, these banks use savings contributions from their members to invest in low-risk and highly liquid assets such as public bonds and private securities. The interest earned from these investments is then credited to their members' accounts.[26] Currently, mutual savings banks are subject to requirements that are similar to those applied to conventional banks under Chap. 19, Title 12 of the United States Code.[27]

It is important to note that savings and loan associations operate as a self-help financing scheme. These associations primarily accept initial deposits and regular savings contributions from their members. They can also borrow loans from other financial institutions.[28] Savings and loan associations offer loans and bank-type credit cards to their members, provided they have sufficient collateral.[29] It has been noted that members of savings and loan associations are mostly working-class individuals residing in small communities.[30] Currently, savings and loan associations are required to comply with reserve requirements, capital adequacy ratios, and lending limits in order to ensure the safety of their operation in accordance with Chap. 12 and Chap. 19, Title 12 of the United States Code.[31]

Another financing scheme involves credit unions providing loans to their members. Credit unions primarily accept initial deposits and regular savings to promote thrift among their members. Credit unions typically offer small, uncollateralized personal loans with low interest rates and issue bank-type credit cards to their members.[32] It has been noted that membership in a credit union is usually limited to individuals within the same group, such as employees of a company or individuals within a well-defined neighborhood, community, or rural area. Social pressure among credit union members can serve as collateral for their loans. Federally chartered credit unions are regulated by the Federal Credit Union Act (1934, as amended).[33] They are required to comply with requirements for lending limits, interest rate caps, and credit insurance to ensure the safety and soundness of their operation.[34]

In addition to commercial banks and thrift institutions, finance companies also serve as a source of small funds for individuals and businesses. It is worth noting

---

[26] See Mason (2004, p. 17), Malloy and Lovett (2019, p. 294) and Barth et al. (2010, p. 116).

[27] See Malloy and Lovett (2019, p. 299) and the United States Code, Title 12.

[28] See Mason (2004), Malloy and Lovett (2019, p. 301) and Barth et al. (2010).

[29] Durkin et al. (2014, p. 70).

[30] See Mason (2004, p. 266).

[31] See the United States Code.

[32] See US. Bureau of Federal Credit Unions (1957, p. 1), Malloy and Lovett (2019) and Durkin et al. (2014).

[33] See the United States Code, Title 12, Chapter 14.

[34] See National Credit Union Administration.

that, unlike commercial banks and thrift institutions, finance companies neither take deposits nor accept savings from their customers. Instead, they obtain funds from other sources such as bank loans and by issuing corporate bonds and commercial papers.[35] Finance companies provide individuals with various types of loans, including consumer loans and student loans, and also offer lines of credit or credit cards.[36] It has been observed that finance companies may approve smaller loans compared to commercial banks, but they typically charge higher interest rates. Borrowers with a low credit score or no credit history and no collateral are likely to be subject to very high interest rates. However, if borrowers have collateral to secure their loans, they may have the opportunity to negotiate the interest rates with finance companies.[37] The regulations governing the operation of finance companies are primarily embodied in federal and state statutes. Finance companies are subject to provisions on interest rates, service fees, information disclosure, and consumer protection in lending transactions under the Truth in Lending Act (1968, as amended), the Fair Credit Billing Act (1975, as amended), the Equal Credit Opportunity Act (1974, as amended), and the Fair Credit Debt Collection Act (1977, as amended).

It should be noted that leasing companies can be a source of funds for small firms.[38] Leasing companies mobilize capital from several sources such as bank loans and by issuing corporate bonds. As lessors, they provide customers, known as lessees, with capital leases for purchasing fixed assets, equipment, or machinery. The lessees then lease these assets from the lessors and pay monthly leasing fees. The lease terms can be medium term (from one year to three years in length) or longer term (more than three years in length). At the end of the lease term, the lessees have the option to acquire ownership of the assets at a percentage of the original price or for a nominal amount.[39]

It has been noted that life insurance companies also serve as a source of small funds for individuals who have a whole life insurance policy. These companies

[35] See Mylenbusch (1999, p. 29), Reinhard (2010, p. 23) and Durkin et al. (2014, p. 174).

[36] See Federation of American Scientists (2021, p. 1).

[37] See Sherman (2012, p. 10), Mylenbusch (1999, p. 29), Reinhard (2010) and Durkin et al. (2014, p. 178).

[38] It should be noted that according to Generally Accepted Accounting Principles No. 13, which were published by the Financial Accounting Standards Board (FASB) and took effect as of January 1, 1977, a capital lease must meet any one of the following conditions: (1) ownership of the asset is transferred to the lessee by the end of the lease term; (2) the lease contains an option to purchase the asset at the end of the lease at a percentage of the original price or for a nominal amount; (3) the term of the lease is equal to or greater than 75% of the useful life of the asset; and (4) the present value of the lease payments is equal to or greater than 90% of the fair market value of the asset. FASB is an independent, private-sector, not-for-profit organization that establishes financial accounting and reporting standards for public and private companies and not-for-profit organizations within the United States in the public's interest. The organization was established in 1973, and it is recognized by the United States Securities and Exchange Commission as the designated accounting standard setter for public companies. See Financial Accounting Standards Board (2025).

[39] See Vance (2005, p. 28) and Sherman (2012, p. 134).

allow policyholders to borrow against the accumulated cash value of their insurance policies. The cash value of insurance policies represents the amount that borrowers could receive if they decide to cash in their policies. The interest rates charged by insurance companies for these loans are typically lower than those charged by commercial banks or other financial institutions. Borrowers are required to make payments that include both the principal amount and accompanying interest in accordance with their policy's terms. If they fail to repay the loans, their debts are likely to be deducted from the policy's death benefit upon the borrowers' passing.[40] In the United States, insurance companies obtain their charter from a specific state. Their business operations are regulated individually in each state, and the regulations governing their operations vary from state to state.[41]

Furthermore, loan programs offered by the Small Business Administration (SBA), a federal agency established in 1953, can serve as a source of funding for small businesses. It should be noted that the SBA does not directly provide loans to small businesses. Instead, it provides loan guarantees of up to 85% for businesses seeking loans from SBA lenders, including approved financial institutions and designated lenders.[42] It has been noted that loan guarantees provided by the SBA help to reduce the risk for SBA lenders, which makes it feasible for them to provide loans to start-ups and small firms. In the event of borrower default, SBA lenders are required to make efforts to pursue loan repayment before requesting reimbursement from the SBA. If the default rate of an SBA lender becomes too high, their participation in SBA's loan programs is likely to be discontinued.[43]

It is important to note that SBA loan lenders are divided into three categories, including general, certified, and preferred lenders. General lenders are those with limited experience in providing SBA loans. They are required to submit the information of all loan applicants to the national SBA office for approval before disbursing loans. This process can take several weeks or even months. Certified lenders are those who have experience in providing SBA loans and meet certain requirements for each loan program. They receive a partial delegation of lending authority and are given several days for the turnaround on their applications. Preferred lenders, on the other hand, are chosen from among the best SBA lenders. They can enjoy full authority in making lending decisions, albeit with a lower guarantee rate. The SBA periodically examines their portfolios, and their full authority in making lending decisions is reviewed at least every two years.[44]

It can be seen that the SBA offers several loan programs. These loan programs include the general small business loan program (hereinafter referred to as "7(a) loan program"), microloan program, and real estate and equipment loan program

[40] See Mylenbusch (1999, p. 31) and Burk and Lehmann (2006, p. 78).

[41] See the United States Code, Title 15, Chapter 93.

[42] See the United States Small Business Administration (2025c), Green (2011, p. 1) and Primm and Roncevich (2009, p. 1).

[43] See Rogers (2020, p. 201).

[44] Rogers (2020, p. 202).

(hereinafter referred to as "504 loan program"). It has been noted that depending on the loan program, the SBA may charge SBA lenders a fee from 3% to 3.5% of the loan, which is usually passed on to the borrowers.[45]

It is worth noting that the 7(a) loan program is documented as the most common loan program offered by the SBA, providing bank loans of up to US$ 5 million. The SBA guarantees 85% of loans up to US$ 150,000 and 75% for loans above US$ 150,000. These loans can be used for several purposes, such as purchasing real estate, business equipment and machinery, refinancing existing debt, construction financing, and working capital. While lenders and borrowers have the flexibility to negotiate the interest rate, it must not exceed the interest rate cap set by the SBA. Additionally, lenders must secure collateral when issuing loans exceeding US$ 25,000.[46]

The microloan program provides small and short-term loans to small businesses and certain types of not-for-profit childcare centers. Nonprofit community-based lenders with one year or more of experience in lending and providing training and technical assistance for borrowers can apply to become SBA lenders of micro loans. Eligible lenders will be evaluated and scored based on the documents they submit. Once selected, an SBA lender may borrow a maximum of US$ 750,000 from the SBA during its first year in the microloan program. From the second year of participating in the program, an SBA lender may borrow up to US$ 1.25 million per loan, provided its total program debt does not exceed US$ 5 million at any given time. SBA lenders then provide loans to eligible borrowers in amounts of up to a maximum of US$ 50,000, with a minimum duration of 1 year and a maximum duration of 6 years. Microloans can be used for several purposes, such as working capital, inventory or supplies, furniture or fixtures, machinery or equipment. However, they are ineligible for settling existing debts or acquiring real estate. Interest rates on these loans generally range between 8% and 13%, depending on the SBA lender. It can be noted that the SBA does not review, underwrite, or have the authority to approve or deny microloans.[47]

The 504 loan program provides small businesses with long-term, fixed-rate loans. These loans can be used to purchase major fixed assets such as equipment or real estate for the expansion or modernization of their operations. The loans are made available through Certified Development Companies (CDCs), SBA's community-based partners who regulate nonprofits and promote economic development within their communities. The SBA authorizes CDCs to provide loans to small businesses with the help of third-party lenders (usually banks). For one project of a borrower, a CDC typically finances 40% of the total project costs, a participating lender covers up to 50% of the total project costs, and the borrower contributes the remaining portion of the project costs. Under this loan program, a business must have a tangible net worth not exceeding US$ 15 million and an average net income of US$ 5 million

[45] See the United States Small Business Administration (2025d) and Rogers (2020, p. 202).

[46] The United States Small Business Administration (2025a) and Rogers (2020, p. 203).

[47] See the United States Small Business Administration (2025e).

or less after federal income taxes for the two years preceding the loan application. The maximum amount of a 504 loan is US$ 5 million, and the loan maturity can range from 10 to 20 years. The project assets being financed are used as collateral, and personal guarantees from the owners holding 20% or more ownership are also required.[48]

In the informal micro- and/or small-sized finance sector, capital from family and friends has long been considered a source of small funding for individuals and small firms. This financing scheme allows borrowers to obtain small loans with flexible terms. However, it is important to note that these funds are likely to be very limited.[49]

It has been documented that since the nineteenth century, pawnbrokers have served as a source of capital for low- and moderate-income households. Pawnbrokers offer small, single-payment loans through pawn agreements. Borrowers pawn personal property such as jewelry, musical instruments, electric equipment, or other valuable items as collateral. Pawnbrokers inspect and appraise the value of these items to determine the loan amount. It has been noted that borrowers typically receive loan amounts that are approximately one-third or less of the value of the pawned items. This discrepancy in loan amounts can be attributed to several reasons. For example, pawn loans are likely to be small in size but require the same amount of time and effort to process as larger loans. As a result, pawnbrokers tend to charge high interest rates to generate a favorable return. Additionally, since pawnbrokers take physical possession of the collateral, they bear the responsibility of safeguarding the pawned items and assuming liability for any potential damage or loss. They also must possess knowledge about various items such as jewelry, appliances, equipment, and similar items. This knowledge is essential for accurately assessing the market value of pawned items, identifying potential defects, and distinguishing between genuine items and counterfeits. If borrowers fail to repay the principal amount and the associated interest within a specific time frame, pawnbrokers can sell the pawned items. The operations of pawnbrokers are governed by state regulations.[50]

Since the late nineteenth century, retail consumer lenders (particularly department stores), vendors, and suppliers have offered households and businesses small funds. It has been noted that the practice of door-to-door sales on installment terms, conducted by peddlers hired by large retail stores, attracted households to the realm of department store shopping.[51] The installment payment method gained popularity, particularly among immigrant families who desired goods but lacked the means to pay in cash up-front. Phrases like 'Buy Now, Pay Later' and 'Take Advantage of Our Easy Payment Plan' became prevalent among American

[48] See The United States Small Business Administration (2025b).

[49] See Vance (2005, p. 20) and Rogers (2020, p. 194).

[50] See Durkin et al. (2014, p. 354), Kapoor et al. (2019, p. 162) and Calder (1999, p. 49).

[51] Calder (1999, p. 55).

consumers, as consumer services were promoted.[52] Some major stores have acted as finance companies by offering consumer credit, especially through the issuance of charge cards, to stimulate sales. Cardholders would be granted an unsecured line of credit with a fixed loan amount.[53] It is worth noting that, similar to department stores, vendors and suppliers may also extend favorable trade credit or even provide direct funds to their customers.[54] Loans can be repaid in installments or one lump sum, as agreed upon by the parties involved. It is important to note that timely repayment allows customers to establish a credit history, which can be utilized to access additional trade credit or even secure bank loans.[55]

Furthermore, it is worth noting that customers of start-ups or small firms can serve as a source of capital. Firms can encourage their customers to pay bills in advance. Alternatively, they can negotiate installment payments with customers and request partial payment in advance for their large projects. In some cases, customers of a growing company who rely on the company as a vital resource supplier may choose to finance the development of a specific product in exchange for exclusive distribution rights of the finished product.[56]

It is important to note that in the middle of the nineteenth century, private moneylenders emerged, offering small loans to individuals to make profits. They primarily targeted poor and low-income individuals who faced difficulties in accessing small funds from other sources. It has been noted that due to the high risk and low profitability of lending to poor and low-income individuals, private moneylenders accepted assignments of borrower's wages as collateral and charged high interest rates.[57] Alongside the development of installment credit, loans provided by private moneylenders became a prevalent source of small funds for poor and low-income individuals or those who had fallen behind on their retail installment payments.[58]

It should be noted that since the early 1980s, private moneylenders have introduced payday loans. These loans are typically small in size (US$ 1000 or less), short-term, and require a single payment. It has been noted that payday loans are designed to be repaid on the borrowers' next payday and are offered through physical stores or online websites, depending on state licensing requirements. Targeted borrowers are those who lack credit cards, have low credit scores, no credit history, or who have reached their credit limits. When applying for payday loans, borrowers are generally required to provide their most recent bank statements, pay stubs, and sometimes proof of residence to verify their income and bank accounts. At the time of receiving the loans, borrowers are required to write a personal check for the loan amount plus

---

[52] Calder (1999, p. 20).

[53] See Mylenbusch (1999, p. 35).

[54] See Sherman (2012, p. 11) and Vinturella and Erickson (2013, p. 42).

[55] See Vance (2005, p. 27).

[56] See Sherman (2012, p. 11).

[57] See Calder (1999, p. 50).

[58] Calder (1999, p. 55).

service fees and leave it with the lenders. The lenders agree to delay the presentment of the check for a specific period. Payday loans may carry high interest rates due to implicit additional fees, which make it difficult for borrowers to pay off their debts. Regulations governing payday loans vary widely among different states in the United States. Some states prohibit these loans, while others still permit them.[59]

It is well documented that since the change of the Acceptable Use Policy (AUP)[60] in 1993, the use of the Internet for commercial purposes has experienced significant growth in the United States.[61] Both the supply and demand sides of small funds have used the Internet as a means to establish connections between them. On the demand side, individuals and corporations have increasingly turned to online services for electronic commerce, electronic banking, and electronic collaboration.[62] Meanwhile, on the supply side, conventional banks and other financial institutions have gradually established informational websites and expanded their online banking services,[63] thereby offering a completely different banking delivery model to their customers. This model of banking delivery enables customers to access their accounts and conduct banking transactions at their convenience, as long as they have access to the Internet.[64] Conventional banks and other financial institutions have made efforts to ensure a secure environment for both depositors and borrowers, enabling them to adapt to the new form of banking service.[65]

It is crucial to note that despite the presence of diverse micro- and/or small-sized financing schemes in the United States to provide small loans, a credit gap is likely to persist.[66] From the demand side, some small businesses may find it difficult to access loans provided by financial institutions. This has been attributed to several factors, such as poor credit ratings, unproven track records, or the absence of collateral. It has been noted that the rejection rates for SME loans, which represent the percentage of rejected loan applications compared to the total number of requested SME loan applications, in 2021 and 2022 were 35.9% and 36.6%, respectively.[67] Some other small businesses can be compelled to rely on business credit cards, which can be more expensive than bank loans. However, it should be noted that not all business expenses can be paid using a credit card.[68]

---

[59] See Barr (2007, p. 324), Federation of American Scientists (2021, p. 22) and Consumer Federation of America (2025).

[60] Acceptable Use Policy (AUP) refers to a set of rules that define the rights and responsibilities of computer users and the owner, creator, or administrators of a network, website, or system. Before 1993, the Internet was mainly used for research and educational purposes. See Reilly (1997).

[61] See Seltzer (1995, p. 8), Klotz (2003, p. 11) and Fabrizio and Mowery (2007, p. 308).

[62] Schutzer (1998, p. 169).

[63] See Humphreys (1998, p. 75).

[64] Humphreys (1998, p. 77).

[65] Humphreys (1998, p. 82).

[66] See Mills (2018, p. 40), Nieri (2007, p. 108) and the Federal Reserve System (2019, p. 2).

[67] OECD (2024, p. 225).

[68] See Mills (2018, p. 57).

In addition, unbanked[69] or underbanked[70] individuals have also faced challenges in accessing loans from financial institutions. The Report on the Economic Well-Being of the United States Households in 2018–May 2019, conducted by the Federal Reserve System, revealed that approximately 22% of US adults (about 63 million) fall into the category of being unbanked or underbanked. These individuals are more likely to have low incomes, less education, or belong to a racial or ethnic minority group.[71] It has been noted that unbanked individuals do not possess bank accounts and are more likely to rely on alternative financial services,[72] such as payday loans, money orders, or pawnshop loans, to meet their demand for small funds. Underbanked individuals, on the other hand, have some sort of bank account but lack access to or do not use financial services offered by financial institutions, including credit cards, personal checks, savings accounts, and loans. As a result, they are also likely to rely on alternative financial services. However, it is unlikely that payday loans or pawnshop loans will help borrowers build their credit history, as these loans are generally not reported to national credit reporting companies.[73]

With the advancement of technology and innovation, credit has become available online since 2006 through various online platform lending models.[74] These models include balance sheet lending, marketplace platform lending, and hybrid models.[75] The lending process in these models begins when potential borrowers submit a loan application to lending platforms.[76] Platform service providers then verify information provided by potential borrowers and assess their credit risk. Based on this credit

[69] Unbanked refers to adults who do not have a checking, savings, or money market account at an insured institution. See the Federal Reserve System (2019, p. 25) and Federal Deposit Insurance Corporation (2014, p. 4).

[70] Underbanked refers to adults who have a bank account but often rely on cash and financial services provided by non-bank or alternative financial service providers to manage their finances and fund purchases.

[71] See the Federal Reserve System (2019, p. 25).

[72] Alternative financial service is a term often used to describe the array of financial services offered by providers that operate outside of federally insured banks and credit unions, such as money order (not from a bank or credit union), check-cashing service (not at a bank or credit union), payday loan or paycheck advance, pawn shop or auto title loan, and tax refund advance. See the Federal Reserve System (2019, p. 27).

[73] See Birken (2020).

[74] See Kiisel (2013, p. 130), Mariotto (2016, p. 36), Warren (2016, p. 299).

[75] See Brummer (2020, p. 291) and Akihide and Stagars (2016, p. 31).

[76] It is worth noting that each borrower must disclose or make available to the lending platform, and through the platform to prospective lenders, certain financial and other information, including, among other items, the borrower's credit score (as determined by a credit reporting agency), self-reported income range, debt-to-income ratio, employment status, homeownership status, number of existing credit lines, intended use of funds, and number and/or amount of recent payment defaults and delinquencies. Borrowers may not, however, disclose their identities to prospective lenders or post information that would permit their identities to be determined. See Franson (2023, p. 167).

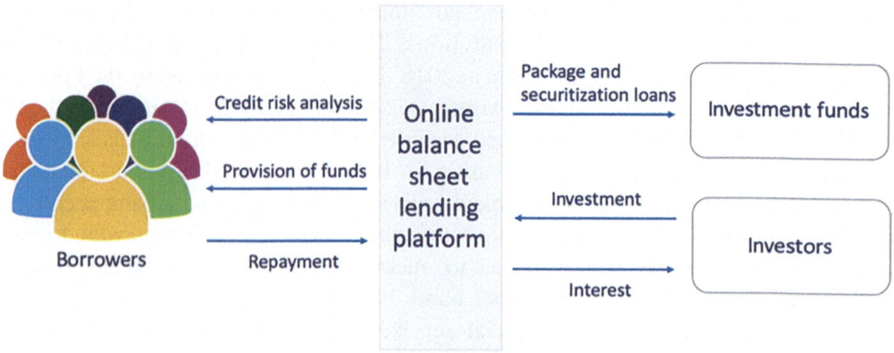


**Fig. 5.1** Online balance sheet lending scheme in the United States (See Working Group Committee on the Global Financial System and the Financial Stability Board (2017, p. 15) and Akihide and Stagars (2016, p. 35))

risk assessment, platform service providers make different decisions depending on the specific lending model.[77]

In the balance sheet lending scheme, platform service providers act as balance sheet lenders. They extend loans to borrowers based on the results of their credit risk evaluation process. However, it should be noted that platform service providers do not possess a banking license. They, therefore, are not allowed to directly accept deposits from investors. Instead, they may raise capital from institutional and private investors through revolving lines of credit and by packaging and securitizing loans for sale to investment funds and other accredited investors. The capital obtained from these investors is subsequently invested in the loans requested by the borrowers (see Fig. 5.1). In this lending model, platform service providers retain the loans on their books as part of their investment portfolios. They assume credit risk if borrowers fail to repay their loans. To mitigate their exposure to borrowers, platform service providers may match loans with short-term or long-term investments, depending on the loan terms. Some platform service providers also implement daily or weekly payment collection methods to monitor and track borrowers' performance.[78]

In the marketplace platform lending scheme, platform service providers match borrowers and lenders through their online lending platforms. If potential borrowers' loan requests meet the requirements of marketplace platforms, they will be posted on the platforms for investors to consider. These investors can include hedge funds, venture capital firms, depository institutions, and retail investors. The posting may include the interest rate,[79] the term of the loans, and the fact that the loans are unsecured. Investors have the flexibility to fund one or multiple loans that match

[77] See Brummer (2020, p. 290).

[78] See Akihide and Stagars (2016, p. 35) and Brummer (2020, p. 291).

[79] It is worth noting that in the early marketplace lending model, an auction marketplace was operated. In this auction marketplace, potential lenders had the opportunity to bid for loans and

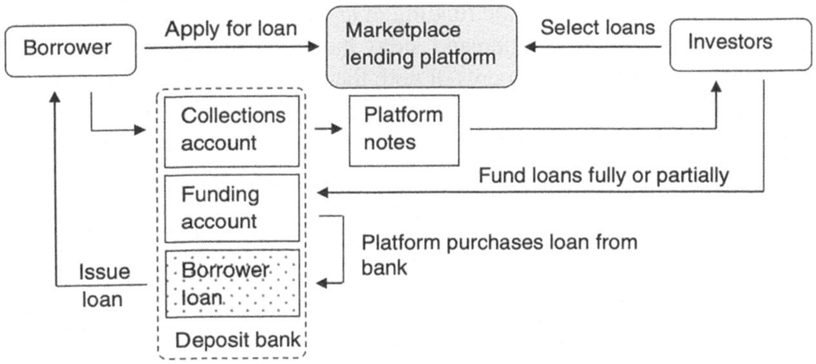


**Fig. 5.2** Marketplace lending scheme in the United States (Akihide and Stagars (2016, p. 33))

their risk appetite or return preference. Alternatively, they may simply determine the size and risk grade of each investment they want to allocate capital to and then await the matching process facilitated by platform service providers. They also have the option to fund an entire loan or a portion of it to manage default risk and diversify their investment portfolio.[80]

In this lending model, platform service providers facilitate money transfers and payment collections between lenders and borrowers. To accomplish this, they use a funding account and a collections account at an affiliated depository bank. The money provided by investor(s) for a loan is transferred to a funding account, while the loan repayments made by the borrower are directed to a collections account. Once the funding account reflects the specified amount from a borrower, the depository bank will grant the loan to the borrower. Simultaneously, the platform service provider purchases the loan from the depository bank at a nominal cost and accepts the loan assignment from the bank accordingly. Subsequently, the platform service provider issues the so-called platform notes to investors based on their funding commitment. Each note reflects a small fraction of the total loan amount. It should be noted that the notes that investors purchase from a lending platform are not secured by any collateral or guaranteed by a third party. The repayment for the platform notes is made by using money in a collections account, where the lending platform collects repayments from the borrower (see Fig. 5.2). It is clear that marketplace lending transactions involve two separate contractual relationships: one between the borrower and the platform in the form of an unsecured loan and the other between the platform and investor(s) in the form of unsecured notes and certificates.[81]

determine the interest rates they were willing to offer. However, in the present model, platform service providers set interest rates based on their evaluation of borrowers' credit risk.

[80] See Brummer (2020, p. 293).

[81] See Akihide and Stagars (2016, p. 33).

As online lending has grown, the funding of small loans has become increasingly complex. Both the supply and demand sides have adapted themselves to hybrid lending models that combine elements of both the balance sheet lending scheme and the marketplace platform lending scheme. For example, some balance sheet lending platforms have developed a business model in which lending platforms sell specific loans to institutional investors and make the loans off the balance.[82]

It should be noted that regulations governing micro- and/or small-sized finance have been incrementally adapted to accommodate the use of the Internet. In recent years, there has been increasing attention on the governance of online platform lending models. These lending models are regulated at both the federal and state levels. They are subject to a range of regulations governing micro- and/or small-sized finance both before and after the AUP in 1993. At present, online P2P lending in the United States is subject to a variety of applicable laws as follows.

State laws regulate licensing requirements for online P2P lending platforms. In the lending scheme shown in Fig. 5.1, where the platform offers consumer loans and does not operate through a funding bank, it is required to obtain a lending license in the state where it serves customers.[83] When a platform offers loans through a funding bank in the lending scheme shown in Fig. 5.2, it may be obligated to acquire state licenses for specific activities, such as loan origination, funding, purchasing, or servicing.[84] These licenses are granted on a state-by-state basis, and the specific requirements can vary accordingly.[85]

Additionally, state laws govern interest rates applicable to P2P loans. Regulations concerning permissible interest rates can vary significantly from state to state. Some states apply uniform laws[86] across all loan types, while others impose different interest rate caps on a range of loan types, such as business loans, education loans, and other loan categories.[87]

P2P lending platforms are required to comply with a number of different federal and state consumer protection laws aimed at promoting transparency, providing truthful information in the lending process, and protecting customers from unfair and abusive practices. These laws include:

---

[82] See Brummer (2020, p. 294).

[83] Brummer (2020, p. 303).

[84] See Franson (2023, p. 115).

[85] Franson (2023, p. 115).

[86] Uniform laws, commonly known as the Uniform Consumer Credit Code (UCCC), were approved by the National Conference of Commissioners on Uniform State Laws in 1968 and revised in 1974. The UCCC is not a federal or state law itself but serves as a model code that states can adopt to create consistent consumer credit laws. Currently, it has been adopted by 11 states to govern consumer credit transactions. The UCCC sets forth regulations concerning the issuance and use of various credit products, ranging from credit cards to mortgages. Its primary objective is to safeguard consumers from fraudulent and unfair lending practices. See Uniform Law Commission (2025b).

[87] See Brummer (2020, p. 297).

(a) the Truth in Lending Act of 1968[88] and its implementing Regulation, Regulation Z,[89] which were initially designed to safeguard consumers by ensuring transparency through disclosures. The Act and Regulation Z have been expanded to impose a wide range of requirements and restrictions on consumer credit.[90] Under these regulations, P2P lending platforms that regularly[91] extend consumer credit[92] are obligated "to provide borrowers with standardized and understandable information concerning terms and conditions of their loans."[93] Lending platforms must "disclose the cost of credit and associated fees, identify annual interest percentage rates, and list the payment schedule (and late fees)."[94] They also have to identify themselves or the entities that are providing credit to the borrowers,[95] as well as offer the borrowers the option to cancel certain types of loans within a specified period;[96]
(b) the Electronic Funds Transfer Act of 1978[97] and its implementing Regulation, Regulation E,[98] which established the fundamental rights and obligations of lending platforms and other parties that involve in electronic fund transfers.[99] These transfers involve the use of electronic terminals, telephones, computers, or magnetic tapes for the purpose of ordering, instructing, or authorizing a lending platform or financial institution to debit or credit a consumer's account.[100] Lending platforms are obligated to disclose specific pieces of information to consumers at the time of signing contracts for electronic fund transfer services or

---

[88] See the United States Code, Title 15, Chapter 41, Subchapter I.

[89] See the Code of Federal Regulations, Title 12, Chapter X, Part 1026.

[90] See The National Credit Union Administration (2021b).

[91] The Code of Federal Regulations, Title 12, Chapter II, Section 226.2(a)(17)(v) provides that: "A person regularly extends consumer credit only if it extends credit (other than credit subject to the requirements of § 226.32) more than 25 times (or more than 5 times for transactions secured by a dwelling) in the preceding calendar year. If a person did not meet these numerical standards in the preceding calendar year, the numerical standards shall be applied to the current calendar year."

[92] The Code of Federal Regulations, Title 12, Chapter II, Section 226.1(c)(1) provides four conditions for consumer credit, including: "(i) The credit is offered or extended to consumers; (ii) The offering or extension of credit is done regularly; (iii) The credit is subject to a finance charge or is payable by a written agreement in more than four installments; and (iv) The credit is primarily for personal, family, or household purposes."

[93] See Brummer (2020, p. 304) and Franson (2023, p. 133).

[94] See Brummer (2020, p. 304). For example, the Code of Federal Regulations, Title 12, subpart C contains rules on disclosures, treatment of credit balances, annual percentage rate calculations, rescission requirements, and advertising for closed-end (installment) loans.

[95] Brummer (2020, p. 304).

[96] For example, the Code of Federal Regulations, Title 12, subpart F provides that once a private education loan is offered and its terms have been adequately disclosed, the lender must allow the borrower 30 calendar days to decide whether to accept such loan.

[97] See The United States Code, Title 15, Chapter 41, Subchapter VI.

[98] See The Code of Federal Regulations, Title 12, Chapter X, Part 1005.

[99] See The Code of Federal Regulations, Title 12, Chapter X, Section 1005.1(b).

[100] See the Code of Federal Regulations, Title 12, Chapter X, Section 1005.3(b)(1).

prior to the first electronic fund transfer.[101] In addition, lending platforms and/or lenders are not allowed to "require a borrower to make payments by electronic means as a condition of obtaining a loan"[102];

(c) the Federal Trade Commission Act of 1914,[103] which was designed to promote fair competition among businesses and safeguard consumers from unfair or deceptive acts or practices in or affecting commerce. The Act has undergone multiple amendments, granting the Federal Trade Commission (FTC) greater authority to address emerging industries and adapt its mission accordingly.[104] Online lending platforms are obligated to comply with Section 5 of the Act,[105] which prohibits unfair or deceptive acts or practices in or affecting commerce. Notably, the Credit Practices Rule[106] was issued by the FTC to safeguard consumers from abusive terms and conditions in credit contracts. Under this Rule, lending platforms are prohibited from including unfavorable terms in loan agreements for borrowers;[107]

(d) the Dodd-Frank Act (2010, as amended),[108] which was designed to enhance consumer protection and increase transparency in the financial markets. The Act established the Consumer Financial Protection Bureau (CFPB) and authorized the CFPB to enact regulations prohibiting unfair, deceptive, and abusive acts or practices.[109] The CFPB has articulated certain standards to identify whether an act or practice is unfair, deceptive, or abusive.[110] Notably, the CFPB is empowered to impose significantly more substantial civil penalties compared

---

[101] See the Code of Federal Regulations, Title 12, Chapter X, Section 1005.7. The required disclosures include liability of lending platforms and consumers, telephone number and address of lending platform, business days of lending platform, types of transfers and limitations, fees, stop payment, confidentiality, error resolution, as applicable.

[102] Although they may provide an incentive for making payments electronically. See Franson (2023, p. 150).

[103] See the United States Code, Title 15, Chapter 2, Subchapter I.

[104] See Duignan (1914).

[105] See the United States Code, Title 15, Chapter 2, Subchapter I, Section 45.

[106] See the Code of Federal Regulations, Title 16, Chapter I, Subchapter D, Part 444.

[107] The Credit Practices Rule prohibits loan agreements from including terms that:

- Require the borrower to generally waive the right to notice and an opportunity to be heard in the event of a lawsuit (confession of judgment clauses)
- Require the borrower to waive the benefit of any laws that protect the consumer's real or personal property from seizure or sale to satisfy a debt (waiver of exemption)
- Assign to the creditor the borrower's wages or earnings unless (a) the borrower may revoke the assignment at any time, (b) the assignment is a preauthorized payment plan established at the time the debt is incurred, or (c) the assignment applies only to wages or earnings already earned at the time of the assignment or
- Pyramid late charges (i.e., impose multiple late charges based on a single late payment)

See Franson (2023, p. 134).

[108] See the United States Code, Title 12, Chapter 53.

[109] See the United States Code, Title 12, Chapter 53, Subchapter V, Section 5491.

[110] See Franson (2023, p. 135).

to the FTC. These penalties can include refunds, restitution, and fines that can amount to US$ 1 million per day for a deliberate violation of the Dodd-Frank Act.[111] It should be noted that online lending platforms may also be subject to state laws pertaining to disclosure obligations;[112]

(e) the Fair Credit Reporting Act (1970, as amended).[113] It can be easily seen that online lending platforms can obtain and utilize consumer reports,[114] alongside their proprietary data and methods, to evaluate loan applications for placement on their platforms. By doing so, they become bound by the regulations outlined in the Act. Under the Act, lenders who utilize consumer credit reports in their loan approval process must have a permissible purpose.[115] They must refrain from sharing customer information with third parties without customers' consent.[116] They also have to implement an identity theft prevention program to safeguard customer information.[117] Additionally, lending platforms are obligated to provide borrowers with specific information regarding their adverse or less favorable lending decisions.[118]

It should be noted that lending platforms may also employ consumer reports to determine interest rates applicable to borrowers. Under the Fair Credit Reporting Act, if a loan is provided to a borrower on less favorable terms compared to a significant number of borrowers, lending platforms must comply with specific disclosure obligations. These obligations include notifying the borrower about the less favorable terms and clarifying that such terms are based on the consumer report. Lending platforms are also required to disclose to the borrower the credit score used in the underwriting, as well as the factors that influenced the credit score;[119]

(f) the Financial Services Modernization Act (1999, as amended),[120] which requires lending platforms to comply with rules and regulations pertaining to the security

---

[111] See Brummer (2020, p. 312).

[112] Brummer (2020, p. 312).

[113] See the United States Code, Title 15, Chapter 41, Subchapter III and the Code of Federal Regulations, Title 12, Chapter X, Part 1022.

[114] See the United States Code, Title 15, Chapter 41, Subchapter III, Section 1681a(d)(1) provides that: "The term "consumer report" means any written, oral, or other communication of any information by a consumer reporting agency bearing on a consumer's creditworthiness, credit standing, credit capacity, character, general reputation, personal characteristics, or mode of living which is used or expected to be used or collected in whole or in part for the purpose of serving as a factor in establishing the consumer's eligibility for (A) credit or insurance to be used primarily for personal, family, or household purposes; (B) employment purposes; or (C) any other purpose authorized under section 1681b of this title."

[115] See the United States Code, Title 15, Chapter 41, Subchapter III, Section 1681b(a)(3)(A).

[116] See the United States Code, Title 15, Chapter 41, Subchapter III, Section 1681b(f).

[117] See the United States Code, Title 15, Chapter 41, Subchapter III, Section 1681c-1.

[118] See the United States Code, Title 15, Chapter 41, Subchapter III, Section 1681m(a) and Brummer (2020, p. 315).

[119] See the United States Code, Title 15, Chapter 41, Subchapter III, Section 1681m(h) and Brummer (2020, p. 319).

[120] See the United States Code, Title 15, Chapter 94, Subchapter I.

of personal information of loan applicants. Accordingly, lending platforms are obligated to inform loan applicants about their policies regarding customers' personal information. They also have to provide loan applicants with an opt-out option before disclosing data to a non-affiliated third party;[121]

(g) the Fair Debt Collection Practices Act (1977, as amended),[122] which provides specific regulations for debt collection. The Act prevents abusive, unfair, and harassing debt collection practices by lending platforms and debt collection agencies. It also limits communication between lending platforms and third parties regarding borrowers' debts and includes requirements for conduct notice and debt validation.[123] In addition, the Racketeer Influenced and Corrupt Organizations Act (1970, as amended)[124] creates both criminal and civil sanctions for lending platforms and debt collection agencies that engage in unlawful debt collection practices;[125] and

(h) the Equal Credit Opportunity Act (1974, as amended),[126] which establishes a legal framework for ensuring equal credit opportunities among borrowers through online lending platforms. The Act prohibits discrimination based on borrowers' race, religion, sex, marital status, age, and source of income in any online lending transaction.[127]

Alongside consumer protection laws, P2P lending platforms are required to adhere to securities laws in the course of their operation. It can be seen that lending platforms can issue financial products, such as securitized loans or platform notes, to investors in order to facilitate the funding of borrower loans. In these cases (i.e., where lending platforms issue securitized loans or platform notes which are deemed to be securities[128]), the platforms become subject to a variety of federal regulations pertaining to disclosure and liability.[129]

[121] See Brummer (2020, p. 323).

[122] See the United States Code, Title 15, Chapter 41, Subchapter V.

[123] See The Federal Trade Commission (2025b) and Brummer (2020, p. 326).

[124] See the United States Code, Title 18, Part I, Chapter 96.

[125] See Brummer (2020, p. 329).

[126] See the United States Code, Title 15, Chapter 41, Subchapter IV.

[127] See The Federal Trade Commission (2025a) and Brummer (2020, p. 334).

[128] It is worth noting that the term "security" means "any note, stock, treasury stock, security future, security-based swap, bond, debenture, evidence of indebtedness, certificate of interest or participation in any profit-sharing agreement, collateral-trust certificate, preorganization certificate or subscription, transferable share, investment contract, voting-trust certificate, certificate of deposit for a security, fractional undivided interest in oil, gas, or other mineral rights, any put, call, straddle, option, or privilege on any security, certificate of deposit, or group or index of securities (including any interest therein or based on the value thereof), or any put, call, straddle, option, or privilege entered into on a national securities exchange relating to foreign currency, or, in general, any interest or instrument commonly known as a "security," or any certificate of interest or participation in, temporary or interim certificate for, receipt for, guarantee of, or warrant or right to subscribe to or purchase, any of the foregoing." See The United States Code, Title 15, Chapter 2A, Subchapter I, Section 77b(a)(1).

[129] See Brummer (2020, p. 351).

Under the Securities Act (1933, as amended), lending platforms that engage in a public offering of securitized loans or platform notes, which are deemed securities,[130] are required to register those loans or notes with the Securities and Exchange Commission (SEC). They are also obligated to provide a prospectus or make it accessible to investors. The prospectus includes a variety of information concerning the offering, including:

(1) A detailed description of the platform and notes
(2) A discussion by management about the platform's performance over the previous 12 months
(3) An overview of the platform's financial condition and financial statements
(4) Material legal proceedings that could impact the platform's financial health
(5) A discussion of the applicable risk factors and
(6) The distribution plan for releasing the securities[131]

---

[130] It should be noted that "[w]hether or not platform notes are securities hinges on whether they comprise 'investment contracts', a category of products enumerated in section 2 of the Securities Act of 1933." However, "the definition of an investment contract is not defined in the statute. Instead, the landmark 1946 Supreme Court case SEC v. Howey provides a framework for such products and holds that investment contracts are financial products that exhibit four characteristics which collectively generate greater risks for investors and warrant enhanced disclosures and investor protections. Specifically, investment contracts are held to be:

(1) An investment of money
(2) In a common enterprise
(3) With an expectation of profits and
(4) To be derived solely from the efforts of others"

See Brummer (2020, p. 352).

The Securities and Exchange Commission (SEC) also holds that "a platform note fall within the definition of 'notes' – a category of instruments designed under section 2 of the Securities Act of 1933 to constitute a 'security' and subject to the United States securities laws. Yet, like investment contracts, notes are not defined in the Securities Act of 1933; and as in the case of investment contracts, the Supreme Court has developed a framework to determine when and under what circumstances an instrument will be considered a 'note', and by extension a security." "The first step involves determining whether the financial instrument in question is one of the following forms of notes that the Court explicitly deems to not be a security, among them:

(1) notes delivered in a consumer financing;
(2) notes secured by a mortgage on a home;
(3) short-term notes secured by a lien on small business or its assets;
(4) short-term note evidenced by accounts receivable;
(5) notes evidencing 'character' loans to bank customers; and
(6) notes evidencing loans from commercial banks for ordinary operations."

If the instrument in question is not among the enumerated list, it will be deemed a security unless it bears a 'strong family resemblance' to one of the categories listed above. Family resemblance is determined by: (1) the motivations of the buyer and seller (for example, whether there is a profit motive); (2) the plan of distribution (whether or not notes are widely offered and sold); (3) the reasonable expectations of the investing public about whether the note is a security; and (4) the existence of an alternate regulatory regime." See Brummer (2020, p. 354).

[131] See Brummer (2020, p. 356).

It is worth noting that lending platforms may be held liable for inaccurate disclosures. Under the Securities Act, investors have recourse against issuers who sell securities through prospectuses that contain untrue statements of material facts or omit material facts.[132]

In a public offering, P2P lending platforms register their notes under Rule 415, which was issued by the SEC.[133] This rule allows lending platforms to file 'shelf' registration statements for a specific amount of a generic category of securities, such as 'notes' or 'debt securities'. These registration statements do not include specific details like maturity dates, interest rates, or other negotiated financial terms that pertain to individual securities. When lending platforms reach agreements with investors for the issuance of specific notes, they can take the requisite amount of notes off the 'shelf' by filing a prospectus supplement with the SEC. The prospectus supplement specifies the amount of notes sold and the applicable negotiated terms.[134]

Alternatively, P2P lending platforms can opt for a private placement of their platform notes under Regulation D, which was issued by the SEC.[135] In this case, they are not required to register their platform notes with the SEC. However, they have to restrict sales of the placement to accredited investors[136] in accordance with Rule 506(c) if they operate online on websites fully accessible to the public. This rule requires lending platforms to take reasonable steps to verify the accredited investor status of the investors.[137]

Another option for P2P lending platforms is that they can engage in small offerings under Regulation A, as amended in 2015 pursuant to the JOBS Act (known as Regulation A+).[138] Their securities offerings are divided into two tiers, including Tier 1, for securities offerings of up to US$ 20 million, and Tier 2, for

---

[132] It is worth noting that to reduce such liabilities, some lending platforms affirmatively disclose that borrower-reported information could be false, and that investors must assume the risk that such information is inaccurate. Brummer (2020, p. 357).

[133] See The Code of Federal Regulations, Title 17, Chapter II, Part 230, Section 415.

[134] See Brummer (2020, p. 358).

[135] See The Code of Federal Regulations, Title 17, Chapter II, Part 230, Regulation D.

[136] The term "accredited investor" includes most institutional investors and individuals who (a) individually, or with their spouse, have a net worth exceeding US$ 1 million exclusive of the value of the person's primary residence (and subject to certain adjustments for "underwater" mortgages), or (b) individually had an income in excess of US$ 200,000 in each of the two preceding years, or had a joint income with spouse in excess of US$ 300,000 in each of those years, and have a reasonable expectation of reaching the same income level in the current year. On August 26, 2020, the SEC adopted amendments to the definition of accredited investor (SEC Release Nos. 33-10824; 34-89669; File No. S7-25-19). The amendments to the accredited investor definition added new categories of natural persons based on professional knowledge, experience, or certifications and added new categories of entities, including a "catch-all" category for any entity owning in excess of US$ 5 million in investments. See Franson (2023, p. 173).

[137] See The Code of Federal Regulations, Title 17, Chapter II, Part 230, Regulation D, Section 506 (c)(2)(ii).

[138] See The Code of Federal Regulations, Title 17, Chapter II, Part 230, Regulation A.

offerings of up to US$ 50 million. Under Regulation A+, lending platforms can offer and sell securities to both accredited and non-accredited investors. However, lending platforms in both the two tiers must provide specified disclosures to investors, submit an offering statement to the SEC, and receive clearance from the SEC before initiating sales.[139]

It is important to note the risk retention requirement under the Dodd-Frank Act (2010, as amended). Since P2P lending platforms package and securitize loans into different risk categories for sale to investors, they are obligated to retain a portion of the loans on their balance sheets. This retention requirement is set at a minimum of 5% of the credit risk of the loans they securitize, as specified in Section 941(b) of the Dodd-Frank Act.[140] Notably, this requirement applies to both public offerings and private placements of asset-backed securities.[141]

P2P lending platforms can also be subject to the Investment Company Act (1940, as amended).[142] The Act defines an investment company as any person engaged in the business of investing in or holding securities[143] that have a value exceeding 40% of the value of its total assets.[144] It can be seen that securitized loans or platform notes issued by lending platforms fall within the definition of securities under the Investment Company Act. Also, P2P lending platforms typically qualify as investment companies. This is because they hold loans acquired through their platforms on their balance sheets, and the value of the loans typically greatly exceeds 40% of the value of their total assets. According to the Investment Company Act, lending platforms, which are deemed investment companies, are required to register with the SEC before selling any of their securities to the public.[145] However, lending

---

[139] The disclosure requirements are broader for Tier 2 issuers than for Tier 1 issuers and, in many respects, resemble those that would apply in a registered public offering by the same company. See Franson (2023, p. 176).

[140] See The Code of Federal Regulations, Title 12, Chapter III, Subchapter B, Part 360, Section 360.6 (b)(5)(A).

[141] It has been noted that this requirement was designed to create incentives for securitizers like lending platforms to carefully monitor the quality of the securitized assets. See Brummer (2020, p. 360).

[142] See The United States Code, Title 15, Chapter 2D, Subchapter I.

[143] The United States Code, Title 15, Chapter 2D, Subchapter I, Section 80a-3(a)(2) provides that "investment securities include all securities except (A) Government securities, (B) securities issued by employees' securities companies, and (C) securities issued by majority-owned subsidiaries of the owner which (i) are not investment companies, and (ii) are not relying on the exception from the definition of investment company in Paragraph (1) or (7) of subsection (c)."

[144] The United States Code, Title 15, Chapter 2D, Subchapter I, Section 80a-3(a)(1) provides that "investment company means any issuer which (A) is or holds itself out as being engaged primarily, or proposes to engage primarily, in the business of investing, reinvesting, or trading in securities; (B) is engaged or proposes to engage in the business of issuing face-amount certificates of the installment type, or has been engaged in such business and has any such certificate outstanding; or (C) is engaged or proposes to engage in the business of investing, reinvesting, owning, holding, or trading in securities, and owns or proposes to acquire investment securities having a value exceeding 40 per centum of the value of such issuer's total assets (exclusive of Government securities and cash items) on an unconsolidated basis."

[145] It should be noted that the registration requirement applies to the investment company itself, rather than to its securities, and the investment company remains obligated also to register the

platforms can resort to several exemptions to escape investment company registration. For example, the exemption under Section 3(b)(1) of the Investment Company Act[146] would be available to lending platforms that claim that their business line is the operation of a website. Another example is the exemption under Section 3(c)(1) of the Investment Company Act. In this example, lending platforms provide their platform notes or securitized loans to less than 100 investors and do not engage in a public offering.

The Investment Advisers Act (1940, as amended)[147] is a significant legal framework that has the potential to apply to P2P lending platforms' activities. The Act defines investment advisers as persons who are professionally compensated for advising others about purchasing securities or providing reports or analyses as to the value of securities.[148] It is worth noting that P2P lending platforms can be considered investment advisers to the extent to which they charge customers for ratings or analyses concerning the notes they issue to investors.[149] Under the Investment Advisers Act, lending platforms that are deemed investment advisers are required to register with the SEC before offering investment advice.[150] They are also subject to detailed disclosures about their business and must comply with numerous rules regarding recordkeeping, client relations, and advertising.[151]

In addition to the aforementioned laws, P2P lending platforms are subject to anti-money-laundering laws and regulations under the Bank Secrecy Act (1970, as amended).[152] They are required to collaborate with the funding bank (see Fig. 5.2) in implementing policies and procedures concerning anti-money laundering. These policies and procedures include (1) establishing a customer identification program to verify the true identities of borrowers; (2) determining whether borrowers are listed as known or suspected terrorists; (3) submitting suspicious activity reports; and (4) implementing an anti-money laundering and information sharing program. It should be noted that P2P lending platforms can be directly subject to these policies

---

securities under the Securities Act. In practice, the investment company can file a single registration statement with the SEC that covers both investment company and securities registration. See Franson (2023, p. 186).

[146]This Section provides that "[a]ny issuer primarily engaged, directly or through a wholly-owned subsidiary or subsidiaries, in a business or businesses other than that of investing, reinvesting, owning, holding, or trading in securities."

[147]See The United States Code, Title 15, Chapter 2D, Subchapter II.

[148]The United States Code, Title 15, Chapter 2D, Subchapter II, Section 80b-1(a)(11) provides that "[i]nvestment adviser means any person who, for compensation, engages in the business of advising others, either directly or through publications or writings, as to the value of securities or as to the advisability of investing in, purchasing, or selling securities, or who, for compensation and as part of a regular business, issues or promulgates analyses or reports concerning securities."

[149]See Brummer (2020, p. 362).

[150]See the United States Code, Title 15, Chapter 2D, Subchapter II, Section 80b-3(a).

[151]See Brummer (2020, p. 362).

[152]See the United States Code, Title 31, Chapter 53, Subchapter III.

and procedures as a money-services business, a securities broker-dealer, an investment company, or an investment adviser.[153]

Furthermore, the Electronic Signatures in Global and National Commerce Act of 2000[154] regulates the use of electronic signatures and electronic records in commercial transactions. The Act also imposes obligations on lending platforms to ensure customers' consent to the terms of the lending service offered.[155]

### 5.1.2 *Japan*

It can easily be seen that the micro- and/or small-sized finance market in Japan has a longer history compared to the market in Vietnam. The origins of the modern system of micro- and/or small-sized financing schemes in Japan can be traced back to the establishment of the modern banking system in the early 1870s.[156] From the supply side, private and public financial institutions, as well as informal credit providers have offered small funding to households and small firms.[157] Private financial institutions, including conventional commercial banks, cooperative-type financial institutions, and other private financial institutions, as well as public financial institutions have provided loans through various financing schemes. Likewise, informal credit providers, such as family members, friends, pawnshops, and private moneylenders, have provided individuals and small firms with small loans through a variety of financing schemes. These financing schemes will be further clarified as follows.

Currently, commercial banks include city banks, regional banks, and second-tier regional banks.[158] These banks receive ordinary and term deposits from depositors to facilitate their lending activities.[159] They can extend small credit to individuals

[153] See Franson (2023, p. 156).

[154] See the United States Code, Title 15, Chapter 96, Subchapter I.

[155] See the National Credit Union Administration (2021a) and Brummer (2020, p. 345).

[156] See Goldsmith (1983, p. 25), Adams and Hoshii (1972, p. 91), The Bank of Japan Economic Research Department (1969, p. 11) and Ogura (2002, p. 1).

[157] See The Institute for Monetary and Economic Studies of the Bank of Japan (1986, p. 163), Alexander and Oh (1989, p. 10), Prindl (1981, p. 6), Tsukahara (2016, p. 3) and Gibbons (2012).

[158] This classification is based on the historical background, location, and customer bases of commercial banks. City banks are located in major cities such as Tokyo, Osaka, and other major cities, while regional banks are typically found in the principal city of a prefecture. Second-tier regional banks were initially established in 1951 as mutual banks and exclusively served SMEs before undergoing conversion to one type of commercial bank, such as city banks or regional banks. See Japanese Bankers Association (2019), Nakamura and Yamada (1996, p. 127) and Tatewaki (2012, p. 117).

[159] It should be noted that an ordinary deposit is used for depositing and withdrawing cash, and there is no minimum deposit amount or maturity requirement. In ordinary deposit accounts, funds can be added or withdrawn at any time, typically through an automatic teller machine (ATM), and they usually earn low-interest rates. On the other hand, a term deposit is an interest-bearing deposit that is

and small firms by means of providing loans, discounting bills and notes, and guaranteeing obligations.[160]

Commercial banks offer borrowers term loans, including short-, medium, and long-term loans, through loan agreements. Under these agreements, they provide borrowers with specific loan amounts within predetermined time intervals. The borrowers are then responsible for repaying both the principal amounts and the accompanying interest as agreed upon by the parties. Bank loans can be secured or unsecured.[161]

They also engage in bill and note discounting through discounting agreements. Discounted bills and notes can serve various purposes, such as commercial bills being issued to settle payments in commercial transactions. Another example is the issuance of promissory notes for the purpose of borrowing from banks, where borrowers act as issuers and banks act as payees. Under discounting agreements, commercial banks purchase outstanding bills and notes at their face value and deduct fees and the accrued interest amount until the maturity date. The payment made by commercial banks for discounted bills and notes can be deemed a form of providing loans to the beneficiaries of these bills and notes. It is worth noting that loans on bills and notes are typically short-term and commonly used to provide working capital for businesses.[162]

Another financing scheme through which commercial banks extend credit is a bank guarantee. In this scheme, commercial banks act as guarantors, ensuring the fulfillment of financial obligations on behalf of their customers in the event that their customers fail to meet their commitments, either partially or in full. Commercial banks collect repayments for their guarantees from the guaranteed customers, who are known as the primary obligors, as agreed upon by the parties. Bank guarantees can be either secured or unsecured.[163]

In addition, commercial banks provide small funding through the issuance of credit cards by their nonbank subsidiaries, which are credit card companies. This enables cardholders to indirectly borrow money from commercial banks in order to make their purchases.[164] It has been noted that credit cards were initially introduced

---

held for a specified period. The term can be short-term (usually less than one year), medium-term (from one to three or five years), or long-term (over three or five years). Term deposits generally offer higher interest rates compared to ordinary deposits. However, if a withdrawal is made before the maturity date, the interest rates applicable to ordinary deposits are likely to be applied. See Nakajima (2013, pp. 107–108).

[160] See The English translation of the Banking Act of Japan (Act No. 59 of 1981, as amended), Article 10.

[161] See Yoshino et al. (2019, p. 93) and The Institute for Monetary and Economic Studies of the Bank of Japan (1986, p. 175).

[162] See Teranishi (1994, p. 104).

[163] See The Institute for Monetary and Economic Studies of the Bank of Japan (1986, p. 189).

[164] See Nakajima (2013, p. 152), Gordon (2012, p. 75), Bank of Japan (2012, p. 273), Japanese Bankers Association (2012, p. 20).

in Japan in 1960.[165] Cardholders are typically required to have a Japanese bank account and provide their personal information, including name, residence, employment status, and proof of income,[166] to obtain an ordinary card with a low credit limit. Certain occupations and a good credit history may enable them to qualify for Gold, Platinum, or Black cards, which offer a wider range of premium services and higher credit limits.[167] A cardholder can choose to make a purchase payment in a single transaction or split it into multiple installments by requesting the credit card terminal at the point of sale to facilitate this. However, the more installments a cardholder chooses and the longer the installments last, the higher the amount of interest they are likely to be required to repay.[168] It has been said that although commercial banks can indirectly provide unsecured loans through credit cards, the principal amounts of these loans are usually limited to a specific amount, such as JP¥ 100,000 or so. In cases where cardholders have low creditworthiness or a low credit score, commercial banks may require personal collateral, such as an individual guarantee or a guarantee from a credit guarantee association or a related company.[169]

It is worth noting that long-term credit banks provided individuals and small firms with long-term credit through lending agreements. The banks were initially established in 1952 and played a significant role in providing loans to corporations before their collapse in 1998. They were permitted to issue bank debentures and accept deposits from the government, public bodies, and other depositors to mobilize capital for their lending operations.[170]

Trust banks also provide long-term credit for machines, equipment, and long-term working capital to individuals and small firms.[171] It is documented that these banks started their operations in the early twentieth century.[172] At present, they conduct banking operations similar to commercial banks, including accepting deposits and providing loans, while also undertaking trust services.[173] The Act on Engagement in Trust Business Activities by Financial Institutions (Act No. 43 of 1943, as amended)[174] and the Trust Business Act (Act No. 154 of 2004, as

---

[165] See Japanese Bankers Association (2012), Mann (2002, p. 1074) and Mann (2001, p. 17).

[166] Typically, a certificate of employment or a copy of the salary income withholding certificate is required as proof of income.

[167] See Yasuda (2020), Batino and Jordan (2020).

[168] See Mann (2001) and Yasuda (2020).

[169] See The Institute for Monetary and Economic Studies of the Bank of Japan (1986, p. 177) and Tatewaki (2012, p. 110).

[170] See Espig (2003, p. 2) and the Japan Times (1998).

[171] See The Institute for Monetary and Economic Studies of the Bank of Japan (1986, p. 203), Tatewaki (2012, p. 113) and Nakamura and Yamada (1996, p. 126).

[172] See Trust Companies Association of Japan (2025).

[173] See Tatewaki (2012, p. 116) and the Institute for Monetary and Economic Studies of the Bank of Japan (1986, p. 206).

[174] The English translation of the Act on Engagement in Trust Business Activities by Financial Institutions of Japan (Act No. 43 of 1943, as amended).

amended)[175] provide requirements for licensing, operation, and supervision of trust banks.

It should be noted that conventional commercial banks are subject to various requirements, including minimum capital requirements, reserve requirements, capital adequacy ratios, lending limits, and interest rate ceilings, under the Banking Act (Act No. 59 of 1981, as amended). They are also obligated to perform due diligence and fulfill other obligations to safeguard the legitimate rights of their customers and ensure the safety and stability of their operations.[176]

Besides conventional commercial banks, leasing companies also offer small finance to businesses. These companies provide finance leases through simple finance lease and sale and lease-back schemes. In a simple finance lease scheme, a business selects an asset or equipment and applies for a finance leasing service provided by a leasing company. The leasing company, as a lessor, uses its funds to purchase the equipment or asset designated by the business, acting as a lessee, then leases it out to the lessee.[177] In contrast, in a sale and lease-back scheme, a business obtains funds by selling its equipment or asset to a leasing company, which then leases the equipment or asset back to the business. In this arrangement, the leasing company assumes the role of the lessor, while the business becomes the lessee.[178] It can be seen that in both of these finance lease schemes, the lessor provides the lessee with the necessary funding to acquire the leased equipment or asset. The lessor then collects the funding and the cost arising from the lease by receiving lease payments from the lessee in accordance with the leasing contract signed by both parties. It has been noted that, in general, the leasing contract is non-cancelable over the lease term, and the lease term is usually medium or long term.[179]

Insurance companies can serve as a source of small loans.[180] They collect insurance premiums from policyholders and provide them with small loans under insurance contracts.[181] It has been noted that life insurance companies began offering life insurance combined with home loans in 1966. This allowed the insured to receive a home loan equal to the face value of their policies. It is worth noting that only individuals under a certain age are eligible for this loan, as repayment is canceled in the event of the borrower's death.[182] In the course of their operations, insurance companies are required to meet capital and solvency margin requirements

---

[175] The English translation of the Trust Business Act of Japan (Act No. 154 of 2004, as amended).

[176] See the English translation of the Banking Act of Japan (Act No. 59 of 1981, as amended), Article 12-2, Paragraph 2.

[177] See Japan Leasing Association (2025a).

[178] Nihei (2020).

[179] See Japan Leasing Association (2025a) and Japan Leasing Association (2025b).

[180] See Tatewaki (2012, p. 128) and The Institute for Monetary and Economic Studies of the Bank of Japan (1986, p. 247).

[181] See the English translation of the Insurance Business Act of Japan (Act No. 105 of 1995, as amended), Article 265–228, Paragraph 2.

[182] See Adams and Hoshii (1972, p. 203).

to ensure the soundness of their operations under the Insurance Business Act (Act No. 105 of 1995, as amended).[183] They are also required to establish insurance policyholder protection funds to cover expenses related to their business activities, including lending.[184] Additionally, loans extended by an insurance company to a policyholder must not exceed 10% of the company's total assets.[185]

It is important to note that consumer credit in Japan, which has its roots in the 1950s, involves individuals and firms procuring small funds from various consumer credit companies.[186] These companies include credit card companies, manufacturer-affiliated credit companies, installment finance companies, and credit-related business companies, such as department stores, merchants, and loan-guarantee companies.[187] Consumer credit companies can offer consumer loans directly to borrowers through loan agreements or credit cards. They also provide borrowers with sale credit for purchasing durable goods, such as electronic devices, furniture, and automobiles.[188] Loans provided by consumer credit companies can be either secured or unsecured. It is noted that consumer credit companies typically develop customer information systems to collect and maintain customers' information, including their credit repayment track records, for loan decision-making.[189] They are required to safeguard the legitimate rights of their customers under the Installment Sale Act (Act No. 159 of 1961, as amended).[190] They are also obligated to handle credit data appropriately and implement fraud prevention measures under the Protection of Personal Information Act (Act No. 57 of 2003, as amended).[191]

In addition to the aforementioned micro- and/or small-sized finance providers, cooperative financial institutions are also a source of small loans. The modern history of cooperative financial institutions in Japan is considered to have started in the nineteenth century.[192] These institutions include credit associations (which are called *shinyo kinko* in Japanese language), credit cooperatives (which are called *shinyo kumiai* in Japanese language), and agricultural and fisheries cooperatives. They provide loans through various financing schemes, as outlined below.

---

[183] See Takahashi et al. (2019, p. 249).

[184] See the English translation of the Insurance Business Act of Japan (Act No. 105 of 1995, as amended), Article 265-32, Paragraph 1.

[185] See the English translation of the Insurance Business Act of Japan (Act No. 105 of 1995, as amended), Article 97-2 and the General Insurance Association of Japan (2025).

[186] See Harner (2000, p. 130) and Gordon (2012, p. 63).

[187] Japan Consumer Credit Association (2025).

[188] See Tatewaki (2012, p. 131).

[189] See Mann (2002, p. 1081), Harner (2000) and Tatewaki (2012, p. 132).

[190] See the English translation of the Installment Sales Act of Japan (Act No. 159 of 1961, as amended).

[191] See the English translation of the Protection of Personal Information Act of Japan (Act No. 57 of 2003, as amended).

[192] See Klinedinst and Sato (1994, p. 509).

Credit associations provide loans through loan agreements. Initially established to cater to the funding needs of SMEs, credit associations have gradually expanded their services to include loans for workers. The purpose of loans provided by credit associations is to foster mutual assistance among their members. It is noted that the operations of credit associations nowadays are similar to those of commercial banks. Credit associations accept deposits from both members and non-members and primarily provide loans to their members. They can offer loans to non-members, but they are required to restrict the share of loans to non-members to 20%. Additionally, credit associations are subject to capital adequacy requirements and other banking regulations.[193]

Credit cooperatives were established in various regions under the Small and Medium-Sized Enterprise Cooperatives Act (Act No. 181 of 1949, as amended), aiming at providing mutual relief among small business owners and workers. Credit cooperatives accept deposits and installment savings from their members, as well as from spouses or relatives who share the same livelihood with them. They also accept deposits from the state, local governments, and other not-for-profit juridical persons, as well as other non-members.[194] Credit cooperatives primarily provide loans and discounted financing for negotiable instruments to both members and non-members.[195] They are required to collect and maintain customers' information, including their credit repayment track records.[196] It is noted that credit cooperatives are unlikely to require collateral to secure the loans they offer. However, they monitor the operations of borrowers to ensure timely repayments.[197]

Agricultural cooperatives were established under the Agricultural Cooperative Act (Act No. 132 of 1947, as amended),[198] aiming at supporting farming activities and improving the livelihoods of farmers.[199] Agricultural cooperatives accept deposits and installment savings from their regular members, who are farmers, as well as from associate members,[200] who are non-farmers.[201] Agricultural cooperatives offer loans, discounted financing for negotiable instruments, and guarantees to

---

[193] See Nakamura and Yamada (1996, p. 128), Tatewaki (2012, p. 119) and Yoshino and Hesary (2017, p. 9).

[194] See the English translation of the Small and Medium-Sized Enterprise Cooperatives Act of Japan (Act No. 181 of 1949, as amended), Article 9-8, Paragraph 1 and Paragraph 2.

[195] The English translation of the Small and Medium-Sized Enterprise Cooperatives Act of Japan (Act No. 181 of 1949, as amended), Article 9-8, Paragraph 1 and Paragraph 2.

[196] See the English translation of the Small and Medium-Sized Enterprise Cooperatives Act of Japan (Act No. 181 of 1949, as amended), Article 10-2.

[197] See Tatewaki (2012, p. 121) and Fukuyama et al. (1999, p. 474).

[198] The English translation of the Agricultural Cooperatives Act of Japan (Act No. 132 of 1947, as amended).

[199] See Tatewaki (2012, p. 126).

[200] Who are called jun kumiai-in in Japanese language.

[201] See the English translation of the Agricultural Cooperatives Act of Japan (Act No. 132 of 1947, as amended), Article 10 and Article 12 and Kazuhito (2013).

their members.[202] To ensure operational safety, agricultural cooperatives are subject to several requirements, including reserve requirements, capital adequacy ratios, and lending limits.[203]

It is worth noting that fisheries cooperatives can serve as a source of small loans. The origins of these cooperatives can be traced back to 1886 when they were established based on the associations of coastal fishermen. The contemporary fisheries cooperatives were later established under the Fisheries Cooperatives Act (Act No. 242 of 1948, as amended).[204] According to this Act, there are three types of cooperatives in the fishing industry, including fishery cooperatives, fishery production cooperatives, and marine products-processing cooperatives. Among these cooperatives, fishery cooperatives and marine products-processing cooperatives are permitted to extend loans. They primarily accept deposits from their members and provide loans to support them in sales operations, ice production, and refrigeration. Similar to agricultural cooperatives, fisheries cooperatives are required to meet several requirements, including reserve requirements, capital adequacy ratios, and lending limits when providing loans to their members.[205]

It is important to note the establishment of the Postal Savings System (hereinafter referred to as "PSS"), which is a government-operated banking system based in post offices. The system was established in 1875 with the aim of promoting thrift and savings among workers and enhancing national welfare. The system accepted five types of savings, including ordinary savings, fixed-mount savings, fixed-term savings, installment savings, and housing installment savings. The terms of these savings could range from six months to ten years. The system provided postal loans using postal savings as collateral. Postal loans must be less than either 90% of the deposited amount or JP¥ 1 million, whichever is lower. In April 2001, the government decided to cease the operation of PSS due to the maturing of Japan's economy and the gradual decline in the role of postal loans.[206]

The government also established the Fiscal Investment and Loan Program (hereinafter referred to as "FILP"), a long-term, low-interest investment and loan initiative by the government, in 1953. FILP aims to achieve several policy objectives, including providing financial support for SMEs, facilitating the construction of hospitals and welfare facilities, offering scholarship loans, and acquiring overseas resource concessions. FILP procures capital through issuing FILP and government-guaranteed bonds, as well as from dividends on government-held shares. The program allows government-affiliated financial institutions to provide extended, fixed-rate, and low-interest loans that are not typically available from the private

[202] See the English translation of the Agricultural Cooperatives Act of Japan (Act No. 132 of 1947, as amended), Article 10.

[203] See the Institute for Monetary and Economic Studies of the Bank of Japan (1986, p. 236).

[204] See the English translation of the Fisheries Cooperative Act of Japan (Act No. 242 of 1948).

[205] See The Institute for Monetary and Economic Studies of the Bank of Japan (1986, p. 238).

[206] See Cargill and Yoshino (2003, p. 8) and The Institute for Monetary and Economic Studies of the Bank of Japan (1986, p. 288).

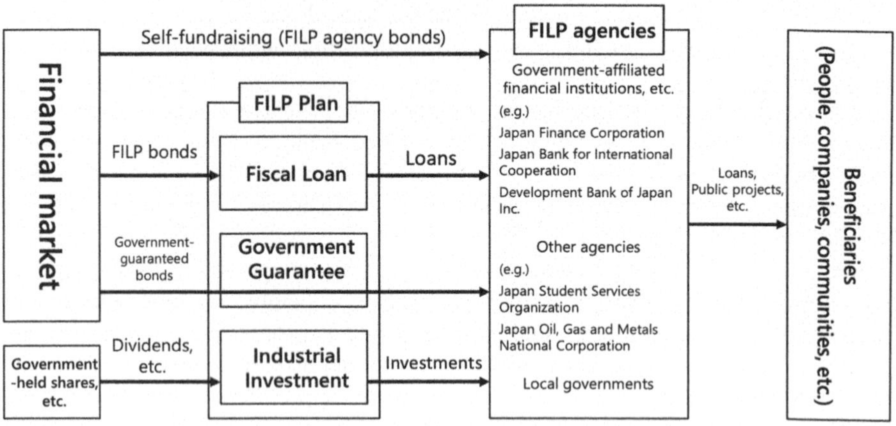


**Fig. 5.3** Financing scheme of FILP (The Ministry of Finance of Japan (2021, p. 2))

sector. Additionally, FILP serves as a source of long-term risk capital, which the private sector may refrain from providing due to high risks.

FILP agencies, which include government-affiliated financial institutions, other agencies, and local governments, offer loans to individuals and companies (see Fig. 5.3). Loans provided by FILP agencies can be either secured or non-secured. For example, the Japan Finance Corporation, one of the government-affiliated financial institutions, can provide loans of up to JP¥ 72 million to business start-ups that are within their first year of operation. The interest rate for loans without collateral is 2% per year, while the rates for loans secured by collateral or guaranteed by a third party range from 1.16% to 1.95% per year.[207]

In the informal credit sector, small loans have been provided for a long time by family members, relatives, neighbors, and friends, as well as through rotating savings and credit associations, pawnshops, and moneylenders. It is widely known that family members, relatives, neighbors, and friends have provided loans to borrowers through loan agreements. These loans can be secured or unsecured, and the terms of the loans can vary.

Rotating savings and credit associations, known as *mujin-ko* or *tanomoshi-ko* in Japanese, emerged in Japan between the twelfth and thirteenth centuries. These associations typically provided funds to low-income households without requiring collateral and interest payments. In a rotating savings and credit association, a group of individuals would gather, contribute a certain sum of money, and provide loans to the group members. They would regularly attend member meetings, contribute a certain amount of money, and take turns receiving the full amount collected at each meeting. If a member who had not received a fund failed to fulfill their obligations to the association, they would lose the right to receive a fund. In the case of a member who had received a fund but later failed to fulfill their obligations, they would face

[207] See Yamori et al. (2013, p. 75), Japan Finance Corporation (2023) and SME Japan (2025).

punishment from the other members. It has been documented that rotating savings and credit associations primarily relied on monitoring mechanisms enforced by kinship, religion, and local community ties. As these associations grew larger and included more members who were total strangers, moral hazard issues among them increased. Because of this, the Japanese government reorganized these associations in 1915.[208] Consequently, rotating savings and credit associations gradually ceased their operations.[209]

Pawnshops provide loans to individuals through pawn agreements. In Japan, there were both private and public pawnshops. It has been noted that private pawnshops existed in the thirteenth century or earlier, while the first public pawnshop was opened in 1912.[210] Public pawnshops were established under the Public Pawnshop Law of 1927 (*Koeki shichiya ho*), whereas private pawnshops were regulated by the Pawnshop Control Law of 1895 (*Shichiya torisihmari ho*). The key differences between public and private pawnshops were the interest rates charged on loans[211] and loan limits[212]. Nowadays, pawnshops are established in accordance with the Pawnbroker Business Act (Act No. 158 of 1950),[213] requiring approval from the Public Safety Commission of each prefecture where pawnshops operate. Borrowers can obtain loans from pawnshops by pledging an item of value, such as jewelry, precious metals, watches, and brand-name goods, as collateral. For the initial borrowing from a pawnshop, borrowers are very likely to be required to present their identity documents, such as a driver's license, passport, or certificates issued by public organizations. Pawnshops appraise the value of pawned items to make decisions on loan amounts that could be provided to borrowers. If borrowers are unable to return their loans by the due date, pawnshops have the right to sell the pawned items to recover the money.[214]

Following the change of the AUP in 1993, broadband Internet services have been commercially available in Japan.[215] Since then, both the supply and demand sides of small funds in Japan have embraced the use of the Internet. Over time, conventional banks and other financial institutions, such as credit unions, insurance companies,

---

[208] Accordingly, there were strict limitations imposed on the amount of the pot, the amount of the premium (contribution), the duration of the operation, and the number of members in rotating savings and credit associations. For instance, a rotating savings and credit association was not allowed to exceed a duration of five years, and the value of one unit of the pot should be below JP¥ 10,000.

[209] See Dekle and Hamada (2000, p. 79) and Izumida (2018, p. 166).

[210] See Skully (2019, p. 364) and Ryuichi (1983).

[211] The Public Pawnshop Law mandated a lower interest rate for public institutions than their private counterparts. See Inoue (2022, p. 8).

[212] The Public Pawnshop Law imposed a maximum loan amount of 10 yen per loan and 50 yen per household to prevent individuals other than the low-income class from exploiting public pawnshops. See Inoue (2022, p. 8).

[213] See the English translation of the Pawnbroker Business Act of Japan (Act No. 158 of 1950).

[214] See Pawnshop Daishin (2025).

[215] See Sunahara and Esaki (2008, p. 4), Coates and Holroyd (2003, p. 92).

and consumer credit companies, have transitioned to offering their services directly via the Internet.[216]

Notably, alongside technological advancements, the social online lending business has been developed in Japan. Social online lending platforms have been facilitating online social networks to connect borrowers and lenders since 2007.[217] Several big names in the lending business include Maneo (established in 2007),[218] Bankers (SBI Social Lending established in 2008 and was absorbed by Bankers in 2022),[219] and AQUSH (established in 2009).[220]

In a social online lending scheme, potential borrowers[221] register for membership and apply for loans through social lending platforms. These platforms subsequently verify the information provided by potential borrowers and evaluate their creditworthiness. If the lending platforms approve borrowers' loan requests, they enter into a loan contract with borrowers. After that, borrowers' loan requests are uploaded to lending platforms for potential investors to consider. Investors who are interested in investing in loans available on social lending platforms are required to sign silent partnership agreements[222] with the lending platforms (see Fig. 5.4). Under the silent partnership agreements, funds provided by investors (known as the silent partner) are considered the property of the lending platforms (known as the business operator).[223] If a lending platform generates a profit on a loan, investors associated with that loan are entitled to receive a portion of the profit. However, they do not have direct claims to funds provided to or collected from borrowers.[224] It is worth noting that, in the event of lending platforms' bankruptcy, investors may encounter unforeseen losses. This is because they would only have a general claim against the bankruptcy estate and receive repayment on a pro rata basis along with other general creditors.[225]

It can be seen that the development of regulations pertaining to micro- and small-sized finance in Japan reflects a gradual adaptation to incorporate the utilization of the Internet. In recent times, there has been a growing focus on the governance of

---

[216] See Ochiai and Iwatani (2002, p. 56), Kitamura et al. (2004, p. 378) and Baba and Hisada (2002, p. 53).

[217] See Adhikary et al. (2018, p. 52), Fujimoto (2008), Dhir and Popescu (2016).

[218] See Maneo (2023).

[219] See SBI Social Lending (2023) and Bankers (2025a).

[220] See AQUSH (2023).

[221] It is worth noting that potential borrowers are required to meet all the criteria established by lending platforms in order to become members. For instance, Bankers requires individuals to: (a) be aged 20 to 75; (b) be residents of Japan; (c) possess a My Number; (d) not be associated with anti-social forces; and (e) not fall under the applicable cases outlined in the Act on Prevention of Transfer of Criminal Proceeds. See Bankers (2025b).

[222] See The English translation of the Commercial Code of Japan (Act No. 48 of 1899, as amended), Article 535.

[223] Japan's Commercial Code (Act No. 48 of 1899, as amended), Article 536, Paragraph 1.

[224] See Samitsu (2017).

[225] Samitsu (2017).

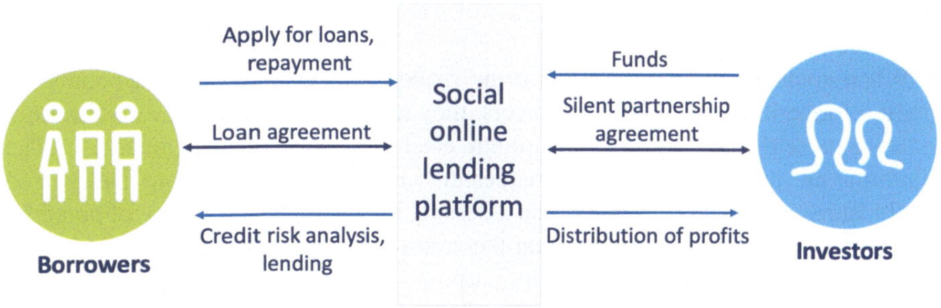


**Fig. 5.4** Social online lending model in Japan (See Adhikary et al. (2018, p. 53) and Samitsu (2017))

social online lending platforms, which are subject to a range of regulations pertaining to micro- and small-sized finance, both before and after the change of the AUP in 1993. Currently, social online lending in Japan is governed by several applicable laws, which include the following.

The Money Lending Business Act (Act No. 32 of 1983, as amended)[226] regulates lending services provided by social online lending platforms. Under the Act, lending platforms are required to register and obtain a money lender's license before providing loans to borrowers.[227] Before concluding a loan contract with borrowers, social online lending platforms must investigate issues concerning borrowers' repayment capacity, such as income or profits or other financial resources, credit, the status of borrowings, repayment plans, and any other matters. Lending platforms are obligated to make use of the credit information held by a Designated Credit Bureau in carrying out their investigations.[228] They are required to disclose and explain loan conditions to borrowers, which encompass loan amounts, interest rates, loan terms, repayment methods, penalties, and any other relevant conditions.[229] In particular, they must provide borrowers with documents that disclose these loan conditions and other pertinent details of the loan contracts upon their conclusion.[230] It is worth noting that loan contracts that have an interest rate exceeding 109.5% per

[226] See the English translation of the Money Lending Business Act of Japan (Act No. 32 of 1983, as amended).

[227] See the English translation of the Money Lending Business Act of Japan (Act No. 32 of 1983, as amended), Article 3 provides that "[a] person who intends to engage in the Money Lending Business, where the person intends to engage in business and establishes business offices or other offices within two or more prefectural areas, must be registered by the Prime Minister, or where the person intends to engage in business and establishes a business office or other office within only one prefectural area, be registered by the prefectural governor who has jurisdiction over the locations of the business office or other office."

[228] See Japan's Money Lending Business Act (Act No. 32 of 1983, as amended), Article 13.

[229] See Japan's Money Lending Business Act (Act No. 32 of 1983, as amended), Article 14.

[230] See Japan's Money Lending Business Act (Act No. 32 of 1983, as amended), Article 17.

annum (or 109.8% per annum in the case of a leap year, with a daily interest rate of 0.3%) are considered void.[231]

When social online lending platforms request Designated Credit Bureaus for credit information on potential borrowers, they must obtain the borrowers' consent in advance, either in writing or through electronic or magnetic means.[232] The platforms are prohibited from: (1) requesting credit information from Designated Credit Bureaus for purposes other than assessing the repayment capacity of potential borrowers; and (2) using or disclosing the credit information obtained from Designated Credit Bureaus to third parties for purposes other than assessing the repayment capacity of potential borrowers.[233]

Additionally, to protect the legitimate rights of borrowers, lending platforms are obligated to: (a) introduce associations that are found to be capable of providing borrowers with consultation, advice, or any other support concerning their borrowings or repayments in a proper and reliable manner;[234] (b) avoid solicitation that is deemed inappropriate, considering the borrowers' knowledge, experience, property status, and the purpose of the loan contract, to ensure sufficient protection of their interests;[235] and (c) implement measures to ensure the appropriate handling of borrowers' information, which is obtained during their lending operations.[236] Lending platforms are prohibited from engaging in the following activities: (1) concluding an excessive loan contract for an individual borrower for a loan that exceeds the repayment capacity of a potential borrower; (2) making false statements or withholding important information from borrowers regarding loan contracts; and (3) engaging in deceptive practices, wrongful actions, or any other unjust acts beyond the aforementioned items.[237]

Social online lending platforms or those entrusted with debt collection under loan contracts are prohibited from engaging in the following actions, which may intimidate individuals or disrupt their personal and business lives: (1) contacting or visiting borrowers' residences during socially inappropriate hours without justifiable grounds; (2) contacting borrowers at their workplaces or any other locations without justifiable grounds; (3) disclosing borrowers' borrowing or personal information to third parties; (4) requesting borrowers to raise funds from sources other than themselves; (5) requesting third parties to fulfill borrowers' obligations; (6) persistently requesting the assistance of third parties in the collection of claims after being

[231] See Japan's Money Lending Business Act (Act No. 32 of 1983, as amended), Article 42, Paragraph 1.

[232] See Japan's Money Lending Business Act (Act No. 32 of 1983, as amended), Article 41-36, Paragraph 1.

[233] See Japan's Money Lending Business Act (Act No. 32 of 1983, as amended), Article 41-38, Paragraph 1.

[234] See Japan's Money Lending Business Act (Act No. 32 of 1983, as amended), Article 12-9.

[235] See Japan's Money Lending Business Act (Act No. 32 of 1983, as amended), Article 16, Paragraph 3.

[236] See Japan's Money Lending Business Act (Act No. 32 of 1983, as amended), Article 12-2.

[237] See Japan's Money Lending Business Act (Act No. 32 of 1983, as amended), Article 12-6.

refused cooperation; (7) continuing to demand performance from borrowers despite them appointing legal representation or initiating legal proceedings; and (8) informing borrowers of the intention to use prohibited language or conduct the deeds mentioned in item (4).[238]

The Interest Rate Restriction Act (Act No. 100 of 1954, as amended)[239] and the Act Regulating the Receipt of Contributions, Receipt of Deposits, and Interest Rates (Act No. 195 of 1954, as amended)[240] govern the interest rates imposed by social online lending platforms. The Interest Rate Restriction Act specifies the maximum allowable interest rates for loans as follows: (a) 20% per annum if the principal amount is less than JP¥ 100,000; (b) 18% per annum if the principal amount exceeds JP¥ 100,000 but is less than JP¥ 1,000,000; and (c) 15% per annum if the principal amount exceeds JP¥ 1,000,000.[241] The Acts cover not only explicit payments to which lenders and borrowers agree to refer to as "interest" but also charges, fees, and similar payments deemed interest.[242] Any additional funds received by the lender in relation to the loan, such as rewards, discount charges, commissions, inspection fees, or similar payments, are considered interest, with the exception of expenses related to contract conclusion and performance obligations.[243] Additionally, any payment received by the lender in connection with the loan, regardless of its name, such as honorarium, fee, or inspection fee, is considered interest.[244] It is important to note that loans with an interest rate exceeding 20% per year may lead to criminal penalties under the Act Regulating the Receipt of Contributions, Receipt of Deposits, and Interest Rates.[245]

In addition to the aforementioned laws, social online lending platforms are subject to the Financial Instruments and Exchange Act (Act No. 25 of 1948, as amended).[246] Under this Act, their operations are deemed to be financial instrument business[247] as these platforms are involved in facilitating investment opportunities

[238] See Japan's Money Lending Business Act (Act No. 32 of 1983, as amended), Article 21-1.

[239] See the English translation of the Interest Rate Restriction Act of Japan (Act No. 100 of 1954, as amended).

[240] See the English translation of the Act Regulating the Receipt of Contributions, Receipt of Deposits, and Interest Rates of Japan (Act No. 195 of 1954, as amended).

[241] See Japan's Interest Rate Restriction Act (Act No. 100 of 1954, as amended), Article 1.

[242] See Sugimura et al. (2017).

[243] See Japan's Interest Rate Restriction Act (Act No. 100 of 1954, as amended), Article 3.

[244] See Japan's Act Regulating the Receipt of Contributions, Receipt of Deposits, and Interest Rates (Act No. 195 of 1954, as amended), Article 5-4, Paragraph 4.

[245] See Japan's Act Regulating the Receipt of Contributions, Receipt of Deposits, and Interest Rates (Act No. 195 of 1954, as amended), Article 5.

[246] See the English translation of the Financial Instruments and Exchange Act of Japan (Act No. 25 of 1948, as amended).

[247] See Japan's Financial Instruments and Exchange Act (Act No. 25 of 1948, as amended), Article 2, Paragraph 8, item (v).

under silent partnership agreements.[248] Lending platforms can engage in the self-offering of units in investment funds and participate in the private placement of interests in investment funds. They are required to register their business and obtain a Financial Instruments Business Operator Subsection 2 license.[249]

When soliciting investors to enter into silent partnership agreements, lending platforms are required to disclose information. They can engage in public offerings[250] or private placements to solicit investors.[251] Lending platforms that engage in public offerings must file a Securities Registration Statement before soliciting investors if the total offering amount is JP¥ 100 million or more.[252] They must provide detailed and comprehensive information concerning their offerings and companies.[253] They are also obligated to provide a prospectus or make it accessible to investors.[254] It should be noted that filing a Securities Registration Statement triggers continuous disclosure obligations, including providing annual reports, semi-annual or quarterly reports, and extraordinary reports. Lending platforms are prohibited from: (1) providing false information, conclusive assessments of uncertain matters, or misleading information to investors; (2) visiting or contacting unsolicited investors; (3) soliciting investors without prior confirmation of their willingness; (4) continuing to solicit customers who have expressed unwillingness or request not to be solicited; and (5) engaging in other acts that harm investor protection, transaction fairness, or confidence in the Financial Instruments Business.[255] It is worth noting that the Financial Instruments and Exchange Act also prohibits lending platforms from providing guarantees to investors.[256]

In the course of providing investment management, the platforms are obligated to faithfully work on behalf of investors and exercise due care to safeguard the interests of investors.[257] In addition, they have to establish robust compliance frameworks

---

[248] See Japan's Financial Instruments and Exchange Act (Act No. 25 of 1948, as amended), Article 2, Paragraph 2, item (xii).

[249] See Japan's Financial Instruments and Exchange Act (Act No. 25 of 1948, as amended), Article 28, Paragraph 2, item (ii).

[250] When the number of investors is 500 or more.

[251] When the number of investors is 499 or less.

[252] See Japan's Financial Instruments and Exchange Act (Act No. 25 of 1948, as amended), Article 5 and Article 23-3.

[253] See Japan's Financial Instruments and Exchange Act (Act No. 25 of 1948, as amended), Article 36.

[254] See Japan's Financial Instruments and Exchange Act (Act No. 25 of 1948, as amended), Article 13.

[255] See Japan's Financial Instruments and Exchange Act (Act No. 25 of 1948, as amended), Article 38.

[256] See Japan's Financial Instruments and Exchange Act (Act No. 25 of 1948, as amended), Article 39, Paragraph 1.

[257] See Japan's Financial Instruments and Exchange Act (Act No. 25 of 1948, as amended), Article 42, Paragraph 1.

and internal control systems to ensure compliance with the Act's provisions and prevent illegal activities.[258]

It is worth noting that compliance with both the Financial Instruments and Exchange Act and the Money Lending Business Act can lead to conflicts of interest between investors and borrowers on social online lending platforms. The Money Lending Business Act mandates borrower anonymity, while the Financial Instruments and Exchange Act requires disclosure to protect investors. Information disclosed to investors includes details about borrowers' loan purposes, collateral, and anonymized borrower descriptions and comments.[259] An illustrative case highlighting the conflict between disclosure under the Financial Instruments and Exchange Act and borrower anonymity under the Money Lending Business Act involves Minnano Credit, an online lending platform established in June 2015.[260] The company raised JP¥ 4500 million from investors, promising to invest the proceeds in a diversified portfolio of promising SMEs. However, the proceeds were actually channelled to a single entity affiliated with Minnano Credit, which was concealed from investors through the exploitation of disclosure loopholes. As a result, the company faced administrative sanctions, including a one-month suspension of business activities. It is noted that this case serves as a tangible example of the conflict arising from the competing principles of disclosure and anonymity.[261]

Another case that highlights the violation of the Financial Instruments and Exchange Act involves SBI Social Lending. On February 5, 2021, the social lending company confirmed concerns about its lending operations to a specific borrower. To investigate these concerns, SBI Holdings, the parent company, established a third-party committee consisting of independent experts.[262] The committee's investigation report, dated April 28, 2021, revealed that SBI Social Lending had used false or misleading information to solicit funds for 39 loan contracts with a total loan amount of more than JP¥ 38.3 billion between May 2017 and October 2020. Over the course of two years from November 2018 to December 2020, the company collected JP¥ 20.7 billion from investors, promising to finance the development of solar power plants and rental apartments. However, the committee discovered that JP¥ 12.9 billion of the collected funds had been diverted to other purposes.[263] Considering these findings, the Financial Services Agency imposed administrative sanctions, including a one-month suspension of business activities.[264] On May 24, 2021, SBI

[258] See Japan's Financial Instruments and Exchange Act (Act No. 25 of 1948, as amended), Article 25.

[259] See Nemoto et al. (2019, p. 9).

[260] See Minnano Credit (2023).

[261] See Nemoto et al. (2019).

[262] See SBI Holdings (2021).

[263] See SBI Social Lending (2021a, p. 25).

[264] See Kanto Finance Bureau (2021) and the Mainichi (2021).

Social Lending announced the closure of its business and committed to returning the collected funds to investors who were impacted by these illicit practices.[265]

## 5.2 The United States and Vietnam's Approaches to Risk Diversification Compared

### *5.2.1 Collateral*

In the United States, collateral has long been used to diversify the credit risk borne by lenders, as mentioned in Sect. 5.1.1.

Collateral can include a wide range of assets. In the United States, assets that can be used as collateral are divided into two main categories, including personal property (which refers to property other than real property, such as objects, money, valuable papers, and property rights) and real property (such as land and buildings).[266] Currently, the Uniform Commercial Code (hereinafter referred to as "UCC")[267] provides a statutory framework governing personal property that can be used as collateral. According to the UCC, personal property that can be used as collateral includes: (1) proceeds to which a security interest attaches; (2) accounts, chattel paper, payment intangibles, and promissory notes that have been sold; and (3) goods that are the subject of a consignment.[268] Additionally, the laws of the state where real property is located will be applied to real property that can be used as collateral.[269]

In both the United States and Vietnam, like many other countries globally, collateral can take various forms. It can be movable or immovable, tangible or intangible, and existing or to be formed in the future. For example, in the United States, proceeds to which security interest attaches can include:

(A) Whatever is acquired upon the sale, lease, license, exchange, or other disposition of collateral.
(B) Whatever is collected on, or distributed on account of, collateral.
(C) Rights arising out of collateral.

[265] See SBI Social Lending (2021b).

[266] See Mellor et al. (2024)

[267] Uniform Commercial Code is a comprehensive set of laws governing all commercial transactions in the United States. It is not a federal law, but a uniformly adopted state law. It is essential for the interstate transaction, and businesses can enter into contracts with confidence that the terms will be enforced in the same way by the courts of every American jurisdiction. A substantial revision to Article 9 was completed in 1998 and adopted in all states. The latest amendment of the article was issued in 2010. See Uniform Law Commission (2025a).

[268] See Uniform Commercial Code, Article 9-102, Paragraph 12.

[269] See Florack et al. (2022).

(D) To the extent of the value of collateral, claims arising out of the loss, nonconformity, or interference with the use of, defects or infringement of rights in, or damage to, the collateral or
(E) To the extent of the value of collateral and to the extent payable to the debtor or the secured party, insurance payable by reason of the loss or nonconformity of, defects or infringement of rights in, or damage to, the collateral.[270]

Additionally, in both the United States and Vietnam, specific requirements are established for property that can be used as collateral and the perfection (validity and enforceability) of a security interest. The establishment of security interests for most categories of personal property in the United States are governed by state laws, which often adopt provisions from the UCC. To establish enforceable security interests in personal property:

(a) The lender must provide value to the grantor of the security interest.
(b) The grantor must have rights in the collateral or the power to transfer rights in the collateral to the lender and
(c) Either the grantor must execute a security agreement providing a description of the collateral or, in the case of certain types of collateral, the collateral must be in the possession or control of the lender.[271]

It has been noted that, in order to be enforceable, a security interest must be perfected by the lender. There are four following methods of perfecting a security interest under the UCC:

(a) Filing a financing statement with a description of the collateral in the appropriate state filing office (typically takes place in the state filing office where the borrower is located)
(b) Possession (as for certain tangible assets)
(c) Establishing control (typically by entering into control agreements in the case of deposit accounts, letter of credit rights, investment accounts, and electronic chattel paper) and
(d) Automatic perfection (as for certain other personal property)[272]

If multiple lenders have successfully perfected security interests in the same collateral, the UCC outlines rules to determine which lender holds priority over the other security interests. Generally, this determination is based on a first-in-time rule, where the lender who first filed or perfected their security interest takes priority. However, there are special rules for acquisition finance, known as purchase-money priority, and specific priority rules apply to certain types of collateral, such as promissory notes, investment securities, and deposit accounts, when a security interest is perfected through possession or control.[273]

---

[270] See Uniform Commercial Code, Article 9-102, Paragraph 64.
[271] See Florack et al. (2022) and Uniform Commercial Code, Article 9-203, Paragraph (b).
[272] Florack et al. (2022) and Uniform Commercial Code, Article 9-203, Paragraph (b).
[273] See Mellor et al. (2024).

It is worth noting that, to establish a security interest in assets not governed by the UCC (such as real property and certain kinds of intellectual property), it is common for the involved parties to create separate collateral documents or mortgages in accordance with the relevant regulations in the jurisdiction that governs the particular property.[274]

Furthermore, in both the United States and Vietnam, depending on the type of security property and the parties involved in a security transaction, additional regulations may apply. For example, a security transaction between a conventional bank and its affiliate[275] is subject to the Code of Federal Regulations (hereinafter referred to as "CFR").[276] Another example relates to the valuation of real property, where appraisers must comply with regulations under the Financial Institutions Reform, Recovery and Enforcement Act of 1989[277] and utilize the Uniform Standards of Professional Appraisal Practice (USPAP).[278] One other example involves the use of intellectual properties, such as patents and patent applications, trademarks and trademark applications, copyrights and copyright applications, and trade secrets. In this case, the Patent Act (1952, as amended),[279] the Trademark Act (1946, as amended),[280] and the Copyright Act (1976, as amended)[281] can be applied.

As a form of collateral, credit guarantees have been developed in the United States with the development of both private and public types. The differences between the United States and Vietnam in terms of credit guarantees are outlined as below.

While private credit guarantees provided for SMEs in Vietnam are commonly referred to as downstream guarantees, private credit guarantees provided for SMEs in the United States are commonly categorized into three types, including downstream guarantee, upstream guarantee, and cross-stream guarantee. Among these types, a downstream guarantee involves a parent company guaranteeing the debts of its subsidiaries. Upstream guarantee involves a subsidiary guaranteeing the debts of its parent company, while cross-stream guarantee involves a subsidiary guaranteeing the debts of its sister company.[282]

---

[274] See Florack et al. (2022).

[275] Affiliate means any entity that controls, is controlled by, or is under common control with conventional banks. See The Code of Federal Regulations, Title 12, Chapter I, Section 28.11.

[276] See the Code of Federal Regulations, Title 12, Chapter II, Section 223.14.

[277] See the United States Code, Title 12, Chapter 34.

[278] The Uniform Standards of Professional Appraisal Practice (USPAP) are the recognized ethical and performance standards for the appraisal profession in the United States. See the Appraisal Foundation (2025).

[279] Regulating inventions in many technology areas. See The United States Code, Title 35.

[280] Regulating trademarks and other source identifiers. See The United States Code, Title 15, Chapter 22, Subchapter I.

[281] Regulating all forms of creative expression, including software, movies, books, and other media properties. See The United States Code, Title 17.

[282] See Mellor et al. (2024, p. 15).

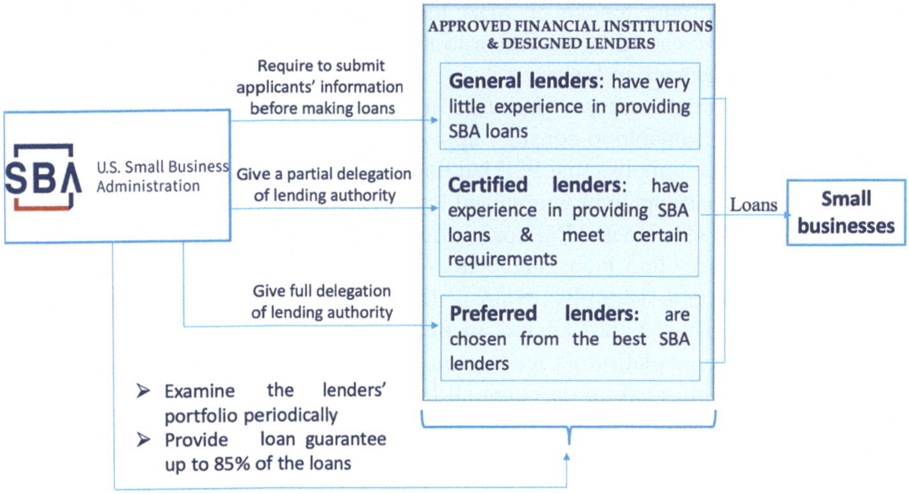


**Fig. 5.5** Loan guarantee provided by the SBA

It can be seen that private guarantees can be used to secure SMEs' loans via P2P lending schemes. It has been noted that in the United States, there are generally no additional limitations or restrictions specifically applicable to the aforementioned types of private credit guarantees beyond the requirements that apply to guarantees in general.[283] However, it is worth noting that a guarantee can be invalidated by a bankruptcy court if it is determined to be a fraudulent transfer.[284] This can occur if, at the time the guarantee is provided, the guarantor is insolvent and does not receive reasonably equivalent value in return for the guarantee.[285] Furthermore, when private guarantees are used to secure SMEs' loans via P2P lending schemes, security interests also need to be perfected by P2P lenders in accordance with current laws to ensure enforceability.

Another difference is that the public guarantee model in the United States (see Fig. 5.5) is more sophisticated in comparison with the public guarantee models in Vietnam.

As mentioned in Sect. 5.1.1, the SBA provides credit guarantees through approved financial institutions or designated lenders. In practice, if borrowers default, SBA lenders are expected to diligently pursue repayments before seeking reimbursement from the SBA. If an SBA lender's default rate becomes excessively high, they may face discontinuation from participating in SBA loan programs. Furthermore, in the event of credit default, SBA lenders may receive up to 85% guarantee from the SBA for the defaulted loans. It can be seen that this mechanism of

[283] See Florack et al. (2022, p. 15).

[284] Under Section 548 of the Federal Bankruptcy Code. See The United States Code, Title 11, Chapter 5, Subchapter III, Section 548.

[285] See Mellor et al. (2024, p. 15) and Florack et al. (2022).

selecting and classifying lenders in SBA loan programs is likely to help reduce lenders' risk and increase their incentive to thoroughly evaluate borrowers' creditworthiness before extending loans.

To explore potential measures for mitigating risks faced by lenders in P2P lending in Vietnam, it is reasonable to consider applying the guarantee mechanism used in SBA loan programs. Suppose that P2P lending platforms are classified and selected by a guarantor to participate in guaranteed loan programs. Suppose also that a P2P lending platform is selected and P2P loans offered via its platform can be guaranteed. In this scenario, providing loan guarantees for P2P loans is likely to enhance the platform's incentive to carefully evaluate the creditworthiness of potential borrowers. It can also assist P2P lenders in mitigating the risk of adverse selection which results from the platform's inadequate due diligence performance and provision of inaccurate information on potential borrowers' creditworthiness. Additionally, when the guarantor periodically reviews the list of loans provided through the P2P lending platform, it is likely to mitigate the risk of financial loss for P2P lenders in the event of the platform's temporary or permanent cessation. However, as mentioned in Sect. 1.2, if potential borrowers are non-banked or underbanked and they apply for loans via the platform for the first time, the platform is hardly able to have their track records. This can lead to an increased default rate for the lending platform. As a result, the likelihood of the lending platform being selected by the guarantor is likely to be reduced, and it is highly unlikely that P2P loans provided via the platform will be guaranteed. Furthermore, it is also highly unlikely for P2P borrowers to easily find guarantors willing to guarantee their repayment of P2P loans.

### 5.2.2 *Due Diligence*

Due diligence has long been used in the United States to diversify the risk associated with micro- and/or small-sized financing schemes as discussed in Sect. 5.1.1. It can be seen that there are several similarities between the United States and Vietnam concerning due diligence. These similarities are outlined below.

Due diligence in both the United States and Vietnam involves KYC or e-KYC. In the United States, a range of entities that are deemed financial institutions and nonfinancial trade and businesses are subject to the Bank Secrecy Act (1970, as amended) and the relevant regulations.[286] They are required to conduct KYC or e-KYC to verify customer identification data. They are also obligated to maintain records of collected data and keep track of customers' business transactions to ensure their financial activities are consistent with their business operations.[287]

[286] See The United States Code, Title 31, Subtitle IV, Chapter 53, Subchapter II, Article 5312.

[287] Brummer (2020, p. 426), Mulligan (1998, p. 2358) and Office of the Comptroller of the Currency (2025b).

Due diligence in both countries can also involve credit scores. Under the US Fair Credit Reporting Act (1970, as amended), credit reporting companies provide credit scores for individuals, while business credit reporting companies offer credit scores for businesses.[288] These companies frequently collect data from various sources, including financial institutions, public records,[289] and other sources, to compile credit reports that include credit scores. For example, three major national credit reporting agencies, namely, Equifax, Experian, and TransUnion, gather lending information and can provide annual credit scores for millions of individuals.[290] Business credit reporting companies like Dun & Bradstreet, Experian Commercial, and Equifax Small Business also collect data and provide credit scores for millions of businesses.[291]

It is worth noting that credit ratings issued by credit rating agencies can be utilized in due diligence in the United States and Vietnam. In the United States, credit rating agencies have expanded their opinions on borrowers' creditworthiness since the 1930s.[292] The main regulations governing the provision of credit ratings by credit rating agencies are the Credit Rating Agency Reform Act (2006, as amended) and the Dodd-Frank Act (2010, as amended). Under the Credit Rating Agency Reform Act, credit rating agencies are required to register with the SEC to become nationally recognized statistical rating organizations (hereinafter referred to as "NRSROs").[293] According to the Dodd-Frank Act, NRSROs must meet the following requirements for a transparent credit rating process: (1) disclose and publish ratings and track records, allowing users to assess accuracy and compare performance among NRSROs; (2) provide clear and informative track records for investors with varying levels of sophistication, covering multiple years and types of credit ratings; (3) notify users of any changes or errors in methodologies that could affect ratings; and (4) publish detailed information on assumptions, data reliability, limitations, risks,

[288] See Federal Trade Commission (2025) and Malloy and Lovett (2019, p. 223).

[289] Such as property or court records.

[290] It is worth noting that rated individuals have the right to request one free copy of their credit report each year from each of the three major consumer reporting companies (Equifax, Experian, and TransUnion). These companies also cooperate with Fair Isaac Corporation to provide FICO scores, a particular brand of credit score. FICO scores take into account data in five areas to determine creditworthiness, including payment history, current level of indebtedness, types of credit used, length of credit history, and new credit accounts. See Board of Governors of the Federal Reserve System (2025) and FICO (2023).

[291] See Carbajo (2018).

[292] Credit rating was first used by the United States regulators to limit the riskiness of assets held by regulated entities under the Securities Act in 1933, the Securities Exchange Act in 1934, and the Investment Company Act in 1940. See Hemraj (2015, p. 108).

[293] At present, among nine credit rating agencies which registered as NRSROs, S&P, Moody's, and Fitch are the biggest companies that provided around 2 million credit ratings, accounting for about 95% of the total outstanding credit ratings of all NRSROs in 2019. See the United States Securities and Exchange Commission (2021) and Office of Credit Ratings (2020, p. 11).

and use of third-party due diligence services with each credit rating.[294] Additionally, NRSROs must mitigate conflicts of interest by reviewing and revising credit ratings if an employee who previously worked for the issuer or related parties was involved in the rating process within one year.[295] Furthermore, rating analysts are required to pass qualifying exams and engage in continuing education to enhance the quality of credit ratings.[296]

It can be seen that despite the aforementioned similarities between the United States and Vietnam concerning due diligence, the employment of due diligence by P2P lending platforms in the United States is more likely to be facilitated. It is apparent that credit scores provided by diverse credit reporting companies, as well as credit ratings issued by credit rating agencies, can play an important role in this facilitation.

### *5.2.3 Risk Limiting Measures*

Credit limits have long been employed in the United States to limit the risk borne by lenders.[297] Regulations on credit limits applied to conventional banks are issued in both the United States and Vietnam. For example, in the United States, total loans and extensions of credit are regulated as follows:

> A national bank's or savings association's total outstanding loans and extensions of credit to one borrower may not exceed 15% of the bank's or savings association's capital and surplus, plus an additional 10% of the bank's or savings association's capital and surplus, if the amount that exceeds the bank's or savings association's 15% general limit is fully secured by readily marketable collateral, as defined in § 32.2(v). To qualify for the additional 10% limit, the bank or savings association must perfect a security interest in the collateral under applicable law and the collateral must have a current market value at all times of at least 100% of the amount of the loan or extension of credit that exceeds the bank's or savings association's 15% general limit.[298]

Additionally, quantitative limitations are imposed on bank affiliate lending transactions. Banks are not allowed to lend more than 10% of their capital stock and surplus to a single affiliate, or more than 20% to the aggregate of all affiliates.[299]

---

[294] It should be noted that the activities of credit rating agencies are fundamentally commercial in character and should be subject to the same standards of liability and oversight as apply to auditors, securities analysts, and investment bankers. See the United States Dodd-Frank Act of 2010, Section 931 (3) and Section 932 (a) (5) (q).

[295] See the United States Dodd-Frank Act of 2010, Section 932 (a) (4) (h) (4) (A).

[296] See the United States Dodd-Frank Act of 2010, Section 936 and Hemraj (2015, p. 140).

[297] It is worth noting that restrictions on the lending of national banks to a single borrower were first enacted in 1863 as part of the National Currency Act. See the Harvard Law Review Association (1985, p. 430).

[298] See the Code of Federal Regulations, Title 12, Chapter I, Part 32, Section 32.3 (a).

[299] See the United States Code, Title 12, Chapter 3, Subchapter X, Section 371c (a) (1).

However, the aforementioned lending limits are subject to certain exceptions, depending on the reliability and strength of the collateral, as well as the liquidity of the loan obligations involved.[300] For example, loans arising from the discount of commercial or business paper, loans secured by US obligations (such as bonds, notes, certificates of indebtedness, or treasury bills of the US government), or loans secured by segregated deposit accounts are not subject to the above lending limits.[301]

### 5.2.4 Risk Sharing

It can be seen that, in comparison with Vietnam, the United States has a long history and extensive experience concerning loan syndication. The syndicated loans market in the United States started in the late 1980s, while the first document regulating syndicated loans in Vietnam was issued in 2011. Additionally, Vietnam has not yet established a secondary market for syndicated loans, whereas syndicated loans in the United States have been provided in both the primary and secondary markets since the 1990s.[302]

In 1995, the Loan Syndications and Trading Association was formed to develop best practices, market standards, and trading documentation in order to promote the development of the syndicated loans market and help spread the credit risk caused by one borrower among multiple lenders.[303] The approach to diversification of risk borne by lenders by using the secondary market in the United States is introduced in Sect. 5.2.7.

### 5.2.5 Provisional Funds

Provisional funds have long been employed in the United States to offset bad debts. Banks' provisional funds were initially regulated in 1947 to absorb loan losses. These losses can be from loans that are identified as bad loans and good loans that later become uncollectable.[304]

There are several notable similarities between the United States and Vietnam in terms of employing provisional funds to mitigate the risk borne by lenders in lending transactions. Provisional funds in both countries include specific provisions and general provisions. Specific provisions are intended to absorb losses from specific

[300] See Malloy and Lovett (2019, p. 199).

[301] See the Code of Federal Regulations, Title 12, Chapter I, Part 32, Section 32.3 (c).

[302] See Marsh and Virmani (2024, p. 2).

[303] See Marsh and Virmani (2024, p. 1).

[304] See Walter (1991, p. 26).

bad loans, while general provisions are intended to absorb potential losses from good loans that later become uncollectable.[305]

However, in Vietnam, provisional funds are primarily determined based on qualitative and quantitative debt classification, whereas in the United States, various techniques have been employed. For example, before the mid-1970s, banks were encouraged to use the constant percentage-of-loans technique,[306] which required them to set target levels for the ratio of their loan loss provision to total loans. They would then add to the provision whenever the ratio fell below target levels. From the mid-1970s to the mid-1980s, banks used peer equivalent and loss history techniques, setting provisional funds based on peer banks' levels or historical loan losses.[307] In the mid-1980s, banks applied the loan analysis technique, estimating provisions for different loan categories based on historical losses and the knowledge of individual loan categories.[308] During 1998–2003, the incurred loss method was introduced in the Generally Accepted Accounting Principles.[309] This method estimates loan loss provision based on historical information and current economic events.[310] In 2016, the Financial Accounting Standards Board (FASB) introduced the current expected credit losses method, using historical data, current conditions, and forecasts that affect the collectability of the remaining loans to estimate credit losses.[311]

### 5.2.6 Credit Insurance

Credit insurance has long been employed as a method to mitigate losses borne by lenders in the United States. Historically, several states, including New York, New Jersey, and Louisiana, passed the first statutes permitting the provision of credit insurance between 1885 and 1886.[312] Since 1955, the National Association of Insurance Commissioners (NAIC) has drafted legislation to assist states in effectively regulating the credit insurance industry.[313]

Similar to credit insurance in Vietnam, credit insurance in the United States is not a legal requirement in lending transactions. Lenders and borrowers are free to negotiate the purchase of credit insurance. Lenders may purchase credit insurance and/or require borrowers to pay credit insurance premiums to secure loans.

---

[305] See Walter (1991, p. 21).

[306] It is worth noting that this technique does not require banks to determine expected future loan losses.

[307] See Walter (1991, p. 26).

[308] See Walter (1991, p. 27).

[309] This method was adopted by the SEC.

[310] See Gnanarajah (2018).

[311] See Alpert (2021) and the Federal Reserve System (2020).

[312] See Hanna (1931, p. 522) and Brown (1969, p. 440).

[313] See Brown (1969, p. 449).

However, in Vietnam, there are currently no specific regulations governing credit insurance apart from the general regulations in the Law on Insurance Business 2022. Meanwhile, in the United States, the NAIC has proposed several model acts regarding credit insurance. For example, the Creditor-Placed Insurance Model Act (1996) establishes a legal framework for creditor-placed insurance. This type of insurance refers to insurance that lenders unilaterally purchase after credit transactions, providing coverage for collateralized personal property against various risks, such as fire, theft, or collision, that could impair lenders' interests or affect the value of collateral. This insurance is acquired when the borrowers fail to provide the necessary physical damage insurance as required in lending agreements.[314] Another example is the Consumer Credit Insurance Model Act (2001), which was proposed to create a legal framework for consumer credit insurance[315] issued or sold in connection with loans or other credit transactions.[316] This Model Act includes regulations on policy provisions, premiums and refunds, insurer duties, enforcement, and penalties.

### 5.2.7 *Secondary Market*

It has been noted that loans are actively traded in the United States, with the secondary loan market emerging in the 1990s and becoming a vibrant, dealer-driven market.[317] Banks have been motivated to reduce their exposure to borrowers and engage in regulatory capital arbitrage by selling loans rather than holding them until maturity. Although loans are not considered securities, they can be issued to qualified institutional buyers under Rule 144a of the Securities Act (1993, as amended),[318] and they are traded similarly to other debt securities on over-the-counter (OTC) markets.[319]

It can be seen that, in comparison with Vietnam, the United States has extensive experience concerning the secondary loan market. In 1995, the Loan Syndication Trading Association (LSTA) was established to foster the growth of the secondary loan market. The LSTA plays a leading role by developing policies and guidelines, promoting standardization of loan documentation, and ensuring equitable market practices. It introduced a monthly dealer quote-based secondary mark-to-market

[314] See Creditor-Placed Insurance Model Act (1996), Section 3 (G).

[315] Consumer credit insurance is a general term used to refer to any or all of credit life insurance, credit accident and health insurance, credit unemployment insurance, or any other insurance specifically defined in this Act in accordance with the Consumer Credit Insurance Model Act, Section 2 (B) (2).

[316] See Consumer Credit Insurance Model Act, Section 2 (A) (2).

[317] Marsh and Virmani (2024).

[318] See Anthony et al. (2017, p. 11).

[319] See Santosa and Nigro (2009, p. 1411) and Practical Law (2014, p. 26).

process in 1996 to value loans, enhancing market liquidity and transparency. In collaboration with Thomson Reuters Loan Pricing Corporation, LSTA formed the first secondary mark-to-market pricing service in 1999, providing daily US secondary market prices for loan participants. Additionally, the creation of the S&P/LSTA Leveraged Loan Index and the availability of bank loan ratings by rating agencies further facilitated the development of the secondary loan market in the United States. Furthermore, the LSTA has published complete credit agreements to facilitate transactions among market participants.[320]

## 5.3 Japan and Vietnam's Approaches to Diversification Compared

### *5.3.1 Collateral*

Collateral has long been considered an effective method to diversify credit risk faced by lenders in Japan, as mentioned in Sect. 5.1.2. The practice of commercial banks securing loans with collateral was standardized in 1962 when the Federation of Bankers Associations published uniform bank loan contracts.[321] Currently, collateral is primarily regulated by the Civil Code (1896, as amended) and related regulations.

It can be seen that Japan and Vietnam share several similarities in the practice of using collateral to diversify lenders' credit risk in lending transactions. One similarity is the wide range of assets that can be used as collateral in both countries. In Japan, collateral can include immovables,[322] movables,[323] receivables,[324] shares, and other securities,[325] as well as intellectual property rights.[326] Another similarity is that collateral can be movable or immovable, tangible or intangible, and existing or to be formed in the future. For example, in Japan, both immovables and movables, as well as receivables and future receivables, can serve as collateral for pledges.[327] Additionally, in both Japan and Vietnam, there are specific requirements and

[320] See Marsh and Virmani (2024).

[321] See Kitagawa and Kurasawa (1994, p. 107).

[322] Land and any fixtures thereto are immovables. See the English translation of the Civil Code of Japan (Act No. 89 of 1896, as amended), Article 86, Paragraph 1.

[323] Things other than immovables are movables (for example, automobiles, machinery, equipment, inventory, and other movables). See Japan's Civil Code (Act No. 89 of 1896, as amended), Article 86, Paragraph 2.

[324] Such as trade loan claims, lease receivables, claims for fees, trade receivables, and other receivables.

[325] Other securities include bonds and trust beneficial interests.

[326] Such as patent rights, trademark rights, design rights, and copyrights. See Suehiro (2023).

[327] See Japan's Civil Code (Act No. 89 of 1896, as amended), Article 352 and Article 356.

regulations regarding property that can be used as collateral and the perfection (validity and enforceability) of security interests. Furthermore, depending on the type of security property and the parties involved in a security transaction, additional regulations may apply.

In Japan, the typical forms of security interest and perfection requirements corresponding to several types of assets are set out below.

Firstly, immovables can be used as collateral in Japan. It has been noted that the most common form of security over an immovable is a mortgage.[328] A mortgage "gives the secured creditor a preferential right relating to the value of the mortgaged property, and allows it to receive payments from the proceeds of the mortgaged property before other creditors."[329] It is worth noting that secured obligations can be specified in fixed mortgages or designated as a certain group of unspecified obligations, which are commonly referred to as blanket mortgages.[330] To perfect a mortgage, it must be registered with the relevant legal affairs bureau in compliance with the Real Property Registration Act (2004, as amended)[331] and other applicable laws governing registration.[332] Under current laws, land and buildings built on it are considered distinct forms of real property.[333] Therefore, the process of establishing and perfecting a mortgage is necessary for both land and buildings individually.[334]

Secondly, movables can also be used as collateral according to Japanese laws. It has been noted that the most common forms of security for movables are pledges and security assignments.[335] Under the Civil Code (1896, as amended), to perfect a pledge over a movable property, actual delivery of the property to the obligee[336] and continuous possession of the property by the pledgee are required.[337] On the other hand, the creation of a security assignment can become effective through delivery

[328] See Aoyama and Matsuda (2022, p. 99) and Suehiro (2023).

[329] See Ueno and Yamamoto (2023, p. 4). Japan's Civil Code (Act No. 89 of 1896, as amended), Article 369, Paragraph 1 provides that: "[a] mortgage has the right to have the mortgagee's claim satisfied prior to other obligees out of the immovables that the obligor or a third party provided to secure the obligation without transferring possession."

[330] See Aoyama and Matsuda (2022). Japan's Civil Code (Act No. 89 of 1896, as amended), Article 398 bis 2, Paragraph 1 and Paragraph 2 provide that:

(1) Mortgages may be created, by an establishing act, in order to secure unspecified claims of a certain scope, up to the limit of a maximum amount.
(2) The scope of the unspecified claims to be secured by the mortgage under the provisions of the preceding paragraph (hereinafter referred to as 'revolving mortgage') must be prescribed by limiting the scope to claims arising from specific contracts with the obligor for continuous transactions or other claims arising from certain kinds of transactions with the obligor.

[331] See the English translation of the Real Property Registration Act of Japan (Act No. 123 of 2004).

[332] See Japan's Civil Code (Act No. 89 of 1896, as amended), Article 370.

[333] See Japan's Civil Code (Act No. 89 of 1896, as amended), Article 177.

[334] See Yusuke Suehiro (2023).

[335] See Ueno and Yamamoto (2023, p. 5) and Aoyama and Matsuda (2022).

[336] See Japan's Civil Code (Act No. 89 of 1896, as amended), Article 344.

[337] See Japan's Civil Code (Act No. 89 of 1896, as amended), Article 352.

and continuous possession[338] or registration.[339] Movable properties can serve as collateral either as individual assets or as a collection of assets. In the case of a collection, it must be adequately identified by specifying the asset type, location, and other relevant criteria.[340]

Thirdly, collateral can include receivables. In a lending transaction, a lender and borrower can establish a security agreement to create a security interest over receivables. Within such an agreement, it is crucial to adequately identify the target receivables, specifying their type, date of origination, and any other relevant details as applicable. If the target receivables are expected to be generated in the future, it is necessary to specify the time period during which the receivables will be created in the security agreement.[341] The creation of a security interest over receivables can take the form of a pledge or a security assignment. The lender can perfect the pledge or security assignment through two methods: (a) sending a date-certified notice to, or obtaining a date-certified consent from, the debtor of the receivables;[342] or (b) registering the pledge or security assignment.[343]

Fourthly, it should be mentioned that collateral can also include shares. In Japan, the most prevalent form of security over shares is through pledges. For listed shares, pledges can be established and perfected by registering them within the book-entry system administered by the Japan Securities Depositary Center, Inc.[344] On the other hand, for shares in unlisted companies, pledges are considered established upon delivery of the share certificates to the secured creditor. The perfection of these security interests can be achieved through either (1) continuous possession by the pledgees[345] or (2) requesting the issuing companies to record the pledges on their shareholder ledgers.[346]

---

[338] See Japan's Civil Code (Act No. 89 of 1896, as amended), Article 178.

[339] See The English translation of the Act on Special Provisions for the Civil Code Concerning the Perfection Requirements for the Assignment of Movables and Claims of Japan (Act No. 104 of 1998, as amended), Article 3, Paragraph 1 provides that: "[i]f a corporation assigns movables (excluding movables for which a warehouse receipt, a bill of lading or a multimodal bill of lading is issued; the same applies hereinafter), and a registration of assignment is made in a registration file of movables assignment with regard to the assignment of the movables, it is deemed that the movables have been delivered as set forth in Article 178 of the Civil Code."

[340] This allows lenders to include movable properties acquired in the future as part of the security. See Aoyama and Matsuda (2022).

[341] See Suehiro (2023).

[342] See Japan's Civil Code (Act No. 89 of 1896, as amended), Article 364 and Article 467, Paragraph 1.

[343] See Japan's Act on Special Provisions for the Civil Code Concerning the Perfection Requirements for the Assignment of Movables and Claims (Act No. 104 of 1998, as amended), Article 4, Paragraph 1 and Article 14.

[344] See Japan's Civil Code (Act No. 89 of 1896, as amended), Article 520 bis 7 and Suehiro (2023).

[345] See the English translation of the Company Act of Japan (Act No. 86 of 2005, as amended), Article 147, Paragraph 2.

[346] See Japan's Company Act (Act No. 86 of 2005, as amended), Article 147, Paragraph 1.

As a form of collateral, credit guarantees have long been developed in Japan with the development of both private and public types. The differences between Japan and Vietnam regarding credit guarantees are outlined below.

It can be seen that private guarantees in Japan include guarantees provided by individuals (hereinafter referred to as "personal guarantees")[347] and guarantees provided by corporations. The Civil Code (1896, as amended) provides detailed regulations pertaining to personal guarantees. Accordingly, individuals acting as guarantors for personal guarantees must possess the legal capacity and sufficient financial resources to fulfill the guaranteed obligation.[348] Guarantees are deemed legally binding and enforceable only when they are established in writing or in an electronic or magnetic record.[349] In addition, in the case of revolving guarantees,[350] the guarantee contract must specify the maximum amount of the guaranteed obligation.[351] The date of a revolving guarantee contract should be crystallized within five years from the signing date.[352] In the case of a guarantee contract where the principal obligation is a loan obligation assumed for business or a revolving guarantee contract that includes a loan obligation assumed for business, the contract is considered ineffective unless the guarantor expresses their intention to fulfill the guarantee obligation. This expression of intention must be done through a notarial instrument, which should be prepared within one month prior to the conclusion of the contract.[353] Furthermore, the guarantor must be provided by the obligor (or debtor) with information and explanations regarding specific matters, such as the economic condition of the debtor, the amount to be repaid for the debt, and the occurrence of an event of default.[354]

While private credit guarantees provided by corporations in Vietnam are commonly known as downstream guarantees, private credit guarantees provided by

[347] It is worth noting that in practice, personal guarantees are commonly utilized in commercial transactions. For example, a representative director or majority owner of a small firm provides guarantees when the firm is granted a loan. See Ueno and Yamamoto (2023, p. 15).

[348] See Japan's Civil Code (Act No. 89 of 1896, as amended), Article 450, Paragraph 1.

[349] See Japan's Civil Code (Act No. 89 of 1896, as amended), Article 446, Paragraphs 2 and 3.

[350] A revolving guarantee is an agreement where the principal obligation comprises one or more unidentified obligations within a specified scope. See Japan's Civil Code (Act No. 89 of 1896, as amended), Article 465 bis 2, Paragraph 1.

[351] See Japan's Civil Code (Act No. 89 of 1896, as amended), Article 465 bis 2, Paragraph 2.

[352] See Japan's Civil Code (Act No. 89 of 1896, as amended), Article 465 bis 3, Paragraph 1. It is worth noting that the principal obligation under a contract for revolving guarantee by an individual for loans becomes crystallized in the following cases: (a) the lender files a petition for compulsory execution or enforcement of a security right for a payment obligation regarding any property of the guarantor or the principal obligor, and the procedure for compulsory execution or enforcement is initiated; (b) the guarantor or the principal obligor receives an order commencing bankruptcy proceedings; or (c) the relevant principal obligor or guarantor passes away. See Japan's Civil Code (Act No. 89 of 1896, as amended), Article 465 bis 4.

[353] See Japan's Civil Code (Act No. 89 of 1896, as amended), Article 465 bis 6, Paragraph 1.

[354] See Japan's Civil Code (Act No. 89 of 1896, as amended), Article 465 bis 10.

corporations in Japan are typically categorized into three types, including downstream guarantee, upstream guarantee, and cross-stream guarantee. In principle, guarantee contracts in Japan must be in written or electronic form,[355] and the guarantors should have sufficient financial resources to fulfill the guarantee obligation.[356] It has been noted that, in general, there are no specific statutory limitations or restrictions on credit guarantees by corporations in Japan, except the possibility of avoidance in upstream guarantees. In practice, the granting of upstream guarantees typically requires the consent of any minority shareholders of the guarantors.[357]

Another notable difference is that Japan has a long history and extensive experience regarding public guarantees in comparison with Vietnam. The public guarantee system in Japan dates back to the establishment of the Credit Guarantee Corporation of Tokyo in 1937.[358] Credit Guarantee Corporations (CGCs) receive financial support from local governments and provide credit guarantees to assist SMEs and micro-enterprises[359] in accessing loans from financial institutions (see Fig. 5.6). To limit the risk faced by CGCs when providing credit guarantees, maximum guarantee limits are established. For corporations, the maximum limits for general guarantees, unsecured guarantees, and privately placed bond guarantees are set at JP¥ 200 million, JP¥ 80 million, and JP¥ 450 million, respectively. For cooperatives, the maximum limits for general guarantees and unsecured guarantees are set at JP¥ 400 million and JP¥ 80 million, respectively.[360]

CGCs conduct credit checks on enterprises to determine guarantee eligibility. They accept credit guarantee applications from SMEs and micro-enterprises through financial institutions or directly. When applications are submitted through financial institutions, CGCs conduct credit checks on enterprises and issue guarantee certificates upon their approval of guarantees. For direct applications, CGCs facilitate loans through financial institutions and issue guarantee certificates upon loan

---

[355] See Japan's Civil Code (Act No. 89 of 1896, as amended), Article 446.

[356] See Japan's Civil Code (Act No. 89 of 1896, as amended), Article 450.

[357] This is due to the fact that directors of guarantor companies have a duty of care and other obligations under corporate laws, which can affect their decisions regarding the approval of upstream guarantees. See Aoyama and Matsuda (2022, p. 10).

[358] Currently, there are 51 Credit Guarantee Corporations operating throughout Japan under Japan's Credit Guarantee Corporation Act (Act No. 196 of 1953). See Japan Federation of Credit Guarantee Corporations (2022, p. 2).

[359] SMEs and micro-enterprises eligible for credit guarantees provided by CGCs must meet certain criteria based on the number of regular employees or paid-up capital. For instance, enterprises in the manufacturing industry with a paid-up capital of up to JP¥ 300 million or employing not more than 300 employees, or enterprises in the services industry with a paid-up capital of up to JP¥ 50 million or employing not more than 100 employees, fulfill these requirements. See Japan Federation of Credit Guarantee Corporations (2022, p. 7).

[360] Japan Federation of Credit Guarantee Corporations (2022, p. 8).

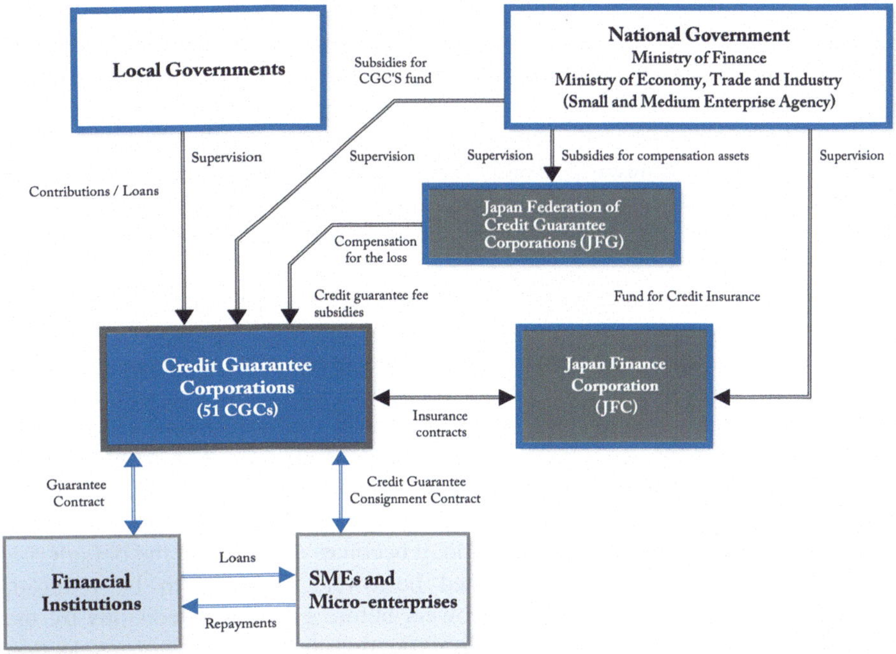


**Fig. 5.6** The Credit Supplementation System in Japan (Japan Federation of Credit Guarantee Corporations (2022, p. 5))

approval. Financial institutions disburse loans based on the certificates, and SMEs and micro-enterprises repay according to the loan terms. If SMEs and micro-enterprises default, CGCs repay financial institutions. CGCs then collect outstanding amounts from SMEs and micro-enterprises while assisting them in their recovery.[361]

It is worth noting that the public credit guarantee system in Japan utilizes responsibility-sharing methods between CGCs and financial institutions to distribute the credit risk associated with providing loans to SMEs and micro-enterprises. Financial institutions can choose between the partial guarantee method and the burden charge method. Under the partial guarantee method, CGCs typically guarantee 80% of individual loans, while financial institutions assume the remaining 20% risk. On the other hand, under the burden charge method, CGCs provide a 100% guarantee for individual loans, and financial institutions subsequently pay CGCs a burden charge of approximately 20% of the guaranteed payment.[362]

It should be noted that the credit guarantee system in Japan combines the credit guarantee system provided by CGCs with the credit insurance operated by the Japan

[361] Japan Federation of Credit Guarantee Corporations (2022, p. 6).

[362] Japan Federation of Credit Guarantee Corporations (2022, p. 9).

Finance Corporation (JFC).[363] This arrangement allows CGCs to seek insurance coverage from JFC[364] when they are unable to recover the guaranteed funds from SMEs and micro-enterprises. The comprehensive insurance contract between CGCs and JFC ensures that all guarantees are automatically insured, enabling CGCs to diversify their credit risk and preventing them from selectively choosing which guarantees are to be insured.[365] Additionally, JFC provides partial reimbursement based on the insurance coverage ratio,[366] which likely promotes risk sharing between CGCs and JFC and mitigates moral hazard in CGCs' assessment of guarantee applications.[367]

For the purpose of exploring potential measures to mitigate risks faced by P2P lenders in Vietnam, the author suggests considering the application of Japan's public credit guarantee mechanism. This would involve a guarantor providing guarantees to SMEs in Vietnam to access P2P loans via online lending platforms. Implementing such a system could include measures such as (1) conducting credit checks on P2P borrowers prior to guarantee decisions; (2) implementing responsibility-sharing methods between the guarantor and P2P lenders and/or lending platforms; and (3) allowing the guarantor to obtain insurance coverage from insurance companies. In this scenario, it becomes evident that the default risk faced by P2P lenders due to defaulted borrowers is likely to be reduced. Conducting credit checks on P2P borrowers before guarantee decisions by the guarantor may also assist P2P lenders in mitigating the risk of adverse selection resulting from inadequate due diligence performed by P2P lending platforms. Additionally, this practice may help minimize the risk of financial loss faced by P2P lenders in the event of temporary or permanent cessation of P2P lending platforms' operations. However, it is important to note that if potential borrowers are non-banked or underbanked and applying for loans via P2P platforms for the first time, assessing their creditworthiness may be challenging. In such cases, P2P loans provided through lending platforms may not be guaranteed.

---

[363] Japan Finance Corporation (JFC) was established on October 1, 2008, following the enactment of the Japan Finance Corporation Act (Act No. 57 of 2007) and the merger of four policy-based financing institutions: the National Life Finance Corporation (NLFC), the Agriculture, Forestry and Fisheries Finance Corporation (AFC), the Japan Finance Corporation for Small and Medium Enterprise (JASME), and the International Financial Operations of the Japan Bank for International Cooperation (JBIC). In April 2012, the Japan Bank for International Cooperation Act was enacted, resulting in the separation of the Japan Bank for International Cooperation (JBIC) from JFC. See Japan Finance Corporation (2024, p. 47).

[364] See The English translation of the Small and Medium-sized Enterprise Credit Insurance Act of Japan (Act No. 264 of 1950, as amended).

[365] See Kuroda (2020, p. 252).

[366] It is worth noting that 70–90% of the repaid amount is reimbursed to the CGC as insurance money by JFC. See Japan Federation of Credit Guarantee Corporations (2022, p. 7).

[367] See Kuroda (2020).

### 5.3.2 *Due Diligence*

In Japan, due diligence has also been employed as means to mitigate risk in lending transactions. Several similarities concerning due diligence in Japan and Vietnam are outlined as follows.

One similarity is that due diligence in both countries involves KYC or e-KYC. In Japan, KYC or e-KYC is primarily regulated by the Criminal Proceeds Transfer Prevention Act (Act No. 22 of 2007, as amended).[368] Accordingly, a variety of specified business operators[369] are required to conduct KYC or e-KYC and maintain transaction records. For example, financial institutions have to perform KYC or e-KYC before opening deposit accounts for large cash transactions exceeding JP¥ 2 million or for cash remittances exceeding JP¥ 100,000.[370] The collected information may include individuals' names, domiciles, and dates of birth, as well as companies' names, principal places of business, and the identities of those who have substantial control over companies.[371] The methods of information verification for non-face-to-face transactions may include sending transaction-related documents to customers' addresses by registered mail or receiving copies of verification documents like driver's licenses or passports. Additionally, online verification methods can also be employed, such as receiving facial photos and images of verification documents like driver's licenses or passports, receiving facial photos and IC chip storage information, receiving verification document images or IC chip storage information along with bank inquiries, and receiving verification document images or IC chip storage information with a specified amount of money transferred to customers' accounts.[372]

Another similarity relates to the provision of credit information to facilitate due diligence. Japan has credit information bureaus that provide credit information to facilitate the due diligence of financial institutions. These major bureaus are the Personal Credit Information Center,[373] Japan Credit Information Reference Center

368 See The English translation of the Criminal Proceeds Transfer Prevention Act of Japan (Act No. 22 of 2007, as amended).

369 Including financial institutions, financial leasing operators, credit card operators, real estate agencies, dealers in precious metals and stones, telephone receiving service providers, telephone forwarding service providers, judicial scriveners, certified administrative procedures specialists, certified public accountants, certified public tax accountants, and lawyers.

370 See National Policy Agency (2016).

371 See Saito and Sekine (2020, p. 123).

372 See Ohno and Tsunematsu (2019).

373 It is worth noting that the first Personal Credit Information Center was established in 1973 by the Tokyo bankers association, followed by 24 other centers across Japan. On October 17, 1988, all these centers were consolidated into a unit of the Japanese Bankers Association, providing services to its 1088 member institutions, including commercial banks, financial institutions, bank-affiliated credit card companies, and guarantee companies throughout the country. See Japanese Bankers Association (2025c).

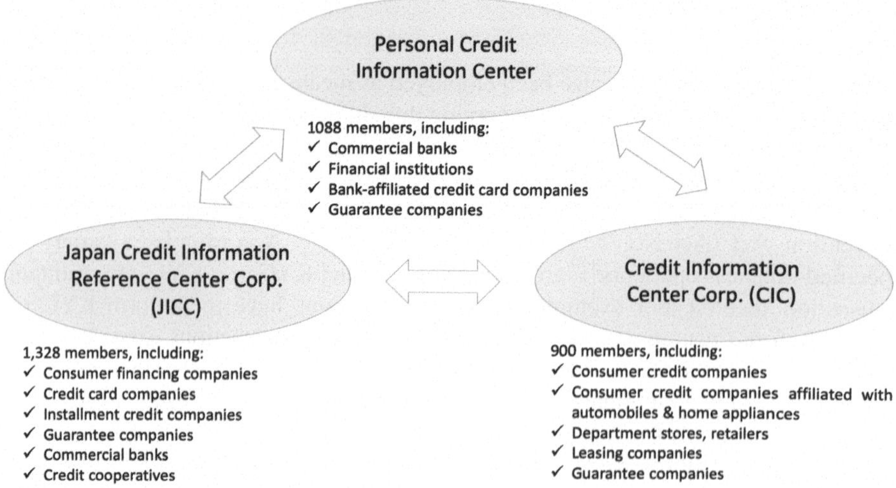


**Fig. 5.7** The shared Credit Information Network System

Corp. (hereinafter, "JICC"),[374] and Credit Information Center Corp. (hereinafter, "CIC").[375] It has been noted that these bureaus have collected and stored a lot of personal credit information as well as provided credit information to their member financial institutions.[376] In March 1987, these three bureaus started a shared credit information system (Credit Reporting Information Network—hereinafter, "CRIN") (see Fig. 5.7).[377]

One other similarity is the employment of credit ratings in due diligence. In Japan, credit rating agencies[378] assign credit ratings under the Financial Instruments and Exchange (Act No. 25 of 1948, as amended).[379] Each rating agency "must set a policy and methodology for determining credit ratings and for providing them or

[374] JICC was established in June 1986 by the Federation of Credit Bureaus of Japan to provide credit information to its 1328 member institutions, including consumer financing companies, credit card companies, installment credit companies, guarantee companies, commercial banks, and credit cooperatives. Its mission is to support the sound development of the consumer credit market. See Japan Credit Information Reference Center Corp. (2025).

[375] CIC was established in September 1984 by the Japan Consumer Credit Industry Association. It currently has 900 member institutions, including consumer credit companies, automobile and home appliances affiliates, department stores, retailers, leasing companies, and guarantee companies, as of March 2021. See Credit Information Center (2025).

[376] See Japanese Bankers Association (2025b).

[377] See Japanese Bankers Association (2025a).

[378] Such as Japan Credit Rating Agency (JCR) and Nippon Investors Service (NIS). See Japan Credit Rating Agency, Ltd. (2025) and Rating and Investment Information, Inc. (2025).

[379] See Financial Services Agency (2010).

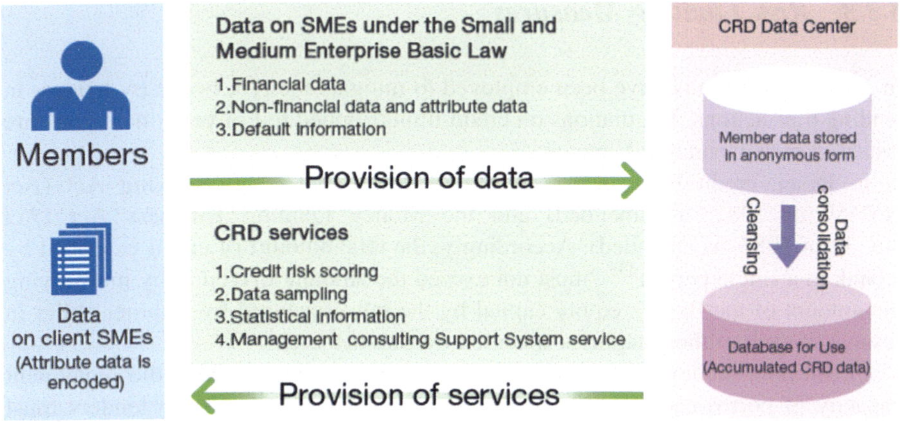


**Fig. 5.8** The structure of CRD

making them available for inspection."[380] Additionally, they are required to establish an operational control system to ensure the fair and appropriate performance of their credit rating services. The system should include measures for assigning individuals with expert knowledge and skills, managing business quality, preventing investors' interests from being harmed with the aim of benefiting the credit rating agencies themselves or individuals associated with their ratings, and other measures to ensure the proper execution of business.[381]

On the other hand, a significant difference in the employment of due diligence between Japan and Vietnam is the existence of a rich and nationwide database on SMEs in Japan, which facilitates CGCs' credit guarantee-providing process. In March 2001, the Credit Risk Database (hereinafter referred to as "CRD") was established as a voluntary association of mainly CGCs throughout Japan. It collects and compiles business data on SMEs and assesses their financial condition. In June 2009, CRD became the CRD Association, which includes credit guarantee corporations, government-affiliated and private financial institutions, and private credit rating agencies as members. CRD members provide financial and nonfinancial data and default information on SMEs to the CRD system. The CRD then checks and cleanses the data for accuracy, accumulates data from the same borrowers, analyzes credit risk information on SMEs, and provides this information to its members (see Fig. 5.8).[382]

[380] See Japan's Financial Instruments and Exchange (Act No. 25 of 1948, as amended), Article 66 bis 36.

[381] See Japan's Financial Instruments and Exchange (Act No. 25 of 1948, as amended), Article 66 bis 33.

[382] See Kuwahara et al. (2020, p. 99) and Credit Risk Database (2025).

### 5.3.3 Risk Limiting Measures

In Japan, credit limits have been employed to mitigate the risk borne by lenders in lending transactions. Regulations on credit limits applied to conventional banks are issued in both Japan and Vietnam.

In Japan, credit limits are primarily regulated under the Banking Act (Act No. 59 of 1981, as amended) and the Money Lending Business Act (Act No. 32 of 1983, as amended). Accordingly, the total amount of credit extended by a bank to a single person[383] "must not exceed the amount arrived at by multiplying the amount of the Bank's equity capital by the ratio specified by Cabinet Order in respect of each of the categories specified by Cabinet Order."[384]

In addition, money lenders must not extend a loan that exceeds the repayment capacity of borrowers. Before entering into a loan contract, money lenders must investigate matters concerning the repayment capacity of borrowers, such as income, profits, other financial resources, credit, the status of borrowings, and repayment plans.[385] Furthermore, money lenders are prohibited from providing a loan that exceeds the base amount, which is obtained by dividing the total amount of the relevant individual customer's annual salary and other regular income similar thereto by three.[386]

### 5.3.4 Risk Sharing

It is clear that Japan has a long history and extensive experience concerning loan syndication compared to Vietnam. Syndicated loans have been used in Japan since the 1970s to enable borrowers to access large loans and assist lenders in sharing credit risk among syndicated lenders. After being launched on the primary market, syndicated loans can be traded on the secondary market.[387]

In January 2001, the Japan Syndication and Loan Trading Association was established[388] to promote the proper development of both the primary and secondary syndicated loan markets.[389] The Association provides standard formats for

383 A single person includes any other person uniquely related to that single person as specified by Cabinet Order.

384 See Japan's Banking Act (Act No. 59 of 1981, as amended), Article 13, Paragraph 1.

385 See Japan's Money Lending Business Act (Act No. 32 of 1983, as amended), Article 13, Paragraph 1.

386 See Japan's Money Lending Business Act (Act No. 32 of May 13, 1983, as amended), Article 13, Paragraph 2.

387 See Nakajima (2013, p. 150).

388 With over 70 members, mainly financial institutions and institutional investors.

389 See Hamada (2004, p. 18) and Japan Syndication and Loan-Trading Association (2024).

syndicated loan contracts and develops rules for market participants to follow.[390] The approach to the diversification of risk borne by lenders by using the secondary market in Japan is introduced in Sect. 5.3.7.

### 5.3.5 *Provisional Funds*

Provisional funds have long been employed in Japan to absorb loan losses of commercial lenders and mitigate credit risk.[391]

Japan and Vietnam share several commons in terms of employing provisional funds to mitigate credit risk. Provisional funds in both countries include specific provisions and general provisions. Specific provisions are set aside to cover potential losses on specific loans that are classified as nonperforming or impaired, while general provisions are made to cover potential losses on performing loans in the overall loan portfolio.

It is readily apparent that, in Vietnam, provisional funds are primarily determined based on qualitative and quantitative debt classification, while in Japan, several techniques have been used. Before 1987, Japan followed a rule-based approach for loan loss provisioning,[392] requiring all banks to maintain a minimum 5% fund against loans based on government guidelines.[393] In 1987, this percentage was raised to 10%.[394] In 2002, the Financial Services Agency introduced the discounted cash flow method for loan loss provisioning, aimed at large borrowers facing special attention and bankruptcy risks.[395] This method estimates credit losses by using discounted future cash flow projections, considering factors like the borrower's creditworthiness, economic conditions, and probability of default. It assesses the expected cash flows from the loan and the potential loss severity in case of default. Currently, banks' provisional funds are established in accordance with Japanese Generally Accepted Accounting Principles (JGAAP). Under JGAAP, banks are required to establish and maintain provisional funds periodically, based on the classification of debts and assessment of credit risks.[396]

[390] See Japan Syndication and Loan-Trading Association (2025).

[391] See Packer and Zhu (2012, p. 5).

[392] See Abbott (1989, p. 236).

[393] See Abbott (1989, p. 235).

[394] See Abbott (1989, p. 237).

[395] See Kawai (2004).

[396] See Ernst and Young (2011, p. 3).

### 5.3.6 *Credit Insurance*

Credit insurance has been employed to mitigate the risk in lending transactions in Japan. Similar to credit insurance in Vietnam, credit insurance in Japan is a business activity of non-life insurance companies. It is not legally required in lending transactions in Japan. Lenders and borrowers have the discretion to negotiate and decide whether to purchase credit insurance as part of their loan agreements.

However, it has been noted that credit insurance in Japan involves the provision of several types as follows. Firstly, installment sales credit insurance covers all risks of failure to collect installment sales debts. Insurance companies can provide coverage for up to 50% of the eventual loss.[397] Secondly, employees' housing loan credit insurance protects employers or creditors who offer housing loans to their employees as part of their benefit program from losses resulting from the employee's or debtor's inability to repay the loans. This insurance can also extend coverage to employers who act as guarantors for their employees, reimbursing them in case of employees' failure to repay the housing loans to financial institutions. Thirdly, employees' general loan credit insurance provides coverage for losses suffered by employers or creditors who offer various types of personal loans[398] (excluding housing loans) to their employees. Fourthly, personal loan credit insurance is accessible to financial institutions that offer unsecured loans to individuals.[399]

Additionally, when CGCs agree to guarantee loans, which are granted by financial institutions for SMEs and micro-enterprises, the guarantees are insured through credit insurance under the Small and Medium-sized Enterprise Credit Insurance Act (Act No. 264 of 1950, as amended).[400] In these situations, CGCs pay the required insurance premiums. If SMEs and micro-enterprises are unable to repay their loans to financial institutions by the designated deadline, CGCs assume responsibility for repaying the loans on their behalf.[401] The JFC reimburses CGCs with 70–90% of the repaid amount as insurance coverage,[402] and CGCs are then obligated to make efforts to reclaim the repaid amount from SMEs and micro-enterprises.[403] It has been noted that credit insurance provided by the JFC not only prevents moral hazard at CGCs but also contributes to the soundness of their business operations. It also

[397] This could involve the outstanding amount reduced by any subsequent recoveries, including the value of retrieved goods, along with the expenses incurred during the recovery process.

[398] Such as loans for education, marriage, and childbirth.

[399] See Kobayashi et al. (2016, p. 158).

[400] See Japan's Small and Medium-sized Enterprise Credit Insurance Act (Act No. 264 of 1950, as amended).

[401] See Japan Federation of Credit Guarantee Corporations (2022, p. 7).

[402] Japan Federation of Credit Guarantee Corporations (2022, p. 7).

[403] See Japan's Small and Medium-sized Enterprise Credit Insurance Act (Act No. 264 of 1950, as amended), Article 7.

plays an important role in facilitating the flow of funds to SMEs and diversifying the credit risk borne by financial institutions.[404]

It can be seen that Japan has a long history and extensive experience concerning credit insurance in comparison with Vietnam. The combination of credit insurance provided by JFC and credit guarantee offered by CGCs has helped financial institutions, as lenders, diversify their credit risk when providing loans for SMEs and micro-enterprises.

### 5.3.7 Secondary Market

In Japan, loans from banks and other financial institutions can be traded and transferred to diversify credit risk among investors and primary lenders.

Similar to Vietnam, Japan also has a company established for the purpose of handling banks' bad loans. In Japan, the Cooperative Credit Purchase Company was established by commercial banks in 1992 for that purpose.[405] This company purchased bad loans from commercial banks, which are secured by collateral, and then it rented and/or sold the collateral to repay the banks. While the company handled the rental and sale of collateral and revenue collection from bad loans, the respective banks remained responsible for any shortfalls in collected revenue and the initial purchase price of the bad loans. From July 1998, the company was able to buy loans without recourse against banks; however, it has been noted that the process of how the company managed bad loans after purchasing them from banks remained unclear.

However, in comparison with Vietnam, Japan has extensive experience in establishing a secondary loan market to diversify credit risk borne by primary lenders. In February 1993, the Ministry of Finance in Japan introduced a framework for the establishment of special-purpose companies. These companies acquire restructured loans by exchanging them for a set number of shares in the new entities. The assessed worth at the time of transfer is determined by subtracting the contracted cash flow from the loans, using a market interest rate for calculation. Because the special-purpose entities do not change the claim on the ultimate obligors, banks can exert pressure on nonbank entities to restructure their operations while also potentially benefiting from recovery. The valuation of transferred loans and the losses experienced depend on the rate at which agreed-upon cash flows are discounted.[406]

It has been noted that the primary method of transferring loans in the secondary loan market in Japan is the outright transfer of loan receivables. In this process, loan receivables can be transferred without needing the approval of borrowers, unless specified differently in loan contracts. The transfer of the associated security package

[404] See Kuroda (2020, p. 252).

[405] See Ito (2012, p. 92) and Packer (1994, p. 3).

[406] See Packer (1994, p. 3).

might occur with or without the consent of the security provider and other lenders, contingent upon the nature of the security interest—whether it is a fixed or blanket security.[407]

An alternative method in the secondary loan market in Japan that has also been noted is participation. In this arrangement, loan receivables and security packages are not legally transferred to participants. Instead, participants indirectly benefit from security packages through lenders' enforcement. Participants assume the credit risks associated with both existing lenders and borrowers. If existing lenders face insolvency, participants retain a contractual claim against lenders for the owed amounts under participation agreements.[408]

## 5.4 Interim Conclusion

As outlined in Chap. 4, Vietnam has various micro- and/or small-sized financing schemes in place, designed to provide loans to households and small businesses. Despite these efforts, a credit gap still persists within society. On the other hand, the United States and Japan, which also have various micro- and/or small-sized financing schemes, have managed to navigate their credit gaps by effectively utilizing these schemes. With the advancement of technological innovations, all three countries have embraced the use of the Internet to facilitate micro- and/or small-sized finance. However, the primary differences stem from their distinct histories and levels of experience in this field. Vietnam has a relatively brief history and limited experience with micro- and/or small-sized financing schemes, as these initiatives began to develop following the "Đổi Mới" reform in 1986. In contrast, the United States and Japan have a long-standing history and extensive experience, particularly in the utilization of the Internet for commercial purposes, which began in 1993. Vietnam had only seven years of experience with micro- and/or small-sized finance before embracing the Internet for commercial purposes, whereas the United States and Japan had over a century of experience in this field. Additionally, in Vietnam, the experience of using the Internet to match borrowers and lenders is relatively recent, and this practice was initiated from the onset of Internet use. The simultaneous growth of the middle class and the demand for small funds from small businesses and families has prompted both supply and demand sides to adapt to using the Internet for financial transactions. On the other hand, in both the United States and Japan, the regulations governing small finance have not been entirely separate from pre-1993 regulations, even after the commercial use of the Internet became widespread. The regulations governing small finance in these countries have incrementally evolved to accommodate Internet usage.

[407] See Aoyama and Matsuda (2022, p. 104).

[408] Aoyama and Matsuda (2022, p. 104).

As also mentioned earlier, diverse approaches to risk diversification in micro and/or small-sized financing schemes in Vietnam, the United States, and Japan include methods such as collateral, due diligence, risk limiting, risk sharing, provisional funds, credit insurance, and participation in the secondary market. The most significant disparities between the approaches to risk diversification in micro- and/or small-sized financing schemes in Vietnam, the US, and Japan pertain to their historical development and level of experience. While Vietnam has a brief history and limited experience with risk diversification in micro- and/or small-sized financing schemes, the United States and Japan have a long history and extensive experience in this area.

By applying the legislative experience of the United States and Japan to risk diversification related to micro- and/or small-sized finance via P2P lending platforms in Vietnam, the author found that certain strategies can be beneficial. Specifically, the approaches to risk diversification in micro- and/or small-sized financing schemes in the United States and Japan are likely to help mitigate one or several risks to which participants in P2P lending in Vietnam are exposed. For example, the application of the guarantee mechanism used in the United States's SBA loan programs could potentially assist P2P lenders in Vietnam. It can help in mitigating several risks, including the risk of adverse selection, which results from the platforms' inadequate due diligence performance and provision of inaccurate information about potential borrowers' creditworthiness. Furthermore, it can also reduce the risk of financial loss in the event of the temporary or permanent cessation of the platforms' operations. The application of Japan's public credit guarantee mechanism to P2P lending schemes in Vietnam is also likely to help P2P lenders mitigate several risks. These risks may include default risk caused by borrowers failing to meet their debt obligations, the risk of adverse selection resulting from inadequate due diligence performed by P2P lending platforms, and the financial risk faced by P2P lenders in the event of temporary or permanent cessation of the platforms' operations. Moreover, applying a combination of loan syndication and a secondary loan market, as practiced in the United States and Japan, could help P2P lenders in Vietnam mitigate liquidity risk and financial loss. Such loss could be caused by borrowers defaulting and by temporary or permanent cessation of the lending platforms' operations.

Based on these findings, the author suggests that Vietnam could draw lessons from the experiences of the United States and Japan in order to consider its regulatory approaches to the P2P lending business, thus encouraging the sector's sound development. More detailed suggestions will be presented in Chap. 8.

Despite the implementation of various risk diversification strategies in micro- and/or small-sized financing schemes in Vietnam, P2P lenders continue to face challenges in diversifying their risks when providing small loans through online lending platforms.

As mentioned earlier, Vietnam lacks a public organization equivalent to the United States's SBA, which offers credit guarantees to help SMEs access loans. Additionally, the Credit Supplementation System in Japan cannot be easily adapted for use in Vietnam. While Vietnam does have local credit guarantee funds for SMEs in its provinces, these funds are not consolidated into a single system as is the case with the CGCs in Japan. Additionally, in Vietnam, there is no organization that performs a role similar to that of JFC, which insures credit guarantees offered by CGCs with the aim of diversifying the default risk of SMEs defaulting on their loans. Although it may be possible to establish a guarantee system in Vietnam similar to the SBA system in the United States or the Credit Supplementation System in Japan, the problem arises when potential borrowers are non-banked or underbanked. When these individuals apply for loans via lending platforms for the first time, without a track record, it is likely to make guaranteeing P2P loans difficult. Unless a mechanism like the guarantee associations in Japan, which provides guarantees at a reasonable fee even to borrowers without a track record, is also implemented, it will be challenging to offer such guarantees.

As also mentioned in Chap. 3, in Vietnam, lenders using P2P lending platforms—and potentially the platforms themselves if acting on behalf of the lenders—face challenges in enhancing the effectiveness of their due diligence. This is primarily due to several factors: lack of access to credit information held by the Credit Information Center; absence of support from credit information companies; limited credit ratings from credit rating companies; and the costs associated with establishing internal credit scoring systems to assess potential borrowers' credit risk. If P2P lending platforms were to operate in the United States, the execution of due diligence would likely be facilitated by the availability of diverse credit reporting companies and credit ratings issued by credit rating agencies. If P2P lending platforms were to operate in Japan, the execution of due diligence would likely be facilitated by the methods of KYC and e-KYC, regulated by laws, and a rich, nationwide database on SMEs (the CRD). However, it is clear that the prerequisites found in the United States and Japan for facilitating due diligence are lacking in Vietnam.

In terms of risk mitigation strategies, many of the ones used in the United States and Japan are not immediately adoptable in Vietnam. For example, in the United States, credit limits can be established based on collateral reliability and strength, as well as loan obligation liquidity. In Japan, they can be based on a borrower's repayment capacity and a base amount calculated by dividing an individual's annual salary and other regular income by three. However, implementing these measures in Vietnam's P2P lending might be challenging due to the likelihood of P2P loans being unsecured and the potential costs of establishing individual credit limits.

Both the United States and Japan have established practices for creating provisional funds. However, applying these practices in Vietnam's P2P lending may be challenging due to a lack of experience, undeveloped accounting practices, and the absence of tax incentives. Lending platforms likely lack incentives to establish provisional funds from their own contributions, and fees collected from P2P lenders and/or borrowers to create these funds could deter their use of the platforms.

Furthermore, practices observed in the United States and Japan, such as offering syndicated loans and establishing a secondary loan market—although not specific to P2P lending—could potentially facilitate risk diversification in Vietnam's P2P lending. However, as mentioned earlier, Vietnam's first debt trading floor is not expected until 2026. Moreover, in the context of P2P lending, selling defaulted loan receivables on the secondary market is likely to be challenging unless priced very low, ultimately leaving P2P lenders bearing the losses from such defaults.

Given the above analysis, it becomes clear that while the objectives of individual risk diversification measures employed in the United States and Japan are applicable to Vietnam's P2P lending context, their direct implementation may not be feasible. Therefore, it is essential to explore new strategies aimed at similar risk mitigation objectives. To identify potential measures for risk diversification in Vietnam's P2P lending—even after adopting measures from the United States and/or Japan—it might be first useful to explore the potential of a mutual funding scheme, in which P2P lenders support one another in mitigating risks inherent in P2P lending. Secondly, there is a need for empirical research to find out the social facts surrounding the P2P lending business. Accordingly, Chap. 6 introduces the concept of a mutual funding scheme, while Chap. 7 presents an empirical research on Vietnamese P2P lending industry.

## References


Abbott GC (1989) Loan loss provisioning. Intereconomics 24:233–240

Adams TFM, Hoshii I (1972) A financial history of the new Japan. Kodansha International, Tokyo

Adhikary BK, Kutsuna K, Hoda T (2018) Crowdfunding: lessons from Japan's approach. Springer, Singapore

Akihide I, Stagars M (2016) Marketplace lending, financial analysis, and the future of credit: Integration, profitability and risk management. Wiley, New York

Alexander AJ, Oh KD (1989) The development and structure of consumer credit in Japan. Rand, California

Alpert G (2021) Loan loss provision. https://www.investopedia.com/terms/l/loanlossprovision.asp. Accessed 20 Mar 2025

Anthony J, Docherty P, Lee D, Shamsuddin A (2017) Liquidity commonality in the secondary corporate loan market. Econ Lett 161:10–14

Aoyama H, Matsuda Y (2022) Japan. In: Nassiri A (ed) The lending and secured finance review, 8th edn. Law Business Research Ltd.

AQUSH (2023) About AQUSH. https://www.aqush.jp/aboutUs. Accessed 12 Jun 2023

Baba N, Hisada T (2002) Japan's financial system: its perspective and the authorities' roles in redesigning and administering system. https://www.imes.boj.or.jp/research/papers/english/me20-2-3.pdf. Accessed 20 Mar 2025

Baker McKenzie (2024) Global financial services regulatory guide – United States of America. https://www.bakermckenzie.com/en/insight/publications/guides/global-fsr-guide. Accessed 20 Mar 2025

Bank of Japan (2012) Clearing and settlement systems in Japan. https://www.boj.or.jp/en/paym/outline/pay_boj/pss1212a.pdf. Accessed 20 Mar 2025

Bankers (2025a). https://holding.bankers.co.jp/. Accessed 20 Mar 2025

Bankers (2025b) FAQ. https://www.bankers.co.jp/faq/faq.html. Accessed 20 Mar 2025

Barr MS (2007) Banking the poor: policies to bring low- and moderate-income households in the United States into the financial mainstream. In: Anderloni L, Braga MD, Carluccio EM (eds) New frontiers in banking services: emerging needs and tailored products for untapped markets. Springer, Berlin

Barth JR, Li T, Lu W (2010) Bank regulation in the United States. CESifo Econ Stud 56(1): 112–140

Batino T, Jordan M (2020) The ultimate guide to debit and credit cards in Japan. https://www.bfftokyo.com/how-to-make-a-debit-or-credit-card/. Accessed 20 Mar 2025
Billingsley R, Gitman LJ, Joehnk MD (2013) Personal financial planning, 13th edn. South-Western College Publishing, Ohio
Birken EG (2020) The costs of being unbanked or underbanked. https://www.forbes.com/advisor/banking/costs-of-being-unbanked-or-underbanked/. Accessed 20 Mar 2025
Board of Governors of the Federal Reserve System Consumers' guide: credit reports and credit scores. https://www.federalreserve.gov/creditreports/pdf/credit_reports_scores_2.pdf. Accessed 20 Mar 2025
Brigham EF, Houston JF (2015) Fundamentals of financial management, 14th edn. Cengage Learning, Boston
Brown PW (1969) Credit insurance: abuse and reform. Bost Coll Law Rev 10(2):439–458
Brummer C (2020) Fintech law in a nutshell. West Academic Publishing, Minnesota
Burk JE, Lehmann RP (2006) Financing your small business. Sourcebooks Inc, Illinois
Calder L (1999) Financing the American dream: a cultural history of consumer credit. Princeton University Press, New Jersey
Carbajo M (2018) What makes up a small business credit report? https://www.sba.gov/blog/what-makes-small-business-credit-report. Accessed 20 Mar 2025
Cargill TF, Yoshino N (2003) Postal savings and fiscal investment in Japan: the pss and the filp. Oxford University Press, Oxford
Coates K, Holroyd C (2003) Japan and the internet revolution. Palgrave Macmillan, New York
Constand RL, Osteryoung JS, Nast DA (1991) Asset-based financing and the determinants of capital structure in the small firm. In: Yazdipour R (ed) Advances in small business finance. Springer, California
Consumer Federation of America (2025) How payday loans work. https://paydayloaninfo.org/how-payday-loans-work/. Accessed 20 Mar 2025
Credit Information Center (2025) History. https://www.cic.co.jp/en/history.html. Accessed 20 Mar 2025
Credit Risk Database (2025) Structure of CRD. https://www.crd-office.net/CRD/en/structure/index.html. Accessed 20 Mar 2025
Creditcards (2025) Luxury card™ credit cards. https://www.creditcards.com/luxury-card/. Accessed 20 Mar 2025
Dekle R, Hamada K (2000) On the development of rotating credit associations in Japan. Econ Dev Cult Change 49(1):77–90
DeMatteo M (2021) Black cards are the ultimate status symbol - but what are they? https://www.cnbc.com/select/what-is-a-black-card/. Accessed 20 Mar 2025
Dhir H, Popescu G (2016) P2P lending in Japan. https://lending-times.com/2016/11/08/p2p-lending-in-japan/. Accessed 12 Jun 2023
Duignan B (1914) Federal Trade Commission Act. https://www.britannica.com/event/Federal-Trade-Commission-Act. Accessed 20 Mar 2025
Durkin TA, Elliehausen G, Staten ME, Zywicki TJ (2014) Consumer credit and the American economy. Oxford University Press, New York
Ernst & Young (2011) JGAAP-IFRS comparison. https://www.eyjapan.jp/services/assurance/ifrs/issue/ifrs-others/other/pdf/ifrs-jgaap-comparison-v30-E.pdf. Accessed 20 Mar 2025
Espig P (2003) The demise of a banking dinosaur: long-term credit bank. Chazen Web J Int Bus 3(1)
Fabrizio KR, Mowery DC (2007) The federal role in financing major innovations: information technology during the postwar period. In: Lamoreaux NR, Sokoloff KL (eds) Financing innovation in the United States, 1870 to the present. The MIT Press, Massachusetts
Federal Deposit Insurance Corporation (2014) 2013 FDIC national survey of unbanked and underbanked households. https://www.fdic.gov/household-survey/2013-fdic-national-survey-unbanked-and-underbanked-households#:~:text=2013%20FDIC%20National%20Survey%20of%20Unbanked%20and%20Underbanked%20Households,-Share%20This%3A&text=The%

202013%20household%20survey%20results,of%20the%20mainstream%20banking%20system. Accessed 20 Mar 2025
Federation of American Scientists (2021) An overview of consumer finance and policy issues. https://fas.org/sgp/crs/misc/R45813.pdf. Accessed 20 Mar 2025
Federal Trade Commission (2025) Fair Credit Reporting Act. https://www.ftc.gov/enforcement/statutes/fair-credit-reporting-act. Accessed 20 Mar 2025
FICO (2023) Frequently asked questions about fico scores. https://www.fico.com/en/resource-access/download/50381. Accessed 20 Mar 2025
Financial Accounting Standards Board (2025) About the FASB. https://www.fasb.org/facts/. Accessed 20 Mar 2025
Financial Services Agency (2010) FSA publishes English translations of regulation on credit rating agencies. https://www.fsa.go.jp/en/news/2010/20100331-4.html. Accessed 20 Mar 2025
Florack A J, Dworkin C M, Jackson L V, Troconis A (2022) Banking & Finance 2022 USA: law & practice and USA: trends and development. https://www.davispolk.com/insights/articles-books/banking-finance-2022-usa. Accessed 20 Mar 2025
Franson M (2023) The regulation of marketplace lending: a summary of the principal issues. https://www.chapman.com/media/publication/15093_Chapman-Regulation-of-Marketplace-Lending-2023.pdf. Accessed 20 Mar 2025
Fukuyama H, Guerra R, Weber WL (1999) Efficiency and ownership: evidence from Japanese credit cooperatives. J Econ Bus 51(6):473–487
Fujimoto T (2008) Social lending takes root in Japan. https://japantoday.com/category/features/executive-impact/social-lending-takes-root-in-japan. Accessed 20 Mar 2025
Gallagher TJ, Andrew JD (2007) Financial management: principles and practice, 4th edn. Pearson College Div, New Jersey
Gibbons D (2012) Taking on the money lenders: lessons from Japan. https://silo.tips/download/taking-on-the-money-lenders-lessons-from-japan. Accessed 20 Mar 2025
Gnanarajah R (2018) Banking: current expected credit loss (CECL). https://fas.org/sgp/crs/misc/R45339.pdf. Accessed 20 Mar 2025
Goldsmith RW (1983) The financial development of Japan, 1868-1977. Yale University Press, Connecticut
Gordon A (2012) Credit in a nation of savers: the growth of consumer borrowing in Japan. In: Logemann J (ed) The development of consumer credit in global perspective. Palgrave Macmillan, New York
Green CH (2011) The SBA loan book: the complete guide to getting financial help through the small business administration, 3rd edn. Adams, Massachusetts
Gup BE (2011) Banking and financial institutions: a guide for directors, investors, and borrowers. Wiley, New Jersey
Hamada T (2004) The growth of loan syndication in Japan. Cap Res J 7(1):12–20
Hanna J (1931) Credit insurance. Univ PA Law Rev 79(5):521–548
Harner SM (2000) Japan's financial revolution and how American firms are profiting. Routledge, New York
Hemraj M (2015) Credit rating agencies: self-regulation, statutory regulation and case law regulation in the United States and European Union. Springer, Switzerland
Humphreys K (1998) Banking on the web. In: Cronin MJ (ed) Banking and finance on the internet. Wiley, New York
Inoue T (2022) Health impacts of public pawnshops in industrializing Tokyo. https://arxiv.org/pdf/2305.09352. Accessed 20 Mar 2025
Ito T (2012) The stagnant Japanese economy in the 1990s: the need for financial supervision to restore sustained growth. In: Hugh T. Patrick and Takeo Hoshi (eds) Crisis and change in the Japanese financial system. Springer, Massachusetts
Izumida Y (2018) The kou in Japan: a precursor of modern finance. In: Adams DW, Fitchett DA (eds) Informal finance in low-income countries. Routledge, New York

Japan Consumer Credit Association (2025) About JCA. https://www.j-credit.or.jp/en/association/. Accessed 20 Mar 2025
Japan Credit Information Reference Center Corp. (2025) About JICC. https://www.jicc.co.jp/aboutus. Accessed 20 Mar 2025
Japan Credit Rating Agency, Ltd. (2025) Company information. https://www.jcr.co.jp/en/service/company/company.html. Accessed 20 Mar 2025
Japan Federation of Credit Guarantee Corporations (2022) Credit guarantee system in Japan. https://www.zenshinhoren.or.jp/document/Credit_Guarantee_System_in_Japan_2022.pdf. Accessed 20 Mar 2025
Japan Finance Corporation (2023) Overview of operation. https://www.jfc.go.jp/n/english/operations.html#sme. Accessed 12 Jun 2023
Japan Finance Corporation (2024) 2024 Japan finance corporation annual report. https://www.jfc.go.jp/n/english/report/pdf/jfc2024e_0.pdf. Accessed 20 Mar 2025
Japan Leasing Association (2025a) Characteristics of finance lease. https://www.leasing.or.jp/english/information/finance.html. Accessed 20 Mar 2025a
Japan Leasing Association (2025b) Classification of leases. https://www.leasing.or.jp/english/information/kind.html. Accessed 20 Mar 2025b
Japan Syndication and Loan-Trading Association (2024) Introduction. https://www.jsla.org/english. Accessed 20 Mar 2025
Japan Syndication and Loan-Trading Association (2025) Publication of the "Mandate Letter, Confidentiality Pledge, and Letter of Intent to Participate (JSLA 2025 Edition)". https://www.jsla.org/shared_topics/5842. Accessed 20 Mar 2025
Japanese Bankers Association (2012) Payment systems in Japan. https://www.zenginkyo.or.jp/fileadmin/res/en/banks/payment-systems/paymentsystems.pdf. Accessed 20 Mar 2025
Japanese Bankers Association (2019) Types of Banks (as of December 2019). https://www.zenginkyo.or.jp/en/banks/financial-institutions/. Accessed 20 Mar 2025
Japanese Bankers Association (2025a) A framework of shared credit information network system (CRIN). https://www.zenginkyo.or.jp/en/pcic/appendix/appendix-01-2/. Accessed 20 Mar 2025
Japanese Bankers Association (2025b) Credit Information Bureaus in Japan. https://www.zenginkyo.or.jp/en/pcic/appendix/appendix-01/. Accessed 20 Mar 2025
Japanese Bankers Association (2025c) Role of personal credit information center. https://www.zenginkyo.or.jp/en/pcic/info-center/. Accessed 20 Mar 2025
Kanto Finance Bureau (2021) Administrative sanctions for SBI Social Lending. http://kantou.mof.go.jp/kinyuu/pagekt_cnt_20210512001.html. Access 12 Jun 2023
Kapoor JK, Dlabay LR, Hughes RJ and Hart MM (2019) Personal finance, 13th edn. McGraw Hill India, New York
Kawai M (2004) Reform of the Japanese banking system. https://ideas.repec.org/p/hst/hstdps/d05-102.html. Accessed 20 Mar 2025
Kazuhito Y (2013) Understanding the Japan agricultural cooperatives. https://www.nippon.com/en/currents/d00082/. Accessed 20 Mar 2025
Kiisel T (2013) Getting a small business loan: financing your main street business. Apress, New York
Kitagawa H, Kurasawa Y (1994) Japan: development and structural change of banking system. In: Patrick HT, Park YC (eds) The financial development of Japan, Korea, and Taiwan. Oxford University Press, New York
Kitamura Y, Suto M, Teranishi J (2004) Reflections on the new financial system in Japan: participation costs, wealth distribution and security market-based intermediation. In: Fan JPH, Hanazaki M, Teranishi J (eds) Designing financial systems in East Asia and Japan. Routledge, New York
Klinedinst M, Sato H (1994) The Japanese cooperative sector. J Econ Issues 28(2):509–517
Klotz RJ (2003) The Politics of internet communication. Rowman & Littlefield Publishers, Maryland

Kuroda A (2020) Credit supplementation system for unlocking sme and startup access to finance: the case of Japan. In: Yoshino N, Hesary FT (eds) Unlocking sme finance in ASIA: roles of credit rating and credit guarantee scheme. Routledge, New York

Kobayashi N, Umekawa Y, Mikami T, Okuda S (2016) Insurance law in Japan, 3rd edn. Kluwer Law International, Netherlands

Kuwahara S, Yoshino N, Sagra M, Farhad TH (2020) Establishment of the credit risk database: concrete use to evaluate the creditworthiness of smes. In: Unlocking sme finance in Asia: roles of credit rating and credit guarantee schemes. Routledge, New York

Malloy MP, Lovett WA (2019) Banking and financial institutions law in a nutshell, 9th edn. West Academic Publishing, Minnesota

Maneo (2023) Company Profile. https://www.maneo.jp/apl/aboutus?page=company. Accessed 12 Jun 2023

Mann RJ (2001) Card-based payment systems in the United States and Japan. https://www.imes.boj.or.jp/research/papers/english/01-E-02.pdf. Accessed 20 Mar 2025

Mann RJ (2002) Credit cards and debit cards in the United States and Japan. Vanderbilt Law Rev 55(4):1055–1108

Mariotto C (2016) Competition for lending in the internet era: the case of peer-to-peer lending marketplaces in the USA. Digiworld Econ J 103(3):35–58

Marsh B, Virmani T (2024) Loan syndications and trading: an overview of the syndicated loan market. https://iclg.com/practice-areas/lending-and-secured-finance-laws-and-regulations/01-loan-syndications-and-trading-an-overview-of-the-syndicated-loan-market. Accessed 20 Mar 2025

Mason DL (2004) From buildings and loans to bail-outs: a history of the American saving and loan industry 1831-1995. Cambridge University Press, New York

Mellor T, Weinstein K, Denhup R (2024) USA: lending & secured finance laws and regulations 2024. https://iclg.com/practice-areas/lending-and-secured-finance-laws-and-regulations/usa. Accessed 20 Mar 2025

Mills KG (2018) Fintech, small business & the American dream: how technology is transforming lending and shaping a new era of small business opportunity. Springer, Switzerland

Minnano Credit (2023) Company Profile. https://msetsu.com/en/company#companyInfo. Access 12 June 2023

Mulligan D (1998) Know your customer regulations and the international banking system: towards a general self-regulatory regime. Fordham Int Law J 22(5):2324–2372

Mylenbusch D (1999) CliffsNotes getting a loan. Cliffs Notes, California

Nakajima Y (2013) Banking business in Japan. https://glim-re.repo.nii.ac.jp/?action=repository_action_common_download&item_id=2823&item_no=1&attribute_id=22&file_no=1. Accessed 20 Mar 2025

Nakamura M, Yamada K (1996) Financial institutions of Japan. In: Hayakawaa S (ed) Japanese financial markets. Woodhead Publishing, Cambridge

National Policy Agency (2016) Act on prevention of transfer of criminal proceeds. https://www.npa.go.jp/sosikihanzai/jafic/pdf/e_leaf20161001.pdf. Accessed 20 Mar 2025

Nemoto N, Storey D, Huang B (2019) Optimal regulation of p2p lending for small and medium-sized enterprises. https://www.adb.org/publications/optimal-regulation-p2p-lending-small-and-medium-sized-enterprises. Accessed 20 Mar 2025

Nieri L (2007) Access to credit: the difficulties of households, in new frontiers in banking services: emerging needs and tailored products for untapped markets. Springer, Berlin

Nihei Z (2020) Financial restructuring basics - how to rescue distressed companies, lecture notes taken during the Japanese Business Law in Practice course at the LL.M Program in International Economic and Business Law, Kyushu University on December 19, 2020

Ochiai D, Iwatani M (2002) Individual investors and the investment– savings balance. In: Ujiie J (ed) Japanese financial markets, 2nd edn. Woodhead Publishing, Cambridge

OECD (2024) Financing smes and entrepreneurs 2024: an OECD scoreboard. https://www.oecd.org/en/publications/financing-smes-and-entrepreneurs-2024_fa521246-en.html. Accessed 20 Mar 2025

Office of Credit Ratings (2020) Annual report on nationally recognized statistical rating organizations as required by section 6 of the Credit Rating Agency Reform Act of 2006. https://www.sec.gov/files/2020-annual-report-on-nrsros.pdf. Accessed 20 Mar 2025

Office of the Comptroller of the Currency (2025a) Bank Secrecy Act (BSA). https://www.occ.treas.gov/topics/supervision-and-examination/bsa/index-bsa.html. Accessed 20 Mar 2025

Office of the Comptroller of the Currency (2025b) Bank Secrecy Act (BSA) & related regulations. https://www.occ.treas.gov/topics/supervision-and-examination/bsa/bsa-related-regulations/index-bsa-and-related-regulations.html. Accessed 20 Mar 2025

Ogura S (2002) Banking, the state and industrial promotion in developing Japan, 1900-73. Palgrave Macmillan, Hampshire

Ohno N, Tsunematsu (2019) Japan: amendment to the act on prevention of transfer of criminal proceeds. https://www.iflr.com/article/b1lmxb9jyx90zk/japan-amendment-to-the-act-on-prevention-of-transfer-of-criminal-proceeds. Accessed 20 Mar 2025

Packer F (1994) The disposal of bad loans in Japan: a review of recent policy initiatives. https://core.ac.uk/download/pdf/161436077.pdf. Accessed 20 Mar 2025

Packer F, Zhu H (2012) Loan loss provisioning practices of Asian banks. https://papers.ssrn.com/sol3/papers.cfm?abstract_id=2038215. Accessed 20 Mar 2025

Pawnshop Daishin (2025) Smart cashing by pawnshop. https://psdaishin.jp/daishin-global.htm. Accessed 20 Mar 2025

Practical Law (2014) Finance multi-jurisdictional guide: United States. https://www.acc.com/sites/default/files/resources/upload/US%20Lending%20InfoPak_FINAL%2012.3.14.pdf. Accessed 20 Mar 2025

Primm S, Roncevich T (2009) SBA loan application guide. Upstart Business Consulting Group, Washington, D.C.

Prindl AR (1981) Japanese finance: a guide to banking in Japan. Wiley, New Jersey

Rating and Investment Information, Inc (2025) Corporate history. https://www.r-i.co.jp/en/docs/company/history.html. Accessed 20 Mar 2025

Reilly RA (1997) Transforming the paradigm for crafting acceptable use policy: managing the electronic commons. https://core.ac.uk/download/pdf/286363364.pdf. Accessed 20 Mar 2025

Reinhard M (2010) Commercial mortgages 101: everything you need to know to create a winning loan request package. AMACOM, New York

Rogers S (2020) Entrepreneurial finance: finance and business strategies for the serious entrepreneur, 4th edn. McGraw Hill, New York

Ryuichi S (1983) The emergence of private pawn shops: Japanese government policy. https://d-arch.ide.go.jp/je_archive/society/wp_je_unu59.html. Accessed 20 Mar 2025

Sahni RA, Byrne T (2020) Banking regulation 2020 in USA. In: Hsu PC, Bahar R (eds) Global legal insights - banking regulation 2020, 7th edn. Global Legal Group, London

Saito T, Sekine T (2020) Banking Regulation 2020 in Japan. In: Hsu PC, Bahar R (eds) Global legal insights - banking regulation 2020, 7th edn. Global Legal Group, London

Samitsu A (2017) Structure of p2p lending and investor protection: analyses based on an international comparison of legal arrangements. https://www.boj.or.jp/en/research/wps_rev/lab/lab17e06.htm. Accessed 20 Mar 2025

Santosa JAC, Nigro P (2009) Is the secondary loan market valuable to borrowers? Rev Econ Financ 49(4):1410–1428

SBI Holdings (2021) Notice Regarding the Establishment of a Third-Party Committee. https://www.sbigroup.co.jp/news/2021/0205_12325.html. Accessed 20 Mar 2025

SBI Social Lending (2021a) About our future business operation. https://www.sbi-sociallending.jp/pages/press210524. Access 12 Jun 2023

SBI Social Lending (2021b) Report. https://www.sbi-sociallending.jp/assets/pdf/report210428.pdf. Access 12 Jun 2023

SBI Social Lending (2023) Company Information. https://sbsl.bankers.co.jp/pages/aboutus. Accessed 2 May 2023

Schutzer D (1998) Foundations for electronic commerce: standards and strategic alliances. In: Cronin MJ (ed) Banking and finance on the internet. Wiley, New York

Seltzer R (1995) The way of the web. Seltzer Books

Sherman AJ (2012) Raising capital: getting money you need to grow your business, 3rd edn. HarperCollins Publishers, New York

Skully MT (2019) The development of the pawnshop industry in East Asia. In: Bouman FJA, Hospes O (eds) Financial landscapes reconstructed: the fine art of mapping development. Routledge, New York

SME Japan (2025) How to obtain a loan for your new business in Japan. https://www.smejapan.com/japan-business-guides/how-to-obtain-a-loan-for-your-new-business-in-japan/#JFCloan_overview. Accessed 20 Mar 2025

Suehiro Y (2023) Japan: lending & secured finance laws and regulations - Japan 2023. https://iclg.com/practice-areas/lending-and-secured-finance-laws-and-regulations/japan. Accessed 20 Mar 2025

Sugimura K, Itatani M, Bessho M (2017) Scope of maximum interest rate regulations. https://www.boj.or.jp/en/research/wps_rev/lab/lab17e01.htm/. Accessed 20 Mar 2025

Sunahara H, Esaki H (2008) Brief history of internet deployment in Japan. In: Esaki H, Sunahara H, Murai J (eds) Broadband internet deployment in Japan. IOS Press, Tokyo

Takahashi S, Yamamoto K, Sakemi T (2019) Japan. In: Rogan P (ed) The Insurance and Reinsurance Law Review, 7th edn. Gideon Roberton, London

Tatewaki K (2012) Banking and finance in Japan: an introduction to the Tokyo market. Routledge, London

Teranishi J (1994) Japan: development and structural change of the financial system. In: Patrick HT, Park YC (eds) The financial development of Japan, Korea, and Taiwan. Oxford University Press, New York

The Appraisal Foundation (2025) What is USPAP? https://www.appraisalfoundation.org/imis/TAF/Standards/Appraisal_Standards/Uniform_Standards_of_Professional_Appraisal_Practice/TAF/USPAP.aspx#:~:text=What%20is%20USPAP%C2%AE%3F,profession%20in%20the%20United%20States. Accessed 20 Mar 2025

The Bank of Japan Economic Research Department (1969) Money and banking in Japan (trans: Nishimura S). Macmillan Publishers, London

The Code of Federal Regulations, Title 12, Chapter X. https://www.ecfr.gov/. Accessed 20 Mar 2025

The English translation of the Act on Engagement in Trust Business Activities by Financial Institutions of Japan (Act No. 43 of 1943, as amended). https://www.japaneselawtranslation.go.jp/en/laws/view/2662/en. Accessed 20 Mar 2025

The English translation of the Act on Special Provisions for the Civil Code Concerning the Perfection (Act No. 89 of 1896). https://www.japaneselawtranslation.go.jp/en/laws/view/3464/en. Accessed 20 Mar 2025

The English translation of the Act Regulating the Receipt of Contributions, Receipt of Deposits, and Interest Rates of Japan (Act No. 195 of 1954, as amended). https://www.japaneselawtranslation.go.jp/en/laws/view/1880/tb. Accessed 20 Mar 2025

The English translation of the Agricultural Cooperatives Act of Japan (Act No. 132 of 1947, as amended). https://www.japaneselawtranslation.go.jp/en/laws/view/4031. Accessed 20 Mar 2025

The English translation of the Banking Act of Japan (Act No. 59 of 1981, as amended). https://www.japaneselawtranslation.go.jp/en/laws/view/2689/en. Accessed 20 Mar 2025

The English translation of the Civil Code of Japan (Act No. 89 of 1896, as amended). https://www.japaneselawtranslation.go.jp/en/laws/view/3494#je_pt3ch1sc4at7. Accessed 20 Mar 2025

The English translation of the Commercial Code of Japan (Act No. 48 of 1899, as amended). https://www.japaneselawtranslation.go.jp/en/laws/view/4293. Accessed 20 Mar 2025

The English translation of the Company Act of Japan (Act No. 86 of 2005, as amended). https://www.japaneselawtranslation.go.jp/en/laws/view/3206/en#je_pt2ch2sc3sb3at2. Accessed 20 Mar 2025
The English translation of the Criminal Proceeds Transfer Prevention Act of Japan (Act No. 22 of 2007, as amended). http://www.japaneselawtranslation.go.jp/law/detail/?printID=&re=02&vm=03&id=1659&lvm=02. Accessed 20 Jul 2023
The English translation of the Financial Instruments and Exchange Act of Japan (Act No. 25 of 1948, as amended). https://www.japaneselawtranslation.go.jp/en/laws/view/2355/en. Accessed 20 Mar 2025
The English translation of the Fisheries Cooperative Act of Japan (Act No. 242 of 1948). https://www.japaneselawtranslation.go.jp/en/laws/view/4031. Accessed 20 Mar 2025
The English translation of the Insurance Business Act of Japan (Act No. 105 of 1995, as amended). https://www.japaneselawtranslation.go.jp/en/laws/view/4090. Accessed 20 Mar 2025
The English translation of the Installment Sales Act of Japan (Act No. 159 of 1961, as amended). https://www.japaneselawtranslation.go.jp/en/laws/view/3942/en. Accessed 20 Mar 2025
The English translation of the Interest Rate Restriction Act of Japan (Act No. 100 of 1954, as amended). https://www.japaneselawtranslation.go.jp/en/laws/view/4046/en. Accessed 20 Mar 2025
The English translation of the Money Lending Business Act of Japan (Act No. 32 of 1983, as amended). https://www.japaneselawtranslation.go.jp/en/laws/view/3224. Accessed 20 Mar 2025
The English translation of the Pawnbroker Business Act of Japan (Act No. 158 of 1950). http://www.japaneselawtranslation.go.jp/law/detail/?vm=2&re=02&id=467&lvm=01. Accessed 18 Jun 2021
The English translation of the Protection of Personal Information Act of Japan (Act No. 57 of 2003, as amended). https://www.japaneselawtranslation.go.jp/en/laws/view/4241. Accessed 20 Mar 2025
The English translation of the Real Property Registration Act of Japan (Act No. 123 of 2004). https://www.japaneselawtranslation.go.jp/en/laws/view/2016. Accessed 20 Mar 2025
The English translation of the Small and Medium-Sized Enterprise Cooperatives Act of Japan (Act No. 181 of 1949, as amended). https://www.japaneselawtranslation.go.jp/en/laws/view/3830#je_ch2sc1. Accessed 20 Mar 2025
The English translation of the Small and Medium-sized Enterprise Credit Insurance Act of Japan (Act No. 264 of 1950, as amended). https://www.japaneselawtranslation.go.jp/en/laws/view/498. Accessed 20 Mar 2025
The English translation of the Trust Business Act of Japan (Act No. 154 of 2004, as amended). https://www.japaneselawtranslation.go.jp/en/laws/view/3488. Accessed 20 Mar 2025
The Federal Reserve System (2019) Report on the economic well-being of U.S. households in 2018 - May 2019. https://www.federalreserve.gov/publications/files/2018-report-economic-well-being-us-households-201905.pdf. Accessed 20 Mar 2025
The Federal Reserve System (2020) Frequently asked questions on the new accounting standard on financial instruments - credit losses. https://www.federalreserve.gov/supervisionreg/topics/faq-new-accounting-standards-on-financial-instruments-credit-losses.htm. Accessed 20 Mar 2025
The Federal Trade Commission (2025a) Equal Credit Opportunity Act. https://www.ftc.gov/enforcement/statutes/equal-credit-opportunity-act. Accessed 20 Mar 2025
The Federal Trade Commission (2025b) Fair Debt Collection Practices Act. https://www.ftc.gov/legal-library/browse/rules/fair-debt-collection-practices-act-text. Accessed 20 Mar 2025
The General Insurance Association of Japan (2025) Investment regulation. https://www.sonpo.or.jp/en/regulations/004.html?fbclid=IwAR0oMe4kcInSZp844MvBUWJq0JHB6rPv_1rV1KB0lopd81zpehEirbIA29k. Accessed 20 Mar 2025
The Harvard Law Review Association (1985) The policies behind lending limits: an argument for a uniform country exposure ceiling. Harv Law Rev 99(2):430–449

The Institute for Monetary and Economic Studies of the Bank of Japan (1986) The Japanese financial system (trans: Robert AF). Clarendon Press, Oxford

The Japan Times (1998) Government nationalizes long-term credit bank of Japan. https://www.japantimes.co.jp/news/1998/10/23/national/government-nationalizes-long-term-credit-bank-of-japan/. Accessed 20 Mar 2025

The Mainichi (2021) Japan gov't orders unit of financial firm sbi to halt operations. https://mainichi.jp/english/articles/20210609/p2g/00m/0bu/040000c. Access 12 Jun 2023

The Ministry of Finance of Japan (2021) Overview of fiscal investment and loan program 2021. https://www.mof.go.jp/english/policy/filp/FILP_overview2021.pdf. Accessed 20 Mar 2025

The National Credit Union Administration (2021a) Electronic Signatures in Global and National Commerce Act (E-Sign Act). https://www.ncua.gov/regulation-supervision/manuals-guides/federal-consumer-financial-protection-guide/compliance-management/deposit-regulations/electronic-signatures-global-and-national-commerce-act-e-sign-act. Accessed 20 Mar 2025

The National Credit Union Administration (2021b) Truth in Lending Act (Regulation Z). https://www.ncua.gov/regulation-supervision/manuals-guides/federal-consumer-financial-protection-guide/compliance-management/lending-regulations/truth-lending-act-regulation-z. Accessed 20 Mar 2025

The United States Code, Title 12. https://www.law.cornell.edu/uscode/text. Accessed 20 Mar 2025

The United States Securities and Exchange Commission (2021) Current NRSROs. https://www.sec.gov/ocr/ocr-current-nrsros.html. Accessed 20 Mar 2025

The United States Small Business Administration (2025a) 7(a) loans. https://www.sba.gov/funding-programs/loans/7a-loans. Accessed 20 Mar 2025

The United States Small Business Administration (2025b) 504 loans. https://www.sba.gov/funding-programs/loans/504-loans. Accessed 20 Mar 2025

The United States Small Business Administration (2025c) About SBA. https://www.sba.gov/about-sba. Accessed 20 Mar 2025

The United States Small Business Administration (2025d) Loans. https://www.sba.gov/funding-programs/loans. Accessed 20 Mar 2025

The United States Small Business Administration (2025e) Microloans. https://www.sba.gov/funding-programs/loans/microloans. Accessed 20 Mar 2025

Trust Companies Association of Japan (2025) Origins of trusts in Japan and the enactment of the Trust Act and the Trust Business Act. https://www.shintaku-kyokai.or.jp/en/trusts/trusts02_01.html. Accessed 20 Mar 2025

Tsukahara O (2016) SME financing in Japan. https://www.fsa.go.jp/frtc/20061205/08.pdf. Accessed 20 Mar 2025

Ueno H, Yamamoto T (2023) Lending and taking security in Japan: overview. https://uk.practicallaw.thomsonreuters.com/4-500-9220?transitionType=Default&contextData=(sc.Default). Accessed 20 Mar 2025

Uniform Law Commission (2025a) Uniform Commercial Code. https://www.uniformlaws.org/acts/ucc. Accessed 20 Mar 2025

Uniform Law Commission (2025b) Uniform Consumer Credit Code. https://www.uniformlaws.org/committees/community-home?communitykey=0f8dc75f-b418-4378-9641-486bb12813ff. Accessed 20 Mar 2025

US. Bureau of Federal Credit Unions (1957) Federal credit unions: cooperative thrift and credit. U.-S. Government Printing Office, Washington, D.C.

Vance DE (2005) Raising capital. Springer, New York

Vinturella JB, Erickson SM (2013) Raising entrepreneurial capital, 2nd edn. Elsevier, London

Walter JR (1991) Loan loss reserves. Econ Rev 77(4):20–30

Warren WS (2016) The frontiers of peer-to-peer lending: thinking about a new regulatory approach. Duke L & Tech Rev 14(1):298–316

Working Group Committee on the Global Financial System and the Financial Stability Board (2017) Fintech credit: market structure, business models and financial stability implications. https://www.bis.org/publ/cgfs_fsb1.htm. Accessed 20 Mar 2025

Yamori N, Kondo K, Tomimura K, Shindo Y, Takaku K (2013) Japanese banking regulations and sme finance under the global financial crisis. Japanese J Monet Financ Econ 1(1):59–90
Yasuda S (2020) A guide to credit cards in Japan: choosing, applying and using a credit card in Japan. https://tokyocheapo.com/living/choosing-a-credit-card-in-japan/. Accessed 20 Mar 2025
Yoshino N, Hesary FT (2017) Solutions for small and medium-sized enterprises' difficulties in accessing finance: Asian experiences. https://www.adb.org/publications/solutions-smes-difficulties-accessing-finance-asian-experiences. Accessed 20 Mar 2025
Yoshino N, Nakabayashi S, Morgan PJ (2019) Japan's financial system and its challenges. In: Volz U, Morgan PJ, Yoshino N (eds) Routledge handbook of banking and finance in Asia. Routledge, New York

# Chapter 6
# Mutual Funding as a New Tool for Risk Diversification

Despite discussions in government and academic circles about how to diversify the risks borne by lenders in P2P lending schemes in Vietnam, risk diversification remains a compelling topic. This is because P2P lenders still face substantial risks associated with lending small funds through online lending platforms, as mentioned in the previous chapter. Although it is not easy to eliminate these risks, we can, to some extent, mitigate or reduce them.

Given the substantial risks associated with lending small funds through online lending platforms, it is worth considering how P2P lenders might mitigate these risks. One potential solution is considering the concept of 'mutual help', which does not emerge arbitrarily but draws from Vietnam's long-standing sociocultural traditions. Historically, Vietnamese communities have relied on mutual assistance—such as informal savings groups, reciprocal labor exchanges, and communal risk-sharing—to support one another in times of financial or social hardship. These practices are deeply embedded in the country's social culture and continue to influence community behavior today.[1]

The rationale for applying mutual help to P2P lending arises from the regulatory gap that currently exists in Vietnam. While P2P lenders and conventional commercial bank depositors may appear similar—both entrust funds with the expectation of earning interest—their legal protections are vastly different. It is easy to observe that depositors in conventional commercial banks benefit from robust regulatory safeguards, including deposit insurance and oversight mechanisms. In contrast, P2P lenders can hardly enjoy comparable legal protection; their investments in P2P loans are neither insured nor effectively regulated, leaving them vulnerable to borrower defaults and potential misconduct by platform service providers.

In this context, mutual help can offer a culturally resonant and practically relevant mechanism for collective risk mitigation. Rather than relying solely on platform service providers or legal reforms, P2P lenders may benefit from participating in

[1] See Tuan et al. (2014), The Vietnam Veterans Association (2023) and Dat (2025).



Y. H. Nguyen, *Regulating Peer-to-Peer Lending in Vietnam*,
https://doi.org/10.1007/978-981-96-9505-8_6

lending schemes that allow for peer-to-peer support. This approach does not replace regulation but provides an interim or complementary strategy grounded in Vietnamese communal norms. The concept of mutual help will be elaborated further below.

## 6.1 Mutual Help as the Foundation for Mutual Funding

Mutual help is commonly considered a form of assistance based on natural modes of bonding and affiliation between human beings.[2] People facing common problems in life, such as financial, housing, or health problems, may come together and form mutual help groups to support one another.[3] These groups can be established by individuals within regional societies (national affiliation, local affiliation, or both) or by individuals with no organizational affiliation to address various life challenges.[4] It is worth noting that, in terms of organization, mutual help groups can be either peer-led or professionally led.[5] Their members may include both those who have overcome common problems and those seeking solutions to such problems.[6] In general, mutual help can be categorized into three major types, including reciprocity, redistribution, and unidirectional help, depending on the direction of actions taken within mutual help groups.[7] Reciprocity primarily involves labor exchange, where members of mutual help groups assist each other with hard work like planting rice, cutting rice, and re-roofing houses (see Fig. 6.1). An example of reciprocity action can be observed in the group-based rice farming practices of Vietnamese farmers in the

---

[2] See Gidron and Chesler (1994, p. 3), Spade (2020, p. 7) and Zimmerman et al. (1991, p. 252).

[3] For instance, in agricultural villages in Japan, relatives formed mutual help groups to assist each other when one of the group members needed help in building or repairing the roof of a house. In return, the member reciprocated by assisting others at various times. Similarly, in the United States, alcoholics established mutual help groups where they met regularly to share information and offer psychological support to each other. See Onda (2013, p. 533) and Pistrang et al. (2008, p. 110).

[4] For example, during the early 1980s, Vietnamese veterans, particularly those who had experienced post-traumatic stress disorder, formed mutual support groups in different local areas, such as villages, communes, or towns, to provide assistance in treating the disorder. In 1989, the Vietnam Veterans Association was founded by veterans from across the nation, with the goal of uniting and motivating all veterans to actively engage in the nation's construction and defense. The association aimed to safeguard veterans' interests and legitimate rights while offering mutual aid in their daily lives. See Gressard (1986, p. 74) and The Vietnam Veterans Association (2023).

[5] The rice farming groups established by Vietnamese farmers in the early twentieth century in the Mekong Delta, based on kinship, neighborship, and/or friendship, serve as an example of peer-led mutual help groups. In contrast, the Vietnam Veterans Association, established by Vietnamese veterans across the country under the leadership of the Communist Party of Vietnam, can be seen as an example of professionally led mutual help groups. Moreover, within the informal financial sector, Vietnamese individuals have the option to create mutual help groups, which are organized either by the members themselves or with the assistance of an NGO and/or a formal credit institution. See Tuan et al. (2014, p. 69), The Vietnam Veterans Association (2023) and Dat (2025).

[6] See Borkman (2021, p. 10), Roberts et al. (1999, p. 842) and Meissen et al. (1991, p. 429).

[7] See Onda (2017, p. 163).

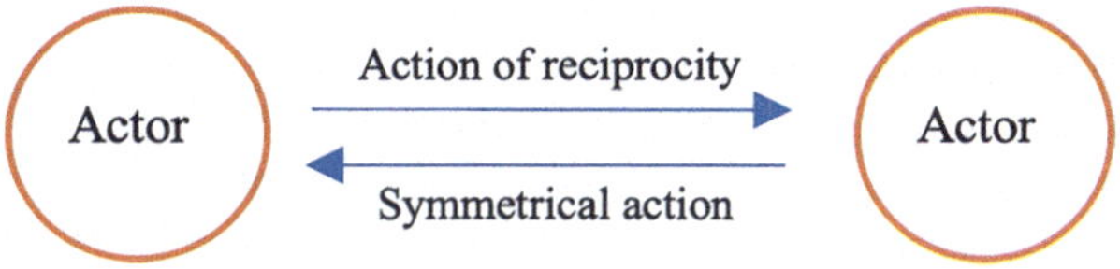


**Fig. 6.1** Reciprocity help (See Onda (2018, p. 4))

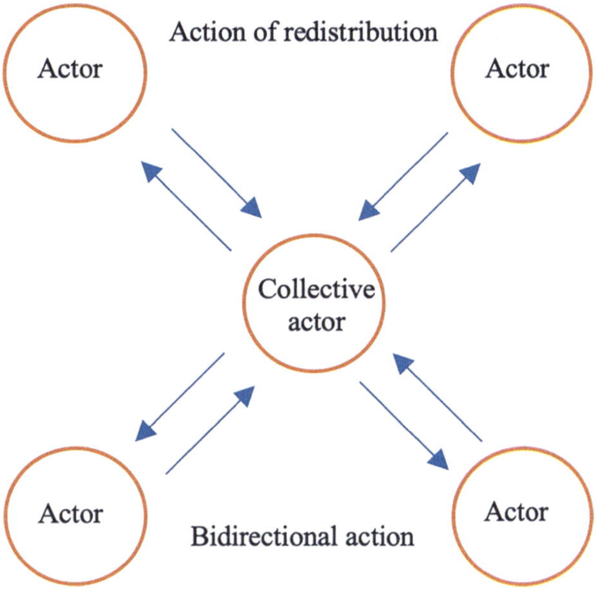


**Fig. 6.2** Redistribution (See Onda (2013, p. 533))

Mekong Delta during the early twentieth century. These farmers established labor exchange groups based on kinship, neighborship, and/or friendship to provide mutual support.[8]

Redistribution refers to schemes where manpower, goods, and money are gathered and allocated among mutual help group members (see Fig. 6.2). For example, historically in Japan, families in villages that shared common areas such as mountains, forests, or seas would contribute their labor to tasks like repairing and cleaning roads and canals, thereby maintaining these shared resources. In exchange, they would be granted the right to utilize the resources of the mountain, forest, or sea.[9] Another example of redistribution can be observed in Vietnam, where individuals who are familiar with and trust each other form tontine groups (known as Ho, Hui, Bieu, or Phuong). These groups regularly collect modest contributions from their members to provide mutual assistance. The funds accumulated from the group members are consolidated into a shared pool within each tontine group. Group members then take turns accessing or borrowing from this collective fund. The

[8] See Tuan et al. (2014).

[9] See Onda (2013, p. 534).

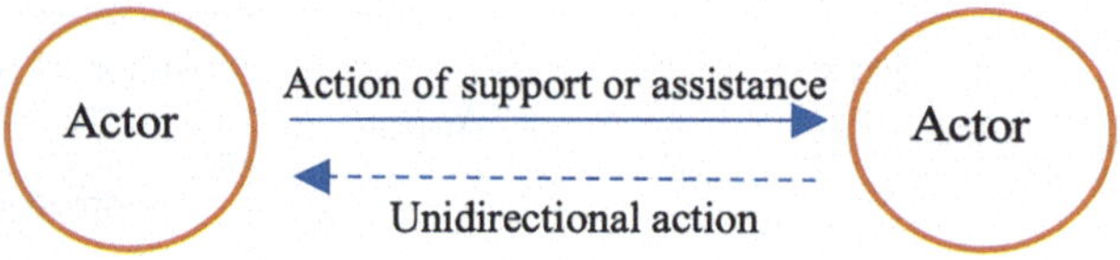


**Fig. 6.3** Unidirectional help (See Onda (2013, p. 533))

interest rates and loan amounts extended to group members can be determined through consensus among all members, by means of a bidding process, or by the group's designated organizer.[10]

Finally, unidirectional help refers to help given without the expectation of reciprocity, such as unidirectional support at wedding or funeral ceremonies, where assistance is provided without the need for labor or monetary exchange (see Fig. 6.3).

Among the three types of mutual help, redistribution can be used to create mutual help groups that assist individuals struggling to borrow small amounts of money. In these mutual help groups, all members agree to contribute to and maintain a common pool of money in exchange for the right to borrow some money from the pool.[11] By establishing such lending schemes through mutual help groups, group members can create a mechanism for cooperation and support among each other. This cooperation and support can be fostered through regular group meetings (for example, weekly or monthly), during which members contribute a small amount each time to lend funds to those in need, discuss financial issues, and share experiential knowledge about using and managing small funds.[12] It is important to note that the personal familiarity among group members and the level of social integration among them play important roles in building confidence, sustaining mutual trust among group members, and mitigating the risks faced by them.[13]

Notably, the mitigation of risk faced by group members in lending schemes deployed by mutual help groups can be achieved as follows. Firstly, these lending schemes are likely to assist group members in increasing the effectiveness of the use of loans borrowed from the common pool, thanks to the discussion and sharing of experiential knowledge among them. This can potentially reduce the risk of default for members acting as borrowers. Additionally, these lending schemes can mitigate the risk to which group members acting as lenders are exposed. This is because if any group members default on loans borrowed from the common pool, they are very likely to lose the money they have contributed to the pool and face the threat of social punishment and peer pressure from other group members. Such sanctions, along with the fear of losing contributed money, are likely to motivate borrowers to be

[10] See Pham and Lensink (2007) and Wolz et al. (2001, p. 30).

[11] See Onda (2013, p. 1).

[12] See Roberts et al. (1999, p. 845), Gidron and Chesler (1994, p. 14) and Ibrahim (2020, p. 32).

[13] See Roberts et al. (1999, p. 846).

conscious of their usage of borrowed funds and actively seek ways to ensure their repayment obligations.[14]

Nowadays, online mutual help groups have been established among people facing common life challenges.[15] In order to gain an understanding of whether online lending schemes employed by mutual help groups, or online mutual funding schemes (hereinafter referred to as "mutual funding schemes," or simply, "mutual funding," for the purpose of convenience), can assist individuals providing and seeking small funds within these groups to mitigate their risks, the next sections will examine the risks inherent in mutual funding schemes and the possibility of employing these schemes to mitigate the risks faced by P2P lenders in Vietnam.

## 6.2 Understanding of Mutual Funding

In order to understand the risks inherent in mutual funding, the notion of mutual funding cannot be missing. Based on the idea of mutual help, a mutual funding scheme is established as an investment or credit scheme for pooling money, where a specific number of investors or lenders form and/or join a group. These individuals contribute a specified amount of money regularly (for example, weekly or monthly) via an online lending platform to provide small funds or funding support to group members in need.

It can be seen that mutual funding schemes carry several major risks. Firstly, there is an information gap between individuals seeking funds (or, potential borrowers) and those providing funds (or, potential lenders) within mutual funding schemes, which might put potential lenders at risk of making wrong lending decisions. Like any face-to-face mutual help scheme, mutual funding schemes are established with the main purpose of providing mutual help among group members. Their members may include individuals in regional societies (national affiliation, local affiliation, or both national and local affiliation) who know much about each other, as well as those who have no organizational affiliation and know very little about each other. This is evident in Vietnam, where there have been cases in which members of tontine groups did not know each other well. They placed their trust in the tontine holders or organizers and contributed their funds to the common pools.[16] It should be noted that in mutual funding schemes, mutual funding members might be easily solicited by online lending platforms, and they are very likely to have no organizational affiliation with each other or know very little about one another. Due to this information gap, lenders in mutual funding schemes can hardly make good lending decisions.

[14] See Onda (2013, p. 540) and Allen and Babus (2010, p. 377).

[15] See Salem et al. (1997, p. 192).

[16] However, the tontine holders then ran away with all the money from the common pools. See Linh and Dương (2018).

In order to reduce the information gap between lenders and borrowers in a mutual funding scheme, platform service provider may exercise due diligence to evaluate potential borrowers' creditworthiness. However, this solution may not be effective in the case of unbanked or non-banked individuals applying for loans through a mutual funding for the first time. On the other hand, it is easy to see that personal relationships among scheme members of lending schemes deployed by face-to-face mutual help groups can significantly contribute to creating confidence and mutual trust among group members, as well as imposing social punishment and peer pressure on defaulted borrowers. This suggests that personal relationships among members of a mutual funding can help mutual funding members, to some extent, mitigate such an information gap. Indeed, repeated lending through a mutual funding enables potential lenders to gather more information about potential borrowers over time, which can improve personal relationships among them. It has also been observed that, based on the information about potential borrowers that potential lenders know and the degree of personal relationships among them, potential lenders can make lending decisions that fit the initially unobserved risk characteristics of potential borrowers.[17]

It is not surprising that the assets contributed to a common pool by lenders in either a face-to-face mutual help scheme or a mutual funding scheme through an online lending platform are excessively exposed to the risk of borrower default. This is because lenders voluntarily contribute their assets into the common pool to provide funding support to other group members for the purpose of helping each other. In the case of borrower default, the pool is exposed to the risk of being lost partly or fully. Since lenders' assets are pooled, they are exposed to the risk of losing their money corresponding to their contribution to the pool. Suppose that one borrower in a face-to-face mutual help group's lending scheme fails to repay their loan, the corresponding lenders are very likely to share the loss of the loan. Likewise, in an online mutual funding scheme, if one borrower defaults, the corresponding lenders can hardly share the loss of the defaulted loan with any other party apart from the scheme members. It should be noted that even though a mutual funding can be established via online lending platforms, the lenders can hardly claim responsibility from the platform service provider, as examined in the preceding chapter.

In addition to the aforementioned risks, the pooled fund in a mutual funding scheme is very likely to be too small compared to the total demands of potential borrowers, which can make it difficult to maintain the scheme's existence and operation. The gap between the supply of funds and the demand for loans may arise due to the lack of group members with idle assets who are willing to contribute their assets into the common pool for lending to those in need within the same group. Similar to a face-to-face mutual help group's lending scheme, the primary source of funds for the common pool of a mutual funding is the group members themselves. The inability to sustain a steady membership may pose a continual threat to the

[17] See Sedai et al. (2021, p. 2).

survival and smooth operation of the mutual funding.[18] Additionally, a significant gap between the supply of and demand for funds can occur if a large number of group members seek to borrow from the pool, and their demand exceeds the size of the pool at a certain point in time. If the pooled fund is too small to meet the considerable demand for funds from potential borrowers, it might reduce the incentive for group members to maintain their membership in the mutual funding. This is particularly likely because members of a mutual funding typically face a common difficulty in borrowing small funds to meet various needs in life, similar to members in lending schemes of face-to-face mutual help groups. However, it is worth noting that, in face-to-face mutual help groups, personal relationships among group members are typically embedded in kinship, friendship, comradeship, neighborhood, or regional community. These relationships can increase the confidence and mutual trust among individuals facing common problems, motivating them to form mutual help groups and attract more potential members to join and support one another.[19] Likewise, in a mutual funding scheme, it can be seen that personal relationships among scheme members can help increase the number of members joining the scheme, which, in turn, contributes to the growth of the pooled fund. By fostering confidence and trust, these personal relationships can play an important role in the success and sustainability of the mutual funding scheme.

Based on the above analysis, it can be easily presumed that the business operations and loan usage by borrowers in a mutual funding scheme are poorly monitored, which is likely to increase the credit risk borne by lenders. Unlike lending schemes of face-to-face mutual help groups, where lenders are likely to closely monitor the business operations and loan usage by borrowers to put peer pressure on them and induce them to use their loans effectively, such monitoring can hardly be realized in mutual funding schemes. This is because members of a mutual funding scheme are often recruited through online lending platforms, and they may have limited knowledge about each other, as discussed earlier. However, it can be observed that active monitoring of business operations and loan utilization by borrowers in a mutual funding scheme is achievable when there is an enhancement in the personal relationships among scheme members. Indeed, by engaging in regular discussions about financial challenges and exchanging experiential knowledge regarding the utilization and management of small funds, lenders and borrowers with strong personal relationships within a mutual funding scheme are likely to be more capable of closely monitoring business operations and loan utilization by borrowers.[20] Notably, inadequate monitoring of borrowers' business operations and loan utilization within a mutual funding scheme might stem from the absence of professional management in the organization of the scheme. In the absence of such professional management, lenders struggle to consistently gather information about borrowers' business operations and loan usage. They are also unable to systematically analyze this

[18] See Meissen et al. (1991, p. 438).

[19] See Salem et al. (1997, p. 191) and Gidron and Chesler (1994, p. 14).

[20] See Stiglitz (1990, p. 351).

information to implement necessary changes to loan conditions based on borrowers' risk characteristics.

Furthermore, akin to borrowers in lending schemes within face-to-face mutual help groups, borrowers participating in a mutual funding arrangement are highly likely to possess minimal or no collateral to secure their loans. This circumstance could potentially expose lenders to the risk of partial or complete loss of their invested funds. This is because individuals involved in mutual funding typically encounter challenges when attempting to borrow small funds to fulfill various life needs. As previously mentioned, these members often make regular modest contributions in exchange for the privilege of borrowing small funds from the shared pool. It can be readily assumed that borrowers within a mutual funding scheme are highly likely to consist of impoverished or low-income individuals who possess limited or negligible collateral to secure their loans. The loans extended through the scheme are expected to be unsecured, thereby exposing the shared pool of the scheme to the potential risk of partial or complete loss. Moreover, lenders are prone to possessing minimal or no collateral to recover loans from borrowers who default, which could potentially subject them to the risk of partial or complete loss of their invested funds. In practice, as per the Hai Phong City People's Court, which is authorized to handle cases linked to lending within tontine groups in the city, lenders face significant challenges in recovering their loans when borrowers default. This is due to the fact that defaulted borrowers who have become insolvent generally lack the assets needed to meet their repayment obligations. In certain instances, if defaulted borrowers possess jobs and incomes, lenders might have the possibility to gradually recover the debts.[21]

It is important to note that within a mutual funding scheme, borrowers are prone to experiencing either minimal or excessively stringent sanctions in the event of loan default. On the one hand, unlike lending schemes within face-to-face mutual help groups, members of a mutual funding scheme can be recruited through online lending platforms. Consequently, they may have limited knowledge about each other, resulting in a lack of substantial social sanctions imposed on borrowers who default. It is evident that borrowers who have defaulted may be excluded from upcoming lending schemes implemented by the lending platform and/or prohibited from borrowing future loans from lenders who incurred losses due to their defaults. However, if borrowers fail to repay the borrowed funds, whether intentionally or unintentionally, the lenders are then burdened with the losses stemming from the defaulted loans. On the other hand, let's consider a scenario where defaulted borrowers are widely recognized by other members of the group. In this scenario, defaulted borrowers could potentially be excluded from forthcoming lending schemes implemented by the lending platform and/or be denied the opportunity to borrow future loans from both the lenders who experienced losses due to their default and the other group members. Additionally, they are highly likely to experience peer pressure and encounter social repercussions from other group members,

[21] See The People's Court of Hai Phong City (2020).

including criticism and ostracism.[22] It can be observed that these sanctions are excessively severe for individuals who are unable to repay their loans due to incapacity, as opposed to deliberate non-repayment. From the above analysis, it is evident that personal relationships between defaulted borrowers and other group members in a mutual funding arrangement play a crucial role in enforcing the aforementioned social penalties on defaulted borrowers.

## 6.3 Mutual Funding as a Technique for Risk Diversification

Based on the analysis above, it is reasonable to propose that mutual funding schemes can provide a method to aid P2P lenders in mitigating risks when offering small loans through online lending platforms. The mitigation of risks faced by P2P lenders through the utilization of mutual funding, as well as the limitations of this approach, are outlined below.

On the one hand, personal relationships between members of a mutual funding scheme deployed by an online lending platform can, to a certain extent, help mitigate the risks faced by P2P lenders. One of the risks that potential lenders in P2P lending schemes in Vietnam are likely to face is making wrong lending decisions, as examined in Sect. 3.2.1. This risk can be mitigated by utilizing personal relationships among members of a mutual funding scheme. The reason is that personal relationships among members of a mutual funding scheme can help diminish the information gap between potential lenders and potential borrowers. Once potential lenders acquire more information about potential borrowers, they are likely to be in a better position to differentiate between healthier borrowers and riskier ones, leading to improved lending decisions.

Personal relationships among members of a mutual funding scheme can also aid P2P lenders in mitigating the credit risk caused by defaulted borrowers and/or the temporary or permanent cessation of platform service providers' operations by distributing the risk among a larger number of lenders. This is because personal relationships within a mutual funding scheme are likely to nurture confidence and mutual trust among the members. This, in turn, can motivate them to attract more potential members to join the scheme, thereby increasing the size of the pooled fund. The more members join a mutual fund, and the larger the size of a pooled fund becomes, the more lenders are likely to collectively share the credit risk caused by a defaulted borrower.

It is worth noting that credit risk faced by P2P lenders in a mutual funding scheme can be reduced through the close monitoring of P2P borrowers' business operations and loan utilization. This monitoring can be achieved by enhancing personal relationships among members of the scheme. Indeed, regular discussions about financial difficulties and the sharing of experiential knowledge regarding the use and

[22] See Onda (2013).

management of small funds between lenders and borrowers who have strong personal relationships within a mutual funding can help lenders gain a better perspective on observing borrowers' business operations and loan usage. With such an improved position, P2P lenders can readily implement necessary changes or adjust lending conditions to prevent and/or mitigate credit risk.

Furthermore, personal relationships among members of a mutual funding scheme play an important role in exerting peer pressure and social consequences on defaulted borrowers, potentially assisting P2P lenders in reducing the default they face. As mentioned above, if defaulted borrowers are familiar to other group members, they are more likely to experience peer pressure and social consequences from their peers, such as condemnation and ostracism. This may motivate P2P borrowers to exercise more caution in utilizing the loans borrowed from the shared pool and strive to repay their debts in the event of default.

On the other hand, the effectiveness of credit risk mitigation for P2P lenders through a mutual funding scheme might be constrained by several reasons. For example, because the main source of funds for the shared pool in a mutual funding scheme comes from the voluntary contributions of P2P lenders, these contributed funds are highly susceptible to the default risk resulting from defaulted borrowers. If a borrower defaults on a loan, the common pool becomes vulnerable to the risk of losing the corresponding amount. In such a case, P2P lenders are very likely to incur a loss from the defaulted loan. Another example is that P2P borrowers are very likely to possess little or no collateral to secure their loans. Since borrowers in a mutual funding typically face difficulties in obtaining small funds to meet various life needs, the loans provided through this scheme are highly likely to be both small and unsecured. If a borrower defaults on a loan, the corresponding lenders are likely to have minimal or no collateral to recover the lent money, thus making it highly probable that they will bear the loss of the defaulted loan.

Given the analysis above, it can be readily presumed that personal relationships among members of a mutual funding scheme, in the absence of professional management overseeing its operations, could be a significant factor contributing to the scheme's limitations. As stated in Sect. 6.1, in terms of organization, mutual help groups can be categorized as either peer-led or professionally led. Building on this concept, it becomes apparent that professional management of a mutual funding endeavor can involve entrusting the task to skilled members or organizing it among the members themselves, with the assistance of the platform service provider or a professional institution. Personal relationships among members of a mutual funding, without professional management overseeing its operation, are unlikely to effectively mitigate the risks faced by P2P lenders. While such relationships can aid potential lenders in making informed lending decisions by narrowing the information gap between them and potential borrowers, it remains improbable that all potential lenders within a mutual funding possess comprehensive knowledge of potential borrowers' information. This is because group members participating in a mutual funding scheme through an online lending platform are highly likely to lack any organizational affiliation with one another or possess minimal knowledge about each other. Suppose there are several potential lenders who have strong relationships with multiple potential borrowers in a mutual funding scheme. Without professional management overseeing the operation of a mutual funding, the collection and systematic analysis of valuable information on potential borrowers becomes challenging, thereby limiting the ability of all potential lenders to make improved lending decisions. Another example is that personal relationships between members of a mutual funding without professional management can scarcely contribute to the enhancement of peer monitoring among the members. This monitoring is crucial for preventing and/or mitigating the default risk stemming from borrowers who fail to meet their obligations. This is because, in the absence of professional management, the prospect of regular discussions concerning financial difficulties and the exchange of experiential knowledge regarding the utilization and management of small funds between lenders and borrowers with strong personal relationships within a mutual funding is unlikely to materialize. As a result, the challenge of gaining a more advantageous position for closely and consistently monitoring borrowers' business operations and loan utilization is likely to impede lenders from enacting necessary changes or adjusting lending conditions based on borrowers' risk profiles.

In Vietnam's contemporary urbanized society, where heavy reliance on the Internet is prominent, the creation of a mutual funding scheme through an online lending platform might not align well for various reasons, as detailed below. In answer to the escalating requirement for modest loans within Vietnamese society, an increasing number of online lending platforms have emerged, particularly in major cities such as Hanoi, Ho Chi Minh, and Da Nang. Furthermore, a growing number of Vietnamese citizens, including both lenders and borrowers without the requisite sophistication, have been encouraged to participate in lending schemes via online lending platforms.[23] As indicated in Sects. 3.2.1 and 3.2.2, these individuals are susceptible to the risks[24] linked with online lending platforms. Similarly, platform service providers are prone to the risks associated with the Internet, as discussed in Sect. 3.2.3.[25] It is worth noting that due to the increasing solicitation of Vietnamese citizens by online lending platforms to participate in P2P lending schemes, they are more likely to lack any organizational affiliation with each other or possess limited knowledge about one another. The diminished likelihood of personal relationships among members of mutual funding schemes is likely to create challenges in mitigating the associated risks. Moreover, given that members of a mutual funding are

[23] See Hùng and Nhung (2020).

[24] For example, P2P lenders and borrowers are exposed to the risk of being solicited to enter into an unfair service contract by a platform service provider. Another example is that P2P lenders and borrowers are at risk of having their personal information misappropriated by platform service providers and/or stolen by hackers.

[25] For example, platform service providers are at risk of identity fraud committed by P2P lenders and borrowers using P2P lending platforms for the purpose of stealing money, money laundering, terrorist financing, or other illicit activities, and the risk of having their platforms attacked by spies and hackers for the purpose of stealing personally identifiable information of P2P lenders and borrowers using their platforms, interrupting the operation or even destroying the operating system of the lending platforms.

usually individuals facing challenges in obtaining small funds to fulfill various life needs, there could be a shortage of group members possessing available assets and the willingness to contribute those assets to the collective pool for the role of lenders. In the meantime, even as the number of middle-class individuals in Vietnamese society with some available assets who could contribute to the collective pool of a mutual funding scheme rises,[26] it is probable that they would seek to invest for profit rather than in return for the right to borrow small funds from the shared pool.[27] Due to this, lacking a legal framework for the operation of P2P lending platforms, both platform service providers and members of mutual funding schemes face challenges in enticing more middle-class individuals to participate, thereby expanding the size of the shared pools. This challenge is likely to impede the distribution of default risk arising from a single defaulted borrower across a larger number of lenders.

It is important to note that in Japan, a mutual funding scheme is legally structured as a credit cooperative.[28] A credit cooperative can be formed with the aim of fostering mutual support among its members, and all participants have the option to voluntarily join or leave the credit cooperative.[29] Credit cooperatives can both receive deposits or installment savings from members and extend loans to them.[30] In practice, credit cooperatives primarily operate within specific locations, and they may not necessarily demand collateral. However, they closely oversee borrowers' business activities and loan utilization to guarantee loan repayment, as discussed in Sect. 5.1.2. In a society characterized by active financial activities, the regulations under Japan's Banking Act (Act No. 59 of 1981, as amended) and Financial Instruments and Exchange Act (Act No. 25 of 1948, as amended) are applicable with necessary modifications. In the case of traditional mutual funding schemes, the implementation of the Banking Act (Act No. 59 of 1981, as amended) signifies that these schemes take on a highly institutional nature and bear a resemblance to commercial banks. On the contrary, for contemporary crowdfunding through lending or investment, the Financial Instruments and Exchange Act (Act No. 25 of 1948, as amended) is directly applicable.[31] These regulations suggest the inadequacy of mutual funding schemes in the context of the vibrant financial activities within the current society. As a result, such quasi-bank institutions might forfeit the advantage of personal relationships.

---

[26] See An (2021).

[27] This is because middle-class people's demand for small funds can often be met by commercial banks, as mentioned in Sect. 2.1.2.

[28] See Japan's Small and Medium-Sized Enterprise Cooperatives Act (Act No. 181 of 1949, as amended), Article 3, Item 2.

[29] See Japan's Small and Medium-Sized Enterprise Cooperatives Act (Act No. 181 of 1949, as amended), Article 5, Paragraph 1.

[30] See Japan's Small and Medium-Sized Enterprise Cooperatives Act (Act No. 181 of 1949, as amended), Article 9 bis 8, Paragraph 1.

[31] See Motoyanagi (2022).

## 6.4 Interim Conclusion

In this chapter, mutual help is first considered. It is categorized into three main types, including reciprocity help, redistribution, and unidirectional help. Among the three types of mutual help, the chapter found that redistribution can be used to create mutual help groups that assist individuals struggling to borrow small amounts of money. In these mutual help groups, members agree to contribute to a shared fund in exchange for the right to borrow from it when needed. This arrangement can foster a system of mutual support, reinforced by regular group meetings where members not only contribute financially but also discuss financial concerns and exchange experiential knowledge on how to effectively use and manage small loans.

Such practices enhance the risk mitigation capacity of a group lending scheme in several ways. First, shared learning and peer advice can improve how members use borrowed funds, thereby reducing the likelihood of default. Second, the structure of the group itself discourages delinquency: members who default risk losing their own contributions and facing informal sanctions such as social pressure and reputational damage. These internal incentives promote responsible borrowing and repayment behavior. As a result, redistribution-based mutual help groups can potentially offer a culturally grounded and functionally effective model for reducing financial risks in small-scale lending.

To explore potential measures for diversifying the risk borne by P2P lenders in Vietnam, the chapter further examines a mutual funding scheme. This scheme involves pooling money contributed by a group of investors or lenders and providing it to participants in need of finance via an online lending platform. The chapter found that personal relationships among participants in a mutual funding can contribute to the mitigation of risks borne by P2P lenders. This is because (1) personal relationships between participants in a mutual funding scheme can help bridge the information gap between individual potential borrowers and lenders; (2) confidence and mutual trust among participants in a mutual funding scheme, built upon their personal relationships, can attract more potential participants, thereby increasing the size of the pooled fund. The growth of the pooled fund can mitigate vulnerabilities against borrower defaults and potential suspension or cessation of platform service providers' operation; (3) such personal relationships can enable P2P lenders to closely monitor P2P borrowers' business operations and loan usage, thereby potentially reducing unexpected default risks caused by P2P borrowers; and (4) such personal relationships play an important role in imposing peer pressure and social punishments on defaulted borrowers, thereby mitigating the risk caused by defaulted borrowers.

In consideration of the above discussions, the author proposes that the risks faced by P2P lenders in Vietnam can be mitigated by implementing the characteristics of a mutual funding scheme (that is, personal relationships among participants) thereto. Challenges in implementing mutual funding in Vietnam's P2P lending schemes will be examined in Chap. 7 and empirical testing the feasibility of mutual funding as a risk diversification will be conducted in Chap. 8.

## References

Allen F and Babus A (2010) Networks in finance. In: Kleindorfer PR, Wind YJ and Gunther RE (eds) The network challenge: strategy, profit, and risk in an interlinked world. Wharton School Pub.

An P (2021) Vietnam among world's fastest middle class growth nations. https://e.vnexpress.net/news/business/data-speaks/vietnam-among-world-s-fastest-middle-class-growth-nations-4351459.html. Accessed 20 Mar 2025

Borkman T (2021) Self-help/mutual aid groups and peer support: a literature review. Brill Academic Publishers, Leiden

Dat TT Analysis of the informal credit sector in Vietnam. https://www.gdrc.org/icm/viet-dat_tran.html. Accessed 20 Mar 2025

Gidron B and Chesler M (1994) Universal and particular attributes of self-help: a framework for international and intranational analysis. In: Lavoie F, Barkman T and Gidron B (eds) Self-help and mutual aid groups: international and multicultural perspectives. Routledge, New York

Gressard CF (1986) Self-help groups for Vietnam veterans experiencing posttraumatic stress disorder. J Spec Gr Work 11(2):74–79

Hùng NM and Nhung TTH (2020) The status quo of the p2p lending sector in Vietnam. https://tapchicongthuong.vn/bai-viet/thuc-trang-hoat-dong-cho-vay-ngang-hang-tai-viet-nam-76652.htm. Accessed 20 Mar 2025

Ibrahim H (2020) Structured savings and asset ownership: the role of rotating savings and credit associations among African immigrants in the United States. J Sociol Soc Welf 47(2):29–57

Japan's Small and Medium-Sized Enterprise Cooperatives Act (Act No. 181 of 1949, as amended). https://www.japaneselawtranslation.go.jp/en/laws/view/3830. Accessed 20 Mar 2025

Linh N and Dương H (2018) Nạn giật hụi, bể hụi nở rộ khắp nước [The collapse of tontine groups boomed across the country]. https://plo.vn/nan-giat-hui-be-hui-no-ro-khap-nuoc-post504657.html. Accessed 20 Mar 2025

Meissen GJ, Gleason DF and Embree MG (1991) An assessment of the needs of mutual help groups. Am J Community Psychol 19:427–442

Motoyanagi Y (2022) Fundraising and disclosure, lecture notes taken during the Japanese business law in practice course at the LL.M Program in International Economic and Business Law, Kyushu University on April 2, 2022

Onda M (2013) Mutual help networks and social transformation in Japan. Am J Econ Sociol 72(3): 531–564

Onda M (2017) Mutual help networks in globalization: reconsideration of a rotating credit system in modern capitalism. J Fac Sociol 20(2):163–180

Onda M (2018) Micro finance in traditional mutual help networks in East Asia: a comparison of rotating savings and credit associations in Japan, South Korea, China, and Taiwan. J Fac Sociol 28(2):1–25

Pham TTT and Lensink R (2007) Lending Policies of Informal, Formal and Semiformal Lenders. Econ Transit Institutional Chang 15(2):181–209

Pistrang N, Barker C and Humphreys K (2008) Mutual help groups for mental health problems: a review of effectiveness studies. Am J Community Psychol 42(1-2):110–121

Roberts LJ, Salem D, Rappaport J, Toro PA, Luke DA and Seidman E (1999) Giving and receiving help: interpersonal transactions in mutual help meetings and psychosocial adjustment of members. Am J Community Psychol 27(6):841–868

Salem DA, Anne BG and Reid C (1997) Mutual help goes on-line. J Community Psychol 25(2): 189–208

Sedai AK, Vasudevan R and Pena AA (2021) Friends and benefits? endogenous rotating savings and credit associations as alternative for women's empowerment in India. World Dev 145(2): 1–23

Spade D (2020) Mutual aid: building solidarity during this crisis and the next. Verso Books, London

Stiglitz JE (1990) Peer monitoring and credit markets. World Bank Econ Rev 4(3):351–366

The People's Court of Hai Phong City (2020) Chơi hụi, họ, tình trạng vỡ hụi, vỡ họ với những hệ lụy để lại [Taking part in Hui, Ho, the collapse of Hui, Ho, and the consequences]. https://haiphong.toaan.gov.vn/webcenter/portal/haiphong/chitiettin?dDocName=TAND140839. Accessed 20 Mar 2025

The Vietnam Veterans Association (2023) Điều lệ Hội Cựu Chiến Binh Việt Nam [The Charter of the Vietnam Veterans Association]. http://www.cuuchienbinh.com.vn/. Accessed 30 July 2023

Tuan LA, Cottrell A and King D (2014) Changes in social capital: a case study of collective rice farming practices in the mekong delta, Vietnam. J Vietnamese Stud 9(2):68–99

Wolz A, Tri PM and Kirsch OC (2001) Promotion of self-help in rural Vietnam. https://www.sai.uni-heidelberg.de/intwep/fia/VW-breit30.pdf. Accessed 20 Mar 2025

Zimmerman MA, Reischl TM, Seidman E, Rappaport J, Toro PA and Salem DA (1991) Expansion strategies of a mutual help organization. Am J Community Psychol 19(2):251–278

# Chapter 7
# Challenges in Implementing Mutual Funding in Vietnam's P2P Lending Schemes

## 7.1 Challenges in P2P Lending from a Lender's Perspective

Mutual funding schemes offer several advantages over the current P2P lending schemes in Vietnam. For example, while P2P lenders and borrowers participating in a P2P lending scheme are not likely to have personal relationships with each other, participants in a mutual funding scheme are more likely to have personal relationships with one another, as outlined below. As mentioned in Sect. 6.2, individuals often face challenges in accessing small funds. In response to these challenges, they come together to establish a mutual funding scheme for mutual support. Both lenders and borrowers, as scheme participants, cooperate and support each other through regular group meetings. During these meetings, each of them contributes a small amount to a shared pool each time. This pool is then used to provide small funds individually to those in need within the scheme. Lenders can borrow from the pool, becoming borrowers, and once they have repaid their loans, they can resume as lenders. During regular group meetings, both lenders and borrowers can discuss their individual financial difficulties and share experiential knowledge about using and managing small funds. These personal connections between lenders and borrowers within a mutual funding scheme are likely to help bridge the information gap between them to a certain extent. As a result, this may reduce the risk of wrong lending decisions for those acting as lenders. Additionally, personal relationships among participants (including both lenders and borrowers) in a mutual funding scheme are likely to foster confidence and mutual trust among them. This trust is likely to motivate scheme participants to recruit more members to the scheme, as discussed in Sect. 6.3. As more participants join a mutual funding scheme, the defaults caused by individual borrowers are spread among a larger group, including lenders and non-defaulting borrowers. Furthermore, since both lenders and borrowers in a mutual funding scheme collectively contribute to a shared pool, they all share the credit risk caused by defaulted borrowers. When a borrower is at risk of default, both lenders and other borrowers in the scheme might exert peer pressure

 
Y. H. Nguyen, *Regulating Peer-to-Peer Lending in Vietnam*,
https://doi.org/10.1007/978-981-96-9505-8_7

and apply social sanctions, such as condemnation and ostracism, on that individual. As detailed in Sect. 6.3, personal relationships within the scheme, particularly between lenders and borrowers as well as among borrowers themselves, are crucial for applying peer pressure and imposing social consequences on those who default. Such peer pressure and social consequences can motivate borrowers to use loans from the shared pool prudently and address any repayment defaults promptly. This diligence and effort can potentially help participants in the scheme reduce the likelihood of defaults.

Another advantage is that participants in a mutual funding scheme share profits and jointly bear losses. In a P2P lending scheme, individual P2P lenders can either manually invest in loans available on the platform or wait for the platform to automatically match them with one or more borrowers, as mentioned in Sect. 1.1. In either method, each lender is solely responsible for bearing the risk of default from the borrower(s) to whom they lent. In contrast, in a mutual funding scheme, a specific number of investors or lenders regularly contribute a predetermined amount of money to a shared pool. This pool is then used to provide financial support or small funds to scheme members in need. Profits from lending activities are distributed among participants in the scheme, while losses from defaults are collectively borne by them. Sharing these losses among participants is the essence of risk diversification within the scheme. The model presented in Sect. 1.2, which explains how default risk from one borrower is shared among lenders, illustrates this risk diversification.

Considering the favorable features of a mutual funding scheme mentioned previously, it might be worthwhile to explore integrating them into the current P2P lending scheme, with the necessary adjustments. The feasibility of integrating each feature, particularly in achieving risk diversification for P2P lenders, will be examined below.

Suppose personal relationships were to be established among P2P lenders or between P2P lenders and borrowers. Additionally, suppose individual potential P2P borrowers were to establish a tight personal relationship with one or more P2P lenders. If personal relationships were to be established among individual P2P lenders, they would likely be able to share information with one another. Even though their individual information might be limited, they could collectively gain more specific insights into the potential risks associated with individual borrower candidates. However, such information sharing seems feasible in practice if the P2P lending platform provides information obtained from one lender to the other lenders. P2P lenders would be able to utilize such information to distinguish between borrowers with low and high default risks, thereby potentially mitigating the risk of making wrong lending decisions. Once a borrower defaults, they may be excluded from future borrowings if the relevant information is shared by lenders. However, the same results can be achieved if the P2P lending platform excludes a once-defaulted borrower from joining the platform for a certain period of time or permanently. Therefore, it seems that personal relationships among lenders might not be necessary. In sum, it seems that personal relationships among lenders or between lenders and borrowers are not always necessary for sharing information about potential defaulting borrowers, applying pressure to motivate due repayments, or excluding defaulted borrowers from the lending scheme. Moreover, considering that there likely are no personal relationships between lenders and borrowers before they join the P2P lending platform, it might not be realistic for either the P2P lending platform, lenders, or borrowers to expend cost and labor to establish such relationships.

Next, the author will examine the plausibility of incorporating the feature of sharing both profits and losses from the mutual funding scheme into a P2P lending scheme. P2P borrowers are unlikely to contribute any money, unlike borrowers in a mutual funding scheme. Considering this, expecting P2P lenders to share profits from loans with borrowers would be unrealistic. As detailed in Sect. 6.2, participants in a mutual funding scheme contribute to a shared pool with dual motivations: they seek to generate profits and want the ability to borrow when necessary. Conversely, middle-class individuals in Vietnam possessing idle assets, who might become P2P lenders, primarily pursue their own profits when participating in P2P lending schemes. They usually do not face significant hurdles in accessing small funds. Therefore, they might not be attracted to mutual funding schemes where members act both as lenders and borrowers. Given this context, it may not be practical for individual P2P lenders and borrowers to jointly share lending profits and bear losses from defaults. Insights from interviews detailed in Sect. 7.4.2 support this inclination. In sum, P2P lenders may be hesitant to share both profits and losses with fellow lenders and borrowers within the same P2P lending scheme.

In sum, it might not be realistic for P2P lenders to share profits and losses with P2P borrowers. However, sharing profits and losses solely among P2P lenders within the same scheme could help stabilize their returns and diversify the credit risk they bear. Suppose that P2P lenders join a P2P lending platform and collectively contribute funds to a common pool. This pool can then be allocated to provide loans to borrowers joining the same platform. Profits from loans are distributed among P2P lenders, while losses from defaults are collectively shared by them. This pool can then be allocated to provide loans to borrowers within the system. Profits from lending activities are distributed among P2P lenders, while losses from defaults are collectively shared by them. P2P lenders may contribute varying amounts and opt for diverse loan durations, such as 3 months, 6 months, or 1 year. Similarly, P2P borrowers can apply for various loan amounts and the same range of durations via a P2P lending platform. Loan applications from P2P borrowers are matched with the available funds in the common pool.

However, individual lenders might be hesitant to accept the decisions of other peer lenders regarding the utilization of the common pool, as there is no guarantee that they will all make equally wise lending decisions. Likewise, individual borrowers might be hesitant to share the same funds with other borrowers, as there is no guarantee that they all have equally low default risks. They would dislike the idea that someone else's default could increase their current or future borrowing interest rates or worsen other terms. If lendings were to be made from the common pool, both lenders and borrowers might expect someone with far greater ability to assess potential borrowers and monitor borrowers to control the pool.

If P2P lenders choose to establish a common pool and share profits and losses with other lenders, entrusting professional management with borrower assessment, lending decisions, and borrower monitoring seems like a readily conceivable solution for stabilizing the risks, even if it may moderate peak profits. Lenders may not always have rational or moderate preferences, which can make them hesitant to accept such a solution. In addition, the lack of professional management of loans and borrowers is likely to make potential lenders wary of entering the P2P lending business. Therefore, it is conceivable that lenders might still be open to such a solution. Nonetheless, ingenuity in a detailed scheme to attract them might be necessary. Such a detailed scheme and the benefits of implementing it for other stakeholders (i.e., borrowers and platform service providers) will be discussed in the upcoming sections.

## 7.2 Challenges in P2P Lending from a Borrower's Perspective

Adopting the solution proposed in the previous Section, which involves implementing professional management over common pool operations, can have positive implications for P2P borrowers, as discussed in this Section. Assuming that a significant number of potential lenders prefer their lending to be managed by professional experts rather than managing it themselves, it is probable that a lending scheme involving a pool of funds under professional management will attract more funds, though this is not guaranteed. A larger pool of funds might increase the number of borrowers who can access financing and/or enlarge the amount individual borrowers can obtain.

Additionally, professional management of lending may exclude potential borrowers with low creditworthiness. However, on the other hand, the ability to stabilize risks might make it possible for even those with lower creditworthiness to participate in the scheme.

Furthermore, professional management of lending might accelerate the timing of declaring default for borrowers facing difficulties. While this may reduce the opportunity for borrowers to turn their business around, it could also prevent the tragedy of borrowers overextending themselves to the point of being unable to recover.

In consideration of the discussion above, while professional management of lending might have both advantages and disadvantages for borrowers, one cannot deny the possibility that it could assist borrowers in acting more rationally.

## 7.3 A Platform Service Provider's Perspective

Establishing a common pool with contributions from multiple lenders and then allocating these funds across various borrowers can be a complex task. This includes, but is not limited to, managing a diverse portfolio of funds, ensuring efficient allocation of funds, maintaining regulatory compliance, overseeing repayment management, diversifying risks, and communicating with stakeholders such as lenders and borrowers. Given these complexities, it is almost inevitable that a professional management approach is essential for the efficient and safe operation of such a lending model.

Under current laws in Vietnam, professional management involving the handling of a diverse portfolio of funds entrusted by individuals and organizations is permitted only by entities specifically authorized by the Law on Credit Institutions 2024 and the Law on Securities 2019. These authorized organizations include commercial banks,[1] general finance companies,[2] specialized finance companies,[3] people's credit funds,[4] MFIs,[5] securities companies,[6] and securities investment fund management companies.[7] They are required to establish trust contracts with clients before managing or overseeing their properties.[8] They are also obligated to ensure the efficient use of trust property, to inform trustors sufficiently and promptly about the performance of fiduciary duties, and to transfer all legal benefits and related documents to trustors as agreed upon in the trust contracts and in accordance with related laws.[9]

Platform service providers are not allowed to manage funds entrusted by individual P2P lenders because, as previously mentioned, they are not among the authorized organizations. Clearly, when a common pool is formed using contributions from multiple lenders, and these funds are distributed to numerous lending opportunities—encompassing multiple borrowers and potentially several lendings to a single borrower—a platform service provider engaging in such professional management will prompt the application of financial regulations to that provider. In order to enable P2P lendings to utilize a professionally managed common pool, it is crucial to introduce laws demanding sufficient qualifications for platform service providers. These qualifications should ensure that lenders can confidently entrust them with such professional management.

---

[1] See Vietnam's Law on Credit Institutions 2024, Article 113.

[2] See Vietnam's Law on Credit Institutions 2024, Article 119, clause 1.

[3] See Vietnam's Law on Credit Institutions 2024, Article 124, clause 1.

[4] See Vietnam's Law on Credit Institutions 2024, Article 126, clause 4 (a).

[5] See Vietnam's Law on Credit Institutions 2024, Article 130, clause 1.

[6] See Vietnam's Law on Securities 2019, Article 88.

[7] Vietnam's Law on Securities 2019, Article 88.

[8] See Circular No. 35/VBHN-NHNN of Vietnam, Article 4, clause 1 and Vietnam's Law on Securities 2019, Article 90, clause 2.

[9] See Circular No. 30/2014/TT-NHNN of Vietnam (amended in 2016), Article 4, clause 1 and Vietnam's Law on Securities 2019, Article 90.

## 7.4 Practical Measures for Mitigating Issues in P2P Lending Schemes

### *7.4.1 Exploring a New Contractual Model for Lending*

As discussed in earlier sections, the establishment of a common pool could be one of the potential solutions to reduce the risks faced by P2P lenders. This pool would comprise contributions from lenders within the same lending scheme, with both profits and losses being distributed among them. In this Section, we will explore measures to make the setting up of such a common pool feasible.

In a P2P lending scheme, individual potential lenders typically do not have personal relationships with each other, as highlighted in Sect. 6.1. The absence of personal relationships makes it unrealistic for them to negotiate with each other to establish a common pool of funds.

Unless facilitated by a platform service provider, establishing such a common pool between individual potential lenders would likely be impossible. Therefore, it would be insightful to examine a scenario where a platform service provider establishes a pool and entices potential lenders to contribute their funds to the pool.

Under this scenario, the platform service provider is unlikely to successfully solicit potential lenders unless they provide these lenders with the information they are likely to demand. The author attempts to enumerate that information. To gain clues for this purpose, the author refers to items that would likely be included in the terms and conditions of a typical loan agreement, as well as borrowers' representations and warranties that are generally included in such agreements. This is because these items can reasonably be assumed to correspond to the profits that the lender is likely to obtain, the mechanisms for obtaining profit, potential losses that the lender might incur, and the uncertainties faced by the lender, especially those that the lender should be concerned about or is likely to be concerned about.

It can be seen that the typical terms and conditions of a small loan agreement are likely to include, but are not limited to, Parties Involved, Principal Amount, Interest Rate, Payment Terms (which may cover the monthly payment amount, due date, acceptable payment methods, and payment destination), Loan Term, Late Payment Policy, Events of Default, Prepayment, Collateral, Fees, Insurance, Assignment, and Dispute Resolution. Additionally, the typical representations and warranties by the borrower of a small loan agreement are likely to include the following items, though this list is not exhaustive: Borrower's Authority and Capacity to Borrow, Valid and Binding Obligation, No Conflicts, Financial Statements or Conditions, No Material Adverse Change, No Pending or Threatened Litigation, No Insolvency, Regulatory Compliance, No Delayed Tax Payment, Accuracy of Information, No Default, Use of Loan Proceeds, Collateral, No Undisclosed Liabilities, and Insurance.

Given these typical terms and conditions of a small loan agreement, it is crucial for platform service providers to provide potential lenders with information disclosure as follows:

**Parties Involved**: Suppose that a certain number of potential lenders will contribute to a common pool arranged by a Platform Service Provider to facilitate loans to borrowers. The Provider must, at least, determine the contractual parties who will establish the pool and those who will own the properties included in the pool. Additionally, the Provider must specify who will be the lender for each individual loan launched from the pool.

For example, the pool may be arranged simply as a bookkeeping entry. The contributed property might continue to be attributed to each individual lender who contributed. Moreover, a lending to a single borrower might merely be an aggregation of multiple loans from several lenders participating in the pool. This scheme appears to require highly intricate calculations. Considering this, the effort required to implement this scheme may be significant and cannot be overlooked.

Alternatively, the pool can be established by individual lenders making monetary contributions to the provider or another service provider designated by the provider. These contributions are processed via individual contracts, where each one is established between a single lender and the designated service provider. When money is contributed to the pool, it may be attributed to the service provider. As a result, individual lenders might relinquish their direct rights to those funds. Instead, they acquire a claim, which grants them the right to request the service provider to distribute the pool's profits and losses and return any remaining assets. A form of silent partnership agreement, known in Japanese as "Tokumei Kumiai Keiyaku" (often translated as a "silent partnership"), is provided for in Article 536 of the Commercial Code of Japan (Act No. 48 of 1899, as amended).[10] This agreement has been widely used in Japan over the years for various funding purposes, including aircraft finance, real estate finance, venture capital, small lending, and more, serving as a prime example of such a scheme. In this scheme, contributor losses are limited to at most the amount they contributed or committed. However, the pool cannot escape the risk of being seized by the service provider's creditors.

Additionally, the pool can be established either jointly by the lenders or by both the lenders and the platform service Provider, with monetary contributions from all involved parties. These contributions are made through a single multiparty contract, in which every lender, and potentially the Provider, become parties to it. The money contributed to the pool remains under the joint ownership of all the contributors, while individual contributors cannot use or rescind such money at their respective discretion. The utilization of the pool's fund is managed and controlled by the specific party (presumably, the service Provider, or a fund manager appointed by

---

[10]The Commercial Code of Japan, Article 536 provides that:

(1) A silent partner's contribution is part of the assets of the proprietor.
(2) A silent partner may only make money and other assets the subject matter of the contribution.
(3) A silent partner may not be engaged in executive management of the proprietor's business and may not act as the proprietor's representative.
(4) A silent partner holds no rights against or obligations towards a third party in connection with the actions of the proprietor.

the service Provider). The pool becomes the lender in every lending to the borrowers. The profit and loss of the fund are jointly attributed to the contributors, but allocated to individual contributors periodically. A form of a cooperative agreement is provided for in Article 504 of the Civil Code 2015.[11] This agreement has been widely used in Vietnam for various funding purposes, primarily for business and investment cooperation, without the need to establish a formal legal organization. It serves as an example of such a scheme. Similarly, a form of a partnership agreement, known in Japanese as "Kumiai Keiyaku," is provided for in Article 667 of the Civil Code of Japan (Act No. 89 of 1896, as amended).[12] Also a derivative form of Kumiai Keiyaku is provided by other specific laws such as Limited Liability Partnership Act (Act No. 40 of 2005, as amended)[13] and Limited Partnership Act for Investment (Act No. 90 of 1998, as amended).[14] This agreement has been widely used in Japan over the years for various funding purposes, mainly for venture capital and private equity investments, serving as another example of such scheme. In this scheme, the pool may be segregated from the assets specific to the service Provider, making it less susceptible to threats posed by the service Provider's creditors. However, in the event of a loss incurred by the pool, unless a limited liability partnership is adopted, there is a risk that contributor losses may exceed the amount they contributed or committed.

Furthermore, individual lenders may be able to constitute a pool by assigning money to a trust company or a commercial bank licensed for trust operations for the purpose of trust. The properties in the pool solely belong to the trustee, and the lenders will have the right to demand that the trustee distribute the profit and loss of the pool. The loans will be made in the name of the trustee but can be managed by the service provider instead of the trustee itself. In Vietnam, entrusted loans are commonly facilitated through commercial banks licensed for trust, providing an example of such a scheme. Similarly, lending trust, known as "Kashitsuke Shintaku" in Japanese and commonly offered by commercial banks licensed for trust business in Japan, serves as another example of such a scheme. In general, trust structures seem to provide a fairly secure means of protecting the pool. However, there is a significant concern about whether the high costs associated with trust companies or trust banks can be covered by the interests obtained from the relatively small and short-term loans provided in the P2P lending scheme, as envisioned.

---

[11] Vietnam's Civil Code 2015, Article 504 provides that: "1. A cooperation contract means an agreement between natural and/or juridical persons regarding property contribution, effort to perform certain jobs, the same benefit and mutual responsibility. 2. Each cooperation contract must be made in writing."

[12] The Civil Code of Japan, Article 667 provides that:

(1) A partnership contract becomes effective when each of the parties promises to make a contribution and engage in a joint undertaking.
(2) The subject of the contribution may be services.

[13] The Limited Liability Partnership Act of Japan (Act No. 40 of 2005, as amended).

[14] The Limited Partnership Act for Investment of Japan (Act No. 90 of 1998, as amended).

**Principal Amount:** The Provider must determine the total amount of money that each lender can or should contribute to the pool, specifically both the minimum and maximum amounts in both words and numbers. Additionally, the Provider must determine the minimum and maximum amounts of individual loans, as well as the maximum total loans that can be extended to a single borrower. It is obvious that these conditions are much related to the scope of risk for individual lenders.

**Interest Rate:** The Provider must determine the interest rate applicable to individual loans. This can be set at a fixed rate or determined by a formula. The minimum and maximum interest rates can also be established. Additionally, lenders may expect the Provider to present the expected Internal Rate of Return in advance.

**Payment Terms:** The Provider must specify whether loan repayments will be made in installments or as a lump sum, and establish a policy on the repayment schedule and timing. They must also define the monthly or periodic distribution or allotment of repayment amounts that individual lenders can expect to receive, which includes both the principal amount and the interest. Additionally, the Provider must set the due date, determine acceptable payment methods, and designate the payment destination for individual loans, as well as for the distribution to the lenders.

**Loan Term:** The Provider must establish methods for determining the loan terms for individual loans. Additionally, the Provider must determine the duration individual lenders must wait after contributing to the pool before they are allowed to withdraw their contributions from the pool.

**Late Payment Policy:** The Provider must determine the delayed interest and late charges applicable to late payments. The Provider must further determine the methods for allocating losses caused by late payments among lenders. Additionally, the Provider must determine how delays in distributions from the pool to the lenders should be addressed, and the extent to which, and from which resources, lenders are compensated.

**Events of Default:** The Provider must not only specify the events of default for individual loans but also define situations that lead to borrowers being excluded from the lending scheme due to their failure to perform their commitments or adhere to other stipulated conditions.

**Prepayment:** The Provider must specify the conditions for early refundment to lenders from the pool, in addition to the prepayment of individual loans. The conditions for such early refundment include situations where an adequate borrower cannot be found or when the collection of loans occurs faster than anticipated.

**Collateral:** The individual loan agreements may stipulate whether borrowers need to provide collateral. However, if the loans are sourced from a pool funded by the lenders, the Provider must determine who will execute the security interests. Additionally, the Provider must establish a procedure to bear the costs of executing these interests from the pool and report them to the lenders.

**Fees:** Establishing and maintaining the pool incurs costs. Additionally, there are charges for professional management related to lending, collection, and bookkeeping. To cover these expenses, the Provider must determine what types and amounts of fees will be collected from the lenders.

**Insurance:** The lenders are likely to demand that the Provider obtain insurance to protect the pool from potential damages and losses.

**Assignment:** It may be necessary to provide a means for lenders to assign their rights to receive profit distributions and fund refundments from the pool to other lenders, in order to bridge the gap between the terms of individual loans and the investment periods of individual lenders in the pool.

**Dispute Resolution:** It is necessary to establish dispute resolution procedures not only for disputes between parties to the loan agreement and between lenders and Providers but also for disputes among lenders who are contributors to the pool.

Assuming that individual loans are provided from the pool, in addition to the borrower's representations and warranties in the loan agreement, there is a need to represent and warrant the legality of the pool, the Provider's legal authority to maintain and manage the pool, and the legality and legal authority of those providing professional management for the operation of the pool.

Based on the discussion above concerning the Parties Involved, establishing a common pool either jointly by the lenders or by both the lenders and the Provider seems more practical than other alternatives. However, lenders will likely expect the Provider to implement measures limiting their liabilities and potential losses. Also, it seems viable to reference the experience of other jurisdictions, including the United States and Japan. However, based on the considerations discussed above regarding the terms and conditions, as well as the representations and warranties, it suggests that to implement such a scheme, we must elaborate on the terms and conditions applicable to the pool. On the other hand, it is also suggested that such implementation is well within the capability of law practitioners. Additionally, the legality and regulations applicable to the parties responsible for the establishment, placement of contributors' interest, management, and operation must be examined.

### *7.4.2 Learning from the Experiences of the United States and Japan: Potential Measures Based on Comparative Insights*

This research focuses on finding solutions to mitigate or diversify the risk borne by lenders in P2P lending in Vietnam. Considering the new contractual model for lending discussed in the previous section, it becomes apparent that introducing a collective pool of funds to help diversify lenders' risks would transform the nature of the current 'peer-to-peer' (P2P) lending scheme, moving away from its traditional individual-based approach. This is because the funds contributed to the pool are managed in a way that prevents individual lenders from controlling their individual interests in the pool, as mentioned above, and the manager of the pool substantially acts as the lender in transactions with borrowers. In contrast to the current P2P lending scheme, where the relationship between a lender and a borrower could be one-to-one, one-lender-to-multiple-borrowers, or multiple-lenders-to-one-borrower (as mentioned in Sect. 1.1), in a lending scheme with a collective pool, the relationship becomes one-lender-to-multiple-borrowers, with the pool or its manager being deemed as the lender.

However, this shift is not likely to materially disadvantage investors who contribute to a collective pool of funds for lending, in spite of making conventional P2P lending investments. If a number of lenders choose to contribute to a collective pool of funds for lending, rather than participating in conventional P2P lending, the status of individual lenders is likely to change in several aspects as follows:

(i) Applicable interest rates: The applicable interest rates for lenders contributing to a collective pool are unlikely to be determined on an individual lender basis. Instead, they are likely to be decided unilaterally by the pool manager in accordance with the predetermined and current conditions of the pool.
(ii) Default probabilities: The probabilities of default can be distributed across a portfolio of loans provided from the pool, rather than being borne by individual loans made by individual lenders. The overall default probabilities can be influenced by the risk profiles of the borrowers who receive loan(s) from the pool, as well as by the predetermined and current conditions of the pool.
(iii) Stabilization: The diversification of risk associated with a portfolio of loans provided from the pool is likely to enhance the stability of returns and minimize the impact of adverse events on individual lenders.
(iv) Management cost: In cases where lenders contribute to a collective pool, it is reasonable to expect that they entrust its management to the platform service provider or a fund manager appointed by the provider. This arrangement can lead to cost savings for individual lenders by reducing the operational costs and time involved in managing individual loans independently. However, it is important to note that the management cost might be determined based on both the predetermined and current conditions of the pool, and could also be set unilaterally by the pool's manager.

The legality and regulations applicable to the parties responsible for establishing and managing a collective pool of funds for lending, as well as protecting the interests of contributors will be examined below.

According to current Vietnamese laws, specifically the Law on Securities 2019 and relevant regulations, fund management companies[15] are permitted to establish public funds, manage securities investment funds,[16] and publicly offer fund certificates to investors.[17] Public funds established by fund management companies are

[15] Circular No. 99/2020/TT-BTC of Vietnam, Article 2, clause 3 provides that: "A fund management company means an enterprise that has been licensed by the State Securities Commission to establish and engage in operations including securities trading, securities investment fund management, securities investment portfolio management, and securities investment consulting services."

[16] See Vietnam's Law on Securities 2019, Article 73, clause 1 and Circular No. 99/2020/TT-BTC, Article 2, clause 3.

[17] Vietnam's Law on Securities 2019, Article 100, clause 1 provides that: "The establishment of public funds and public offering of fund certificates shall be conducted by securities investment

regulated as securities investment funds that publicly offer fund certificates.[18] Additionally, securities investment funds managed by fund management companies are regulated as funds that are established through capital contributions by investors for investments in securities or other assets, including real estate.[19] Moreover, fund certificates offered by fund management companies are regulated as securities[20] that certify their holders' ownership of a stake in a securities investment fund.[21]

To be established, a fund management company must meet specific legal requirements provided by the Law on Securities 2019 and relevant regulations to obtain a license from the State Securities Commission. These requirements are separated from the requirements for establishing a public fund by a fund management company, and they include the following:[22]

(i) The company's minimum charter capital must be VN₫ 25 billion.[23]
(ii) The company's shareholders or contributing members[24] must be individuals or organizations that are qualified for the establishment and management

fund management companies in accordance with Article 108 of this Law and must be registered with the State Securities Commission" and Circular No. 99/2020/TT-BTC, Article 14, clause 1 provides that: "Securities investment fund management companies are permitted to mobilize funds domestically and overseas to establish and manage securities investment funds."

[18] Vietnam's Law on Securities 2019, Article 4, clause 38 provides that: "Public fund means a securities investment fund that publicly offers fund certificates."

[19] See Vietnam's Law on Securities 2019, Article 4, clause 37. Securities investment funds can invest in the following assets: (a) deposits at commercial banks as stipulated by banking laws; (b) money market instruments, including financial instruments and negotiable instruments as prescribed by law; (c) government debt instruments, government-backed bonds, and municipal bonds; (d) listed shares, shares registered for trading, bonds listed on the stock exchange, and public fund certificates; (e) unlisted shares of issuers operating under the laws of Vietnam; shares of joint-stock companies or stakes in limited liability companies; (f) rights arising in connection with securities held by securities investment funds; (g) eligible real estate as prescribed in the Law on Real Estate Business; and (h) other securities and assets as stipulated by law. See Circular No. 98/2020/TT-BTC of Vietnam, Article 5, clause 2 and Article 24, clause 2.

[20] Vietnam's Law on Securities 2019, Article 4, clause 1 provides that:

Securities means assets, including the following types:

(a) Shares, bonds, and investment fund certificates;
(b) Warrants, secured warrants, share purchase rights, and depository receipts;
(c) Derivatives;
(d) Other types of securities as stipulated by the Government.

[21] Vietnam's Law on Securities 2019, Article 4, clause 4.

[22] See Vietnam's Law on Securities 2019, Article 75.

[23] See Decree No. 155/2020/ND-CP of Vietnam, Article 175, clause 3.

[24] According to Article 71, clause 2 of the Law on Securities 2019 of Vietnam, a fund management company can take the form of either a joint-stock company or a limited liability company. "A shareholder" means an individual or organization that holds at least a share of a joint-stock company. "A contributing member" means an individual or organization that holds part or all of the charter capital of a limited liability company. See Vietnam's Law on Enterprises 2020, Article 4, clause 3 and clause 29.

of enterprises in Vietnam as prescribed by the Law on Enterprises.[25] Additionally, shareholders or contributing members that are organizations must have demonstrated profitable business operations in the two years preceding the year in which the license is applied for, and must have had their latest annual financial statement audited, receiving unqualified opinions. Shareholders or contributing members who hold 10% or more of the charter capital of a fund management company and their related persons (if any) must not hold more than 5% of the charter capital of another fund management company.

(iii) If the fund management company is organized as a multimember limited liability company,[26] it must have at least two contributing members that

[25] Vietnam's Law on Enterprises 2020, Article 7, clause 2 provides that:

The following organizations and individuals do not have the right to establish and manage enterprises in Vietnam:

(a) State authorities and People's armed forces using state-owned assets to establish enterprises to serve their own interests;
(b) Cadres, civil servants, and public employees;
(c) Commissioned officers, non-commissioned officers, career military personnel, military workers and public employees in agencies and units of the Vietnam People's Army; commissioned officers, non-commissioned officers and police workers in police authorities and units, except for those designated and authorized as representatives to manage state-owned stakes in state-owned enterprises or to manage state-owned enterprises;
(d) Executive officers and managers of state-owned enterprises, except those who are designated as authorized representatives to manage state-owned stakes in other enterprises;
(dd) Minors; people with limited legal capacity; incapacitated people; people having difficulties controlling their behaviors; organizations that are not juridical persons;
(e) People who are facing criminal prosecution, kept in temporary detention, serving an imprisonment sentence, serving an administrative penalty in a correctional institution or rehabilitation center, has limited legal capacity or is incapacitated, is not able to control his/her own behaviors, is banned by the court from holding certain positions or doing certain works; other cases prescribed by the Law on Bankruptcy and the Anti-corruption Law.
(f) Juridical persons that are banned from business operations or certain fields as prescribed by the Criminal Code.

[26] Vietnam's Law on Enterprises 2020, Article 46, clause 1 provides that: "A multi-member limited liability company means an enterprise that has from two to fifty members that are organizations or individuals. A member's liability for the enterprise's debts and other liabilities shall be equal to the amount of capital that member contributed to the enterprise."

are organizations. If it is organized as a single-member limited liability company,[27] its sole member must be a commercial bank,[28] insurance company,[29] securities company,[30] or foreign organization that meets the

[27] Vietnam's Law on Enterprises 2020, Article 74, clause 1 provides that: "A single-member limited liability company is an enterprise owned by a single organization or individual (hereinafter referred to as the owner). The owner's liability for the company's debts and other liabilities shall be equal to the company's charter capital."

[28] Vietnam's Law on Credit Institutions 2024, Article 4, clause 23 provides that: "A commercial bank refers to a bank authorized to engage in all banking operations and other business activities under this Law with the aim of generating profit."

[29] Vietnam's Law on Insurance Business 2022, Article 4, clause 17 provides that: "An insurance company refers to an enterprise that is established, managed, and run as per this Law and other relevant laws to do business in the insurance, reinsurance, and reinsurance cession sector."

[30] Circular No. 121/2020/TT-BTC of Vietnam, Article 2, clause 1 provides that: "A securities company refers to an enterprise licensed by the State Securities Commission to perform one or several services or business activities as prescribed in Article 72, clause 1, and Article 86, clause 1, 2, 3, 4, and 5 of the Law on Securities 2019,"

Vietnam's Law on Securities 2019, Article 72, clause 1 provides that: "Securities Companies are licensed to perform one, several, or all of the following businesses:

(a) Securities brokerage;
(b) Proprietary trading;
(c) Securities Underwriting Guarantees; and
(d) Securities investment consultancy" (translated by the State Securities Commission of Vietnam),

Vietnam's Law on Securities 2019, Article 86, provides that:

1. A securities company licensed to provide securities brokerage services may:
    (a) Receive and manage securities trading accounts of individuals; distribute securities or act as securities distribution agent; manage securities trading accounts; manage other enterprises' lists of securities holders;
    (b) Provide online securities trading services; provide or cooperate with credit institutions in granting loans for the purchase of securities or securities lending; provide or cooperate with credit institutions in advancing payments for securities; engage in securities depository services; offset and process securities payments; offer other derivative-related services.
2. A securities company licensed for proprietary trading may trade securities on its proprietary trading account, make investments, contribute capital, and issue or offer financial products.
3. A securities company licensed for securities underwriting may provide securities offering consultancy services; perform pre-offering procedures; act as an agent for securities depository, payment, and transfer; provide consultancy on restructuring, consolidation, acquisition, and rearrangement of enterprises; provide consultancy of enterprise administration, and business strategies; provide consultancy on offering, listing, and registration of securities; provide consultancy on enterprise equitization.
4. A securities company licensed to provide securities investment consultancy services may provide services for its clients in accordance with Clause 32 Article 4 of this Law.
5. In addition to the services specified in Clause 1, 2, 3, and 4 of this Article, a securities company may provide other financial services in accordance with this Law after submitting a written report to the State Securities Commission. The State Securities Commission is

requirements specified by law.[31] In the case that the fund management company is organized as a joint-stock company,[32] it must have at least two founding shareholders that are organizations. Additionally, the total capital contributed by organizations must be at least 65% of the fund management company's charter capital, with contributions from commercial banks, insurance companies, and securities companies constituting a minimum of 30% of the company's charter capital.

---

entitled to suspend or terminate the provision of other financial services by a securities company if they do not conform to the law or pose a risk to the securities market system...

[31] Vietnam's Law on Securities 2019, Article 77 provides that:

1. Foreign investors may contribute capital, purchase shares, and acquire stakes in securities and fund management companies under the following conditions:
   (a) A foreign investor that is an organization satisfying the requirements outlined in Clause 2 of this Article, along with its related parties, may hold up to 100% of the charter capital of a securities or fund management company. If the requirements in Clause 2 of this Article are not fully met, the foreign investor, along with its related parties, may only hold up to 49% of the charter capital.
   (b) A foreign investor that is an individual and their related parties may hold up to 49% of the charter capital of a securities or fund management company.
2. In order for a foreign organization to hold 100% of the charter capital of a securities or fund management company through capital contribution or share/stake purchase, the organization must:
   (a) Be licensed and have been continuously operating in the field of banking, securities, or insurance for at least two years prior to the year in which capital is contributed or shares/stakes are purchased;
   (b) Have the licensing authority in their home country and the State Securities Commission engaged in a mutual or multilateral agreement regarding information exchange, management, inspection, and supervision of securities activities and the securities market; and
   (c) Demonstrate profitability in the two years prior to the year in which capital is contributed or shares/stakes are purchased, and have the latest annual financial statement audited with unqualified opinions.

[32] Vietnam's Law on Enterprises 2020, Article 111, clause 1 provides that: "A joint-stock company is an enterprise in which:

(a) The charter capital is divided into units of equal value called shares;
(b) Shareholders can be organizations and individuals; the minimum number of shareholders is three, and there is no limit on the maximum number of shareholders;
(c) A shareholder's liability for the company's debts and liabilities is equal to the amount of capital contributed to the company by the shareholder;
(d) Shareholders may transfer their shares to other persons except for the cases specified in Article 120, clause 3 and Article 127 clause 1 of this Law."

(iv) The company's premises are adequate for its business operations.[33] Additionally, the company's equipment and technologies are adequate for its business operations.[34]
(v) There are one General Director (or Director),[35] at least five employees having a certificate in fund management,[36] and at least one employee responsible for compliance and
(vi) The company's draft charter conforms to current laws.

It can be seen that fund management companies can establish and manage public funds which are pools of funds contributed by investors, as well as engage in soliciting investors for investment in securities through public offerings of fund

---

[33] According to Decree No. 155/2020/ND-CP of Vietnam, Article 176, clause 3, the company must provide suitable premises for its departments and working units, as well as trading facilities that align with their business operations. Additionally, it must possess a valid premises lease contract or documentation demonstrating its ownership or the right to use the premises.

[34] According to Decree No. 155/2020/ND-CP of Vietnam, Article 176, clause 3, the company must have a server, network equipment, employee computers, telephone systems/switchboards, printer (s), fax machine(s), tables and chairs, projection equipment, transaction software, safes, a backup system, an information and document storage system, as well as a security and confidentiality system.

[35] The company's General Director (or Director) must not be facing criminal prosecution, serving an imprisonment sentence, or be banned from businesses related to securities. They must not have incurred any administrative penalties for securities-related offenses in the last six months prior to the application date. They must also possess a Certificate in Fund Management and at least four years of experience working in specialized departments of finance, securities, banking, or insurance organizations or in finance, accounting, or investment departments of other organizations.

[36] According to Law on Securities 2019 of Vietnam, Article 97, clause 2 and Decree No. 155/2020/ ND-CP of Vietnam, Article 213, clause 3, a Certificate in Fund Management will be issued to an individual who meets the following criteria:

(i) Possesses full legal capacity, is not facing criminal prosecution, and is not banned from businesses related to securities
(ii) Holds a bachelor's degree or above
(iii) Holds securities-related qualifications, including a Certificate of Training in Securities and the Securities Market, a Certificate of Training in Regulations on Securities and the Securities Market, a Certificate of Training in Securities Analysis and Investment, a Certificate of Training in Securities Brokerage, and a Certificate of Training in Securities Investment Counseling, or equivalent certificates
(iv) Holds a Certificate of Training in Financial Counseling, a Certificate of Training in Securities Underwriting, and a Certificate of Training in Financial Statement Analysis, or equivalent certificates
(v) Holds a Certificate of Training in Fund and Asset Management
(vi) Successfully passes the test for a Securities Practicing Certificate. Foreign individuals who possess legally recognized securities-related qualifications from overseas and have practiced as securities professionals overseas must also pass the test on Vietnam's regulations concerning securities and the securities market and
(vii) Has a minimum of three years of experience working in sales, investment, finance, or accounting departments of enterprises or in organizations operating in the field of finance, banking, insurance, securities, or audit, or holds a valid securities practicing certificate issued overseas

certificates. However, to establish a public fund, a fund management company must adhere to specific procedures for the initial public offering of fund certificates. The current regulations for a public offering, as outlined below, consist of multiple detailed requirements and stringent adherence to these requirements.

The initial public offering of fund certificates must meet the following conditions: (1) the total value of the offered fund certificates must be VN₫ 50 billion or more; (2) the offering must be overseen by a supervisory bank; (3) the fund management company must have a detailed plan for the issuance of fund certificates and the utilization of capital generated by the offering; and (4) the fund certificates offered to the public must be listed on the securities exchange following the conclusion of the offering, except in cases where open-end fund certificates[37] are offered.[38]

Additionally, the fund management company is required to register with the State Securities Commission and obtain a certificate for the public offering of fund certificates.[39] Subsequent to receiving this certificate, the company is obligated to disclose information about its offering to the public in order to solicit potential investors.[40] It must engage in investor solicitation for a minimum of 20 days and can do so for up to 90 days from the effective date of the certificate of public offering of fund certificates.[41] Following this time frame, the company is obliged to report the results of the offering to the State Securities Commission.

A public fund can be successfully established if the following conditions are met: (a) there are at least 100 investors, not including professional investors,[42] solicited to

---

[37] Open-end fund certificates refer to certificates that confirm the holder's ownership of a stake in an open-end securities investment fund. These certificates have to be redeemed at the request of the investors who own them. See Vietnam's Law on Securities 2019, Article 4, clause 39.

[38] See Vietnam's Law on Securities 2019, Article 15, clause 5.

[39] See Circular No. 98/2020/TT-BTC of Vietnam, Article 13, clause 1.

[40] See Circular No. 98/2020/TT-BTC of Vietnam, Article 13, clause 2.

[41] See Circular No. 98/2020/TT-BTC of Vietnam, Article 14.

[42] Vietnam's Law on Securities 2019, Article 11 provides that:

> 1. Professional investors are individuals or entities with adequate financial capacity or the necessary qualifications concerning securities. These investors include:
>
> (a) Commercial banks, foreign bank branches, finance companies, insurance companies, securities companies, securities investment fund management companies, securities investment companies, securities investment funds, international financial institutions, off-budget financial funds, and state-owned financial institutions permitted to buy securities as prescribed by relevant laws;
>
> (b) Companies that have contributed charter capital of more than VND 100 billion, listed companies, or companies that have securities registered on the securities trading system;
>
> (c) Holders of securities practicing certificates;
>
> (d) Individuals holding a portfolio of listed and registered securities worth at least VND 2 billion as confirmed by a securities company;
>
> (dd) Individuals whose taxable income in the latest year is at least VND 1 billion according to their tax declaration documents submitted to tax authorities or tax deduction documents from their income payer.

invest in fund certificates; and (b) the total value of fund certificates sold is at least VN₫ 50 billion.[43]

It is clear that, along with the complexity and stringency of regulations governing public offerings, the associated costs[44] are likely to be substantial. As a result, pursuing the immediate goal of raising funds, limited both in their amount and in the number of contributors, may not be the most suitable strategy for a platform service provider.

Besides the establishment of a public fund by a fund management company, professional investors can collectively establish a private fund through a capital contribution contract.[45] The establishment of a private fund is required to meet the following conditions: (1) the contributed capital is not smaller than VN₫ 50 billion; (2) there are from two to 99 contributors who are all professional investors; (3) the private fund is managed by a fund management company; and (4) the private fund's assets are deposited at one depository bank that is independent from the fund management company.[46] However, it is worth noting that potential investors contributing to a pool for providing P2P loans may not always be professional investors. In light of this consideration, it may not be feasible for platform service providers to contemplate the establishment of a private fund for pursuing the immediate goal of raising funds from both professional and non-professional investors.

According to the Law on Securities 2019, "securities" means assets, including shares,[47] bonds,[48] fund certificates, warrants,[49] secured warrants,[50] share purchase

---

[43] See Vietnam's Law on Securities 2019, Article 108, clause 1.

[44] For example, the payment for the service of overseeing the offering by a supervisory bank, the cost of applying for the public offering certificate issued by the State Securities Commission, and the cost of information disclosure.

[45] See Vietnam's Law on Securities 2019, Article 113, clause 1.

[46] See Vietnam's Law on Securities 2019, Article 113, clause 2.

[47] Shares are securities that certify the lawful rights and interests of their holders to a portion of the share capital of the issuer. See Vietnam's Law on Securities 2019, Article 4, clause 2.

[48] Bonds are securities that attest to the lawful rights and interests of their holders in a portion of the issuer's debt. See Vietnam's Law on Securities 2019, Article 4, clause 3.

[49] Warrants are securities that are issued together with bonds or preference shares and bestow upon their holders the right to buy a certain amount of common shares at a specified price over a specific period of time. See Vietnam's Law on Securities 2019, Article 4, clause 5.

[50] Secured warrants are securities secured by collateral and issued by a securities company. They allow their holders to have the right to buy (call option) or the right to sell (put option) the securities to their issuer at a specified strike price prior to or on a specified date, or receive the difference between the strike price and the underlying security price at that time. See Vietnam's Law on Securities 2019, Article 4, clause 6.

rights,[51] depository receipts,[52] derivatives,[53] and other kinds of securities defined by the government. Among these types of securities, fund certificates share several similarities with the interest in a fund dedicated to P2P lending. For example, both fund certificates and the interest in a fund within a pool, to which lenders contribute for providing P2P loans, can be characterized as representing either the capital contribution (by investors to an investment fund or by lenders to a pool of funds) or the capital contributors' ownership stake in a portion of an investment fund or a pool of funds. Additionally, the interest in a fund for P2P lending can be deemed as an asset that potentially benefits P2P lenders in the future, specifically based on the profits generated from P2P lending. In light of these similarities, it might be more conservative to deem the interest in a fund for P2P lending as a security.

Furthermore, in the course of managing securities investment funds, fund management companies must fulfill several obligations. These obligations include: (1) acting as an authorized representative and/or on behalf of its trustors to exercise the rights of ownership of their funds in a truthful and prudent manner;[54] (2) promulgating procedures for the management of securities investment funds, internal control procedures, a valuation manual, conditions and procedures for calling, conducting, and ratifying decisions of General Meetings of Investors of funds, and a code of professional ethics for each working position;[55] (3) adhering to the code of professional ethics, and conducting their management duties with impartiality, truthfulness, and voluntary commitment for the best interests of their trustors;[56] and (4) implementing a risk management system and disseminating procedures, strategies, and policies of risk management in conformity with each securities investment fund.[57]

Additionally, fund management companies are subject to a range of mandatory requirements to ensure the proper management of securities investment funds. These requirements include: (1) investing trust funds in accordance with current regulations, the charter of securities investment funds, and trust contracts; (2) entering into a supervisory contract with a supervisory bank for public securities investment funds; (3) timely and accurately maintaining records of ownership of properties

---

[51] Share purchase rights refer to a type of securities issued by joint-stock companies with the aim of granting existing shareholders the right to purchase new shares under specific conditions. See Vietnam's Law on Securities 2019, Article 4, clause 7.

[52] A depository receipt means a type of securities issued based on securities of an organization that is lawfully established and operating in Vietnam. See Vietnam's Law on Securities 2019, Article 4, clause 8.

[53] Derivatives are financial instruments in the form of contracts, including options, futures, and forwards, that determine the rights and obligations of the contract parties to pay and transfer a specific quantity of underlying assets at a specified strike price prior to or on a specified date in the future. See Vietnam's Law on Securities 2019, Article 4, clause 9.

[54] See Circular No. 99/2020/TT-BTC of Vietnam, Article 10, clause 1.

[55] See Circular No. 99/2020/TT-BTC of Vietnam, Article 10, clause 2.

[56] See Circular No. 99/2020/TT-BTC of Vietnam, Article 10, clause 3.

[57] See Circular No. 99/2020/TT-BTC of Vietnam, Article 10, clause 4.

within securities investment funds at the supervisory bank; (4) implementing an independent system for managing individual trustors' accounts and the company's assets; adequately and punctually retaining accounting books and transaction documents related to trustors' funds; efficiently consolidating information about funds of each trustor and the depository where such funds are kept; (5) allowing the supervisory bank to inspect and consolidate information about the management of securities investment funds; and (6) appointing at least two fund executives having the Certificate in Fund Management, a minimum of two years of asset management experience, and no prior administrative penalties for securities-related offenses to manage and administer investments of each securities investment fund.[58] Moreover, fund management companies must uphold the confidentiality of trustors' information[59] and comply with anti-money laundering regulations.[60] They must also assume liability for losses incurred by trustors due to their own faults[61] or failures to fulfill their obligations.[62] It is important to note that fund management companies are not permitted to use properties in public funds managed by them to provide loans or guarantees for loans.[63]

In accordance with the Civil Code 2015, funds can be contributed to a common pool for providing P2P loans either by the lenders alone or jointly by both the lenders and the platform service provider through a single multiparty cooperative contract, as mentioned in the previous section. In this scenario, the provider can provide the necessary information to solicit potential lenders to participate in a cooperative contract. The funds contributed to the common pool shall be considered as property owned in common[64] by cooperative parties.[65] These parties shall not be allowed to withdraw their contributed funds before the termination of the cooperation contract, unless all the parties agree otherwise.[66] They can benefit from the yield and income

[58] See Circular No. 99/2020/TT-BTC of Vietnam, Article 10, clause 5.

[59] See Circular No. 99/2020/TT-BTC of Vietnam, Article 10, clause 19.

[60] See Circular No. 99/2020/TT-BTC of Vietnam, Article 10, clause 15.

[61] For example, the faults of fund management companies' employees, problems, or errors in their technical system or business process.

[62] See Circular No. 99/2020/TT-BTC of Vietnam, Article 10, clause 13.

[63] See Vietnam's Law on Securities 2019, Article 110.

[64] Vietnam's Civil Code 2015, Article 209 provides that:

1. Ownership in common is multiple ownership whereby each owner's share of the ownership rights with respect to the multiple ownership property is specified.
2. Each of the owners in common has rights and obligations with respect to the multiple ownership property corresponding to its share of the ownership rights, unless otherwise agreed.

[65] See Vietnam's Civil Code 2015, Article 506, clause 1.

[66] See Vietnam's Civil Code 2015, Article 506, clause 3.

generated through lending from the pool, as well as engage in decisions regarding the performance of the cooperation contract and the monitoring of lending activities.[67] Additionally, they can appoint a representative to conduct lending activities under the cooperative contract on their behalf.[68] These parties are jointly responsible for common liabilities through their shared property. They shall be held accountable with their own property, based on their individual contributions to the pool, if the common funds within the pool are inadequate to fulfill their common obligations under or arising from the cooperative contract, unless otherwise specified by the cooperation contract or prescribed by law.[69] A cooperative party can withdraw from the cooperative contract under any of the following circumstances: (a) meeting the conditions specified in the cooperation contract, or (b) providing a valid reason with the consent of more than half of the total cooperative parties.[70] Cooperative parties withdrawing from the cooperative contract have the right to reclaim their contributed funds and allocated profits, but they must also settle any outstanding obligations under the cooperative contract.[71] In contrast, a natural person or legal entity can become a new cooperative party with the consent of over half of the total cooperative parties, unless the cooperative contract specifies otherwise.[72]

It can be seen that P2P lenders can legally contribute funds jointly to a pool through a single multiparty cooperative contract under the Civil Code 2015 to provide P2P loans. However, if they frequently engage in lending to P2P borrowers and derive the majority of their income from providing P2P loans, the lending transactions from the pool may no longer be considered civil transactions. They could face accusations of conducting banking activities illegally without a banking license, as highlighted in Sect. 2.2. On the other hand, if P2P lenders entrust their funds within the common pool to a credit institution licensed for lending operations, it might be a viable option for them to maintain the pool and continue providing P2P loans. However, as mentioned earlier, although the loans provided from the pool can be managed by the platform service provider, there is a significant concern that the costs associated with trust banks may not be commensurate with the revenues generated from P2P lending.

In light of the above-mentioned regulations and considerations, it can be seen that platform service providers must meet complex and detailed requirements to be eligible for establishing and managing investment funds, as well as soliciting lenders to contribute funds to a pool. At present, the interest in a fund for P2P lending is not regulated as a security. Platform service providers may only become eligible for soliciting lenders either through public offerings or private placements, establishing a pool funded by lenders and managing such a pool if the interest in a fund for P2P

[67] See Vietnam's Civil Code 2015, Article 507, clause 1 and clause 2.

[68] See Vietnam's Civil Code 2015, Article 508, clause 1.

[69] See Vietnam's Civil Code 2015, Article 509.

[70] See Vietnam's Civil Code 2015, Article 510, clause 1.

[71] See Vietnam's Civil Code 2015, Article 510, clause 2.

[72] See Vietnam's Civil Code 2015, Article 511.

lending can be regulated as a security. However, by drawing insights from the regulatory experiences of the United States and Japan in P2P lending, investor solicitation, and the establishment and management of investment funds, Vietnam may discover practical solutions for formulating regulations that are well-suited for its own P2P lending practices.

For example, as mentioned in Sect. 5.1.1, securitized loans or platform notes publicly offered by P2P lending platforms in the United States are considered securities. Similarly, in Japan, rights derived from a partnership contract stipulated in the Civil Code (Act No. 89 of 1896, as amended), a limited partnership agreement for investment provided for in the Limited Partnership Act for Investment (Act No. 90 of 1998), and a limited liability partnership agreement detailed in the Limited Liability Partnership Act (Act No. 40 of 2005), as well as interests in TK agreements (Tokumei Kumiai Keiyaku), which are often used as a vehicle to launch social lending and crowdfunding, are deemed to be securities.[73] Specifically, interests in collective investment schemes (commonly referred to as investment funds) established based on partnership contracts are considered as securities and are subject to the Financial Instruments and Exchange Act (Act No. 25 of 1948, as amended). According to this Act, the rights to receive dividends of profits or distribution of assets arising from businesses that use cash or securities based on partnership contracts of investors contributing to an investment fund are considered as securities.

In Japan, social lending platforms' operations of establishing investment funds and soliciting investors through public offerings of units in investment funds or through private placements of interests in investment funds, on a regular basis, are deemed to be financial instrument business.[74] The Financial Instruments and Exchange Act also regulates that any person engaging in self-offering of interests in collective investment schemes (investment funds) or self-management of assets contributed by investors (limited to investment in securities) is required to register their business.[75] Especially, for soliciting investors online to contribute to an investment fund, it is required to register as an Electronic Public Offering Service. The registration as type-I small-amount electronic public offering service[76] is applicable

[73] See Japan's Financial Instruments and Exchange Act (Act No. 25 of 1948, as amended), Article 2, Paragraph 2, item (v).

[74] See Japan's Financial Instruments and Exchange Act (Act No. 25 of 1948, as amended), Article 2, Paragraph 8, item (v).

[75] See Japan's Financial Instruments and Exchange Act (Act No. 25 of 1948, as amended), Article 29.

[76] According to Japan's Financial Instruments and Exchange Act (Act No. 25 of 1948, as amended), Article 29 bis 4-2, Paragraph 10, the term "type-I small amount electronic public offering service" means electronic public offering service (limited to handling of public offering or handling of private placement of securities that are not listed on a financial instruments exchange and excluding those specified by Cabinet Order) which satisfies the requirements specified by Cabinet Order as being such handling where the total issue value of the securities and the amount to be paid by the person that acquires the securities are small.

for in cases where a person seeks to only engage in type-I small-amount electronic public offering service from among type-I financial instruments businesses. Meanwhile, the registration as type-II small-amount electronic public offering service[77] is applicable for in cases where a person seeks to only engage in type-II small-amount electronic public offering service from among type-II financial instruments businesses. A type-I or type-II small-amount electronic public offering service provider must publicize its trade name, registration number, and other matters related to its business by means of using an electronic data processing system or by any other means as regulated.[78]

It can be seen that these regulations, with fewer requirements compared to those of traditional fund management and securities businesses, could pave the way for P2P platform service providers in Vietnam to legally engage in soliciting lenders to contribute to an investment scheme for P2P lending, establish funds for P2P lending, and manage such funds, while enabling the government to watch and monitor these businesses.

### *7.4.3 Future Directions in Vietnamese P2P Lending Scheme and Regulation*

As P2P lending usage expands in Vietnam, it is crucial for the country to establish a legal framework that encourages potential lenders to make diligent choices when participating in P2P lending platforms and facilitates the sound development of the lending business, as mentioned in Sect. 1.1. The author discussed the issues concerning the solicitation of potential lenders for investment in P2P lending schemes, the establishment and management of collective funds for such lending, and the legislative experiences of the United States and Japan. In light of these discussions, the author deems it practical and beneficial to adapt Vietnamese regulations to facilitate collective lending through a common pool, while ensuring proper management and reasonable regulation of these pools.

---

[77] According to Japan's Financial Instruments and Exchange Act (Act No. 25 of 1948, as amended), Article 29 bis 4-3, Paragraph 3, the term "type-II small amount electronic public offering service" as used in Paragraphs (1) and (2) means, among electronic public offering service, handling of public offering or handling of private placement of securities (limited to rights set forth in item Article 2, Paragraph [2], item [v] or [vi] which are deemed to be securities pursuant to that paragraph [excluding those that fall under the category of electronically recorded transferable rights] and which are set forth in Article 3, item (iii) or which are not listed on a financial instruments exchange, and excluding those specified by Cabinet Order; hereinafter the same applies in this paragraph) which satisfies the requirements specified by Cabinet Order as being such handling where the total issue value of the securities and the amount to be paid by the person that acquires the securities are small (specifically, an aggregate issue amount of less than 100 million yen per fund, and less than 500,000 yen in investment amount per investor).

[78] See Japan's Financial Instruments and Exchange Act (Act No. 25 of 1948, as amended), Article 29 bis 4-2, Paragraph 8 and Article 29 bis 4-3, Paragraph 3.

Drawing on the legislative experiences of the United States and Japan, Vietnam might consider implementing legislation that enables platform service providers to establish collective pools of funds for the purpose of small lendings, solicit potential lenders to contribute to such pools, and manage them, all under appropriate regulation and supervision. For the purpose of designing such legislation, it would be convenient to deem the interests in a pool for small lendings as securities. This approach would allow for the application, with suitable adjustments, of existing securities regulations to the establishment of collective pools of funds for small lendings and the solicitation of potential lenders to contribute to such pools. Specifically, in order to consider regulations over placements of interests in collective pools for small lendings by platform service providers, it is meaningful to consider the legislative experiences of the United States and Japan. Several specific requirements worth mentioning include the following:

Assuming that it is possible to deem interests in collective pools for the purpose of small lendings as securities, we can consider obligating platform service providers to register their business with the competent authority (i.e., the State Securities Commission of Vietnam) in order to be qualified to engage in the placement of these interests. Vietnam could consider adapting Japan's regulations for type-II small-amount electronic public offering service registration to apply to platform service providers. The application by individual platform service providers for such registration should include the disclosure of details such as the trade name, charter capital, headquarters and offices, employees, and business categories.[79] It is worth noting that Japan's Financial Instruments and Exchange Act (Act No. 25 of 1948, as amended) also sets forth criteria for refusing such registration. These include: (1) false statements in the application or in any accompanying documents; and (2) the applicant falling under specific conditions, such as previous revocation of registration, financial penalties under the Financial Instruments and Exchange Act or other regulations, engagement in businesses against the public interest, insufficient human resources, inadequate system establishment, a corporation with an officer falling under conditions set by a cabinet order,[80] capital or contributions below 10 million yen, absence of a business office in Japan, or non-membership in a financial instrument business association.[81]

In the United States, P2P lending platforms are required to register with the SEC under the Investment Company Act (1940, as amended) and the Investment Advisers Act (1940, as amended), as mentioned in Sect. 5.1.1. These platforms

[79] See Japan's Financial Instruments and Exchange Act (Act No. 25 of 1948, as amended), Article 29 bis 2, Paragraph 1 and Article 29 bis 4-3.

[80] Who are with impaired cognition, decision-making, and communication due to mental issues; undergoing unrecovered bankruptcy; penalized with imprisonment or a severe penalty within the past five years; ex-Financial Instrument Business Operator with revoked registration; discharged or dismissed under the Financial Instruments and Exchange Act; fined for financial law violation or penalized for a crime under the Penal Code (Act No. 45 of 1907, as amended).

[81] See Japan's Financial Instruments and Exchange Act (Act No. 25 of 1948, as amended), Article 29 bis 4.

must submit a statement containing detailed information, including information about each affiliated person (such as name, address, and involvement in other companies), their policies in different activities, the business experience of directors and officers over the past five years, inclusion of information and documents necessary for registering securities or outlining plans for future issuances.[82] Failure to register their business may occur if the SEC finds that their registration statements omit material facts.[83]

To ensure the sound operation of platform service providers and enable effective government monitoring, Vietnam can consider implementing registration requirements for these providers, drawing on regulations similar to those in Japan and the United States. This approach would represent one of the essential measures to achieve these objectives.

Only after business registration, platform service providers are to be permitted to engage in public offerings or private placements of interests in collective pools to solicit potential lenders for P2P lending. Potential lenders solicited to contribute to collective pools for P2P lending by platform service providers might include both professional and non-professional investors.[84] Regulations concerning public offerings or private placements by P2P lending platforms in the United States and Japan can be adapted for formulating similar regulations in Vietnam.

As mentioned in Sect. 5.1.1, in the United States, P2P lending platforms can choose one of the following options: (a) opting for a public offering by filing 'shelf registration statements' for a specific amount of a generic category of securities (platform notes) with the SEC; (b) opting for a private placement of their platform notes to accredited investors; or (c) engaging in small offerings, which include Tier 1 for securities offerings of up to US$ 20 million and Tier 2 for offerings of up to US $ 50 million, to both accredited and non-accredited investors.[85] It is worth noting

---

[82] See The United States Code, Title 15, Chapter 2D, Subchapter I, Section 80a-8(b).

[83] See The United States Code, Title 15, Chapter 2D, Subchapter I, Section 80a-8(e).

[84] The definition of professional investors is governed by Article 11 of Vietnam's Law on Securities 2019, as mentioned in the previous section.

[85] In the United States, an 'Accredited Investor' is an individual or entity falling within certain categories or reasonably believed to fall within these categories at the time of purchasing securities. The categories include: (1) Financial institutions, brokers, dealers, registered investment advisers, insurance companies, registered investment companies, Small Business Investment Companies, and certain other entities; (2) Private business development companies; (3) Certain organizations, corporations, business trusts, partnerships, or limited liability companies with total assets exceeding $5,000,000; (4) Directors, executive officers, or general partners of the issuer; (5) Natural persons with an individual net worth or joint net worth with a spouse exceeding $1,000,000, excluding the value of their primary residence, and individuals with individual income exceeding $200,000 or joint income with a spouse exceeding $300,000 in the past two years; (6) Certain trusts directed by a sophisticated person with total assets exceeding $5,000,000; (7) Entities where all equity owners are accredited investors; (8) Other entities not formed for acquiring securities with investments exceeding $5,000,000; (9) Natural persons holding professional certifications or designations recognized by the SEC; (10) Knowledgeable employees of the issuer; (11) Family offices with assets under management exceeding $5,000,000; and (12) Family clients of a qualifying family office.

that in the case of public offerings, P2P lending platforms are obligated to register their platform notes with the SEC and provide a prospectus or make it accessible to investors. In the case of engaging in small offerings,[86] lending platforms in both Tiers must provide specified disclosures to investors, submit an offering statement to the SEC, and obtain approval before initiating the solicitation of investors.

As mentioned in Sect. 5.1.2, in Japan, when soliciting investors to enter into silent partnership agreements to provide small lendings, a lending platform is required to disclose specific information. This includes the trade name, address, an indication that it is a financial instruments business operator, registration number, an outline of the partnership agreements, any fees, remuneration, or other consideration payable by investors, an indication of any risk that a loss will be incurred due to fluctuations in the money rate, the value of currencies, and quotations on the financial instruments market, along with other related information specified as material particulars

In the realm of securities regulations concerning public offerings and private placements, it is noteworthy that the concept of 'Accredited Investors' in the United States has seemingly served as a model for similar classifications in other countries. For instance, Japan's 'Tekikaku (Qualified) Investors' and Vietnam's 'Professional Investors' bear a resemblance to the American system, suggesting that these countries may have drawn inspiration from the United States's framework in developing their own regulations.

Article 29 bis 5, Paragraph 3 of the Financial Instruments and Exchange Act of Japan provides that 'Qualified Investors', which typically include Tokutei Toushika (Professional Investors), mean Professional Investors or any other person specified by Cabinet Office Order as those being equivalent to Professional Investors and having a close relationship with a Financial Instruments Business Operator (including those that seek to obtain registration under Article 29). Professional Investors include individuals as provided for under Article 34 bis 4 of the Financial Instruments and Exchange Act, including: (1) individuals who are the proprietor of a business and have concluded a silent partnership agreement, or any other individuals specified by Cabinet Office Order as being similar thereto; and (2) individuals other than those set forth in the preceding item, who satisfy the requirements specified by Cabinet Office Order as persons equivalent to Professional Investors, in light of such individuals' knowledge and experience and the state of their assets. For example, the State, the Bank of Japan, juridical persons incorporated by a specific Act of incorporation pursuant to the provisions of any specific Act, Investor Protection Funds, the Deposit Insurance Corporation of Japan, the Agricultural and Fishery Cooperative Savings Insurance Corporation, the Insurance Policyholders Protection Corporation of Japan, Specific Purpose Companies, issuer companies of listed share certificates, stock companies whose stated capital amounts to 500 million yen or more, Financial Instruments Business Operators, or juridical persons that fall under the category of Specially Permitted Business Notifying Persons, and foreign juridical persons are regulated as Qualified Investors under Article 23 of the Cabinet Office Ordinance on Definitions under Article 2 of the Financial Instruments and Exchange Act (Ordinance No. 14 of 1993, as amended).

See The US Code of Federal Regulations, Title 17, Chapter II, Part 230, Regulation D, Section 501, Japan's Financial Instruments and Exchange Act (Act No. 25 of 1948, as amended), Article 29 bis 5, Paragraph 3 and Article 34 bis 4, the Cabinet Office Ordinance on Definitions under Article 2 of the Financial Instruments and Exchange Act (Ordinance of the Ministry of Finance No. 14 of 1993, as amended) of Japan, Article 23 and Vietnam's Law on Securities 2019, Article 11. See also, Financial Services Agency (2025).

[86] Small offerings refer to those of up to US$ 20 million (Tier 1) or US$ 50 million (Tier 2), as mentioned above.

that may impact investors' judgment.[87] Subject to these regulations, P2P lending platforms are permitted to engage in public offerings or private placements to solicit investors.[88] In the case of public offerings, lending platforms must file a Securities Registration Statement with the competent authority if the total offering amount is JP ¥ 100 million or more. They are also obligated to provide a prospectus or make it accessible to investors.[89]

In addition to developing regulations that allow platform service providers to engage in offering interests in collective pools for soliciting potential lenders for P2P lending, but only after meeting certain requirements, Vietnam should also consider the legislative experiences of the United States and Japan in implementing regulations to ensure the proper management of these pools.

In the United States, investment companies managing collective funds are subject to various obligations aimed at protecting investors and ensuring regulatory oversight by the SEC. These obligations include the following: (1) upholding a fiduciary duty, necessitating investment companies to act in the best interests of collective funds and investors;[90] (2) adhering to disclosure requirements, which entail providing detailed and accurate information about collective funds' objectives, strategies, risks, fees, and other pertinent details in collective funds' prospectus and periodic reports;[91] (3) compliance with numerous rules governing recordkeeping, client relations, and advertising;[92] (4) submission of regular reports to the SEC and provision of reports to investors;[93] (5) adherence to specific rules designed to safeguard investors' interests and prevent misappropriation;[94] and (6) establishment and maintenance of effective compliance programs aimed at preventing violations of securities laws.[95]

In Japan, a financial instruments business operator providing type-II small-amount electronic public offering service and managing collective funds for lending are subject to specific requirements for ensuring their proper management and protecting investors. Requirements concerning the operator's transactions with

[87] See Japan's Financial Instruments and Exchange Act (Act No. 25 of 1948, as amended), Article 43 bis 5.

[88] Public offerings involve 500 or more investors, while private placements involve 499 or fewer investors.

[89] See Japan's Financial Instruments and Exchange Act (Act No. 25 of 1948, as amended), Article 13.

[90] See The United States Code, Title 15, Chapter 2D, Subchapter I, Section 80a-35 and Section 80b-6.

[91] See The United States Code, Title 15, Chapter 2D, Subchapter I, Section 80a-10 and Section 80a-17.

[92] See The United States Code, Title 15, Chapter 2D, Subchapter I, Section 80a-12, Section 80a-17, and Section 80a-30.

[93] See The United States Code, Title 15, Chapter 2D, Subchapter I, Section 80a-29.

[94] See The United States Code, Title 15, Chapter 2D, Subchapter I, Section 80a-17 and Section 80a-33.

[95] See The United States Code, Title 15, Chapter 2D, Subchapter I, Section 80a-37.

customers include establishing an operational control system for the fair and appropriate performance of its business or services,[96] being sincere to customers;[97] clarifying transaction conditions to customers in advance,[98] delivering documents concerning a financial instrument transaction contract to customers prior to and upon the conclusion of the contract by means of using an electronic data processing system or by any other means regulated by laws,[99] providing customers with a specific time period to cancel the contract,[100] refraining from making an offer or promise in connection with the compensation of losses incurred by investors,[101] conducting business in a manner appropriate in light of customer knowledge, experience, the state of assets, or purpose for which a financial instruments transaction contract is concluded,[102] and establishing and disclosing a policy and method for executing customer orders.[103] The operator is also subject to requirements regarding accounting[104] and the supervision of the competent authority.[105]

Furthermore, Vietnam should also draw insights from the legislative experiences of the United States and Japan to establish regulations that ensure a sound lending business utilizing collective pools of funds by platform service providers. As mentioned in Sect. 5.1.1, in the United States, platform service providers must secure a lending license in the states where they operate when offering loans through balance sheet lending schemes, or they must operate through a funding bank in the

---

[96] See Japan's Financial Instruments and Exchange Act (Act No. 25 of 1948, as amended), Article 35 bis 3.

[97] See Japan's Financial Instruments and Exchange Act (Act No. 25 of 1948, as amended), Article 36.

[98] See Japan's Financial Instruments and Exchange Act (Act No. 25 of 1948, as amended), Article 37 bis 2.

[99] See Japan's Financial Instruments and Exchange Act (Act No. 25 of 1948, as amended), Article 37 bis 3, Article 37 bis 4, and Article 43 bis 5.

[100] See Japan's Financial Instruments and Exchange Act (Act No. 25 of 1948, as amended), Article 37 bis 6.

[101] See Japan's Financial Instruments and Exchange Act (Act No. 25 of 1948, as amended), Article 39.

[102] See Japan's Financial Instruments and Exchange Act (Act No. 25 of 1948, as amended), Article 40.

[103] See Japan's Financial Instruments and Exchange Act (Act No. 25 of 1948, as amended), Article 40 bis 2.

[104] Financial services providers engaging in Type-II Financial Instruments Business are subject to requirements concerning business books, the submission of business reports to the competent authority, and the creation, maintenance, and making available for public inspection of explanatory documents containing specific details outlined in the business report. See Japan's Financial Instruments and Exchange Act (Act No. 25 of 1948, as amended), Chapter III, Section 3.

[105] Financial services providers engaging in Type-II Financial Instruments Business are subject to regulations concerning the notification of operation suspension, notification of operation discontinuance, changing business methods, or taking necessary measures to improve business operation or the state of assets in accordance with the competent authority's request, and other supervisory measures by the competent authority. See Japan's Financial Instruments and Exchange Act (Act No. 25 of 1948, as amended), Chapter III, Section 4.

case of marketplace lending schemes. Additionally, they are bound by consumer protection laws. Similarly, in Japan, lending platforms that provide small loans through pools contributed by investors must register and obtain a money lender's license under the Money Lending Business Act (Act No. 32 of 1983, as amended) before offering loans. These platforms are also subject to regulations safeguarding borrowers' legitimate rights, as highlighted in Sect. 5.1.2. Considering the experiences of the United States and Japan, Vietnam should contemplate regulations on licensing for lending businesses and the protection of borrowers when formulating regulations for P2P lending platforms. It should be noted that these regulations are based on the assumption that loans are provided by professional non-bank lenders rather than by individual, non-professional peer lenders, while also ensuring the protection of borrowers' interests.

While providing measures to mitigate the risk borne by lenders, Vietnam may also consider implementing measures to protect the interests of borrowers and applying these measures to all forms of small lending. These measures, as commonly understood, often include the limitation of interest rates. As mentioned in Sect. 5.1.1, in the United States, each state has its own usury laws that establish the maximum legal interest rate allowable on loans. These laws are designed to protect consumers from excessively high-interest rates, though the regulations and maximum allowable interest rates can vary significantly from state to state. In Japan, the limitation of interest rates imposed in any lending, including but not limited to social online lending platforms, is strictly regulated under the Interest Rate Restriction Act (Act No. 100 of 1954, as amended) and the Act Regulating the Receipt of Contributions, Receipt of Deposits, and Interest Rates (Act No. 195 of 1954, as amended), as mentioned in Sect. 5.1.2. Drawing from the legislative experience of the United States and Japan, Vietnam should consider regulating the maximum allowable interest rates, encompassing payments that lenders and borrowers explicitly agree to designate as 'interest', as well as charges, fees, and similar payments that, regardless of categorization, functionally amount to interest. Any payment received by lenders in connection with loans, regardless of their name, such as honorarium, fee, or inspection fee, should be considered interest.

The implementation of measures protecting the interests of borrowers should also include preventing the seizure of assets necessary for maintaining a minimum standard of living. In the United States, most regulations stipulating such prevention are provided under the Bankruptcy Code of 1978 (as amended), the Consumer Credit Protection Act of 1968 (as amended), the Social Security Act of 1935 (as amended), and state laws. Under Section 522 of the Bankruptcy Code, when an individual files for bankruptcy, there are exemptions that determine which assets can be protected from liquidation to pay off debts. These exemptions include necessities such as a primary residence, personal belongings, and the debtor's interest, not to exceed US$ 2400 in value, in one motor vehicle.[106] Additionally, under Section 1673 (b) of the Consumer Credit Protection Act of 1968 (as amended), the maximum amount of an

[106] See The United States Code, Title 11, Chapter 5, Subchapter II, Section 522.

individual's disposable earnings that can be garnished is generally limited to 25% of their disposable income or the amount by which their disposable income exceeds 30 times the federal minimum wage, whichever is less.[107] Moreover, the protection of social security benefits and public benefits from seizure is derived from the nature and purpose of these benefits under the Social Security Act (Title 42 of the US Code).[108] This protection is designed to ensure that individuals receiving these benefits have a stable source of income to meet their basic needs.

Similarly, in Japan, comprehensive regulations are in place to protect the interests of borrowers, ensuring the non-seizure of vital assets and guaranteeing individuals the means to maintain a basic standard of living. The Civil Execution Act (Act No. 4 of 1979, as amended) is a prime example, overseeing the safeguarding of essential personal assets and special claims crucial for an individual's livelihood.[109] Article 131 of this Act delineates personal belongings exempt from seizure, encompassing clothes, bedclothes, furniture, kitchen utensils, tatami mats, and more. Additionally, it includes provisions for agriculture and fishing tools, essential occupational instruments, religious items, personal documents, and objects of honor. Article 152 of this Act specifies limitations on the seizure of certain claims. These claims include those that are pertaining to (1) continuous performance received to maintain a person's living; (2) compensation, wages, salary, retirement pension, bonus, or similar remuneration; and (3) retirement allowance or similar remuneration, where again three-quarters of the performance is safeguarded from seizure. The Public Assistance Act (Act No. 144 of 1950, as amended) also restricts the seizure of public assistance benefits, as stipulated in Article 58.[110] Additionally, Article 41 of the Employees' Pension Insurance Act (Act No. 115 of 1954, as amended) protects the right to receive pension insurance benefits and imposes restrictions on their assignment or attachment.[111] Similar protections are extended to national pension insurance benefits under Article 24 of the National Pension Act (Act No. 115 of 1954, as amended).[112] Moreover, Subsection 6 (Article 75 to Article 78) of the National Tax Collection Act (Act No. 147 of 1950, as amended) prevents the seizure of general property (such as clothes, bedding, furniture, kitchen utensils, tatami mats, and fittings that are essential to daily life), wages, social insurance benefits, and assets vital for agriculture and fishing.[113] Furthermore, Article 2 of the Law

[107] See The United States Code, Title 15, Chapter 41, Subchapter II, Section 1673.

[108] See The United States Code, Title 42.

[109] See the Civil Execution Act (Act No. 4 of 1979, as amended) of Japan.

[110] See the Public Assistance Act (Act No. 144 of 1950, as amended) of Japan, Article 58.

[111] See the Employees' Pension Insurance Act (Act No. 115 of 1954, as amended) of Japan, Article 41.

[112] The National Pension Act (Act No. 111 of 1950, as amended) of Japan, Article 24 provides that: "The right to receive benefits cannot be transferred, used as collateral, or seized. However, this does not apply when the right to receive old-age basic pension or additional pension is seized through measures related to delinquent national taxes (including measures based on such examples)."

[113] See the National Tax Collection Act (Act No. 147 of 1950, as amended) of Japan, Article 75, Article 76, Article 77 and Article 78.

Concerning Prohibition of Seizure and Related Matters for Benefit Payments to Low-Income Households Associated with the Use of Contingency Funds in March of Reiwa 5 (2023) (Act No. 64 of 2020) establishes safeguards for the right to receive and the non-seizure of payments and properties associated with low-income household benefits related to the use of contingency funds in March of Reiwa 5 (2023).[114]

Vietnam should also consider implementing regulations to safeguard the essential assets and property of defaulted borrowers from being seized during debt collection.

## 7.5 Interim Conclusion

This chapter outlined the favorable features of a mutual funding scheme, including (a) participants in a mutual funding scheme are more likely to have personal relationships with one another, and (b) they share profits and jointly bear losses.

For the purpose of exploring potential solutions to mitigating the risks borne by P2P lenders, this chapter delved into the feasibility of integrating each of these features into the current P2P lending scheme in Vietnam. It emphasized that there likely are no preexisting personal relationships between lenders and borrowers before they join the lending via a P2P lending platform. It might not be realistic for either the P2P lending platform, lenders, or borrowers to expend cost and labor to establish such relationships. Additionally, it might not align with the expectations or preferences of P2P lenders to share profits and losses with P2P borrowers. However, sharing profits and losses solely among P2P lenders within the same scheme could help stabilize their returns and diversify the credit risk they bear. Given this, the author proposes a potential solution to stabilize the risks faced by P2P lenders: having P2P lenders contribute to a common lending pool where they share both profits and losses with other lenders. This involves entrusting professional management with tasks such as borrower assessment, lending decisions, and borrower monitoring. Since lenders may be hesitant to accept such a solution, ingenuity in a detailed scheme to attract them might be necessary.

This chapter then explained how the proposed solution can benefit other stakeholders, including borrowers and platform service providers. For borrowers, a large pool of funds could enhance accessibility to financing and potentially increase individual borrowing limits. Moreover, stabilizing the risks borne by lenders might open avenues for borrowers with lower creditworthiness to access the lending

[114]The Law Concerning Prohibition of Seizure and Related Matters for Benefit Payments to Low-Income Households Associated with the Use of Contingency Funds in March of Reiwa 5 (2023) (Act No. 64 of 2020) of Japan, Article 2 provides that:

1. The right to receive the payment of the Benefit for Low-Income Households related to the use of contingency funds in March of Reiwa 5 (2023) cannot be transferred, provided as collateral, or seized.
2. The money and other properties received as the Benefit for Low-Income Households related to the use of contingency funds in March of Reiwa 5 (2023) cannot be seized.

scheme. Furthermore, while professional management of lendings may reduce the opportunity for borrowers to turn their business around, it could prevent the tragedy of borrowers overextending themselves to the point of being unable to recover. As for platform service providers, the intricate process of establishing a common pool necessitates a professional management approach for the effective and secure operation of the lending model. Recognizing this, the author recommended the introduction of laws mandating adequate qualifications for platform service providers to ensure their capability for professional management, thereby fostering lender confidence in entrusting them with these responsibilities in the context of P2P lending.

This chapter further investigated the transformation of the nature of "peer-to-peer" lending in the current P2P lending scheme through the establishment of a common pool contributed by lenders for lending.

In a P2P lending scheme, individual potential lenders typically do not have personal relationships with each other. Unless facilitated by a platform service provider, establishing such a common pool between individual potential lenders would likely be impossible. Therefore, this chapter examined a scenario where a platform service provider establishes a pool and entices potential lenders to contribute their funds to the pool. Under this scenario, the platform service provider is unlikely to successfully solicit potential lenders unless they provide these lenders with the information they are likely to demand. The author attempted to enumerate that information by referring to items that would likely be included in the terms and conditions of a typical loan agreement, as well as borrowers' representations and warranties that are generally included in such agreements.

The typical terms and conditions of a small loan agreement are likely to include, but are not limited to, Parties Involved, Principal Amount, Interest Rate, Payment Terms (which may cover the monthly payment amount, due date, acceptable payment methods, and payment destination), Loan Term, Late Payment Policy, Events of Default, Prepayment, Collateral, Fees, Insurance, Assignment, and Dispute Resolution.

Additionally, the typical representations and warranties by the borrower of a small loan agreement are likely to include the following items, though this list is not exhaustive: Borrower's Authority and Capacity to Borrow, Valid and Binding Obligation, No Conflicts, Financial Statements or Conditions, No Material Adverse Change, No Pending or Threatened Litigation, No Insolvency, Regulatory Compliance, No Delayed Tax Payment, Accuracy of Information, No Default, Use of Loan Proceeds, Collateral, No Undisclosed Liabilities, and Insurance.

Also, this chapter explored feasible measures for establishing a collective lending pool. These measures include: (a) a bookkeeping entry system where the pool is a compilation of individual contributions attributed to each lender; (b) individual lenders contributing funds to a designated service provider through individual contracts, relinquishing direct rights in favor of a claim to request profit and loss distribution; (c) joint establishment of the pool by lenders or jointly with the platform service provider, involving a single multiparty contract and the management of the pool by a specific party (presumably, the service provider, or a fund manager appointed by the service provider); and (d) creation of a pool by individual lenders assigning funds to a trust company or licensed bank for trust operations, with the trustee holding sole ownership, and lenders retaining the right to demand profit and loss distribution, allowing loans to be managed by the service provider. Among these measures, the third measure seems more practical than the others. The chapter suggested that to implement such a lending scheme through a collective pool, it is necessary to elaborate on the terms and conditions applicable to the pool. Such implementation is well within the capability of law practitioners.

In light of this, this chapter highlighted that introducing a collective pool of funds to help diversify lenders' risks would transform the nature of the current 'peer-to-peer' lending scheme, moving away from its traditional individual-based approach. This is because the funds contributed to the pool are managed in a way that prevents individual lenders from controlling their individual interests in the pool, as mentioned above, and the manager of the pool substantially acts as the lender in transactions with borrowers.

This chapter then discussed the issues concerning the solicitation of potential lenders for investment in P2P lending schemes, the establishment and management of collective funds for such lending, and the legislative experiences of the United States and Japan. Drawing from the experiences of these countries, the author proposes possible solutions to adapt Vietnamese regulations, aiming to facilitate collective lending through a common pool and promote the sound development of the lending business in the country.

Proposed solutions are: (1) classifying the interests in a pool for small lendings as securities, enabling the application of existing securities regulations with suitable adjustments for the establishment and solicitation of potential lenders; (2) mandating platform service providers to register their business with the competent authority (i.e., the State Securities Commission) for qualification to engage in interest placements; (3) permitting platform service providers, only post-registration, to conduct public offerings or private placements of interests in collective pools in order to solicit both professional and non-professional investors for P2P lending; and (4) introducing regulations to ensure the proper management of these pools by platform service providers.

Furthermore, to facilitate the sound development of the lending business in Vietnam, the author also proposes that Vietnam should impose licensing requirements for lending business conducted by professional non-bank lenders, rather than individual, non-professional peer lenders when formulating regulations for P2P lending business. Additionally, Vietnam should also implement measures to protect the interests of borrowers, applying these measures to every kind of small lending. These measures include (a) limiting interest rates, and (b) preventing the seizure of assets necessary for maintaining a minimum standard of living.

## References

Financial Services Agency FAQ on Financial Instruments and Exchange Act, https://www.fsa.go.jp/en/laws_regulations/faq_on_fiea/section06.html. Accessed 20 Mar 2025

The Code of Federal Regulations, Title 17, Chapter II, Part 230, Regulation D. https://www.ecfr.gov/current/title-17/chapter-II/part-230/subject-group-ECFR6e651a4c86c0174?toc=1. Accessed 20 Mar 2025

The English translation of Circular No. 30/2014/TT-NHNN of the State Bank of Vietnam (amended in 2016) (trans: Thuvienphapluat). https://thuvienphapluat.vn/van-ban/Tien-te-Ngan-hang/Circular-No-30-2014-TT-NHNN-offer-acceptance-trusteeship-performed-credit-institutions-foreign-bank-branches-261952.aspx?tab=1. Accessed 20 Mar 2025

The English translation of Circular No. 35/VBHN-NHNN of Vietnam (trans: Thuvienphapluat). https://thuvienphapluat.vn/van-ban/Tien-te-Ngan-hang/Integrated-document-35-VBHN-NHNN-2016-offer-acceptance-trusteeship-performed-credit-institutions-413092.aspx?tab=1. Accessed 20 Mar 2025

The English translation of Circular No. 98/2020/TT-BTC of Vietnam (trans: Thuvienphapluat). https://thuvienphapluat.vn/van-ban/Chung-khoan/Circular-98-2020-TT-BTC-providing-guidance-operation-of-securities-investment-funds-468889.aspx?tab=1. Accessed 20 Mar 2025

The English translation of Circular No. 99/2020/TT-BTC of Vietnam (trans: Thuvienphapluat). https://thuvienphapluat.vn/van-ban/Doanh-nghiep/Circular-No-99-2020-TT-BTC-operation-of-securities-investment-fund-management-companies-466054.aspx?tab=1. Accessed 20 Mar 2025

The English translation of Circular No. 121/2020/TT-BTC of Vietnam (trans: Thuvienphapluat). https://thuvienphapluat.vn/van-ban/Doanh-nghiep/Circular-121-2020-TT-BTC-prescribing-operation-of-securities-companies-471425.aspx?tab=1. Accessed 20 Mar 2025

The English translation of Decree No. 155/2020/ND-CP of Vietnam (trans: Thuvienphapluat). https://thuvienphapluat.vn/van-ban/Chung-khoan/Decree-155-2020-ND-CP-elaboration-of-some-Articles-of-the-Law-on-Securities-484721.aspx?tab=1. Accessed 20 Mar 2025

The English translation of the Cabinet Office Ordinance on Definitions under Article 2 of the Financial Instruments and Exchange Act (Ordinance of the Ministry of Finance No. 14 of 1993, as amended) of Japan. https://www.japaneselawtranslation.go.jp/en/laws/view/1966/en#je_at31. Accessed 20 Mar 2025

The English translation of the Civil Code of Japan (Act No. 89 of 1896, as amended). https://www.japaneselawtranslation.go.jp/en/laws/view/3494/en. Accessed 20 Mar 2025

The English translation of the Civil Execution Act (Act No. 4 of 1979, as amended) of Japan. https://www.japaneselawtranslation.go.jp/en/laws/view/4272. Accessed 20 Mar 2025

The English translation of the Commercial Code of Japan (Act No. 48 of 1899, as amended). https://www.japaneselawtranslation.go.jp/en/laws/view/2135/en. Accessed 20 Mar 2025

The English translation of the Employees' Pension Insurance Act (Act No. 115 of 1954, as amended) of Japan. https://www.japaneselawtranslation.go.jp/en/laws/view/3554#je_ch3sc1at14. Accessed 20 Mar 2025

The English translation of the Financial Instruments and Exchange Act of Japan (Act No. 25 of 1948, as amended). https://www.japaneselawtranslation.go.jp/en/laws/view/2355/en. Accessed 20 Mar 2025

The English translation of the Law Concerning Prohibition of Seizure and Related Matters for Benefit Payments to Low-Income Households Associated with the Use of Contingency Funds in March of Reiwa 5 (2023) (Act No. 64 of 2020) of Japan. https://elaws.e-gov.go.jp/document?lawid=505AC1000000064. Accessed 20 Mar 2025

The English translation of the Limited Liability Partnership Act of Japan (Act No. 40 of 2005, as amended). https://www.japaneselawtranslation.go.jp/en/laws/view/3826/en. Accessed 20 Mar 2025

The English translation of the Limited Partnership Act for Investment of Japan (Act No. 90 of 1998, as amended). https://www.japaneselawtranslation.go.jp/en/laws/view/3822/en. Accessed 20 Mar 2025

The English translation of the National Pension Act (Act No. 111 of 1950, as amended) of Japan. https://elaws.e-gov.go.jp/document?lawid=334AC0000000141_20230401_505AC0000000003&keyword=%E5%9B%BD%E6%B0%91%E5%B9%B4%E9%87%91%E6%B3%95. Accessed 20 Mar 2025

The English translation of the National Tax Collection Act (Act No. 147 of 1950, as amended) of Japan. https://elaws.e-gov.go.jp/document?lawid=334AC0000000147_20230401_505AC0000000003&keyword=%E5%9B%BD%E7%A8%8E%E5%BE%B4%E5%8F%8E%E6%B3%95. Accessed 20 Mar 2025

The English translation of the Public Assistance Act (Act No. 144 of 1950, as amended) of Japan. https://www.japaneselawtranslation.go.jp/en/laws/view/24#je_ch8at3. Accessed 20 Mar 2025

The English translation of Vietnam's Civil Code 2015 (trans: Thuvienphapluat). https://thuvienphapluat.vn/van-ban/Quyen-dan-su/Law-No-91-2015-QH13-The-Civil-Code-303230.aspx?tab=1. Accessed 20 Mar 2025

The English translation of Vietnam's Law on Credit Institutions 2024 (trans: Thuvienphapluat). https://thuvienphapluat.vn/van-ban/Tien-te-Ngan-hang/Law-32-2024-QH15-Credit-institutions-606780.aspx?tab=1. Accessed 20 Mar 2025

The English translation of Vietnam's Law on Enterprises 2020 (trans: Thuvienphapluat). https://thuvienphapluat.vn/van-ban/EN/Doanh-nghiep/Law-59-2020-QH14-Enterprises/451799/tieng-anh.aspx. Accessed 20 Mar 2025

The English translation of Vietnam's Law on Insurance Business 2022 (trans: Thuvienphapluat). https://thuvienphapluat.vn/van-ban/Doanh-nghiep/Law-08-2022-QH15-insurance-business-524310.aspx?tab=1. Accessed 20 Mar 2025

The English translation of Vietnam's Law on Securities 2019 (translated by the State Securities Commission of Vietnam). http://ssc.gov.vn/webcenter/portal/ssc/pages_r/l/chitit?dDocName=APPSSCGOVVN162142990. Accessed 20 Mar 2025

The United States Code, Title 15, Chapter 2D, Subchapter I. https://www.law.cornell.edu/uscode/text/15/chapter-2D/subchapter-I. Accessed 20 Mar 2025

# Chapter 8
# Empirical Testing the Feasibility of Mutual Funding as a Risk Diversification Tool in Vietnam

## 8.1 The Design of the Empirical Test

This study empirically examines the viability of a mutual funding scheme as a risk mitigation tool for P2P lending schemes in Vietnam. The investigation seeks to explore three key questions: (1) To what extent are potential lenders willing to join a mutual funding scheme established via an online lending platform? (2) What role do personal relationships among participants play in such a scheme? (3) To what extent can professional management overseeing the operation of the scheme sustain lending activity on these platforms?

To explore these questions, the author employed qualitative research methods. This approach was chosen because it is expected that these methods can offer in-depth insights into the social contexts surrounding potential lenders[1] and the reasons and motivations guiding their behavior.[2] Specific data of this kind are absent in existing studies. Therefore, the author's endeavor to obtain such data is crucial for examining the viability of the proposals presented in Chap. 7.

Especially, in-depth interviews were particularly suitable for this study, which seeks to understand the attitudes of potential lenders in Vietnam's P2P lending sector. This suitability stems from two main reasons. First, the study focuses on exploring the personal attitudes of individuals toward a proposed mutual funding scheme. Second, the topic involves sensitive issues related to personal or family assets and decisions about participation in such a scheme. In-depth interviews offer several advantages for this context, notably their flexibility and reliability. They allow the researcher to adapt questions to each interviewee's circumstances by adding, omitting, or modifying them as needed. Additionally, since responses can shape the direction of subsequent questions, this method enables a dynamic and

[1] See Leeuw and Schmeets (2016, p. 158).

[2] See Mack et al. (2005, p. 1).



Y. H. Nguyen, *Regulating Peer-to-Peer Lending in Vietnam*,
https://doi.org/10.1007/978-981-96-9505-8_8

responsive data collection process.[3] Probing and follow-up questions are especially useful for eliciting deeper insights and clarifying vague or incomplete answers.[4]

Semi-structured interviews were selected for this empirical research to strike a balance between consistency and flexibility. This method allowed the researcher to prepare a predefined set of questions to ensure key topics were covered, while also enabling the exploration of additional relevant issues as they arose.[5] The format helped maintain direction and control throughout the interviews.[6] To gain first-hand insights into the attitudes of potential lenders toward a mutual funding scheme in Vietnam, in-depth interviews were conducted. These interviews aimed to explore participants' views on the establishment of mutual funding schemes within the context of P2P lending. Two groups of interviewees were targeted: middle-class individuals who could serve as potential lenders, and practitioners working in the P2P lending industry. The former group was expected to provide personal perspectives on participating in mutual funding schemes via online lending platforms, while the latter offered professional insights into client engagement and operational practices within the sector.

A pre-defined set of guiding questions (see Appendix F) was developed to ensure comparability across interviews while still allowing room for spontaneous follow-up questions. This adaptability enabled the author to probe deeper into relevant areas and clarify ambiguous responses.

Participants were approached through a purposive sampling technique,[7] based on the study's objectives and the relevance of interviewees' backgrounds. Initial contacts were established through the author's personal and professional networks, which proved instrumental in securing cooperation, particularly given the general reluctance among individuals to participate in academic studies involving financial disclosures. Cultural norms in Vietnam, where trust and personal relationships often influence willingness to engage, likely played a significant role in facilitating participation. Follow-up questions were conducted via email or messaging apps when further clarification was required, and this procedure was explained to participants in advance.

Ethical considerations were central to the research process. The study followed the ethical guidelines outlined by Kyushu University's Responsible Conduct of Research program (see Appendix B for the digest version). Each participant received a Participant Information Statement and Consent Form (Appendix C), which clarified the study's purpose, the voluntary nature of participation, data use, and privacy

[3] See Mack et al. (2005, p. 3).

[4] See Bailey (2018, p. 101).

[5] See Bos (2020, p. 34).

[6] Bos (2020, p. 34).

[7] It has been noted that purposive sampling, a widely employed sampling technique, categorizes participants based on predetermined criteria that pertain to a specific research question. The size of the sample, whether predetermined or not, relies on factors like available resources, time, and study goals. In purposive sampling, sample sizes are frequently guided by theoretical saturation, indicating when new data cease to provide further insights. Mack et al. (2005, p. 5).

protections. A Revocation of Consent Form (Appendix D) was also provided, reinforcing participants' right to withdraw at any time. Where interviewees consented to the identification of demographic information or organizational affiliation in future publications, a separate Identifying Company and Interviewee in Future Publication Consent Form was obtained (Appendix E).

A total of eight face-to-face interviews were conducted between May 23 and May 30, 2022, all held in Hanoi. The sample comprised middle-class[8] Vietnamese individuals and representatives from four active P2P lending platforms—Vnvon, Lendbiz, Tima, and VOV247. Hanoi was chosen due to its significance in the P2P lending market and the author's familiarity with its sociocultural context. Interviews were conducted in Vietnamese and typically lasted around two hours. Each session began with a brief overview of the study, followed by discussions guided by the interview outline. While the interviews were based on pre-prepared questions, spontaneous follow-up inquiries were common, allowing participants to elaborate on previously unanticipated yet relevant issues.

Most interviews were audio-recorded with participants' consent; where consent was not granted, detailed notes were taken. Recordings were transcribed promptly after each session to ensure accuracy and retain contextual richness. Selected interview responses and corresponding questions are included in Appendices F and H.

## 8.2 Key Findings and Insights on the Feasibility of Mutual Funding in Vietnam

### *8.2.1 Vietnamese Middle-Class Individuals Encounter Little Challenges in Accessing Small Funds*

Given that middle-income households can access credit services from various sources, including commercial banks as depicted in Fig. 2.2, they encounter little impediments when seeking to borrow small funds to address their daily needs. During the interviews conducted for this research, two interviewees stated that obtaining small loans from banks is a straightforward process:

> Actually, I possess several types of assets, namely, cash, houses, cars, stocks, and gold. Among these, houses account for a significant portion of my total assets. My family owns a house in Hanoi and another in my hometown, which together are valued at approximately VN₫ 7 billion. Obtaining small loans is not a challenge for me due to my ability to easily borrow from several commercial banks where my credit history is favorable. Additionally, I can leverage my salary account to secure loans swiftly from a bank (See Appendix H—Question 1: Answer 1).

[8] In this empirical research, the middle class is defined as individuals with a per capita spending above US$ 15 per day and a wealth over US$ 500,000.

> My assets comprise an apartment in Hanoi and online savings accounts with commercial banks. Additionally, I possess gold, an investment insurance package, and investments in the stock market. Obtaining small loans is convenient for me through my credit card issued by a commercial bank, as well as by borrowing funds from the savings accounts I hold with the bank (See Appendix H—Question 1: Answer 2).

Two additional interviewees mentioned that borrowing money from family members, relatives, friends, and colleagues is a feasible option for them:

> I have the majority of my assets in an apartment, accounting for approximately 80% of my total assets, and a small portion of cash deposited in a bank (around 2% of my total assets). Borrowing small amounts (ranging from VN₫ 20 million to VN₫ 50 million) from family members, relatives, and friends poses no difficulty for me (See Appendix H—Question 1: Answer 3).

> We spent a lot on buying a car and an apartment in Hanoi, and a significant part of my family's cash has been invested in stocks. However, we encounter no challenges in borrowing small loans when needed. Borrowing around VN₫ 50 million from friends and colleagues is quite accessible for us (See Appendix H—Question 1: Answer 4).

## *8.2.2 Vietnamese Middle-Class Individuals Express a Willingness to Invest in a Mutual Funding Scheme*

Among Vietnam's middle-class population, there is a growing demand for investment opportunities, driven by their aspirations to improve their quality of life. This includes seeking better goods and services, especially in sectors such as healthcare, education, living conditions, and entertainment, all of which often carry higher expenses.[9] In Vietnam, typical investment channels encompass the real estate market, the stock market, gold, bank deposits, and investment insurance packages. However, the middle-class demographic typically approaches these investment options with varying levels of caution.

With the broader availability of fintech tools and platforms, P2P lending has emerged as a new source of micro and/or small funding, seeing rapid growth in Vietnam since 2015. A notable surge in online lending platforms has been observed in major cities such as Hanoi, Ho Chi Minh, and Da Nang. When asked whether they would be open to regularly contributing their small assets to a shared pool in return for the opportunities to borrow funds from the same pool, interviewees demonstrated a willingness to invest in the P2P lending market, primarily motivated by the prospect of generating profit rather than simply securing borrowing rights for the future. For example, one interviewee answered:

> I have deposited a portion of my cash in a commercial bank, but the interest I receive is quite low, around 6% or 7% per year. At present, my investments are divided between stocks and gold, though I have experienced losses in the stock market and modest gains from gold.

[9] See Oxford Analytica (2017).

Additionally, I am allocating some of my idle cash to P2P loans in order to generate profit (See Appendix H—Question 2: Answer 1).

My preference is to make regular contributions of small amounts to a pool facilitated by an online lending platform, aiming for profit. This strategy aligns with my goal of diversifying risk within my asset allocation. I think the stock market is not a suitable investment channel for ordinary individuals. Although it seemed attractive last year due to soaring stock market indexes and the new trading system at the Ho Chi Minh City Stock Exchange, this year has been marked by losses for me. Furthermore, the real estate market requires significant capital investment. Currently, the real estate market in Vietnam is facing potential downturn risks. This stems from the challenges real estate businesses encounter in accessing capital sources, with some of them resorting to selling properties and housing at substantial discounts. Several real estate companies have halted or postponed investment endeavors and construction projects (See Appendix H—Question 2: Answer 2).

Similarly, two additional interviewees stated:

I am currently investing in stocks, but it is quite difficult to predict the stock market's trends. I have even lost some money investing in the stock market. Therefore, I would like to explore other profitable investment channels, including a mutual funding by regularly contributing a small amount into a pool. This will help me diversify my investment portfolio (See Appendix H—Question 2: Answer 3).

We have spent a considerable amount on buying a car and an apartment in Hanoi. Most of my family's cash has been invested in stocks, but we have not earned much profit. We are now open to investing in other lucrative avenues to generate additional income, as we are aiming to purchase a house in my hometown (See Appendix H—Question 2: Answer 4).

### *8.2.3 Personal Relationships Are Pivotal in Vietnamese P2P Lending Business*

P2P lending companies face a shortage of potential investors. Usually, these companies depend on the networks of their staff and customers to connect with potential investors. Potential investors are more inclined to participate in P2P lending if they have close affiliations with individuals who have garnered positive experiences in P2P loan investments. Moreover, staff at P2P lending companies are mandated to leverage their connections within the middle-class demographic to attract more investors to their lending business. This was corroborated by information provided by interviewees from two P2P lending companies.

The majority of investors participating in our P2P platform are individual investors. They reside in various provinces across the country, especially in major cities like Hanoi and Ho Chi Minh City. Many of them are investing in short-term loans (6 months) with investment amounts around VN₫ 100 million. Currently, due to the absence of a specific and appropriate legal framework for the operation of P2P lending companies, numerous potential investors are hesitant to join or invest more assets in P2P lending. They perceive it as a risky investment channel for ordinary citizens. However, if those who possess idle assets (or potential investors) have close relationships with our current investors, they are more inclined to join or can be persuaded to participate in our lending business to seek profit. Many investors using our lending platform share close personal relationships with each

> other. Moreover, managers and staff at P2P lending companies are encouraged and sometimes required to leverage their connections within the middle-class demographic to attract more investors to the company's lending business (See Appendix H—Question 3: Answer 1).

> Most investors on our P2P platform are individuals who typically opt for short-term loans (3 months, 6 months, or 9 months). The highest investment through our platform to date has been VN₫ 25 billion, while the minimum investment has been VN₫ 10 million. Many of these investors maintain personal relationships with our staff and/or our existing customers. Initially, some were hesitant to invest in our lending platform due to concerns about potential financial losses. However, witnessing profitable outcomes for investors with whom they share a personal connection has encouraged them to engage in our lending business. Furthermore, certain investors are aware that the borrowers obtaining funds through our lending platform are primarily small SMEs. They know that our company managers have strong relationships with the executives of these SMEs, and in some cases, our company managers even hold a stake in the SMEs. This awareness has bolstered their confidence in investing in our lending platform (See Appendix H—Question 3: Answer 2).

One interviewee mentioned that her investments in P2P loans stemmed from her trust in a close acquaintance: "I decided to invest in P2P lending to seek profit after my sister had a positive experience with this investment model and recommended it to me" (see Appendix H—Question 3: Answer 3).

Similarly, two other interviewees were willing to engage in P2P lending based on recommendations from close acquaintances:

> I would consider investing 20% to 30% of my idle cash into P2P lending if someone with whom I share a close relationship has enjoyed positive experiences with this investment avenue and recommends it to me (See Appendix H—Question 3: Answer 4).

> If someone I have a close relationship with recommends a P2P lending company in which they have achieved successful investments, I am open to investing a small amount of money in loans facilitated by that P2P lending company (See Appendix H—Question 3: Answer 5).

### *8.2.4 The Role of Professional Management in Overseeing the Operation of a Mutual Funding Scheme*

Given the lack of a specific and suitable legal framework for P2P lending companies, professional management overseeing the operation of a mutual funding scheme becomes crucial in mitigating the risks associated with such a scheme. This sentiment is echoed by the insights provided by two interviewees:

> To be honest, having read about scandals involving P2P lending businesses where lenders lost their investments on various platforms, I am hesitant to invest in a mutual funding scheme established through an online lending platform. In addition, I find it challenging to acquire information regarding the current financial and business status of P2P borrowers, as well as their utilization of funds, in the absence of professional management by an independent party or organization overseeing the mutual funding scheme's operation. I would consider investing in a mutual funding scheme if there were substantial regulations governing this lending business, aiming to guarantee a secure environment for investors (See Appendix H—Question 4: Answer 1).

> I believe that having a professional independent party or organization manage the operation of a mutual funding scheme could instill confidence in investors regarding the operations of P2P lending companies. As for myself, I would be inclined to invest more funds if such professional management were implemented through online lending platforms (See Appendix H—Question 4: Answer 2).

It is clear that the absence of professional management overseeing mutual funding schemes significantly causes potential lenders to be hesitant about engaging in the P2P lending business. They likely lack organizational connections or insights into potential borrowers using P2P lending platforms. They, therefore, encounter difficulties in obtaining crucial information about borrowers, such as their current financial and business status and fund utilization. This lack of transparency diminishes their confidence in participating in P2P lending schemes.

## 8.3 Interim Conclusion and Limitations

This chapter describes the primary source of empirical data: targeted in-depth interviews. These interviews took place from May 23, 2022, to May 27, 2022, with 8 interviewees in Hanoi. Conducted in Vietnamese language, each interview lasted approximately two hours on average.

This chapter, through empirical research, highlights several key findings: (1) Vietnamese middle-class citizens encounter no obstacles in accessing small funds; (2) they show a willingness to invest in mutual funding schemes facilitated by P2P lending platforms; (3) personal relationships hold significant importance in Vietnam's P2P lending landscape; and (4) professional oversight of a mutual funding scheme's operation is crucial for risk mitigation within such a scheme.

Significantly, the evidence provided by the interviewees supports the proposal presented in Chap. 7. In Vietnam's increasingly urbanized society, many individuals, who may not necessarily be financially sophisticated, are being encouraged to participate in lending schemes via online lending platforms. As these individuals likely lack organizational affiliation with one another or have minimal knowledge about each other, it is challenging to establish personal relationships among them, which could potentially mitigate the risks associated with their lending. Absent professional management overseeing mutual funding schemes, P2P lenders struggle to obtain information regarding P2P borrowers' current financial status and loan utilization. This lack of information hinders their ability to effectively adjust lending terms and conditions, as well as prepare for potential borrower defaults. Furthermore, middle-class individuals in Vietnam, who have idle assets and are qualified to participate in P2P lending schemes, are inclined to seek profit. However, participants in a mutual funding scheme share both profits and losses. This characteristic might conflict with the preferences of P2P lenders. This potential conflict presents challenges in implementing the features of a mutual funding scheme; therefore, measures to resolve this conflict are essential.

In conducting empirical research for this chapter, the author encountered several limitations beyond her control. These constraints include challenges to research methodology and inherent difficulties in conducting research in Vietnam.

Regarding the limitations of the research methodology, there are several noteworthy points. Firstly, selecting middle-class individuals for interviews posed time constraints, as these individuals are often busy. Therefore, organizing face-to-face interviews with all participants within a limited time frame proved exceedingly challenging. Secondly, while the number of interviews conducted by the researcher in this study offers insights, it might not be comprehensive enough to capture all the nuances of the results. The author initially planned to conduct 12 interviews during the research design stage. However, as explained earlier, difficulties in coordinating with interviewees reduced this to 8 interviews. Nonetheless, since the quality of qualitative research is not primarily determined by the number of participants,[10] the author believes that the research results are still valid.

## References

Bailey CA (2018) A guide to qualitative field research, 3rd edn. SAGE, London

Bos KVD (2020) Empirical legal research: a primer. Edward Elgar Publishing, Cheltenham

Leeuw FL and Schmeets H (2016) Empirical legal research: a guidance book for lawyers, legislators and regulators. Edward Elgar Publishing

Mack N, Woodsong C, Macqueen KM, Guest G and Namey E (2005) Qualitative research methods: a data collector's field guide. Family Health International, North Carolin

Oxford Analytica (2017) Vietnam's growing middle class will test Hanoi. https://www.emerald.com/insight/content/doi/10.1108/OXAN-DB219742/full/html. Accessed 20 Mar 2025

Safary WM and Rosario AH (2022) Introduction to qualitative research in the Asian context. In: Safary WM and Rosario AH (eds) The sage handbook of qualitative research in the Asian context. SAGE, London

[10] It has been noted that qualitative research provides an opportunity for in-depth study. Because qualitative research deals with complex issues, it is not primarily driven by numbers. It gives preference to in-depth exploration instead of a wide coverage that is focused on a large number of research participants. See Safary and Rosario (2022, p. 5).

# Chapter 9
# Conclusion

Online P2P lending has emerged as a new source of small funding in recent years in Vietnam. This lending model can serve as a useful source of micro and/or small funds, by helping to bridge the credit gap that conventional banks often hesitate to fill. However, the online P2P lending scheme poses risks for major participants, especially lenders involved in this type of lending.

The Vietnamese government recently announced its intention to develop a pilot program for P2P lending. However, the research conducted for this book finds that the significant challenges associated with P2P lending, particularly the difficulties faced by platform service providers in diversifying the risks borne by lenders, create hurdles for the government in formulating regulations specifically applicable for the lending business. Upon examining various financing schemes and approaches in Vietnam, this book has identified a range of issues. Among these, a critical issue is the unsatisfactory diversification of lender risks, despite these schemes and approaches being designed with positive objectives, such as promoting financial inclusion or supporting economic growth. This issue seems to be common among other developing countries where the demand for small finance is expanding.[1] It becomes apparent that there is a need for financial schemes that effectively address the issue of unsatisfactory diversification of lender risks. However, it appears that the robust and safe implementation of such schemes is being hindered by the absence of sufficient or desirable regulatory frameworks. One major reason for this lack could be the widespread use of the Internet before Vietnam and other developing countries could establish sophisticated and detailed regulations applicable to small finance and the solicitation of investments from the general public.

The book investigates how integrating features that are likely to be useful in addressing the issue of unsatisfactory diversification of lender risk could potentially

[1] As mentioned in Sect. 1.2, the diversification of risk borne by lenders in P2P lending schemes has been examined by legal scholars across various jurisdictions, and this issue seems to be common among other developing countries, such as Laos, Myanmar, and the Philippines.



Y. H. Nguyen, *Regulating Peer-to-Peer Lending in Vietnam*,
https://doi.org/10.1007/978-981-96-9505-8_9

benefit the participants of the P2P lending scheme in Vietnam. These features have been derived by referencing a mutual funding scheme. The book clarifies that by introducing specific features of a mutual funding scheme, with necessary adjustments, the issue of inadequate risk diversification for lenders can be considerably resolved. These features entail the establishment of a collective pool for lending, where contributors collectively share both profits and losses. In this scheme, professional managers undertake key tasks such as borrower assessment, lending decisions, and borrower monitoring.

The introduction of such features can benefit not only lenders, by enhancing the diversification of risks borne by lenders, but also other stakeholders, including borrowers and platform service providers. Specifically, for borrowers, stabilizing the risks borne by lenders could potentially increase the opportunities for individuals with lower creditworthiness to access the lending scheme. Additionally, a larger pool of funds could enhance accessibility to financing and potentially increase individual borrowing limits. Moreover, while professional management of lending may reduce the opportunity for borrowers to turn their businesses around, it could also prevent the tragedy of borrowers overextending themselves to the point where recovery becomes impossible. As for platform service providers, the use of professional management would be useful for the effective and secure operation of the lending scheme. As a result, there is a need for regulations to ensure platform service providers have the necessary qualifications. This would guarantee their ability to implement professional management effectively.

The thesis further proposes a new contractual scheme between multiple investors and a platform service provider to facilitate the establishment of collective pools for lending. These pools can be established either jointly by the lenders or by both the lenders and the platform service provider, where all involved parties contribute money. These contributions can be made either through a single multiparty contract among all the lenders, or among all the lenders and the provider, or through multiple one-to-one contracts between individual lenders and the provider. In one possible scheme, the money contributed to the pool remains under the joint ownership of all contributors. In another, either the provider or a party designated by the provider holds the ownership, while contributors retain beneficial interests. Alternatively, in a different scheme, the provider or a party designated by the provider manages the funds, while ownership remains with each individual contributor. These are examples of schemes that could be chosen, and it is possible that other viable options exist. In all such schemes, regardless of their specific structure, no individual contributor can use or rescind the contributed money at their discretion. Presumably, the utilization of the pool's funds is managed by the service provider or a fund manager appointed by the service provider. In substance, the pool becomes the lender in every lending transaction to borrowers. This is regardless of the formal legal structure, where either the pool itself, its manager, or the contributors collectively may be recognized as the lender. The profit and loss of the fund are jointly attributed to the contributors, yet they are allocated to individual contributors on a periodic basis. It is evident that this contractual scheme is useful in soliciting investments from the general public for small lending businesses in Vietnam.

The book emphasizes the need for regulations to mitigate significant risks involved in establishing collective pools by soliciting public investments and subsequently maintaining them. From an investor's perspective, those solicited to contribute to collective lending pools will likely expect platform service providers to implement measures that limit their contingent liabilities and potential losses. It is reasonably presumed that the typical terms and conditions of a small loan agreement well reflect the concerns of lenders. Therefore, the book suggests that referencing these typical terms and conditions can be highly beneficial when preparing the terms and conditions applicable to a collective pool for lending. The responsibility for preparing these terms and conditions should be undertaken by legal practitioners. In addition, from the perspective of platform service providers, it is important to consider the legality and regulations applicable to the parties, which may be different entities or individuals, responsible for establishing a collective pool of funds, placing contributors' interests, and managing pooled funds.

The author examined Vietnam's regulations concerning the establishment and management of public funds by fund management companies, as well as the solicitation of investors for investment in securities through public offerings of fund certificates. As a result of this examination, the author found that platform service providers must meet complex and detailed requirements to be eligible for establishing and managing investment funds, and for soliciting lenders to contribute to a fund pool. The author concludes that unless more realistic and lenient regulations are introduced, these stringent requirements may pose significant challenges for platform service providers. Under the current regulations in Vietnam, interest in a fund for lending is not regulated as a security. Platform service providers may become eligible to solicit lenders, either through public offerings or private placements, establish a pool funded by lenders, and manage such a pool, only if the interest in a P2P lending fund is legally deemed a security and the providers adhere to the applicable regulations.

By drawing insights from the regulatory experiences of the United States and Japan in collective lending, investor solicitation, and the establishment and management of investment funds, the book suggests that Vietnam should regulate the interest in a collective pool for lending as a security. In addition, as a result of examining the regulatory experiences of the United States and Japan, the author identified that Vietnam should implement less stringent regulations compared to those applicable to conventional fund management and securities businesses. Such a change would enable platform service providers to legally engage in soliciting investors to contribute to a collective investment scheme for lending, establish funds for lending small loans, and manage such funds.

The original purpose of this book was to explore safer approaches in P2P lending for lenders, aimed at facilitating the sound development of the lending business in Vietnam. However, ultimately, the author has identified that such safer approaches can be found in two dimensions. On the one hand, there is a need to explore legal systems that ensure the safety and appropriateness of small lending provided by both professional and non-professional lenders. The book suggests that in formulating regulations for small lending businesses, Vietnam should impose licensing requirements on professional non-bank lenders conducting lending businesses, rather than on individual, non-professional peer lenders. Additionally, Vietnam should implement measures to protect the interests of borrowers, including (a) limiting interest rates and (b) preventing the seizure of assets necessary for maintaining a minimum standard of living. While these measures have been examined primarily for the purpose of promoting the soundness of P2P lending, it is very likely that they can be applicable to any kind of small lending.

The book further emphasizes the importance of thoroughly examining regulations for funding schemes, with objectives such as protecting the interests of investors and ensuring the appropriate disclosure of significant risks, among others. These schemes encompass not only conventional securities like stocks and bonds but also formats such as partnerships, silent partnerships, and mutual funds. Building on these findings, the book proposes possible solutions to adapt Vietnamese regulations to clarify the legality of collective lending through a common pool and to establish appropriate regulatory measures. This strategy is expected to foster the healthy development of this lending scheme in the country. The book specifically proposes the following solutions: (1) classifying the interests in a common pool for collective lending as securities; (2) mandating platform service providers to register their business with the competent authority (i.e., the State Securities Commission) to be eligible for engaging in interest placements; and (3) permitting platform service providers, only post-registration, to conduct public offerings or private placements of interests in collective pools in order to solicit both professional and non-professional investors for small lending.

This research primarily aims to identify legal solutions that can reduce or diversify the risks faced by lenders in Vietnam's P2P lending scheme. However, this research suggests that the lenders' risks inherent to the P2P lending scheme could be mitigated by transitioning to a collective lending scheme. On the other hand, it is anticipated that the collective lending scheme might introduce different risks. Yet, the book indicates that these risks could potentially be mitigated by adopting the experiences of jurisdictions with extensive experience in regulations for collective investments. The book intentionally excludes detailed measures for borrower protection, as this aspect falls outside the scope of the current study. Developing specific strategies for borrower protection represents a challenge that the author may explore in future work. Moreover, when examining the regulations of the United States and Japan, the author has become aware of the need to pay attention to the measures, such as guidelines, information provisions, and the provision of document forms, to nudge relevant businesses to employ fair and reasonable practices in soliciting potential investors. Since collecting detailed information about these practices and measures is difficult without becoming an insider of governmental agencies or law firms, thoroughly examining these aspects remains a future challenge for the author.

# Appendix A: List of Selected P2P Lending Platforms in Vietnam

 
Y. H. Nguyen, *Regulating Peer-to-Peer Lending in Vietnam*,
https://doi.org/10.1007/978-981-96-9505-8

| No. | P2P platform | Customer | Lending amount (VN₫) | Maturity | Interest rate | Collateral | Due diligence | Sharing/ limiting the risk | Provisional fund | Insurance | Secondary market |
|---|---|---|---|---|---|---|---|---|---|---|---|
| 1 | Huydong (Loanvi)2015 | SMEs | 30–100 million | 3–6–9–12 months | 10–25% per year | No | Yes | No | No | No | No |
| 2 | Trust Circle2016 | Self-selected groups of individuals | Depend on members | Depend on members | Depends on members | No | No | No | No | No | No |
| 3 | Tima2016 | Individuals | 5–500 million | 10–90 days | Depends on matching results | Depend on loan type | Lenders might do themselves | No | No | Yes | Yes |
| 4 | Vaymuon2017 | Individuals | 1–10 million | 7–45 days | 1.5% per month | No | Yes | No | No | Yes | No |
| 5 | Lendbiz2017 | Individuals<br><br>SMEs | Up to 300 million for individuals;100 million–1 billion for SMEs | 3–12 months | Depends on borrowers' credit score | No | Provided information and face-to-face meeting | No | No | Require individual borrowers | Yes |
| 6 | Mofin2017 | Individuals | 1–20 million | Up to 6 months | 19.8% per year | No | Yes | No | No | Might require | No |
| 7 | Eloan2017 | Individuals<br><br>SMEs | 1 million–5 billion | 1–24 months | Depends on borrowers' credit score | Might require | Yes | No | No | Might require | No |
| 8 | Cashwagon 2017 | Individuals | 1–10 million | 91–182 days | 8.1–12% per year | No | No | No | No | No | No |
| 9 | LinkBank2018 | Individuals | 1–10 million | 1–6 months | No information | No | No | No | No | No | No |
| 10 | Growth wealth<br><br>2018 (Temporarily closed) | Individuals SMEs | No information. | No information | 15–20% per year | No information | No information | No information | No information | No information | No information |

| | | | | | | | | | | | |
|---|---|---|---|---|---|---|---|---|---|---|---|
| 11 | Megalend 2018 (Temporarily closed) | No information | No information | No information | No information | No information | Yes | No information | No information | No information | No information |
| 12 | Vnvon2018 | Individuals, SMEs | 100 million–1 billion | 10–90 days | Up to 20% | No | Yes | No | No | Yes | No |
| 13 | InterLoan2018 | Individuals | 1–70 million | 1–6 months | Up to 19% per year | No | Yes | No | No | No | No |
| 14 | Fiin Credit2018 | Individuals | Loans in cash: up to 50 million; Consumer loans: up to 100 million | Up to 30 days | 18–20% per year | Platform guarantees | Using cookies to collect information. from users' devices | No | No | No | Lenders can sell loans partly or fully |
| 15 | Finizi2018 | Individuals | 0.8–1.3 million | 91–180 days | 19.8–72% per year | No | No | No | No | No | No |
| 16 | Robocash2018 | Individuals | 3.5–10 million | 3–6 months | Up to 18.3% per year | No | No | No | No | No | No |
| 17 | Lendbox2018 | Individuals<br>Households | Individual: 1–10 million;Household: up to 100 million | 7–28 days | 18% per year | No | No | No | No | No | No |
| 18 | Vdong 2018 | Individuals | Up to 5 million | 15 days | No information | No | Yes | No | No | No | No |
| 19 | Viet Than Tai 2018 | Individuals | 1–10 million | No information | No information | No | No | No | No | No | No |
| 20 | Oneclickmoney 2018 | Individuals | 1–10 million | Up to 3 months | 2.1% per day | No | No | No | No | No | No |
| 21 | Cash Money 2018 | Individuals | 1–10 million | 10–30 days | 2% per day | No | No | No | No | No | No |
| 22 | Tietkiemonline2019 | Individuals | 1–20 million | No infor. | 8–16% per year | Yes | No | No | No | No | No |

(*continued*)

(continued)

| No. | P2P platform | Customer | Lending amount (VN₫) | Maturity | Interest rate | Collateral | Due diligence | Sharing/ limiting the risk | Provisional fund | Insurance | Secondary market |
|---|---|---|---|---|---|---|---|---|---|---|---|
| 23 | Vaydi2019 | Individuals | 1–5 million | 91–120 days | 18% per year | No | No | No | No | No | No |
| 24 | Cash242019 | Individuals | Up to 15 million | 3 months | 0.94% per day | No | No | No | No | No | No |
| 25 | Cash VN2019 | Individuals | Up to 10 million | Depends on borrower's credit score | 18.5% per year | No | Yes | No | No | No | No |
| 26 | Ucash 2019 | Individuals | 1–10 million | 7–150 days | 2.1% per day | No | No | No | No | No | No |
| 27 | Erig 2019 | SMEs | 10 million–1 billion | 10–90 days | 12–20% per year | The owners of enter-prises guarantee | Yes | No | No | No | No |
| 28 | Doctor Dong 2019 | Individuals | 0.5–10 million | 3–12 months | 12–20% per year | Yes | No | No | No | No | No |
| 29 | Oncredit 2019 | Individuals | 0.5–10 million (no collateral);Up to 500 million (collateral) | Up to 30 days (no collateral); Up to 60 months (collateral) | 1.56% per day | Yes | Using cookies to collect information. from user's devices | No | No | No | No |
| 30 | Money Bank 2019 | Individuals | 1–10 million | 7–30 days | 1.75% per day | No | No | No | No | No | No |
| 31 | Senmo 2019 | Individuals | 0.5–10 million | 10–30 days | 1.85% per day | No | No | No | No | No | No |
| 32 | Avay 2019 | Individuals | 10–70 million | 12–36 months | 2.33–5% per month | No | Using cookies to collect information from users' devices | No | No | Optional | No |

| | | | | | | | | | | | |
|---|---|---|---|---|---|---|---|---|---|---|---|
| 33 | Vamo 2019 | Individuals | 0.5–10 million | Up to 30 days | 20% per year | No | No | No | No | No | No |
| 34 | Uvay 2019 | Individuals | 1.5–10 million | 15 days | 0.67% per day | No | No | No | No | No | No |
| 35 | Tamo 2019 | Individuals | 0.25–15 million | 90–180 days | 12–20% per year | No | No | No | No | No | No |
| 36 | VayVND 2019 | Individuals | 0.5–3 million | No information | No information | No | Using cookies to collect information from user's devices | No | No | No | No |
| 37 | Monily | Individuals | 1 million–10 billion | 7–90 days | 1–1.2% per day | No | No | No | No | No | No |
| 38 | Akulaku | Individuals | 2–8 million | No information | No information | No information | No information | No information | No information | No information | No information |
| 39 | Ivay | Individuals | 10–200 million | 30 days | 1.17–2.9% per month | No | No | No | No | Yes | No |
| 40 | BaGang | Individuals | Up to 4 million | Up to 30 days | No infor. | No infor. | No infor. | No infor. | No infor. | No infor. | No infor. |

(*continued*)

(continued)

| No. | P2P platform | Customer | Lending amount (VN₫) | Maturity | Interest rate | Collateral | Due diligence | Sharing/ limiting the risk | Provisional fund | Insurance | Secondary market |
|---|---|---|---|---|---|---|---|---|---|---|---|
| 41 | Sieudong | Individuals | 0.5–10 million | 3–6 months | Up to 30% per year | No | Using cookies to collect information from user's devices | No | No | No | No |
| 42 | Vaytien a-z | Individuals | 1.5–100 million | 3—12 months | 3.54–6.21% per month | Depends on loan type | No | No | No | No | No |
| 43 | Credit Now | Individuals | Depends on credit score (up to 50 million) | Depends on credit score (up to 48 months) | Depends on credit score (up to 45% per year) | No | Yes | No | No | No | Yes |
| 44 | ATMonline | Individuals | Up to 10 million | 3–6 months | 12% per year | No | No | No | No | No | No |

| | | | | | | | | | | | |
|---|---|---|---|---|---|---|---|---|---|---|---|
| 45 | Vcash | Individuals | 1–20 million | No information | No information | No information | No information | No information | No information | No information | No information |
| 46 | WeMoney | Individuals | 1–50 million | 10–90 days | No information | Yes | No | No | No | No | No |

*Note*: The author collected information on the websites of P2P lending companies and the website of the national business registration portal: https://dangkykinhdoanh.gov.vn/en/Pages/default.aspx

[Light blue box]: No registered information on the national business registration portal

Name: P2P lending platform with foreign capital contribution

# Appendix B: Responsible Conduct of Research

**Responsible Conduct of Research**
Drafted date: March 31, 2015
Last update: May 14, 2021

## Introduction

This learning material is a digest version compiling several different modules to provide you with means for developing a good understanding of "responsible conduct of research" so that you can carry out focused, high-quality research activities. If you are interested in learning more about each topic with detailed descriptions and case examples, read "Responsible Conduct of Research: Fundamentals" also provided by eAPRIN.

## *I. What Is Responsible Conduct of Research?*

Specific practices that can be considered responsible conduct of research vary from discipline to discipline; however, **honesty, accuracy, efficiency, and objectivity** are four important values that bind all researchers together.

The following sections will discuss generally accepted standards regarding responsible conduct of research in the academic domain, including formal regulations set by the national government and informal guidelines set by academic societies.



Y. H. Nguyen, *Regulating Peer-to-Peer Lending in Vietnam*,
https://doi.org/10.1007/978-981-96-9505-8

### 1.1. The Rules of the Road

Responsible conduct of research means the carrying out of research activities in such a manner that meets **the expectations of both the scientific community and society in general**. Researchers should learn about responsible conduct of research to find out what practices meet these expectations and how to act when their behavior may conflict with some of the complex rules for responsible methods of work.

However, it is also important to note that responsible conduct of research is not always well defined. Some are defined through law and institutional policies that must be followed. Others are set out in nonbinding codes and guidelines that should be heeded. Still other responsible practices are commonly accepted by most researchers but not inscribed anywhere.

### 1.2. The Rules for Autonomy for Scientists

Researchers are expected to behave autonomously as individuals or as a part of the scientific community. For example, "On Being a Scientist: Responsible Conduct in Research" (3rd edition),[1] a 2009 booklet published by the National Academy of Sciences in the United States, describes in its preface:

> The scientific enterprise is built on a foundation of **trust**. Society trusts that scientific research results are an honest and accurate reflection of a researcher's work. Researchers equally trust that their colleagues have gathered data carefully, have used appropriate analytic and statistical techniques, have reported their results accurately, and have treated the work of other researchers with respect. When this trust is misplaced and the professional standards of science are violated, researchers are not just personally affronted—they feel that the base of their profession has been undermined. This would impact the relationship between science and society.

Also, the Science Council of Japan (SCJ) formulated the "Statement: Code of Conduct for Scientists" in 2006 as baseline requirements common to all academic disciplines. This statement was developed in order for scientists to gain the public trust and the mandate of the Japanese people, advance independent and autonomous scientific research and promote the healthy development of science, based on the autonomous work of scientists. In 2013, the document was revised (Statement: Code of Conduct for Scientists [2013]).[2]

### 1.3. Responsibilities for Research Institutions

Research institutions such as universities and research centers are expected **to develop organizational mechanisms for ensuring adequate research conduct by promoting effective initiatives** and **to responsibly involve themselves in the prevention of misconduct by creating an environment that discourages misconduct**. To meet such demands, these institutions are required to clearly define managerial responsibilities and establish accountable mechanisms such as organizations that are autonomous and to promote initiatives to prevent missteps before they occur. Key points of the "**Guidelines for Providing Appropriate Responses to Misconduct in Research Activities**"[3] by the Ministry of Education, Culture, Sports, Science and Technology (MEXT) hereinbelow, "Guidelines" include:

- Increasing researchers' awareness through periodical research ethics education
- Appointing a research ethics education officer for each division
- Developing institutional rules for storage and disclosure of research data and practices based thereon
- Developing institutional rules and mechanisms for investigation of (specified) misconduct and establishing an office responsive to whistleblowers, and
- Setting of procedures for appropriate execution and management of budgets for investigating conflicts of interest, etc.

Further, research institutions are responsible for supervising their personnel to ensure compliance with rules for safety so that hazardous materials are used in conformity with legal and regulatory provisions and other applicable rules. Moreover, to conduct research involving human or animal subjects, institutions are responsible for developing mechanisms to ensure compliance with guidelines and the like set by the national government and for providing their researchers, including students, with appropriate learning opportunities.

## *II. Misconduct in Research Activities*

It is important to know what constitutes "misconduct in research activities" (hereinbelow, "Misconduct"), how to report it if you come across it, and how institutions should handle it.

### 2.1. What Is Misconduct in Research Activities?

#### 2.1.1. Definitions

In Japan, the Guidelines* [3] define misconduct in research activities as "an act that contradicts researchers' ethics, distorts the essence or the spirits of research activities and publication of research results," and "impedes normal scientific communication among the members of the scientific community."

Regardless of discipline, Misconduct in the scope of the Guidelines includes fabrication, falsification, and plagiarism relating to data, study findings, and the like present in research results published in a paper submitted to academic journals, caused by a willful act or gross negligence of due care that must have been exercised by an ordinary researcher. The Guidelines call these acts ***Specified Misconduct***. For the sake of simplicity, we will call it *Misconduct* here with the letter "M" capitalized.

- **Fabrication** means making up data, research results, and the like.
  US federal regulations define Misconduct as involving also the preparation of records of research or study that did not take place and making a report of such research or study through a proposal of a research grant, progress report, or the like. The Japanese Guidelines clearly do not state such acts fall under its scope of Misconduct.
- **Falsification** means manipulating research materials, equipment, or processes, or changing data or results obtained from research activities so that the research is not accurately represented. For example, altering an image to change its meaning or eliminating aspects that do not fit the conclusion a researcher is trying to prove is obviously Misconduct (falsification of an image).
  Also, in trying to prove a hypothesis that the researcher has presented, deleting or editing data that seem to fall outside the range of expected results may also be considered Misconduct (inappropriate data selection), in the sense that distorts test results and leads to an incorrect conclusion.
- **Plagiarism** is the appropriation of another researcher's ideas, analysis processes, data, results, manuscripts, or words without obtaining consent from the researcher or giving appropriate credit. Plagiarism is discussed in detail in <u>VI. Handling of Prior Research: Avoiding the Determination of Plagiarism</u> below.

Misconduct in research activities excludes simple, honest mistakes or differences of opinion, e.g., different interpretations of data.

* The Guidelines were originally issued in August 2006 and titled "Guidelines for Responding to Misconduct in Research Activities" by MEXT, and revised in August 2014 and issued as the decision of the Minister of Education, Culture, Sports, Science and Technology. The effective date of the revised Guidelines is April 1, 2015.

### 2.1.2. Actual Scenarios of Misconduct in Research Activities

When we face a Misconduct case, should we consider it exceptional, or one of many? For example, the <u>Office of Research Integrity</u> in the United States received an average of 198 allegations per year between 1992 and 2007.[4] However, there may be many more unreported cases.

In Japan in 2004, a survey was conducted, led by the Science Council of Japan (SCJ). Out of the 838 academic societies that responded to the survey, 27 answered Yes when asked whether a case of fabrication, falsification, or plagiarism had been brought up in meetings of boards of directors or editorial meetings in the past five years.[5] In the majority of cases, discussion had been concerned with deficiencies in procedures or organizational systems for handling suspected cases of Misconduct.

Many acclaimed international academic journals set their own guidelines for misconduct. For example, the Institute of Electrical and Electronics Engineers (IEEE) provides a <u>clear message</u> on its website to its editors, authors, and reviewers concerning issues of plagiarism and other misconduct.

### 2.2. Questionable Research Practices

Misconduct may represent the extreme end of a continuum of behavior, with perfectly responsible research practices representing the other end. Between the two extremes are varying degrees of more or less inappropriate behaviors, collectively termed "**questionable research practice (QRP)**."[6]

Examples of QRPs are:

- Failing to retain significant research data for a reasonable period
- Conferring or requesting authorship on the basis of a specialized service or contribution that is not significantly related to the research reported in the paper and
- Submitting the same manuscript simultaneously to more than one journal (duplicate submission)

## *III. Data Handling*

Data form the foundation of research. Accordingly, the **integrity of data** is paramount.

The first step in good data management is designing an appropriate **research plan** that ensures the collection of meaningful and unbiased data. Doing so is not wasteful of resources, including manpower or funding, and will lead to the protection of your human and animal subjects.

The next steps, proper data collection, retention, and sharing conforming to the research plan are also vital. **Data sharing** makes data available to others for validation. If data are not recorded in a way that allows others to confirm findings, their integrity could be called into question.

In some circumstances, however, data must be withheld from others rather than shared, for example, when securing the **intellectual property** inherent in new inventions, protecting the confidentiality of **human research subjects**, and addressing national security considerations.

### 3.1. Data

Different disciplines have different notions of what constitutes data. However, proper data management is required throughout the research lifecycle, from protocol development to the archiving or disposal of research materials at the end of a project. For data handling, researchers must be prepared to address questions that can arise at any stage.

### 3.2. Legal and Regulatory Compliance

Researchers must comply with **all relevant laws, regulations, and guidelines**. Communication with others in the research community is vital in order to learn the accepted practices and to develop new procedures, if necessary. Noncompliance may result in substantial fines or other punishment.

You are expected to observe, for example:

1. National government statutes and regulations, local government regulations, and administrative guidelines at the national or local government level
2. Certification standards of private bodies (specialized agencies)
3. Policies and rules set by one's institution
4. Ethical standards set by one's profession
5. Social norms

**Compliance** requirements constitute **the minimum standards** for responsible conduct which every scholar must not fall under. Among the above-listed examples, numbers 1 through 3 relate to these. However, only respecting these compliance requirements is not enough for responsible conduct. **Observing ethical standards accepted by specialists of the relevant discipline** is equally important to be a responsible scholar **(your integrity as a researcher rests on it)**.

#### 3.2.1. Privacy and Confidentiality

Data protection requires rules about **who can access information and under what conditions**, as it sometimes involves privacy issues and statutes for protecting personal information. A specific statute that applies to data handling is different depending on **the nature of the data themselves and many other factors**.

Personal identity data, such as names and addresses, are protected by law, and information relating to individuals' health and financial situations are also protected. In Japan, such data are **subject to protection under the law as personal information if they can identify the individual**. Even if the data per se cannot identify a specific individual, if the data "**can be easily consulted with other information and whereby a specific individual can be identified,**" such data are also considered personal information subject to protection by law.

Rules that apply to data protection are different depending on the country. If you conduct your work outside Japan, be aware of the relevant regulations and standards applicable to the particular country you are in.

#### 3.2.2. Legal and Regulatory Compliance in Collecting and Using Data

Many laws, regulations, and guidelines require that researchers obtain permission to collect and use data before beginning a project. Factors that must be considered include: (1) the kind of data to be collected; (2) the origin of the data; and (3) the purposes for which they are collected, or used. You are always encouraged to make use of the expertise of your institution in order to be certain exactly which rules apply. Of particular note, to collect data relating to human subjects, your institution may require you to complete prescribed procedures such as an ethical review. Thus, you should check your institution's policy on data collection in advance of a project.

## 3.3. Data Collection

### 3.3.1. Data Selection

Data selection consists of the process of determining appropriate **data types** and **sources** as well as suitable **instruments** for collection of data. The data selection process generally is unique to each discipline, and is driven primarily by the nature of the project, prior research, and accessibility of data sources.

Establishing clear standards for data selection **in advance of** a project can help to prevent improper data collection practices such as the exclusion of data that do not fit the hypothesis.

### 3.3.2. How Much Data Should Be Collected?

Different disciplines have different standards for how data should be collected and what constitutes acceptable rigor for the reliability and validity of results. This is one reason why a careful prior review of the up-to-date collection of existing literature on a topic is imperative when designing a research plan. To ensure the development of a scientifically and ethically appropriate study design, it is essential to rely on authentic procedures.

You should always consider seeking specialized methodological expertise any time you are uncertain of your abilities with respect to data selection or other related issues. In general, it is unethical to start a research project if you do not have sufficient methodological skills to complete the relevant work, and, you may jeopardize the scientific integrity of the results obtained in such a research project.

### 3.3.3. Collection Methods

Data collection is the process of gathering and measuring variables of interest in an accepted, systematic fashion.

Data collection methods vary by discipline and data type, but the emphasis on ensuring accurate collection remains the same.

Consequences that can arise from improper data collection include:

- The inability to answer questions regarding the objective of the research accurately
- The inability to repeat and validate the study
- Inaccurate findings
- Wasted resources
- Misleading other researchers to pursue fruitless studies
- Misleading public authorities or private companies in poor decision-making
- Causing harm to human and animal subjects

The degree of impact from faulty data collection also varies by discipline and the content of the project. However, effective methods make the detection of errors easier. As in the case of data selection, it is critical that researchers have sufficient methods and skills to collect data properly and all members of the project team are well-informed of these methods and skills. If they do not have it themselves, outside experts should be brought in to review procedures before, during, and after data collection.

For some projects, it may be appropriate to visit the sites where data is collected so that the process can be observed directly. Also, in any project, a regular review and audit of records should be performed to verify that data collection is proceeding according to the prescribed procedures.

## 3.4. Data Management

### 3.4.1. Storage and Protection

Research data must be stored in a secure and safe place at all times both during a research project and after it ends. For this reason, reliable security policies and procedures should be established, taking into account the kinds of data to be stored, respectively.

Also, for information protection, three core elements must be kept in mind: **confidentiality, availability,** and **integrity**.

### 3.4.2. Confidentiality

To ensure the security of confidentiality, it is important to limit information access and disclosure to authorized users and to prevent disclosures to or access by unauthorized ones. In any research field involving human subjects especially, respecting the rights, dignity, and privacy of the subjects is paramount.

In Japan, secure management obligations are imposed on researchers' institutions by statutes and ethical guidelines for the protection of personal information to prevent such information and data from being disclosed. In addition, several ethical guidelines impose confidentiality obligations on principal investigators (PIs) and researchers.

### 3.4.3. Availability

While protection from illegitimate access must always be important, **the greater risk is that the data might become unavailable to anyone**. Therefore, measures such as protection from risks like fire, water, or other environmental damage, or common technical failures like hard disk malfunctions, must be considered. Primary resources, collections, and archives must be preserved in a secure and safe manner appropriate to the material. Adequate records of what is being stored, and where, can enable data to be located quickly when needed, and prevent future loss.

### 3.4.4. Integrity

**Integrity** refers to the trustworthiness of information. It includes the concept that your data have not been changed inappropriately after having been recorded, whether by accident or deliberate misconduct. It also requires that the data actually came from the person or entity that the user believes it did and did not come from a third party in error.

Integrity can even include the integrity of data recording, the notion that the person or entity in question entered the correct information. It is essential to ensure that the record reflects the actual circumstances and under the same circumstances would generate identical data.

A key way to promote data integrity, whether storing or archiving data manually or electronically, is **configuration management**. This involves keeping track of data on all the media and formats used during different stages of the project. For example, in an oral history project, the raw data could consist of a digital recording, which is then transcribed to a digital written document. This is then excerpted for use in a print publication. Configuration management involves keeping track of all these parts and upgrading the data to newer media or formats as necessary during the life of a particular project.

### 3.4.5. Retention and Disposal

Data handling procedures should describe **when**, **how**, and **who** may handle data for **storage**, **retrieval**, **disclosure**, **archive**, and **disposal** purposes.

How long should the data be kept after a project is over? The answer usually depends on:

- The nature of the project, including potential ongoing interest in or need for the data
- Costs of maintaining the data over the long run
- Contracts with or guidelines set by the research sponsor

In Japan, there are no clear requirements for how long research records are to be maintained. Yet, these days, submission rules at many scientific journals require submitted manuscripts to be maintained for a prescribed period after publication. There may also be institutional rules for how long those records are to be maintained.

Retaining data in paper files or as electronic media for a long time after a project's end, however, can increase the chances of unauthorized access. Risks can also increase if institutional management rules for disposal and archival storage of data are ignored when researchers leave the project or the institution or they themselves pass away.

#### 3.4.6. Disposal of Data

Disposal of confidential data requires a great degree of care and technical expertise to ensure that they cannot be retrieved or reconstructed by a third party.

If researchers lack the required expertise and tools, appropriate technical resources from their organization should be sought or a third-party disposal contractor hired. Disposal of data recorded in non-electronic media such as those stored in lab notebooks or paper files can also be requested of the disposal contractor, the same as the case of electronic media.

### 3.5. Data Analysis

#### 3.5.1. Statistical Examination

Data analysis refers to the process of systemically applying statistical or logical techniques to describe, illustrate, condense, and evaluate data. The method of analysis is determined by the approach taken in the data collection and the type of actual data. In data analysis, the most important requirement is the need for the relevant skills.

#### 3.5.2. Identifying Analysis Methods (Before Data Acquisition)

As with data selection criteria, the selection of statistical analysis methods should always **precede data collection**. If delayed until later in the research process, this may increase the risk that analytic choices will be made based on which method produces the most favorable results.

Disciplines have developed accepted practices for data analysis. If one uses an unconventional approach, it is crucial to state clearly that this is being done, explain why, and demonstrate how this new and possibly untested method of analysis is being used, as well as how it differs from more traditional methods.

Whether statistical or nonstatistical methods are used, researchers should be clear (both to themselves and to their readers or reviewers) about the **limitations and possible biases of their methods**. Failure to understand or acknowledge data analysis issues can compromise the integrity of their research.

### 3.6. Publication and Reporting

Publication in scientific journals or reporting to academic conferences is the process of preparing research findings and disseminating them to the scholarly community to make the research results open to criticism. Reporting research findings with exaggeration is never to be tolerated, as it will contribute to overall loss of public trust in the enterprise of science and technology.

Problems relating to the integrity of data reporting and publication include:

- Misrepresentation of data
- Fabrication or falsification of data
- Arbitrary data analysis to obtain a significant result
- Inadequate evaluation of prior research to play up the significance of one's research
- Misleading, biased discussion of observations
- Reporting conclusions not supported by data
- Failure to disclose conflicts of interest
- Plagiarism
- Irrational attribution or non-attribution of authorship

### 3.7. Ownership, Sharing, and Disclosure of Data

Under Japanese law, "ownership" is established only on tangible objects* which have concrete or actual shape, thus it is not established on information which does not have a shape. However, some information, including intellectual properties such as patent and trade secrets, can be owned exclusively on special provisions of statutes. In addition, rules of a research institution may stipulate that information such as research results belong to the institution. As such, in the following, the word *ownership* or *property right* is used in the context of information that is exclusively owned or belongs to a particular person or entity.

* These days, a Material Transfer Agreement (MTA) is often executed for the handling of tangible objects used in research such as cell lines, mice, and vectors.

#### 3.7.1. Ownership Issues

"Ownership" of data generally means **a researcher possesses and has responsibility for information**. It covers a range of **rights and obligations** with respect to data collection and sharing. Information control is subject to restrictions both by technical capabilities to access, create, modify, or package it, and by legal/regulatory constraints.

Rights and obligations that a researcher has in relationship to their ownership of data depend on the data type (for example, health, education, or financial) as well as on the facility where the data are collected. Rights and obligations may also be governed by a "data-use agreement" for a particular study, which sets limits on how the data are handled, including whether they can be transferred to third parties or disposed of at the end of a project.

All researchers and any other members of a research team should make sure that they have fully understood the content of their institution's policies and rules for data ownership.

In Japan, research institutions (such as universities, research centers, and hospitals) often have institutional working regulations and other rules concerning intellectual properties in which **ownership of information** is stipulated. These rules often include provisions regarding "information relating to research results" or "information obtained in the performance of one's duty" in which matters relating to data ownership are stipulated. In addition, some institutions may require written consent such as by "oath" at the time of employment or participation in a project in order to ensure that data ownership belongs to the institution.

Postdoctoral fellows involved in research, for example, might work under the mistaken belief that they own the data they collect. It is important, therefore, to know that the rights to the data obtained by a person who is affiliated with or employed by a university are owned by the university.

Also, rules of universities often stipulate that, when a faculty member conducts a research project under a contract with the university, i.e., as assignment from the university, or is involved in a research project using the university's facility, staff, or funding (this case is also deemed working for hire or work as an employee), the university owns the rights to the data. As for patent rights, an individual employee who is the inventor has the right to obtain a patent, but the university's rules for employee inventions often stipulate that said right is transferred to the university.

If there is a third party sponsor under a collaborative research agreement or a sponsored (contract) research agreement, stipulations regarding intellectual property rights may be included in an agreement with the sponsor or the research funding agency.

In the case of government funded research, the university usually owns the data but often delegates the responsibility for data management to the **principal investigator, PI**. The PI then takes responsibility for data collection, recording, storage, retention, and disposal. When a paper which includes the data is published, the copyright is retained by the PI, who typically transfers it to a journal.

These days, many institutions such as universities and public research institutions lay out institutional rules that require their researchers not to bring data that the researchers do not have the ownership of into the institution's facilities and not to take research data that the institution has the ownership of out of the institution's facility.

In addition, you need to be fully aware that transnational movement, i.e., export or import, of research data may be in violation of legal provisions relating to export control applicable to the relevant countries, and, if convicted, you may be charged with criminal penalties.

#### 3.7.2. Sharing and Disclosure of Data

Sharing of information benefits the research enterprise of the scientific community: Other researchers learn new techniques, gain new perspectives, and avoid repeating unfruitful experiments, thereby not wasting social resources.

Sharing benefits individual researchers as it can lead to collaborations. Yet some information should not be released because of privacy and human subject protection concerns. Also, releasing some data may potentially cause harm to the society.

In addition, releasing unpublished data at an early stage of research can jeopardize a researcher's ability to develop the research based thereon and their advantage to be the first to publish the finding. Data that could lead to a patent also should not be shared before completing certain procedures. However, it can be said that researchers are generally expected to share raw data after publication as long as doing so does not create an undue financial burden.

Researchers may face the dilemma of balancing between two opposing needs, which are a willingness to share data in order to facilitate scientific progress, and an obligation to sponsors, collaborators, and subjects to preserve and protect data from disclosure.

## *IV. Rules for Collaborative Research*

Today, collaborative and multidisciplinary research and cooperation with the industry have increasing importance in research activities, leading to new research fields, expanding the range and depth of research, and presenting innovative approaches to solving conventional problems. As the trend toward more interdisciplinary research continues, researchers will be required to learn theories and concepts or ideas beyond the boundaries of their own expertise.

### 4.1. What Is Collaborative Research?

Traditionally, **collaboration** refers to a cooperative relationship within the same discipline, either within one institution or among different institutions. These days, multidisciplinary collaboration across multiple disciplines has been increasing.

It is important to note that, in order to ensure that such efforts achieve their research goals, it is necessary to **establish and maintain good communication among collaborators and participating institutions**. To this end, **modes of communication suitable for each case must be established**.

## 4.2. What Are Some of the Potential Problems with Collaborative Research?

### 4.2.1. Differences in Understanding Among Researchers

In some cases, researchers participating in a collaborative project have different understandings of what range of budget and data would be shared, how materials are managed, and so forth. In order to avoid such a situation, it is important to have **formal, written, mutual agreements through the administrative offices at each respective university**.

### 4.2.2. Differences in Styles of Research

One collaborator may believe that peer-reviewed papers should be short and should provide a limited amount of data. Another might suggest that more data should be collected and the "story" of the research should be more fully developed before anything is published. Such differences in approach can appear among collaborators in the same or different disciplines. The discipline-specific norms can also influence decisions regarding who should be an author on a paper. In many disciplines, individuals must contribute substantially to the intellectual process of the research before being included. In other disciplines, **co-authorship** might be granted if an individual participated in doing the research at any level.

Also, **technical jargon** exists within a discipline, across disciplines, and within subdisciplines. It can be challenging for researchers to use terminology that is understood across many disciplines.

To deal with these problems, it is critical to put everything on the table for discussion, including what may seem like trivial questions **as early in the relationship as possible**. Many collaborative projects require a **PI** who leads the entire project from this stage. The PI is responsible for the handling of the research grant, collection, and publication of data, and also for more individual levels, such as skill and ethical education of collaborative researchers, as the person who has the ultimate responsibility of the entire project.

### 4.2.3. Differences Between University and Industry Attitudes

When university and industry researchers work together on projects, they **must agree on how the data and resultant materials will be shared or owned**. For example, in a private company, the data and outcome from research can have a potentially direct impact on profits and their other interests. Thus, additional consideration might be needed. In some cases, they might be withheld from publishing. Some universities do not permit the sponsor to hinder or delay the publication of data. Other universities might be willing to forgo some freedom in exchange for funding, access to industry ideas, and opportunities to train students in commercial research endeavors. However, it is important not to execute an agreement that indefinitely restricts publication of research matter.

## 4.3. Criteria for Determining the Termination or Continuation of a Collaboration

Completing a research project does not necessarily signify the end of a collaborative relationship. And the decision to terminate or continue may be predetermined at any time by the end of the funding interval. It can also be stipulated as **a policy** in a **Memorandum of Understanding** (MOU) at the start of collaborative research.

The likelihood of making a significant contribution to a field of study by continuing the project must be balanced by the desire of each collaborator to continue as well as the rationale and cost for continuing the collaboration. But, if there is an unexpected development at the stage that everyone has expected the end of the project as specified in the memorandum, it is also possible that the collaborators may invite new collaborators and circulate a **new memorandum** to restart the collaboration, if necessary.

### 4.3.1. Data Handling When Terminating Research

An important consequence of terminating a collaborative relationship is the need to clarify data ownership issues beyond the relationship. Another issue related to the results of collaboration that might need to be clarified would be an understanding or policy among collaborators on the allocation of credit in future publications.

These issues, including ownership of research results and **degrees of individual researchers' contributions**, should be thoroughly discussed to minimize misunderstandings and disagreements.

## 4.4. The Keys to Successful Collaborative Research

Several key components of a successful collaboration include:

1. **Communication first, second, and throughout**
2. **Discussing in advance who will do what, and understanding that the research may evolve**
3. **Discussing authorship in advance**
4. **Discussing data and material management in advance**
5. **Discussing intellectual properties in advance**
6. **Managing accountability for researchers responsibilities**
7. **Exchanging a memorandum describing policies for these issues**

## *V. Authorship*

The word *public* in English means "common" or "shared." The word **publication** derived from it has a meaning of making it available to the public or to be shared. Whatever the medium, the act of making words or ideas available to the public (publication) is one with certain social and ethical dimensions.

### 5.1. Responsibilities to Human Intellectual Assets

The accumulated corpus of human scientific knowledge contains statements that are both true and false. Knowledge grows slowly, advancing little by little, improving upon past errors. Discovering that a belief is false can also be considered progress.

Therefore, committing Misconduct such as fabrication, falsification, or plagiarism in the publication of research findings or other forms of **inappropriate research conduct** is an act of contaminating the scientific corpus with the inclusion of faulty knowledge.

### 5.2. Inappropriate Authorship

Typical examples of inappropriate behavior relating to **authorship** of a paper will be discussed in what follows. Including someone who does not meet the criteria for authorship among coauthors or excluding a person who meets the criteria from the list of coauthors are forms of inappropriate research conduct, and, in some cases, may even be deemed as *research misconduct*.

#### 5.2.1. Authorship by Authority

Authorship by authority refers to the cases where authority figures in universities or societies have used their status to become authors on a publication without doing the necessary work related to the publication's content. For example, **laboratory directors** might **either implicitly demand or permit their name be placed on each document** developed within their laboratory, without any substantial involvement in the work.

#### 5.2.2. Gift Authorship

Gift authorship refers to the instances where authorship credit is given to colleagues who did not make sufficient contribution to the research, but they need a certain number of published works to obtain a doctorate or they enjoy a close social relationship with the true authors.

#### 5.2.3. Political Authorship

Political authorship refers to situations where authorship credit is distributed to some individuals who did not make any significant contribution to relevant work. A typical example is to list individuals who are known as authority in the relevant field as coauthors so that the submissions can be easily accepted by the academic journals and get published. In many of these cases, these individuals do not know that their names are listed as co-authors.

#### 5.2.4. Ghost Authorship

Ghost authorship refers to the cases where **the individuals who actually wrote the paper do not show up in the authorship list**. Instead, those who were not involved in the project at all or only peripherally associated are included in the authorship list. This type of inappropriate conduct of research usually occurs when companies or organizations want to add credibility to a paper by recruiting the names of prominent researchers.

### 5.3. Order of Authors

Determining the order of authors on a publication can be a source of much conflict. Part of the reason is that in many disciplines, the **first author** is regarded as the most important one assuming that it is the person who made the most significant contribution to the project. However, in some research areas, the **last author** or the "**corresponding author**" may be regarded as the most important. Also, in some contexts, including situations in which the authors are listed alphabetically, the most important role might be that of the "corresponding author," who is the person most responsible for interacting with the journal editor and the reading audience.

Author order should be based on the discussion among the authors themselves as needed, taking into account the common practices of the relevant discipline. It is important to discuss the author order in addition to the prospective publication of article and the list of authors at an early stage of the research and make amendments as needed.

### 5.4. Redundant Publication and Self-Plagiarism

There are other types of inappropriate conduct of research related to authorship and publication practices. These include publishing the same, or similar, paper more than once.

**Redundant publication** (or duplicate publication) is "publication of a paper that overlaps **substantially** with one already published in print or electronic media."

The practice of reusing one's own work and passing it off as though it is a novel finding is sometimes called "**self-plagiarism**."

There are some appropriate justifications for **secondary publication**, but it usually requires some sort of disclosure in print and permission from the relevant journal editors of the first publication and the secondary publication.

Redundant publication (or duplicate publication) wastes valuable resources relating to publication such as the workloads of personnel and other costs, undue burden on reviewers and editors.

In some cases, when graduate student or junior researcher who has just received a doctorate submits a manuscript to a journal, the submission may be considered a redundant publication if a substantial portion of the manuscript overlaps the content of a published doctoral thesis. It is important to check the manuscript submission rules of the journal and have an extensive discussion with a supervisor in advance of the submission.

### 5.5. Fragmentation

Another way to inflate a CV is to divide its results so finely as to generate as many articles as possible. Such fragmentation has come to be called as "salami publication," which is an analogy to the thin slices of salami. In some cases, however, publishing manuscripts of such many fragmented pieces of research results may be permissible, if, and only if, there is a justifiable reason, and their relationship to each other is disclosed in print.

### 5.6. How to Make an Acknowledgment

The act of acknowledging someone in a publication, or presentation, can sometimes raise difficult issues. It is not always clear what kind of contribution warrants an acknowledgment; this often involves judgment and critical thinking. It is necessary to **obtain permission to be acknowledged from all acknowledged individuals**.

## *VI. Handling Prior Research: Avoiding the Determination of Plagiarism*

Plagiarism is one of three major forms of research Misconduct—the other two being fabrication and falsification. The American Historical Association states in its Statement on Standards of Professional Conduct,[7] "the best professional practice for avoiding a charge of plagiarism is always to be explicit, thorough, and generous in acknowledging one's intellectual debts."

### 6.1. Plagiarism

Plagiarism is Misconduct that can occur in any area of learning and scholarship. As discussed above, the Guidelines define plagiarism as follows:

> The appropriation of another researcher's ideas, analysis processes, data, results, manuscripts or words without obtaining consent from the researcher or giving appropriate credit.

### 6.2. Common Knowledge

When a certain piece of information is already known to the general public, the problem of plagiarism does not arise. Whether the information represents common knowledge depends on a number of factors, but especially on the readership (who the readers are of what is written). For example, if a student were to write a science paper and mention that the planet closest to the sun was Mercury, that student would not be expected to indicate the source for that information because the fact is considered common knowledge.

### 6.3. Summarizing and Paraphrasing

In support of their own research, academic authors typically cite the prior work of others. In doing so, they often describe what others have done: Some may cite a part of the manuscript as it is, and others may summarize its contents. At times, authors paraphrase some of the more relevant details of the previous research. Only when citing a part of the manuscript as it is do the authors need to identify the cited phrase by using quotation marks. However, a citation must always be added to indicate the source of the original material when citing a prior work.

In addition, some authors do not add a citation to identify the source of the original material. This case would be classified as **plagiarism**, for although they may be using their own words to convey **others' ideas, they have not *credited* the original source of the ideas**.

There are no **official** rules that define a minimum number of consecutive words that can be used from another source before the practice constitutes plagiarism.

You must keep in mind that a citation that identifies the source must be indicated as clearly as possible, in a manner where the readers can clearly identify the part that is the author's original ideas and the part that is cited from other materials. In some cases, simple indication of the source may *not* be considered an adequate citation.

## *VII. Responses and Procedures Relating to Misconduct in Research Activities*

Today, the emphasis on the responsibilities of individual researchers has been shifted, and each individual is not only expected to stay away from misconduct in research activities ("Misconduct") **but also expected to play a role in preventing others from committing Misconduct**. The "Guidelines for Providing Appropriate Responses to Misconduct in Research Activities" ("Guidelines") explained in *2.1. What is Misconduct in Research Activities?* (above) also focuses on the issues of "whistleblowing." Researchers are required to act very carefully when playing this role, since their decisions may have an extremely serious impact on the honor, social status, and the like, of themselves and that of other persons.

## 7.1. Methods and Procedures to Respond to Misconduct

### 7.1.1. A Report of Allegation

The Guidelines state that all relevant institutions (such as MEXT, universities, research institutions and funding agencies such as the Japan Science and Technology Agency [JST] and the Japan Society for the Promotion of Science [JSPS]) should provide appropriate measures to keep the identity of the whistleblower who attempts to expose Misconduct and details of their allegations confidential.

The following is an excerpt from the Guidelines discussing how allegations should be handled:

> 2 Handling allegations ((iv) to (viii) are omitted):
>
> (i) Allegations should be made directly to the research institution or body in question, by submitting a written document at reception or by phone, fax, e-mail or interview.
>
> (ii) As a general rule, institutions should only entertain allegations from **whistleblowers who disclose their own identity**, who can identify the accused researcher or group, **who can describe the alleged Misconduct in detail, and whose accusations are backed up on scientific and rational grounds**.
>
> (iii) Notwithstanding (ii), when a research institution or other body receives an anonymous allegation it may, depending on its nature, respond to the allegation as though the whistleblower had been identified by name.
>
> 3 Treatment of the whistleblower and the accused ((iii) and (iv) are omitted):
>
> (i) When receiving an allegation, the research institution or body in question **must take appropriate steps to keep the identity of the whistleblower and details of his or her allegations confidential** ... for instance, the whistleblower should be interviewed in a separate room, and communication by phone or e-mail should be done in such a way that the contents of the allegation cannot become known to anyone other than the member of staff receiving the allegations.
>
> (ii) Until results of its investigation are announced, the research institution or body in question **must ensure that all staff involved observe complete confidentiality in order to prevent the identity** of the whistleblower and the accused, **and details** of the allegation and investigation, **from being disclosed to any unrelated persons against the wishes of the whistleblower and the accused**.
>
> (v) Unless the allegations are proved to have been malicious, the research institution or body in question must not fire, transfer, discipline, demote, cut the pay of or otherwise treat the person who has made an allegation in any disadvantageous way for any reason other than that he or she has made an allegation.
>
> (vi) Unless it has fair grounds to do so, the research institution or body in question must not fire, transfer, discipline, demote, cut the pay of or otherwise treat the person against

whom allegations have been made in any disadvantageous way for any reason other than that he or she has been accused.

### 7.1.2. Guidelines for Whistleblowers

In Japan, those who make allegations of research Misconduct are subject to protection, which are specified in administrative guidelines and other policies issued by administrative agencies. For those who wish to report allegations of Misconduct, Michael Kalichman's guidelines[8] (University of California at San Diego) may be instructive in this regard:

***Documentation***: When making an allegation of Misconduct, clear documentation of who did what, and when they did it, is necessary for fair and prompt response to the allegation.

***Perspective***: What might appear to be a serious action could be a misunderstanding. It might be appropriate to talk to peers, senior researchers, or an ombudsperson of the institution, and even make a question to oneself and answer to it, in order to avoid making a reckless allegation.

As soon as someone is involved in a Misconduct allegation, any concerned persons who respond to the allegation should review institutional policies and procedures on the issue. **A whistleblower needs to know who should be apprised of the allegation, what constitutes evidence for or against an allegation, how the evidence should be obtained, who will review the allegation, what the whistleblower's role will be, and how much time the process is expected to take**.

In addition, the Guidelines suggest that research institutions and funding agencies establish offices for receiving Misconduct allegations, and give advice on matters such as responding to allegations appropriately, establishing systems and means for conducting investigations, identifying Misconduct, handling investigation results, handling appeals, and making the results public.

## 7.2. Procedures for Preliminary and Substantial Investigations and Determination

### 7.2.1. Preliminary and Substantial Investigations, Determination, and Sanctions

According to the Guidelines, when a Misconduct allegation arises, unless otherwise specified, it is **the research institution of the accused person that needs to respond to the allegation**.

The research institution of the accused will carry out **a preliminary investigation in order to determine whether the allegation has substance and whether an investigation is warranted**. In the **substantial Investigation, all the facts are recorded in a formal manner and appraised, leading to a finding of Misconduct or to dismissal of the case**. **Sanctions** are then taken against those who are found to be involved in Misconduct, as well as against authors who, although they have not been found guilty of Misconduct, are found to be responsible for research papers whose content reveal Misconduct (hereinafter, "person found guilty"). Sanctions may be taken against the person found guilty, either by a funding agency such as MEXT, or by the university or research institution to which they belong.

To determine whether Misconduct has been committed, it is necessary to provide an opportunity to the accused person for explanation and to consider all evidence comprehensively, including material or scientific evidence obtained through investigations, witness testimonies, and self-admission of the accused. If the accused person wishes to clear their names, they must bear responsibility for producing scientific evidence proving that the research in question was conducted using valid scientific methods and practices, and that their paper is a just reflection of the results of that research. If, when accounting for their research, the accused **fails to produce critical evidence that ought to exist (e.g., if there is missing raw data, experiment or observation notes, experiment materials or reagents), and cannot justify this lack of evidence, Misconduct will be deemed to have taken place**.

7.2.2. Notification and Reporting of Results of Investigation

The institution that has conducted the substantial investigation is required to promptly give notification and reporting of the results of the investigation to the whistleblower and the accused, and to the relevant funding agency and MEXT.

7.2.3. Protection of Whistleblowers and the Accused

Research institutions **have the responsibility to take steps to protect those who have been accused of Misconduct**, as well as those who have made the allegations. They are also called upon to create a working environment where details of allegations can be kept confidential, and where anyone who wishes to make an allegation out of a sense of duty or good conscience can do so without fear of retaliation. Further, the fact that an allegation has been made should never in itself be used as grounds for disadvantageous treatment such as termination of the research project in question. It is important to note that **maintaining complete confidentiality surrounding allegations also protects the rights of the accused individual**.

Furthermore, where Misconduct is deemed to have occurred, research institutions are required to promptly inform the accused that an allegation has been made, must disclose details of the allegation and the evidence (such as data) on which it is based, and **must give the accused persons an opportunity to rebut the allegation**.

According to the Guidelines, if, as a result of the investigation, a determination of Misconduct has been made, a period must be set aside for the accused to lodge an appeal. The Guidelines also lay out procedures by which appeals should be reviewed.

### 7.2.4. Sanctions

When someone is found guilty of Misconduct, sanctions may be taken both by the funding agency and by the institution to which the person belongs.

In Japan, as soon as it is determined that Misconduct has been committed, the persons found guilty are ordered to cease partaking of competitive funds provided to them by their funding agency or institution. In addition, not only the immediate researchers who are determined to have committed the Misconduct, but also other researchers who have been determined to be responsible for the contents of a paper or the like based on the information relating to the Misconduct are subject to sanctions by the funding agency.

Also, persons found guilty face sanctions in accordance with the internal rules of their institution, and are advised to withdraw the offending paper from academic publication. The results of investigation are then made public, including the name of the institution and details of the Misconduct.

Subsequently, a committee to be established in the funding agency will review the case while taking into account such elements as how serious the level of Misconduct was, how flagrant the case is, how deeply involved each person was, and what positions these persons had at the time of Misconduct, and determine sanctions that should be imposed on these persons, such as termination or return of research funds. Then, the funding agency will decide specific sanctions to take such as termination of funds, claiming a refund of research funds or temporary suspension of the person's eligibility to submit an application for competitive funds.

## *VIII. Managing Public Research Funds*

In order to ensure that public research funds are used in an ethical manner, researchers should not act solely out of their own interests, but should make decisions based on the same rules that all members of the society are required to observe, such as those made in legislation and guidelines.

Many individuals need to get involved in the process of scientific research. Administrative personnel have an especially important role to play on the research team. They work alongside researchers, ensuring that taxpayers' money is used in a cost-effective manner, and run the laboratory in a way that allows researchers to concentrate on their work.

Research institutions usually assign administrative personnel specialized in the use and management of public research funds to both the research support and the accounting divisions. These individuals facilitate the flow of accounting information between the funding agency and researchers, and endeavor to prevent misappropriation of public research funds.

### 8.1. Agency Rules and Institutional Rules

Two types of rules apply to research projects: those set forth by the funding agency, and those set forth by the research institution itself based on the agency's rules.[5,6] All research activities fall under these two sets of rules.

### 8.2. Creation of Rules on the Use of Public Research Funds

Japanese government-funded public research funds, such as Grants-in-Aid for Scientific Research, are subsidies that fall under the provisions of the Act on Rationalization of Budget Execution Pertaining to Subsidies, etc. (Subsidies Rationalization Act).[9] If those in receipt of subsidies (PI and research collaborators) violate the Subsidies Rationalization Act, they may face criminal penalties, including imprisonment and fines. Researchers must also take note of the provisions of the "Grants-in-Aid for Scientific Research Program – KAKENHI –Grants-in-Aid for Scientific Research JSPS Fellows Grant Usage Rules (Grant Conditions)."[10]

In 2006, the Council for Science and Technology Policy issued a report entitled On Initiatives to Prevent the Misappropriation, etc. of Public Research Funds,[11] and recommended that the relevant government agencies and research institutions abide by a common set of guidelines that apply to all accounting work. In response to this recommendation, the relevant government agencies formulated codes of best practices, such as the Guidelines on the Management and Audit of Public Research Funds at Research Institutions (Implementation Standards)[12] by the Ministry of Education, Culture, Sports, Science and Technology (MEXT) (Later, it was revised on February 1, 2021[16]). Furthermore, the year prior, in 2005, the Japanese government issued its Guidelines on the Proper Implementation of Competitive Funds,[13] and all relevant agencies (CAO, Cabinet Office; MIC, Ministry of Internal Affairs and Communications; MEXT, Ministry of Education, Culture, Sports, Science and Technology; MHLW, Ministry of Health, Labour and Welfare; MAFF, Ministry of Agriculture, Forestry and Fisheries of Japan; METI, Ministry of Economy, Trade and Industry; Ministry of Land, Infrastructure, Transport and Tourism; and MOE, Ministry of the Environment) collectively established a liaison committee to make arrangements. This liaison committee developed rules to help eliminate grant fraud, misappropriation of competitive funds, unreasonable overlap of grant proposals, and overfunding of particular PIs, as well as rules concerning other forms of research misconduct such as fabrication. Most research institutions have their own rules on an institutional level.[14]

### 8.3. Examples of Misappropriation and Grant Fraud

In Japan, there are penalties for the misappropriation of public research funds: Research funds may be reclaimed and eligibility for grant application may be suspended.[15] The following examples are typical cases, but there are various other forms of misappropriation and grant fraud.

### 8.3.1. Procurement Budget Misappropriation

The most common form of procurement budget misappropriation is a practice known as "depositing": a research institution makes a fake order of goods to a contract supplier, the supplier then submits fake accounting documents to the institution, the institution wire-transfers money to the supplier, and the supplier holds onto the money for a future transaction or pays the institution back in cash.

In some instances where the use of a procurement budget has been deemed fraudulent, the researcher involved was acting out of ignorance, or had been poorly informed by administrative personnel, and the item they were trying to procure could in fact have been purchased legitimately without resorting to making falsified claims.

### 8.3.2. Travel Budget Misappropriation

This form of misappropriation refers to various ways in which researchers use research funds to benefit themselves: They may claim costs unrelated to research under business trip expenses, receive duplicate payments for the same business trip, or pocket the difference between the standard fare written on an invoice and the discounted actual fare using a transaction receipt prepared by the travel agency. Researchers also sometimes pad their travel expenses so that they can use research funds to extend their trip for non-research-related purposes.

### 8.3.3. Personnel Budget Misappropriation

This form of misappropriation typically involves claims for money to be paid to part-time workers. For example, in order to help provide for their living expenses, research assistants may receive pay for part-time work they never did, or may pocket money for personal use by using research funds to remunerate part-time workers and then having the worker refund them directly.

## 8.4. Duplicate or Excessive Public Research Fund Applications and Awards

Unnecessary expenditure could arise if a researcher applies for or receives funding for the same project from more than one public research fund. This is why multiple applications are considered a form of misconduct and a potential waste of taxpayers' money. It is also considered misconduct to receive funding from private corporations in addition to public research funds. When researchers apply for funding for an important project which may appear to overlap with another project, they need to provide a persuasive explanation as to why they consider that the project is not in fact a duplicate, and they must base their arguments on evidence that is as specific as possible.

8.4.1. Effort

When evaluating applications for public research funds, reviewers need to assess **how feasible a proposed project may be**. Feasibility is calculated on the basis of an index, which is counted by multiplying the researcher's competence by the amount of time allotted to the project. In other words, feasibility is equal to the product of quality and quantity.

Any researcher applying for public research funds now has to declare the "**effort**" they intend to devote to the project: They must fill in what percentage of **their total working hours** will be allotted to the project. By requiring applicants to declare their "effort," the Japanese government tries to avoid providing particular researchers or research groups with more funding than they would be able to use effectively.

Many applicants would be tempted to fill in as high a percentage as possible just to get their application approved. However, if the researcher is working on more than one project concurrently, the total time spent on the two (or more) projects could end up exceeding 100% of their total working hours, which is unacceptable. Some researchers, believing that they can work much more than others—working on Saturdays and Sundays and putting in 15-hour days—may be tempted to declare working hours exceeding 100% of their working week. However, all this extra work can be considered to have contributed to achievements that the researcher has already made, the figure filled in on the application should therefore reflect the percentage of the researcher's total working hours *including* overtime.

Applicants are required to declare efforts of a total not exceeding 100%, including research contracted by private companies and non-research activities. Under this limit, applicants are trusted to make the ethical choice for how they declare their efforts for the proposed project. To give an extreme example, a professor working at a medical school clinical department may be very busy with other duties—managing the clinic, seeing patients, training students, and even working part-time at other hospitals—and may not be left with much time to devote to research. Despite this, they may try to win funding by claiming on the application that 100% of working hours will be devoted to the research project in question. This is clearly inappropriate.

## *IX. Conclusion*

Research activities are the driving force of human intellectual endeavors, which require responsible conduct of research, in other words, a good understanding of researchers' ethics and professional practices based on said understanding. We hope that all researchers who carry out their projects recognize that they are responsible for conducting quality research, as they are continuously receiving support and cooperation from a network of people and resources in a variety of forms.

## References


[1]. "On Being A Scientist: Responsible Conduct in Research", edited by the National Academy of Sciences in the U.S. (3rd ed., 2009), published in Japan by *Kagakudojin*

[2]. The Science Council of Japan (SCJ), Statement: Code of Conduct for Scientists (2013)

[3]. MEXT, Guidelines for Providing Appropriate Responses to Misconduct in Research Activities (2014)

[4]. U.S. Department of Health and Human Services, Office of the Assistant Secretary for Health. Office of Research Integrity Annual Report 2010. (2010)

[5]. SCJ, "Scientific Misconduct and Its Prevention – for autonomy of scientific community –" (2005)

[6]. Steneck, N.H. Fostering integrity in research: Definitions, current knowledge, and future directions. *Science and Engineering Ethics* 12, 53-74.(2006)

[7]. American Historical Association, Statement on Standards of Professional Conduct (revised in 2011)

[8]. Kalichman, M. Resources for Research Ethics Education: Whistleblowing (2001)

[9]. Act on Rationalization of Budget Execution Pertaining to Subsidies, etc. (Subsidies Rationalization Act) (2012)

[10]. Japan Society for the Promotion of Science (JSPS), Grants-in-Aid for Scientific Research Program – KAKENHI –Grants-in-Aid for Scientific Research JSPS Fellows Grant Usage Rules (Grant Conditions)

[11. Council for Science and Technology Policy, Cabinet Office, On Initiatives to Prevent the Misappropriation, etc. of Public Research Funds (2006)

[12]. MEXT, Guidelines on the Management and Audit of Public Research Funds at Research Institutions (Implementation Standards) (2014)

[13]. Cabinet Office, Guidelines on the Proper Implementation of Competitive Funds (2012)

[14]. Board of Audit of Japan, On Initiatives to Prevent the Misappropriation, etc. of Public Research Funds (2012)

[15]. MAFF, Guidelines on the Management and Audit of Public Research Funds at Research Institutions (Implementation Standards) (2013)

[16]. MEXT, Guidelines on the Management and Audit of Public Research Funds at Research Institutions (Implementation Standards) (2021)

# Appendix C: Participant Information Statement and Consent Form

| | |
|---|---|
| 九州大学<br>KYUSHU UNIVERSITY | **Participant Information Statement and Consent**<br>*(Please read this consent agreement carefully)* |

You are invited to participate in a study of *a mutual funding scheme deployed through a peer-to-peer lending platform in Vietnam's current context.* I hope to learn about your willingness to join the mutual funding scheme and your opinion about the scheme. You were selected as a potential participant in this study because you are a middle-class individual or practitioner in the P2P lending industry in Vietnam. Your support is essential for the progress of my research, and I sincerely appreciate your cooperation.

In this study, you will answer several questions regarding mutual funding schemes established through online lending platforms. If you decide to take part, kindly propose the most suitable time and location. It will take approximately 1 hour and a half to 2 hours to complete the interview. You might be contacted for follow-up questions or clarifications. Any information obtained in relation to this study and linked to you will be kept confidential and disclosed solely with your permission, unless mandated by law.

Upon your approval, the interview will be audio-recorded. If you agree to the recording by signing the attached Consent Form, it will be kept confidential and will not be disclosed to anyone other than the interviewer, except as mandated by law. In the event of publication, information will be presented in a manner that ensures your identity remains undisclosed, unless you grant written permission by signing the attached Consent Form.

Participating in this study does not pose any expected risks beyond those encountered in everyday life.

Your involvement in this study is entirely optional, and you can choose to exit at any point without facing any consequences. You have the option to skip over any questions, and if you decide to withdraw, you can simply inform the interviewer



Y. H. Nguyen, *Regulating Peer-to-Peer Lending in Vietnam*,
https://doi.org/10.1007/978-981-96-9505-8

without being subjected to any inquiries. Your decision to participate, decline, or withdraw will not affect your status or relationship in any way.

I appreciate your participation in this research and will send you a summary of the key findings once the research is completed by email. I believe this research will help establish a legal framework for the peer-to-peer lending business in Vietnam, facilitating the sound development of the lending business. If you prefer not to receive my report, please signify your choice by checking the relevant box on the following page.

If you have any questions about this study, please feel free to contact Ms. Nguyen Hai Yen (Mailing address: Graduate School of Law, Kyushu University, Room D-316, East Zone 2, 744 Motooka, Nishi-ku, Fukuoka, 819-0395 Japan; Tell: +81-92-802-5406; Mobile: +81-702-327-6109; Fax: +81-92-802-5407; Email: nguyenhaiyen@kyudai.jp).

You will be given a copy of this form to keep.

**PARTICIPANT INFORMATION STATEMENT AND CONSENT *(continued)***

I have received adequate explanations regarding the purpose and nature of this research, and I consent to take part in the study. I acknowledge the freedom to withdraw at any point without facing any penalties. Additionally, I understand that I will be provided with a copy of this form to keep for my records.

I, ________________________________ consent to an interview with Ms. Nguyen Hai Yen of Kyushu University, Japan.

I, ________________________________ ☐ consent/☐ do not consent, to my interview with Ms. Nguyen Hai Yen of Kyushu University, Japan, being tape recorded.

I, ________________________________ ☐ consent/☐ do not consent to my identity and/or that of ________________________ being identified in any future publication.

| Participant's Signature: | Interviewer's Signature: |
|---|---|
| ________________________________ | ________________________________ |
| Name: | Date: |
| ________________________________ | ________________________________ |

Would you like to receive a report of our findings?

☐ No

☐ Yes, please provide email information here: ____________________________

________________________

Ms. Nguyen Hai Yen (Mailing address: Graduate School of Law, Kyushu University, Room D-316, East Zone 2, 744 Motooka, Nishi-ku, Fukuoka, 819-0395 Japan; Tell: +81-92-802-5406; Mobile: +81-702-327-6109; Fax: +81-92-802-5407; Email: nguyenhaiyen@kyudai.jp).

# Appendix D: Revocation of Consent Form

**Revocation of Consent**

I hereby wish to WITHDRAW my consent to participate in the research proposal described above and understand that such withdrawal WILL NOT jeopardize any treatment or my relationship with Kyushu University.

Signature: ______________________ Name: ______________________

Date: ______________________

The section for Revocation of Consent should be forwarded to Ms. Nguyen Hai Yen (Mailing address: Graduate School of Law, Kyushu University, Room D-316, East Zone 2, 744 Motooka, Nishi-ku, Fukuoka, 819-0395 Japan; Tell: +81-92-802-5406; Mobile: +81-702-327-6109; Fax: +81-92-802-5407; Email: nguyenhaiyen@kyudai.jp).



Y. H. Nguyen, *Regulating Peer-to-Peer Lending in Vietnam*,
https://doi.org/10.1007/978-981-96-9505-8

# Appendix E: Consent for Identifying Company and Interviewee in Future Publication

**Consent for Identifying Company and Interviewee in Future Publication**

I, ________________________________

Signature: ________________________________ Name: ________________________________

Date: ________________________________

The section for Consent should be forwarded to Ms. Nguyen Hai Yen (Mailing address: Graduate School of Law, Kyushu University, Room D-316, East Zone 2, 744 Motooka, Nishi-ku, Fukuoka, 819-0395 Japan; Tell: +81-92-802-5406; Mobile: +81-702-327-6109; Fax: +81-92-802-5407; Email: nguyenhaiyen@kyudai.jp).



Y. H. Nguyen, *Regulating Peer-to-Peer Lending in Vietnam*,
https://doi.org/10.1007/978-981-96-9505-8

# Appendix F: List of Sample Interview Questions

**A. For ordinary citizens**

1. What kind of assets do you have (cash, house, car, stocks, etc)? What is the size of the respective assets? What is the value of the respective assets in your view?
2. Do you deposit your cash in banks? How many percentages of your assets do your bank accounts take? Do you have other means to save your cash (i.e., other kinds of deposit accounts)?
   - If yes, do you want to use it through means with higher risk and/or higher return?
   - If not, where do you invest your cash in addition to bank deposits?
3. Do you have any difficulty in borrowing small money/funds?
   - If yes, how often do you have that difficulty? Would you like to utilize a lending service provided by specialized institutions? Why/why not?
   - If not, which means do you usually utilize to solve that difficulty?
4. Are you willing to contribute your small assets regularly into a pool in exchange for the right to borrow some money from the common pool?
   - If yes, how much would you like to/can contribute on a regular basis? Under what condition would you like to lend your contributed money to the other members of the pool? Do you want to have professional management over the pool?
   - If not, what are your main concerns?
5. Under what condition would you like to contribute your small assets regularly into a pool?
6. What are the purposes for you to utilize a pooling scheme via an online platform?

 
Y. H. Nguyen, *Regulating Peer-to-Peer Lending in Vietnam*,
https://doi.org/10.1007/978-981-96-9505-8

**B. For practitioners in P2P lending industry**

1. Who are the main “users” or “subscribers” of P2P lending services (individuals, households, or SMEs) in Vietnam? Do you think the group of P2P lending users or subscribers is growing?
2. Which institutions are actually running P2P lending businesses (P2P lending companies, financial consulting firms, pawnshops)? Do you think the scale and number of P2P lending business institutions are increasing?
3. At the moment, the State Bank is expected to be the competent authority to manage the P2P lending business in Vietnam. What role does the State Bank currently play in supporting institutions running P2P lending business and managing the P2P lending business?
4. How do the P2P lending companies verify users or subscribers’ personal information and assess users or subscribers’ creditworthiness?
5. What are the problems with the current P2P lending scheme? In which direction is the development of the P2P lending business headed?
6. How do you think the current laws and the future regulatory framework function in the P2P lending business practice?
7. In the absence of legal certainty in some respects, do practitioners have a common understanding of the way in which problems of the current P2P lending scheme (for example, the due diligence of potential borrowers and the diversification of risk borne by lenders) are solved in practice?
8. To what extent are you dealing with the problems? Do you have any prior experience?
9. What is the role of personal relationships between the users or subscribers in doing P2P lending business in your viewpoint?
10. What is the role of professional management in doing P2P lending business in your experience?

# Appendix G: List of Sample Interviewees

| No. | Gender | Age | Position | Education | Tentative visiting date |
|---|---|---|---|---|---|
| 1. | Male | 38 | Staff (potential manager) in the Legal and Compliance Department, Military Bank | Master of Finance | May 23, 2022 (Morning) |
| 2. | Male | 42 | Lecturer of Banking and Finance Law Department, Hanoi Law University | PhD of Law | May 23, 2022 (Afternoon) |
| 3. | Female | 38 | Lawyer, Vietthink Law Firm | Master of Law | May 24, 2022 (Morning) |
| 4. | Female | 33 | Staff in the Legal and Compliance Department, BIDV | Bachelor of Finance | May 24, 2022 (Afternoon) |
| 5. | Male | 32 | Senior Manager in the Customers Service Department, Vnvon Co., Ltd. | Bachelor of Finance | May 25, 2022 (Morning) |
| 6. | Female | 27 | Staff, Lendbiz Co., Ltd. | Bachelor of Law | May 25, 2022 (Afternoon) |
| 7. | Male | 29 | Staff, Tima Co., Ltd. | Bachelor of Finance | May 26, 2022 (Morning) |
| 8. | Female | 30 | Staff, VOV247 Co., Ltd. | Bachelor of Finance | May 27, 2022 (Morning) |



Y. H. Nguyen, *Regulating Peer-to-Peer Lending in Vietnam*,
https://doi.org/10.1007/978-981-96-9505-8

# Appendix H: Selected Inquiries and Answers in the Interviews

## Question 1: What is your difficulty in borrowing small money/funds?

| | |
|---|---|
| Answer 1 | Actually, I possess several types of assets, namely, cash, houses, cars, stocks, and gold. Among these, houses account for a significant portion of my total assets. My family owns a house in Hanoi and another in my hometown, which together are valued at approximately VN₫ 7 billion. Obtaining small loans is not a challenge for me due to my ability to easily borrow from several commercial banks where my credit history is favorable. Additionally, I can leverage my salary account to secure loans swiftly from a bank. |
| Answer 2 | My assets comprise an apartment in Hanoi and online savings accounts with commercial banks. Additionally, I possess gold, an investment insurance package, and investments in the stock market. Obtaining small loans is convenient for me through my credit card issued by a commercial bank as well as by borrowing funds from the savings accounts I hold with the bank. |
| Answer 3 | I have the majority of my assets in an apartment, accounting for approximately 80% of my total assets, and a small portion of cash deposited in a bank (around 2% of my total assets). Borrowing small amounts (ranging from VN₫ 20 million to VN₫ 50 million) from family members, relatives, and friends poses no difficulty for me. |
| Answer 4 | We spent a lot on buying a car and an apartment in Hanoi, and a significant part of my family's cash has been invested in stocks. However, we encounter no challenges in borrowing small loans when needed. Borrowing around VN₫ 50 million from friends and colleagues is quite accessible for us. |

 
Y. H. Nguyen, *Regulating Peer-to-Peer Lending in Vietnam*,
https://doi.org/10.1007/978-981-96-9505-8

### Question 2: In which investment channels are you willing to contribute your small assets regularly?

| | |
|---|---|
| Answer 1 | I have deposited a portion of my cash in a commercial bank, but the interest I receive is quite low, around 6% or 7% per year. At present, my investments are divided between stocks and gold, though I have experienced losses in the stock market and modest gains from gold. Additionally, I am allocating some of my idle cash to P2P loans in order to generate profit. |
| Answer 2 | My preference is to make regular contributions of small amounts to a pool facilitated by an online lending platform, aiming for profit. This strategy aligns with my goal of diversifying risk within my asset allocation. I think the stock market is not a suitable investment channel for ordinary individuals. Although it seemed attractive last year due to soaring stock market indexes and the new trading system at the Ho Chi Minh City Stock Exchange, this year has been marked by losses for me. Furthermore, the real estate market requires significant capital investment. Currently, the real estate market in Vietnam is facing potential downturn risks. This stems from the challenges real estate businesses encounter in accessing capital sources, with some of them resorting to selling properties and housing at substantial discounts. Several real estate companies have halted or postponed investment endeavors and construction projects. |
| Answer 3 | I am currently investing in stocks, but it is quite difficult to predict the stock market's trends. I have even lost some money investing in the stock market. Therefore, I would like to explore other profitable investment channels, including a mutual funding by regularly contributing a small amount into a pool. This will help me diversify my investment portfolio. |
| Answer 4 | We have spent a considerable amount on buying a car and an apartment in Hanoi. Most of my family's cash has been invested in stocks, but we have not earned much profit. We are now open to investing in other lucrative avenues to generate additional income, as we are aiming to purchase a house in my hometown. |

### Question 3: What is the role of personal relationships among participants in a P2P lending scheme in your experience?

| | |
|---|---|
| Answer 1 | The majority of investors participating in our P2P platforms are individual investors. They reside in various provinces across the country, especially in major cities like Hanoi and Ho Chi Minh City. Many of them are investing in short-term loans (6 months) with investment amounts of around VN₫ 100 million. Currently, due to the absence of a specific and appropriate legal framework for the operation of P2P lending companies, numerous potential investors are hesitant to join or invest more assets in P2P lending. They perceive it as a risky investment channel for ordinary citizens. However, if those who possess idle assets (or potential investors) have close relationships with our current investors, they are more inclined to join or can be persuaded to participate in our lending business to seek profit. Many investors using our lending platform share close personal relationships with each other. Moreover, managers and staff at P2P lending companies are encouraged and sometimes required to leverage their connections within the middle-class demographic to attract more investors to the company's lending business. |
| Answer 2 | Most investors on our P2P platform are individuals who typically opt for short-term loans (3 months, 6 months, or 9 months). The highest investment through our platform to date has been VN₫ 25 billion, while the minimum investment has been VN₫ 10 million. Many of these investors maintain personal relationships with our staff and/or our existing customers. Initially, some were hesitant to invest in our lending |

*(continued)*

(continued)

| | |
|---|---|
| | platform due to concerns about potential financial losses. However, witnessing profitable outcomes for investors with whom they share a personal connection has encouraged them to engage in our lending business. Furthermore, certain investors are aware that the borrowers obtaining funds through our lending platform are primarily small SMEs. They know that our company managers have strong relationships with the executives of these SMEs, and in some cases, our company managers even hold a stake in the SMEs. This awareness has bolstered their confidence in investing in our lending platform. |
| Answer 3 | I decided to invest in P2P lending to seek profit after my sister had a positive experience with this investment model and recommended it to me. |
| Answer 4 | I would consider investing 20% to 30% of my idle cash into P2P lending if someone with whom I share a close relationship has enjoyed positive experiences with this investment avenue and recommends it to me. |
| Answer 5 | If someone I have a close relationship with recommends a P2P lending company in which they have achieved successful investments, I am open to investing a small amount of money in loans facilitated by that P2P lending company. |

**Question 4: Under what condition would you like to contribute your small money regularly into a pool established via an online lending platform?**

| | |
|---|---|
| Answer 1 | To be honest, having read about scandals involving P2P lending businesses where lenders lost their investments on various platforms, I am hesitant to invest in a mutual funding scheme established through an online lending platform. In addition, I find it challenging to acquire information regarding the current financial and business status of P2P borrowers, as well as their utilization of funds, in the absence of professional management by an independent party or organization overseeing the mutual funding scheme's operation. I would consider investing in a mutual funding scheme if there were substantial regulations governing this lending business, aiming to guarantee a secure environment for investors. |
| Answer 2 | I believe that having a professional independent party or organization manage the operation of a mutual funding scheme could instill confidence in investors regarding the operations of P2P lending companies. As for myself, I would be inclined to invest more funds if such professional management were implemented through online lending platforms. |